The White House World

The

WHITE HOUSE WORLD

Transitions, Organization, and Office Operations

EDITED BY

MARTHA JOYNT KUMAR AND TERRY SULLIVAN

TEXAS A&M UNIVERSITY PRESS • *College Station*

The paper used in this book meets the minimum requirements
of the American National Standard for Permanence
of Paper for Printed Library Materials, Z39.48-1984.
Binding materials have been chosen for durability.

Library of Congress Cataloging-in-Publication Data

Kumar, Martha Joynt.
The White House world : transitions, organization, and office operations /
edited by Martha Joynt Kumar and Terry Sullivan.
p. cm. — (The presidency and leadership ; no. 13)
Includes index.
ISBN 1-58544-223-2 (cloth : perm paper) —
ISBN 1-58544-227-5 (paper : perm paper)
1. Presidents—United States.   2. Presidents—United States—Transition periods.
3. Presidents—United States—Staff.   4. Bush, George W. (George Walker), 1946–
I. Kumar, Martha Joynt.   II. Sullivan, Terry (Terry O.)   III. Title.   IV. Series.
JK 516 .K86 2003
352.23'7'0973—dc21
2002151573

CONTENTS

PART 4
George W. Bush Makes His Transition into Office and into the White House

Introduction

MARTHA JOYNT KUMAR
TERRY SULLIVAN

THE PRESIDENTIAL ELECTION OF 2000 WAS unique in American history, as was the transition that followed it. It was the first presidential election since 1888 in which the winner of the popular vote was not certified as the next president and the only electoral contest in which the Supreme Court was involved in its outcome. The delay in certifying the vote for Gov. George W. Bush led to a transition in which President-elect Bush had thirty-seven days to shift from campaigning to governing, half of the normally allotted time. This truncated transition posed two special challenges. First, a successful transition demonstrated the stability of our political system. Second, with half the time of a normal changeover, a successful start appeared especially difficult to achieve. In this extraordinary environment, the new White House staff needed access to substantive information about the establishment of an administration. The special circumstances were likely to mean special challenges once in office, and a well-functioning White House staff represented an important opportunity to effectively face what might come.

Previous administrations have demonstrated how hard it was to come by that knowledge. Acting as a conduit for information about the start up, operations, and organization of six previous administrations, the materials developed through the White House Interview Program proved to be an

important resource for those entering office. The program is one component of The White House 2001 Project, a two-part initiative funded by The
Pew Charitable Trusts. It was designed to provide incoming White House
staff members with information on the operation of key offices. The other
part of the project, Nomination Forms Online, a computer software program, was created to ease specific difficulties associated with the myriad
forms filled out by presidential appointees to executive-branch positions.[1]

The White House World: Transitions, Organization, and Office Operations
contains edited versions of the briefing materials assembled for incoming
White House staff members and used by them as they prepared for governing. The first three sections of this book contain elements of the original transition work: essays on previous transitions, the environment
defining White House work, and the operations of seven offices carrying
out functions critical to the effective start up of an administration. A final
section revisits the Bush transition of 2001, bringing the scholarly assessments of several experts in the field as well as a retrospective by Clay Johnson, who served as the executive director of the Bush transition.

Modern Presidential Transitions

While forty-three presidents have experienced a transition when coming
into the presidency, organized changeovers lasting two and a half months
have a brief history. The modern presidential transition dates from the
passage of power between Presidents Truman and Eisenhower.[2] That transition involved the first time the outgoing administration developed and
presented information to the incoming one. "Truman set out deliberately
to establish a precedent that the outgoing President is expected to concern
himself with this problem and establish a pattern of conduct for his entire
administration," observed Laurin Henry, who studied twentieth-century
transitions involving a change in party.[3]

In addition, Dwight Eisenhower was the first nonincumbent president
to come into office under the current practice of having approximately
seventy-five days from election in November to inauguration on January 20. From George Washington's second term through Franklin Roosevelt's first, the time between the November election and the inauguration (March 4) was four months. Eisenhower also was the first president
limited to two terms under the Twenty-second Amendment, a constitutional change that substantially altered transition dynamics. A two-term

limit means that with certainty, one can anticipate a presidential transition at least every eight years.

For those who study presidential transitions and those who have served in the early months and years of a presidency, there is an appreciation for the sense of urgency an incoming administration has about getting a team in place and for the important role played by staff in setting up a smooth handoff of power.[4] "The White House is not simply a spoil of victory," observed Harrison Wellford, a former White House official and specialist on presidential transitions. "It's the nerve center of the greatest government in the world and we ought to at least give it the same respect that you do when you take over a second-rate corporation." Wellford, a lawyer specializing in mergers and acquisitions, noted: "When I compare White House transitions and the lack of systems and discipline and preparation that goes into that to what we do when we are taking over a company, it is night and day and, yet, the stakes are so infinitely smaller with the companies than with the White House."[5] The same observation is made by others who have worked in the White House and devoted time and energy to transitions. Without serious advance planning, the president-elect's team cannot acclimate to their new roles or discover useful information about their new posts. When they arrive on inauguration day, they are greeted by no institutional memory, no predetermined organizational structure, no adopted policies, no outline of their responsibilities, and no manual to show how the place works. In short, they arrive to an empty shell.

Governing Opportunities and Hazards Present during the Transition Period

While an empty White House is a difficult place to adjust to, there is every incentive to move quickly when the new administration comes into office. The early months in a presidential term are like no other. "There is a coming together after an election that is a natural and wonderful impulse in America," observed James Cicconi, former White House staff secretary and deputy chief of staff in the Bush administration.[6] "Just by virtue of winning you have a lot of advantages in terms of an inspired democratic electorate," noted Roy Neel, who was chief of staff for Vice President Al Gore and later served President Clinton as deputy chief of staff. "It gives you a lot of wiggle room and a lot of resources."[7] But, observed Michael Jackson, "it doesn't take long for it to erode."[8] Consequently, the early goodwill is a resource to be contemporaneously spent, not just husbanded for an uncertain future occasion. "The capital that you have at the beginning is so precious, and to not get full benefit from it, because clearly it's going to erode after awhile, is a tragic loss," remarked Wellford. "You really can get a lot done if you have a very clear agenda and have set priorities that are commensurate with the political capital you want to spend. And for the most part Reagan did that."[9]

Given the opportunities and the efforts to prepare these incoming presidents, why have so many transitions failed? Four factors are found in the record of recent transitions. First, when there is a "hostile takeover," with the incoming team having defeated those soon to leave, the winners have a tendency to regard with suspicion any information coming from those who lost. "There is an extraordinary hubris which affects every administration that ousts an incumbent," remarked Wellford. "That's the highest of the highs." Even if they had attentively listened to what the departing Bush staff had to tell them, Clinton staffers were not in place for their counterparts to discuss with them what they had learned during their White House years.

Second, by failing to appoint people to the jobs shortly after the election, a president-elect loses an opportunity for the incoming staff to familiarize themselves with the organizational patterns already in place. Because President-elect Clinton waited to appoint his senior staff until the final week prior to the inauguration, many of their counterparts in the Bush White House had already left their posts. From the viewpoint of one Clinton staff member, the result was that the incoming "people were flying blind." Wellford pointed out that "even though there was some very good work done in preparation for their term, there wasn't a consumer ready for it."[10] People simply were not appointed in time to take advantage of the available briefings and briefing materials. Even a "friendly takeover" can have problems if the staff is not appointed until late or if the president-elect believes he wants to establish a system with a different emphasis.

Third, after a successful campaign, incoming staffers often redirect their energies toward moving their campaign apparatus intact into the White House. "There is some built-in momentum that sweeps people along from important positions in a campaign structure into the White House," noted William Galston, who worked in both the 1992 Clinton campaign and the first two years of the Clinton administration. "The general problem is that it is very difficult to tell people who worked their hearts out for you for two years during a presidential campaign, 'Elections are one thing and governance another,'" he said. "'And your youthful zeal, your take-no-prisoners political skills, were just what we needed then, but this is something different.' That's enormously difficult to do."[11] An administration pays a high price when it merely transforms its campaign staff into the major White House senior staff. Doing so naturally creates a partisan operation that cannot make effective use of the initial period of co-operation. With little to restrain their zeal, the campaign staff can commit blunders that long haunt the president and those who follow the first wave of staffers.

Fourth, the problems presented by a lack of institutional memory are compounded by a staff with little White House training. "There are very few people in senior staff positions in the Congress who didn't start out with junior staff positions in Congress," observed William Galston. "There is a training process." When you look at staff patterns at the White House, "the cycle of training and experience is broken, and it's as though you're starting over again with each administration."[12] When the new president and his staff are people with little Washington and no White House experience, their problems are greater still, for they have little sense of where to find information important to the tasks they are about to begin handling.

The White House Interview Program

In order to help the incoming team take advantage of the opportunities present in a transition and avoid its hazards, a group of presidency scholars committed themselves to fusing together four important communities interested in assuring a successful 2001 transition. The White House Interview Program is an outgrowth of the interest in the promotion of governmental effectiveness evinced by these four communities: presidency scholars, a foundation interested in issues of governance, former White House staff, and educational institutions.

Scholarship on presidential changeovers began with Laurin Henry's *Presidential Transitions*, published in 1960. Henry's research covered the partisan transitions that had occurred up to that point in the twentieth century. His work raised the level of interest in and recognition of the importance of that particular period in the development of an administration. In his *Presidential Transitions: Eisenhower though Reagan*, Carl Brauer filled in the details of the five transitions involving a change in party from 1952 to 1981. John Burke in his *Presidential Transitions: From Politics to Practice* completed the century by updating our understanding of individual transitions, including those of Presidents Carter, Reagan, Bush, and Clinton. These three works provided the details we built upon.[13] And, by the accounts of the Bush transition staff, John Burke's book, read in manuscript, was an important source of information about those transitions they were particularly concerned about.[14]

Along with Burke's book manuscript, the program's staff built a basic library on transitions, which we gave to the transition teams of Governor Bush and Vice President Gore during the spring and summer of 2000. That basic library included two other works focusing on issues relating to transitions: James Pfiffner, *The Strategic Presidency: Hitting the Ground Running*, and Charles O. Jones, *Passages to the Presidency: From Campaigning to Governing*. Both provide information on how particular tasks were undertaken over several recent administrations. Knowing White House operations would be our focus, we also gave them copies of Bradley Patterson's *The White House Staff: Inside the West Wing and Beyond* and Karen Hult and Charles Walcott's *Governing from the White House: From Hoover to Johnson*.[15] Based on our discussions with those involved in the transition planning, the Bush transition staff paid special attention to the Burke manuscript, using it as a source for information on those previous transitions they had already identified as critical examples for them.

Presidency scholars are important for the guidance they provide through our organizational base, the Presidency Research Group of the American Political Science Association. Those serving on the group's twenty-five-member board presently include those who write on the White House, the institution of the presidency, and individual presidents: Professors James MacGregor Burns, George Edwards, John Fawcett, Fred Greenstein, Michael Grossman, Erwin Hargrove, Stephen Hess, Karen Hult, Lawrence Jacobs, Charles Jones, Barbara Kellerman, Samuel Kernell, John Kessel, Paul Light, Frank Mackaman, Calvin Mackenzie, Richard Neustadt, James Pfiffner, Richard Pious, Bert Rockman, Georgia Sorenson, Terry Sullivan, Shirley Anne Warshaw, and Stephen Wayne; Prof. Martha Joynt Kumar served as chair. The board discussed goals, provided counsel, and responded to materials produced by the research group.

In addition to providing information to assist incoming staff to effectively settle into their work, this group of scholars is also interested in further developing the project, for accessible information on White House operations lags behind that available for other governmental institutions, especially Congress. The community of presidency scholars has long wanted to build a base of information across administrations on White House office operations. The White House Interview Program has built such a resource through the interviews conducted for the project and the essays written about the functioning of seven White House offices key to the successful start of an administration.

The seven offices studied are ones important to a smooth start for an administration. They are: Chief of Staff, Staff Secretary, Personnel, Counsel, Press, Communications, and Management and Administration. The chief of staff structures White House operations and recruits the staff. The staff secretary monitors the flow of paper to and from the Oval Office as well as manages a system to follow the implementation of presidential orders. The Office of Presidential Personnel recruits and fills out the executive branch. Nominees for executive positions are vetted by the Office of the Counsel to the President, a unit that early in an administration develops ethics guidelines and considers executive orders. The Press Office manages the president's relations with news organizations, while the Office of Communications develops presidential messages and plans out the release of presidential information. The Office of Management and Administration controls salaries, determines the size of staffs, and allocates office space. While many offices have significant roles as an administration begins, these seven White House units are consistently important to the quality of the start of an administration.

Project Planning

Early in the planning for the White House Interview Program, the board of scholars made what turned out to become three significant strategic decisions. First, based on previous attempts to affect the presidential transition, we determined that we needed financial support sufficient to carry the project through a long and complex buildup period, making contacts and developing information resources. Through the efforts of Paul Light, then director, public policy programs, at The Pew Charitable Trusts, we secured their generous support for a three-year grant. In turn, that commitment became a catalyst for other supporting institutions in academia, government, and elsewhere to provide additional resources. The support of The Pew Charitable Trusts made it possible for us to prepare for the 2001 presidential transition with as much dedication and stamina as those who pursued it from the other direction. The long preparation afforded us legitimacy among and repeated contacts with those who would eventually consume our information.

Second, we decided that advice had to resonate with transition planners: our information had to bear the unmistakable footprints of the experiences of those who previously held the offices. Acting as a conduit for information in this way meant more than simply using research to illuminate a process since the advice of those we interviewed constituted prescriptions. Former staff of both parties were frank in their descriptions of the lessons they had learned, including the painful ones.

Third, we concluded that a new administration needed information long before it had won election. The strategic opportunity for useful advice occurred in a window cracked open during the primaries and continuing through the summer of national party conventions. With credentials established through familiarity, we concluded, transition planners and critical campaign officials could and would absorb briefing materials if they got them on their time schedules and in a form convenient to their work rhythms.

Working with Transition Staff

Throughout 1999, as we interviewed former White House staff members, we informed them of the project and our schedule for the release of information. By the spring of 2000, our project was well known among the organizations of the Republican and Democratic candidates. During that spring and early summer, when they approached us for help, we provided books, manuscripts, articles, and government reports to their campaign staffs. In the summer and fall of 2000, we added our essays, organization charts, and some of the project's interviews to senior staff members of the Bush and Gore camps assigned to work on transition issues. Once the election was decided, the remainder of our work went to the new White House team.

Clay Johnson, executive director of the Bush-Cheney transition, asked us to put together our information in briefing books devoted to each of the offices. During the transition period in 2000 and into the early days of the Bush administration in 2001, the directors and their deputies of the seven selected White House offices read through the White House Interview Program's series of "White House Briefing Books." They found a receptive and appreciative audience. Those who came into the offices used the information to prepare themselves for their new responsibilities. "Clay Johnson, who was the head of the transition, gave me the book ["White House Briefing Book" on the Office of Press Secretary], and he encouraged me strongly to read it," said Bush Press Secretary Ari Fleischer two months into the new administration.[16] "And he was right. It is a wealth of information, and it is a wonderful road map to a job I had never done before. Martha [Kumar]'s book should be mandatory reading. It is very helpful." Other office heads found the information they were given to be similarly useful in preparing to assume their new White House roles.

In the latter months of 2000 and the beginning of 2001, journalists and professors nationwide used the essays developed for the briefing books. With the pieces available on the project's website, www.whitehouse2001. org, journalists, professors, and their students used the material to track transition operations. The essays were published separately in three scholarly journals. Except for "A Tale of Two Transitions," which appeared in *Congress and the Presidency,* all of the articles in parts 1, 2, and 3 of the volume were published in *Presidential Studies Quarterly.* The essays in part 4 came out in *PS: Political Science and Politics.* We thank the editors of all three journals for their permission and help with the publication of the pieces.[17]

CBS White House correspondent Bill Plante commented: "This was an enormously useful project. Those of us who have read it, and I have read a great deal of it, find a tremendous amount of inspiration seeing how others handled their jobs."[18] Given the interest in the project from those in three communities—White House staff, scholars, and journalists—we are publishing our materials in order to share the information with others for use in the classroom and for research projects as well. The essays are edited versions of the pieces provided to the incoming staff.

The Elements of the White House Interview Program

The project provided to the incoming staff various types of information, including transcripts of interviews with former White House staff members; essays analyzing presidential transitions and several aspects of White House life; the functions and operations of seven White House offices; organization charts covering the individual offices over a twenty-five-year period; and an address book of former staff members, letting the incoming staff know who served in their posts during the previous six administrations and their predecessors' current contact information.

Interviews with White House Officials

The building blocks of the project are the interviews conducted with former White House officials, including Pres. Gerald Ford. We have seventy-eight interviews completed with seventy-five people interviewed, most of which will be made available through the individual presidential libraries of the administrations in which the staff members served.[19]

The people interviewed come from six administrations, represent the six offices, and portray the different time periods within an administration. Among them are most of the critical people who served in each of the posts under consideration, including deputies as well as those who headed each office. The largest number of interviewees are those who served as chief of staff and their deputies. Among those interviewed thus far by office are: chief of staff—Howard Baker, James Baker, Richard Cheney, Kenneth Duberstein, Alexander Haig, Thomas McLarty, Leon Panetta, Donald Rumsfeld, and Samuel Skinner; press secretary—Marlin Fitzwater, Mike McCurry, Ron Nessen, Jody Powell, and Larry Speakes; communications director—Don Baer, Sidney Blumenthal, David Demarest, David Gergen, Thomas Griscom, James Holland, Ann Lewis, Gerald Rafshoon, Gerald Warren, and Margita White; counsel—A. B. Culvahouse, Lloyd Cutler, C. Boyden Gray, Robert Lipshutz, Abner Mikva, Bernard Nussbaum, and Peter Wallison; personnel director—Douglas Bennett, Constance Horner, Pendleton James, Jerry Jones, Fred Malek, Arnie Miller, Bob Nash, Bonnie Newman, and Chase Untermeyer; staff secretary—Phillip Brady, James Cicconi, Rhett Dawson, Jon Huntsman, Jerry Jones, and Todd Stern; and director of Office of Management and Administration—Richard Harden, Christopher Hicks, Timothy McBride, John Rogers, and Jodie Torkelson.

The interviews focused on the importance of the White House staff to a president and to the success of his administration and covered information in the following areas: how each person came into office and what they knew about their job beforehand, their responsibilities once in office, the functions performed by their office, the relationship of their unit with other White House offices and with other governmental institutions, and White House work life, including the nature of its pressures. Overall, we learned there are more similarities than there are differences among administrations and identified patterns within offices in order for the incoming staff to have a sense of the operating environment of their unit.

Essays on Presidential Transitions, White House Operations,
and Seven Offices

The essays in this book from the original project are divided into three sections. The first section focuses on the nature of presidential transitions. The first essay released by the project was "Meeting the Freight Train Head On," by Martha Joynt Kumar, George Edwards, James Pfiffner, and Terry Sullivan, a piece bringing together points made by former White House staff about the elements of a good start for a new administration. Pendleton James, who handled personnel issues during the Reagan transition and for the first year and a half of the administration, had the following response to this essay: "If the President-Elect reads nothing else about the transition except for these 13 pages, he will be well-prepared. 'Meeting the Freight Train Head On' is an excellent report summarizing what needs to be done. It should be required reading for the President-Elect's staff."[20] John Burke's essays, "Lessons from Past Presidential Transitions" and "Presidential Transitions, 1980 and 1988," provided information lessons and analysis from the record of past transfers of power.

The second section of this book focuses on the environment of the White House. John Kessel's essay, "The Presidency and the Political Environment," summarizes a broad literature on the relationships impinging on the White House, from the interests that make up the Washington community to Congress and the media. This essay is followed by an examination of the conditions of work in the White House. Two essays by Martha Kumar, "The White House Is Like City Hall" and "The Pressures of White House Work Life" describe the complex relationships found inside the White House. Regardless of the nature of the president's campaign organization, his White House staff must reflect a much broader cross section of interests—a "city hall" of interests. In addition, the staff carries out their work under more scrutiny than anyone else.

Essays in the third section examine what directors of the offices and their deputies need to know about the functions performed by their units, the duties exercised by the directors, the ways in which each office has been organized, and the relationships each has with the others within the White House. "Often called 'the president's lawyer,' the counsel's office serves, more accurately, as the *presidency's* lawyer' with tasks that extend well beyond exclusively legal ones," write MaryAnne Borrelli, Karen Hult, and Nancy Kassop in their essay on the White House Counsel's Office.

"These have developed over time, depending on the needs of different presidents, on the relationship between a president and a counsel, and on contemporary political conditions. The more sharply polarized political atmosphere of recent years has led to greater responsibility, as well as heightened political pressure and visibility, for the traditionally low-profile counsel's office." In fleshing out all of these points, the authors elaborate on the patterns in the growth of responsibilities during the thirty-two-year period studied. The essays on the other six offices cover similar analytical ground. The authors of this section found receptive audiences for their works among the incoming White House staff. Such positive evaluation demonstrate the void filled by the essays.[21]

The scholars examining these offices include people who have experience studying White House operations: Steve Wayne, Charles Walcott, and Shirley Anne Warshaw on the Office of Chief of Staff; Karen Hult and Katherine Tenpas on the Office of Staff Secretary; Brad Patterson and James Pfiffner on the Office of Presidential Personnel; Karen Hult, MaryAnne Borrelli, and Nancy Kassop on the Office of Counsel; Charles Walcott, Bradley Patterson, and Peri Arnold on the Office of Management and Administration; and Martha Joynt Kumar on the Press Office and the Office of Communications.

Before releasing the materials, the essays were read for their accuracy by several persons who either headed or worked in the offices. We wanted to make certain the information contained in them reflect White House organization and the central points the new staff should know about their unit. Among those reviewing the piece on the Office of Press Secretary, for example, were former press secretaries for Presidents Clinton, Bush, Reagan, and Ford, including Joe Lockhart, Jake Siewert, Mike McCurry, Marlin Fitzwater, Larry Speakes, and Ron Nessen. We thank all of those who read these essays, for we benefited from their experience and observations.

Organization Charts of the Seven Offices

Our charts laying out the different ways in which the selected offices have been organized are the first created of individual White House offices. Through a close reading of each, one can observe the patterns in the organization of the units. "The organization charts were very useful in organizing communications," said Karen Hughes. "We laid them out and looked at the different ways it had been done."[22]

The charts demonstrate significant differences in White House organi-

zation. There are patterns observed by Democrats and Republicans, for example, in the creation of the Office of Chief of Staff. While Democrats have
been reluctant at the beginning of their administrations to create a strong
chief of staff or, in the case of President Carter, to appoint one at all, Republican presidents have appointed strong chiefs of staff and have done so early
in the transition period. Taken together, the organization charts demonstrate that over the course of the thirty-two years studied, one can observe
the growth in the number of levels within all of the individual offices and
the increase in the number of people working in each. In 1978 the Office of
Chief of Staff had seven people in it, while twenty years later there were
twenty people and the titles of all had become more task specific, including
the title assistant to the president, which later became chief of staff.

While not a part of our initial project design, we developed the organization charts as a resource for new staff members once we found a solid
data source. Using *The Capital Source* published by *National Journal,* which
contains a listing of the offices within the White House and its subunits, we
developed organizational charts for each. *The Capital Source* has been published biannually since 1986 and less regularly beginning in 1978, thus we
have available material for a solid sampling of White Houses. Those setting
up an office were able to easily view some of the different ways in which
their unit has been structured during the last four administrations.

Essays on the Transition of Pres. George W. Bush

In the final section of the book, we provide assessments of the transition
from those who participated in the studies and, in the case of Clay Johnson III, one who organized the early transition operations of Gov. George
W. Bush. In his "The 2000–2001 Presidential Transition: Planning, Goals,
and Reality," Johnson walks us through the team's thinking. John Burke
compares the Bush transition with recent ones in his "The Bush Transition
in Historical Context." G. Calvin Mackenzie analyzes the appointment
process and experience of the Bush team in his essay, "The Real Invisible
Hand: Presidential Appointees in the Administration of George W. Bush."
In "Already Buried and Sinking Fast: Presidential Nominees and Inquiry,"
Terry Sullivan describes the myriad questions appointees face as they prepare to join an administration. George Edwards discusses the early Bush
policy agenda in "Strategic Choices and the Early Bush Legislative Agenda."
Norman Ornstein and John Fortier analyze the congressional relationship
in their essay, "Relations with Congress." The final piece, "The White

Figure 1.

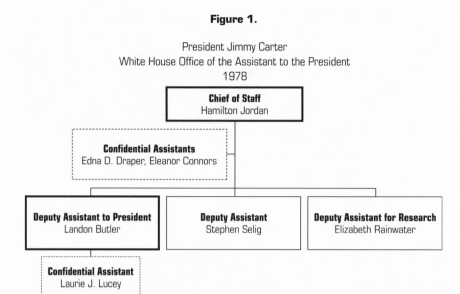

President Jimmy Carter
White House Office of the Assistant to the President
1978

White House Interview Program (whitehouse2001.org). Based on data in *The White House Telephone Directory*, 1978, National Journal Group Inc., Washington, DC. *Key:* ———— = positions with "to the president" in their title; ---------- = staff working for indicated assistant.

House of President George W. Bush: Recruiting and Organizing a Staff," is by Martha Kumar and considers the key decisions shaping the White House staff.

Institutional Support for the White House Interview Program

The success of the White House Interview Program lies in the broad range of talented and committed people and institutions involved in producing its materials. The Pew Charitable Trusts guided our work as well as provided for our funding. During the early stages of the project, Paul Light provided us with creative suggestions for developing information for incoming White House staff. Through his position heading The Presidential Appointee Initiative, Light continues to be one of our strongest and most imaginative supporters. We thank the American Enterprise Institute and its Transition to Governing Project for their help and support for the project. Most especially, we thank Norman Ornstein and John Fortier for their respective efforts in our behalf.

The James A. Baker III Institute for Public Policy has supported the

Figure 2.

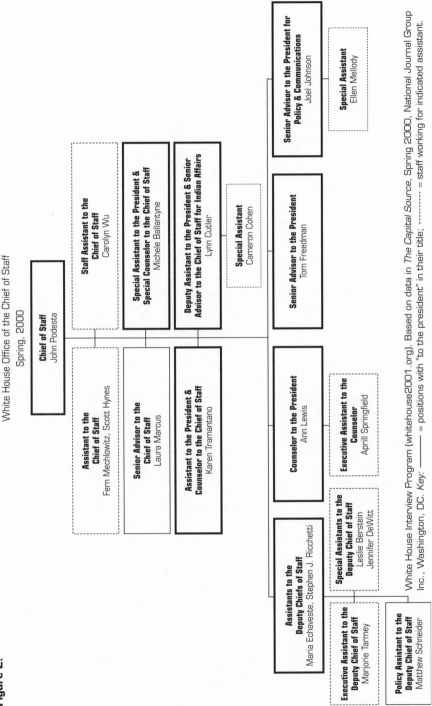

President William Clinton
White House Office of the Chief of Staff
Spring, 2000

Chief of Staff
John Podesta

Staff Assistant to the Chief of Staff
Carolyn Wu

Special Assistant to the President & Special Counselor to the Chief of Staff
Michele Ballantyne

Deputy Assistant to the President & Senior Advisor to the Chief of Staff for Indian Affairs
Lynn Cutler

Special Assistant
Cameron Cohen

Senior Advisor to the President for Policy & Communications
Joel Johnson

Special Assistant
Ellen Mellody

Assistant to the Chief of Staff
Fern Mechlowitz, Scott Hynes

Senior Advisor to the Chief of Staff
Laura Marcus

Assistant to the President & Counselor to the Chief of Staff
Karen Tramantano

Senior Advisor to the President
Tom Freedman

Counselor to the President
Ann Lewis

Executive Assistant to the Counselor
Aprill Springfield

Assistants to the Deputy Chiefs of Staff
Maria Echaveste, Stephen J. Ricchetti

Special Assistants to the Deputy Chief of Staff
Leslie Berstein
Jennifer DeWitt

Executive Assistant to the Deputy Chief of Staff
Marjorie Tarmey

Policy Assistant to the Deputy Chief of Staff
Matthew Schneider

White House Interview Program (whitehouse2001.org). Based on data in *The Capital Source*, Spring 2000, National Journal Group Inc., Washington, DC. *Key:* ———— = positions with "to the president" in their title; -------- = staff working for indicated assistant.

White House 2001 Project in several important ways. The institute provided funding for Professor Sullivan for two years to focus on the project
as well as providing research support through undergraduate and graduate assistants. Over the course of the project, we had significant support
from Secretary James A. Baker III and Ambassador Edward Djerejian, the
institute's honorary chair and director respectively, and associate directors
Prof. Richard Stoll and W. O. King. The institute also organized the Washington Forum on the White House Chief of Staff to coincide with the publication of the "Freight Train" article and to underscore the work of the
White House Interview Program.

We thank the Academy of Leadership at the University of Maryland,
where funds for the White House Interview Program are managed and
from whom we received early support for our project. Over the course of
the grant, we have had several people assisting and supporting us, including Georgia Sorenson, Nance Lucas, Deborah Starobin Armstrong, Michele Giovannini, and Scott Webster. Through the efforts of Prof. Eric
Belgrad, Provost Dan Jones, and Pres. Hoke Smith, Towson University has
provided generous support for Martha Kumar. The University of North
Carolina at Chapel Hill has provided support through its funding of Terry
Sullivan's endeavors and through the excellent graduate students who
worked on the organization charts: Jennifer Hora, Todd McNoldy, Chris-
tine Kelleher, Brian Fogarty, and Jenny Wolack. Stephannie Volk provided
important staff support. At the National Archives and Records Administration, we received important assistance from Sharon Fawcett of the Presidential Library System. Jennifer Velez, who heads the transcription service we are using, has provided us with superior transcriptions of the
interviews. Victor Kovner gave us important advice on the project's interviews and their legal status. And at several turns in the process, Judith
Zouck lent us a helpful hand.

Project Managers Elizabeth Griffith and Ken Simendinger played important roles in the success of our work. In particular, Ken developed the
databases for the project's White House Address Book, organized and
tracked the schedule of interviews and "Deeds of Gift" from our interviewees, oversaw the production of the "White House Briefing Books,"
managed the manuscript of *The White House World*, and worked with authors during the editing process.

It was a true community of people inside and outside of government
working together who made a reality of the White House Interview Pro-

gram. We thank them all for making possible its development and dissemination helpful to those coming into the White House in January 2001.

Notes

1. More complete versions of the briefing materials were released on the White House 2001 Project website, <www.whitehouse2001.org>.

2. Carl M. Brauer, *Presidential Transitions: Eisenhower through Reagan* (New York: Oxford University Press, 1986), p. xv.

3. Laurin L. Henry, *Presidential Transitions* (Washington, D.C.: Brookings Institution, 1960), pp. 696–97. President Truman also set a precedent honored by his successors of having the CIA brief the Democratic and Republican presidential candidates. Henry, p. 689. For a discussion of some of the elements of the Truman-Eisenhower transition, including the liaison work, see Brauer, *Presidential Transitions: Eisenhower through Reagan*, pp. 15–20. See also John P. Burke, *Presidential Transitions: From Politics to Practice* (Boulder, Colo.: Lynne Rienner, 2000), pp. 9, 14, 100, 409.

4. See Burke, *Presidential Transitions;* James P. Pfiffner, *The Strategic Presidency: Hitting the Ground Running* (Chicago, Ill.: Dorsey, 1988); and Charles O. Jones, *Passages to the Presidency: From Campaigning to Governing* (Washington, D.C.: Brookings Institution, 1998).

5. Harrison Wellford, interview with Martha Joynt Kumar, Washington, D.C., Aug. 26, 1997.

6. James Cicconi, Phillip Brady, and Andrew Card, interview with Martha Joynt Kumar, Washington, D.C., Sept. 19, 1997.

7. Roy Neel, interview with Martha Joynt Kumar, July 18, 1997, Washington, D.C.

8. Michael Jackson, interview with Martha Joynt Kumar, Alexandria, Va., July 8, 1997.

9. Harrison Wellford, interview with Martha Joynt Kumar, Aug. 26, 1997, Washington, D.C.

10. Ibid.

11. William Galston, interview with Martha Joynt Kumar, College Park, Md., June 5, 1997.

12. Ibid.

13. See Burke, *Presidential Transitions;* Pfiffner, *Strategic Presidency;* and Jones, *Passages to the Presidency.*

14. In-person and telephone conversations of Martha Joynt Kumar with several people working on transition issues for presidential candidates Al Gore and George W. Bush.

15. Bradley H. Patterson, *The White House Staff: Inside the West Wing and Beyond* (Washington, D.C.: Brookings Institution, 2000); Karen M. Hult and Charles Walcott, *Governing from the White House: From Hoover to Johnson* (Lawrence: University Press of Kansas, 1997). Program members wanted to make use of our expertise and information to help the incoming White House staff learn about their work. The American Political

Figure 3.

Evaluation Questionnaire – White House Interview Program

We would like your help in evaluating the usefulness to you of the following materials, which, except for Interviews with Predecessors, were available both in our White House Briefing Books and on our website. We prefer you fill out the email version of the questionnaire, which you can download from our website [whitehouse2001.org] under the heading "Evaluation." Continue your comments on the reverse side.

- Essays on Presidential Transitions
- Essays on White House Staff
- Office Essays

- Interviews with Predecessors
- Organization Charts of Offices
- White House Address Book

Your Office and Position _____

I. When and Where Did You Get Information?

1. Did you use our materials? ☐ yes ☐ no
2. If yes, which materials did you use? ☐ transition essays ☐ White House essays ☐ office essay ☐ organization charts ☐ White House Address Book ☐ interviews with predecessors.
3. If no, why not? ☐ lack of time ☐ unaware of them ☐ too lengthy ☐ other _____
4. When did you use them? ☐ mostly in the transition ☐ mostly while in office ☐ both
5. Which did you and your staff use most frequently? ☐ electronic copies ☐ paper copies
6. What comparable materials from other sources did you find helpful? Please comment.
   Comments:

II. Which Materials Did You Find Most Useful?

7. Please evaluate the usefulness of our material. Circle your ranking for each item.

	Very Useful	Useful	Indifferent	Not Very Useful	Not at all Useful
Transition Essays	5	4	3	2	1
White House Essays	5	4	3	2	1
Office Essays	5	4	3	2	1
Interviews w/ Predecessors	5	4	3	2	1
Organization Charts	5	4	3	2	1
White House Address Book	5	4	3	2	1

8. Is there information we should add in future editions of our materials? Please comment.
   Comments:

III. Who Used the Materials?

9. What levels of staff were asked to read it? ☐ deputy ☐ assistant and associate ☐ staff assistant
10. What was the most practical application of the material you used? Please comment.
    Comments:

IV. How Were Our Materials Used?

11. Were our materials used as part of an orientation process for your staff? ☐ yes ☐ no
12. Will you use them as new staff join your office? ☐ yes ☐ no
13. Did you talk with your predecessors? ☐ yes ☐ no
14. If yes, what did you learn from them? Please comment.
    Comments:

Providing Answers to Your Questions

Now that you have 180 days behind you, what would you like to know about the challenges ahead of you? This project will provide a way of getting the information you would like to have. We will contact those who previously held your position and ask them a series of questions, some developed by you and the remainder by us. The questions will be asked anonymously and the answers shared with you.

Please use reverse side to continue your written comments

Return this questionnaire to Clay Johnson or email the electronic version to joyntkumar@aol.com

Science Association has a well-established tradition of contributing to the effective functioning of government through the expertise of its members. Frank J. Goodnow, the first president of the association, was an effective proponent of administrative reorganization, and many who followed him also were concerned with the quality of government operations.

Throughout the years, presidents of the association and many scholars in the field of American politics have sought to provide those in government with techniques and information to help them handle their individual responsibilities and overall operations. Whether it was Goodnow, E. E. Schattschneider and his work on political parties, or more recently the projects related to the two hundredth anniversary of the Constitution, the association and its members have a record of seeking to improve the functioning of governmental operations by increasing peoples' knowledge of and appreciation for the functioning of the political system.

16. "Working the West Wing," *Maryland State of Mind,* hosted by Scott Simon, Maryland Public Television, June 7, 2001.

17. The following articles were previously published in scholarly journals: "The Contemporary Presidency: Meeting the Freight Train Head On: Planning for the Transition to Power," *Presidential Studies Quarterly* 30, no. 4 (Dec., 2000); "Lessons from Past Presidential Transitions: Organization, Management, and Decision Making," "The Presidency and the Political Environment," and "The White House as City Hall: A Tough Place to Organize," *Presidential Studies Quarterly* 31, no. 1(Mar., 2001); "The White House Office of Management and Administration," "The Office of the Staff Secretary," "The Office of the Press Secretary" *Presidential Studies Quarterly* 31, no. 2 (June, 2001); "The White House Office of Presidential Personnel," and "The Chief of Staff" *Presidential Studies Quarterly* 31, no. 3 (Sept., 2001); "The Pressures of White House Work Life: 'Naked in a Glass House'" *Presidential Studies Quarterly* 31, no. 4 (Dec., 2001).

The following pieces appeared in *PS: Political Science and Politics* 31, no. 1 (Mar., 2002): "The Bush Transition in Historical Context;" "The Real Invisible Hand: Presidential Appointees in the Administration of George W. Bush;" "Already Buried and Sinking Fast: Presidential Nominees and Inquiry;" "Strategic Choices and the Early Bush Legislative Agenda;" "The 2000–2001 Presidential Transition: Planning, Goals, and Reality."

"A Tale of Two Transitions: 1980 and 1988," appeared in *Congress and the Presidency* 28 (Spring, 2001).

18. "Working the West Wing."

19. The project has worked together with the National Archives and its Office of Presidential Libraries to develop a "Deed of Gift" for the audio discs as well as the transcripts of the interviews. Many of the interviews are now available for review.

20. Letter from E. Pendleton James to Martha Joynt Kumar, July 10, 2000.

21. In a ranking of usefulness, the heads of the offices rated these essays as 5 (very useful) or 4 (useful) on a scale of 5 to 1.

22. Karen Hughes, interview with Martha Joynt Kumar, Washington, D.C., Aug. 27, 2001.

1

The Presidential Transition

Meeting the Freight Train Head On

Planning for the Transition to Power

MARTHA JOYNT KUMAR

GEORGE C. EDWARDS III

JAMES P. PFIFFNER

TERRY SULLIVAN

PRESIDENTIAL CANDIDATES MUST PLAN EARLY for how the winner and his staff will make effective use of his early days in office. Seizing early opportunities eases confirmations, furthers the president's agenda, and affords a new team a valuable reputation for competence. That is the consensus of people who have worked in top White House positions during the Nixon, Ford, Carter, Reagan, Bush, and Clinton administrations. In interviews for the White House Interview Program, many of the sixty-nine staff members expressed a common frustration over the difficulty of organizing an administration when the White House they enter is whistle clean. Their new offices contain empty desks, no files from their predecessors, and a figurative inbox containing expectations the president will deliver on his promises beginning the moment he enters the Oval Office as chief executive. In order to surmount these difficulties and get a fast start as well, both candidates and their teams need to plan early for governing.[1]

Early Opportunities and Hazards

A new president coming into office runs headlong into a series of challenges and deadlines critical to the definition of the new administration. "You have a series of action-forcing deadlines that come up against you

5

like freight trains," observed Harrison Wellford, a veteran participant in the preparation of Democratic presidential candidates. "There are a whole lot of things that happen right there, and for a brand new administration that hasn't done any of this before, these are intimidating challenges." Indeed, the deadlines are daunting. In the seventy-five days between the election November 7 and the inauguration January 20, a new president has to form his White House team, designate fourteen cabinet secretaries, deliver his inaugural address, present his agenda to the nation, and send to Congress a budget of around $1.8 trillion.

If a president-elect fails to use the transition interregnum wisely, he will risk committing some of the same mistakes that set back the new Clinton administration in 1993. "They didn't know who they were going to be working for," commented one Clinton aide about the White House staff. "They didn't know what they were supposed to be doing and, frankly, they were not even clear on the common agenda for the White House and the administration." Early missteps haunted the Clinton administration well into its first term: a slow start on personnel recruitment, delayed designation of the White House staff, poor vetting of some nominees, failure to set priorities, lax handling of FBI files, and mishandling of the firing of career employees of the White House Travel Office. If one does not put together a good team during the transition, one is losing a valuable opportunity to effectively govern, observed Roy Neel, who began the administration serving as chief of staff to Vice President Al Gore. "You're going to stumble and you'll have huge lost opportunities because your first administration, the whole administration, is often defined by your mistakes and your successes in the first year." The Bush administration in 1989, for example, found right off their momentum was slowed by problems associated with the nomination and failure to confirm John Tower to be secretary of defense. "That was a serious bump in the road for us," commented a member of the Bush White House staff. "It was something, first of all, we hadn't anticipated. It preoccupied senior staff attention at the White House for probably two weeks when we couldn't afford to give it attention." It placed in jeopardy their policy initiatives. "If we had stumbled after the Tower problems, I think it would have taken us a long time to recover and it would have jeopardized any momentum we had on the policy side."

The challenge for a president is to take advantage of the early opportunities within the narrow window from the election to the presentation of his budget. The expository period in a presidency is a time when the Washington political community comes together to welcome its new leader and learn about his people and programs. James Baker, chief of staff to Presidents Ronald Reagan and George Bush, described the atmosphere and opportunities of those early days. "There is to some extent a cessation or minimization of the press's adversarial approach to what's going on," he said. "They're more interested in finding out and reporting on what the new administration has in mind. And you don't have people on the other side attacking you. You're pretty free to name your people, make your choices, set your priorities and your objectives. That ends after a hundred days."

Fairly soon the period of cooperation gives way to what has become a hostile relationship between the administration on the one hand and the opposition party, interest groups, and often the press on the other. "The interest groups, whether it's advertising on radio or television or taking out ads or issuing press releases, from day one, from minute one, they launch an attack," observed Kenneth Duberstein, White House chief of staff at the end of the Reagan administration. In order to fashion a system of institutional support, a president needs a team in place that can make the proper connections with the institutions and individuals who form the Washington political community.

How can a new administration avoid a foreseeable train wreck? In our interviews with them, White House staff members who spoke about the transition identified the following as the important elements to getting off to a successful start.

Focus Now on People and Process

The first order of business in preparing the take over of the government is to analyze the jobs a president can fill, to establish the procedures by which the transition team will collect names of appropriate people to fill them, to determine the priorities they should observe in naming people for the posts, and to collect names of possible appointees. The process used to make decisions is critical to the results garnered.

In order to have a smooth transition, an incoming president needs his people in place. Early personnel planning can lay out an infrastructure that will allow the president-elect's team to handle efficiently the thousands of resumes that will pour into transition headquarters beginning the day after the election. The transition personnel director, preferably the director-designate of the Office of Presidential Personnel, should set up a process that involves everyone who ought to have input on appointments and will give the president the range of choices and levels of detail he wants. Since according to the Office of Personnel Management there are 7,303 non-competitive appointments to be made, 1,119 of which are political appointees requiring Senate confirmation, priorities should be set concerning which positions to fill first.[2]

In the case of the Reagan transition, personnel was the early focus for those preparing for office. Pendleton James, with experience as a Nixon personnel office staff member and as a professional headhunter, directed this operation for candidate Ronald Reagan during the summer and fall prior to the 1980 election and later during the first year and a half of his administration. According to James, planning and preparation are essential. "The guys in the campaign were only worried about one thing: the election night. I was only worrying about one thing: the morning after the election," he said. "There is no start up and there is no learning for Presidential Personnel. It has to start its operation the morning after the election." He continued, "Presidential Personnel has to be functional on the first day, the first minute of the first hour."

Establishing priorities in personnel placement begins with the perceived problems the administration must deal with and the positions taken during the campaign. In Ronald Reagan's case the economy was the key issue and was center stage in the appointment process. Pendleton James detailed how they used the appointment process to focus on the issue.

> So we came up with what I called the key eighty-seven. This is going through a planning process and comes out in the planning stage. Obviously, you know you're going to do the cabinet. Obviously, you know you're going to do the White House staff. Then in what order are you going to do the other? So I and my group went through and said, what are the key economic policy-making jobs? Those are the ones we want to address first because, until that person is sworn in, confirmed or appointed, that desk is empty over at Treasury or over at Commerce. Economic policy goes from State Department, Commerce, Treasury; it goes through everybody. It's not just Treasury Department. You want to make certain in the early days to work filling those appointments crucial to your initiatives of the first hundred days.

Handling the processing of names of appointees includes the consideration of the technology the personnel team will use for the handling of resumes coming from every direction. In order to manage the flood, there needs to be a system set up appropriate to dealing with the anticipated volume. In order to stay current, the electronic technology must be in place to meet the tsunami of resumes hitting the president-elect immediately following the election. Processing of names also requires a timeline of what appointments should be made by what times during the transition. Generally, the names of cabinet appointees are released in full before Christmas, with the key posts of state, defense, treasury, and justice attended to shortly after the election. They are sworn in shortly after the inauguration.

The personnel area is the one where the difference is greatest between a "friendly" and a "hostile" transition. When there is a change of party, the White House staff and those serving in political posts throughout the administration all understand they will almost certainly leave office when the new president comes in. The question is who fires them, not whether they will be asked to leave. At the request of the newly elected president, sometimes an outgoing administration will send out notices to those he appointed letting them know the incoming one wants them to vacate their offices. President Bush did that for President Clinton. When there is no change in party, a difficult situation arises as appointed officials must be convinced to leave. When President Bush took office, there were people in the administration who did not want to leave, for they believed they had worked for the Reagan-Bush team. Yet the Bush team wanted to appoint their own people loyal to the new president. "There was a lot of hard feeling between the Reaganites who felt 'Wait a minute, we got you guys elected; why are you being so rude to us and mean to us?'" said one observer of the transition. "They were deeply antagonized by that process. One of the Bush people told me, 'They've had their time in the sandbox; this is our sandbox now.'" When there is a change in party, there is no disagreement over who controls the "sandbox."

Personnel planning during the campaign must be carried on in a low-key manner and coordinated with the head of the campaign. Otherwise, campaign workers may become suspicious that people in a back room are busily dividing the spoils of victory while they are working hard trying to win the campaign. This kind of resentment can be disruptive to a transition, such as in Jimmy Carter's case. The Reagan team learned the lesson well, and according to James, prior to the election their personnel operation was "behind-the-scenes, not part of the campaign and certainly not known to the public." It also was coordinated with Ed Meese, the campaign manager, who daily met with the personnel team at 6:00 A.M. and at 10:00 P.M.

The decision-making process must have the confidence of the whole team. Richard Cheney, who served as chief of staff for President Ford, explained the consequences when people believe the process to be unfair:

> If you don't trust the process, you're going to start looking for ways around it, try to find a friendly congressman who has a good relationship with the president, maybe the chairman of the committee, who can come down and maybe have lunch with the president one day and get him back on track. All of a sudden you have people freelancing, trying to get around the decision-making process because they feel the process lacks integrity. So it's very, very important when you set up the shop to make certain that you have a guaranteed flow—you know what's going in; you know what's coming out. You know when it goes in that it's complete, that everybody's got their shot at the decision memo. You know if there's going to be a meeting, the right people are going to be in the meeting, that the president has a chance to listen to all of that and then make a decision.

If the process is not perceived as fair, people make end runs around the decision makers. "To the extent that you get advocates for a particular point of view running that process, then the process breaks down." That process is established during the transition and the first place it comes up is in sifting through the appointment process.

Avoid Constraining Commitments

The rhythms of the transition are strongly influenced by the commitments the president-elect made during his campaign. In the months running for office, the candidate can ease his passage to power by establishing a clear agenda. At the same time, he can burden himself by making commitments that haunt him after the inauguration. Several recent presidents have found their commitment to reduce the White House staff to be a constraint once they came into office, including Bill Clinton, who promised to cut the White House staff by 25 percent. "Frankly, the only persons who cared about that in 1992 were a handful of people that populate the House Government Operations Committee on the other side," indicated a member of the early Clinton team. "It never made any sense to do that." Other presidents, including Jimmy Carter, faced similar experiences. The effort it takes to fulfill such a promise is seldom worth the small political payoff, but failure to keep the promise itself can be a large embarrassment.

The pledge made during the campaign by Bill Clinton to have a more ethical administration than that of his predecessors proved to be a problem that followed him throughout his administration. According to one Clinton staffer: "Short-sighted is definitely the most diplomatic word I can use for that because you're going to have people in your administration who have made mistakes, you're going to be burned, people are going to have ethical problems, and it just makes you a bigger target. The only person who cared was Ralph Nader, and I'm sure he didn't vote for us." This same person observed, "To a certain extent you could say that a successful transition is rooted in a campaign that is discreet in its promises because those things can come back to bite you."

Likewise, optimistic pledges about political appointments can complicate early months in office. "You don't want to make promises about diversity, for example, in appointments that you can't keep," said one observer of the process. "The problem is not with having a diversity goal; the problem is that you need to have people's expectations calibrated to when you can deliver on that goal," he said. "There's a tendency sometimes to try to deliver on all those promises right way, right in the first two or three weeks, to show that you have made progress in delivering on the symbolic promises that are supposed to define your administration." Fairly soon, however, the new staff realizes it takes a long time to appoint a range of people that reflects the winning coalition and the diversity of America. The easiest way to avoid the problem is to tone down appointment promises during the campaign.

A candidate also needs to be mindful of promises during the campaign, to share influence with the vice president or the first lady. These too can cause difficulties once the candidate takes office. While "two for the price of one" was an attractive promise of making use of a talented wife, once President Clinton came into power and Hillary Clinton took a West Wing office, some new staff were confused about her place in the decision-making process. Promises made during the campaign or the transition about the role of the vice president may need to be rethought once the administration is in office. While President Ford initially gave Vice President Nelson Rockefeller control over the Domestic Policy Council, in the long run it was a decision the president and his staff rethought.

Top White House Staff Come First

The White House staff is the key to an effective presidency, and having a team in place is crucial to an effective transition. Key designations should be made early in the transition, even before cabinet appointments are determined, as the Clinton team learned during its transition. The White House staff extends the reach of a president and increases his capacity to handle the crushing responsibilities of those early weeks and months. "It's crucial in terms of how he's going to function as president, whether or not he's effective," observed Richard Cheney. "A president can do a lot just based on his own personal skills but there's a limit. His reach, his ability to sort of guide and direct the government, to interact with the cabinet, to deal effectively with the Congress, to manage his relationship with the press, all of those are key ingredients to his success."

As the president-elect considers the role of his White House staff, he must think through the general structure of his operation. If the new president reinvents the wheel, adds layers, or jettisons an office, he and his team should have a good rationale for why they are doing so. With the exception of the National Economic Council, the major White House offices have been in place through several cycles of both Democratic and Republican administrations. Before altering the White House structure, the team should have an understanding of what each office brings to the table. An awareness of the different ways in which White House offices have been structured is an important starting place for those coming in.

In order for the new administration to effectively fill the posts necessary to developing and implementing its policies and budget as well as articulate its programs, the president needs to give highest priority to six White House positions. These can be filled at the same time as the important posts of national security adviser and director of the Office of Management and Budget. These two posts are crucial ones, for the president-elect will hear almost immediately from heads of state with their queries about his policies, and at the same time he will need to move immediately on shaping the new administration's budget priorities.

When choosing people for the following six White House posts, former staff members believe a president needs to be aware of particular characteristics of the posts and the people who have successfully filled them. In addition to having the chief of staff as an early choice, the president-elect needs to appoint at approximately the same time the White House personnel director, counsel, legislative affairs director, the director of Management and Administration, and his press secretary. The chief of staff comes first.

Chief of Staff: Personnel, Process, Decision-Making, and Implementation

Literally nothing comes together in a new White House without a chief of staff. Mark Siegel, who served as a deputy to Hamilton Jordan in the Carter White House, described the first meeting of the senior staff following the inauguration of the new president. "When we all got into the Roosevelt Room and sat down, there was literally no one to convene the meeting. You can only imagine sitting around this table. It's 4:00; we're all really new and very excited. It's 4:00; it's 4:01; it's 4:02. People are coughing. Literally there is no one to convene the meeting. Finally this guy named Robert Lipshutz, who was counsel, said in this very Southern accent, 'Well, I'm the oldest person in this room so maybe I'll just get us going.'" Without a chief of staff, a new operation literally cannot get off the ground.

If a president does not choose a chief of staff in the early days following the election, there will be continual jockeying for position and power. In the White House, personnel selection, political strategy, and operational matters all flow from the chief of staff. This person determines who sees the president, what papers are presented to him, and how decisions will be implemented. In addition, the chief of staff sets the tone and the style influencing the ways in which the White House offices do their business.

The position is difficult to fill because the person must have the respect and confidence of the president. The job is so stress-filled and challenging that traditionally the people who serve in the post hold office no more than two or three years. "Everybody wants something from the president, and your job is to say 'no' or to say 'yes, maybe, but,'" observed James Baker. "It's really a tough job because you are at the heart of the political centrifuge and you're subject to all the pulls and tugs. When people can't get at the president, they're going to try and get at the chief of staff, which is the next best thing." At the same time it is a hard job to hold; it needs someone who the president will listen to. While the kind of relationship James Baker had with the two presidents he served was different, in both cases he worked for presidents who listened to his advice and respected the process he created to gather and sift information, to make the most effective use of people surrounding the president, and to craft decisions.

Personnel Director: Recruitment, Job Descriptions, and Appointment Priorities

If there is one White House official who is under the greatest pressure he will receive at the very point when he assumes office, it is the personnel director. In order for a president to fulfill the pledges he makes during the course of the campaign, he needs to staff his administration quickly and get underway with his program. He cannot do that unless he has people holding positions where policy is developed and then later implemented. Since so much of the preparation for the selection of appointees takes place during the transition, past practice has demonstrated there are strong advantages to having the person who later heads the Office of Presidential Personnel be the one who sets up the process during the transition. In the cases of both Pendleton James and Chase Untermeyer, who headed personnel for Presidents Reagan and Bush for approximately the first two years of each administration, their early involvement in the process led to a smooth transition into the White House with no time lost following the inauguration. In addition, their success was based on their commitment to stay in the post for at least the first year and a half of the administration. The personnel director and deputies must be in place for at least that amount of time, otherwise they can be tempted by other opportunities that come their way.

When hiring a personnel director, the president needs a battle-tested person in whom he has confidence to fill the post and identify candidates who meet his criteria. A strong relationship with the president legitimates the process used to choose appointees and thwarts end-runs around the director. In order to weather the storms caused by disappointed supplicants, the personnel director needs to have strong backing from the president, anything less will compromise the process. Chase Untermeyer spoke of the nature of the personnel director's relationship with the president. "The personnel director must be somebody whom the president knows personally and has that degree of confidence not just so that the personnel director can go forth knowing the president has that kind of confidence but also so that everybody else in the system, in the White House, in the departments and agencies, in the press, in the Congress knows that the personnel director speaks with that degree of authority." A director known to have the president's full support can minimize attempted circumventions and thus save time and energy. "It is a discouragement to game playing if it is known that the personnel director has that degree of trust in his relationship to the president that the tendency or the natural force of Washington politics to get around the roadblock and get at the issue through the chief of staff or the legislative liaison or somebody else is lessened."

Legislative Affairs: Prepare the Way for Confirmations, the Policy Agenda, and the Presidential-Congressional Relationship

The president's assistant for legislative affairs needs to be in place soon after the election in order to smooth the path for nominees to executive-branch positions and to work with members of Congress in creating a favorable climate for the president's program on Capitol Hill. A president-elect traditionally meets with congressional leaders early in the transition. His legislative assistant must be on board in time to arrange the meetings and to work especially closely with the leaders of the president's party. If there is a changeover in power in either the House or the Senate, a president-elect needs to prepare for leaders who are going through the same thing he is: a transition. Kenneth Duberstein, who served as legislative liaison and later as chief of staff in the Reagan White House, discussed the importance of passing names through the legislative affairs person before they go up to the Hill. "You're not looking for a veto; you're looking for pitfalls," he said. "You're saving the president problems because if in fact he goes forward with an intent to nominate and a nomination and then it blows up, you are spending chips that you're going to need elsewhere." With so many nominations going up to the Hill once the president comes into office, the legislative liaison needs time to prepare the way. When appointing a person to this post, presidents often choose people who have worked in the legislative shop from a previous administration and are capable of getting off to a rapid start. In addition, the legislative affairs person should be in place in the early days following the election because the president-elect needs to meet with legislative leaders in November. Solid relationships established during the transition will be useful when the president's legislative agenda goes to Congress in the early days of the administration.

Counsel to the President: Vetting Procedures, Ethics and Record-keeping Guidelines, and Executive Orders

The counsel should be named shortly after an election for three purposes. First, that person needs to establish and guide the vetting process for presidential nominees to executive-branch positions; second, the counsel is responsible for establishing any new ethics and record-keeping guidelines the president-elect might want his administration to observe; and third, the counsel can provide advice on the appropriateness of possible executive orders.

For the counsel as well as for the chief of staff, appointments dominate the work of the transition and of the first year. As was the case in the first Bush administration, having a counsel on board during the transition eased the vetting process once the president took office and C. Boyden Gray became counsel to the president. These early days in office also include legal actions a president wants to take, most especially issuing executive orders. The counsel must be in a position to let the president know what he can and cannot do in the areas of appointments, executive actions, and legislation. He will need to establish guidelines for any ethics rules the president wants to institute and instruct staff on record-keeping practices. The counsel will also be required to anticipate and defend against outside legal actions that affect the president and the presidency. Such duties require a special relationship with the president. Lloyd Cutler, who served as counsel to Presidents Carter and Clinton, discussed the kind of person who needs to be chosen for this post, one capable of telling the president "no." "Clearly you want somebody who has his own established reputation, especially now that presidents are put on the defensive so much about their personal past history and peccadilloes and whatever, and someone who is willing to stand up to the president, to say, 'No, Mr. President, you shouldn't do that for these reasons.'"

Press Secretary: Calibrating Press Expectations and Establishing Presidential-Media Relations

The press secretary is important early in an administration because most often the president-elect is taking time off during the transition period and a spokesperson becomes important in representing his interests to the news media and to the public. One of the first orders of publicity business is to calibrate the expectations of reporters and of the public. Once the election takes place, reporters and news organizations wait for quick decisions reflecting the president-elect's priorities in terms of personnel choices for his administration and his policy agenda. It falls to the press secretary to set the stage for the order of decisions and to reduce the expectations reporters inevitably have about the speed of decision making and the announcement of appointments. In addition, he or she works at establishing a productive relationship between the executive and news organizations, most often beginning with an informal meeting of the president with the representatives of news organizations. In early sessions with the president and, more frequently, with the press secretary, reporters lay out their news needs, as those in the new administration make the transition from campaigning to governing, and familiarize the staff with the routines associated with coverage of a president.

Nowhere is the difference between campaigning and governing more pronounced than in the words spoken on behalf of a candidate and of a president. The statements of a president resonate around the world. There is no room for error when speaking on his behalf, which requires a sound knowledge of the federal government. In addition, the person who becomes press secretary must have an understanding of the news needs of electronic as well as print organizations. The person's skill and experience should measure up to the modern demands of what goes out of and what comes in to the White House. In a contemporary administration, the press secretary must deal with the Press Room, with approximately forty reporters continually in place and cameras representing a dozen organizations perched near the driveway ready to roll. When news breaks, the press secretary must understand the effect of words spoken on behalf of the president.

Office of Management and Administration: White House Personnel Slots, Salaries, and Office Space

The Office of Management and Administration is a unit that most often gets publicity only when thing go awry, such as the firing of the career staff in the Travel Office during the early months of the Clinton administration. The office covers a broad array of functions, all related to White House operations. In the words of a former director, Jodie Torkelson, the office is "an organization that has all the cats and dogs. It's the nonpolicy shop. If it's not policy, it fits in there."

The office has an importance all the same. When the new president and his team come into the White House, it is this unit that decides what positions there are to be filled in the lower levels of the White House and the Executive Office of the president, the salaries assigned to each slot, and who will get what desk. "Those three things, number of slots, salaries, and office space, can just drive people nuts," commented Christopher Hicks,

who directed the office during the middle period of the Reagan administration. Decisions made there about staff and salary are "real hard to fix after the fact," said Hicks. Once a job has a set salary level, it is difficult to
lower the amount the next person will be paid. "My point is that that's one
thing that whoever the administrative people are in the transition and the
chief of staff really ought to hammer out before they move into the White
House because, once they've moved into the White House, it's too late."

Learn from Predecessors

There are several ways a new team can learn from predecessors. The most
important source is the outgoing staff. Another method is to bring in
people with White House experience. A third way is learning from those
career employees who work in the Office of Management and Budget and
in the Office of the Executive Clerk.

Outgoing Team

One of the most important transition opportunities an incoming president
and his team has is the outgoing administration. They are a source of valuable information on personnel positions and can be used to take some actions that smooth the way for the incoming administration. One of the
central elements of taking advantage of the interregnum period is to work
with those who are in power; they generally cooperate with the incoming
president. Among the people who had the best start were those who took
the time to speak with their predecessors, as did James Baker. But this can
only happen if the chief of staff is appointed directly following the election.
Once people come into the White House, they lose the time needed to
make those contacts and calls. James Baker found the chiefs of staff who
preceded him to be a useful source of information on how to structure his
office and who might have the needed experience to staff positions. Filling out the White House staff structure must be done quickly. The position
of chief of staff is the one post where people consistently speak with their
predecessors. Not coincidentally, chiefs are appointed early enough to
have sufficient opportunity to talk to others. Other officials are often appointed with so little time before coming in that they cannot speak with
anyone beforehand.

There is a natural divide between the outgoing White House staff and
those members of the incoming administration, who tend not to listen to

the advice the incumbents would like to deliver. Said Richard Cheney: "You really want to help the new crowd. There is an institutional sense of responsibility; you want things to go well. In our case, certainly President Ford, even though he had a fairly bitter battle with Jimmy Carter, felt strongly about having the transition work and that was his charge to us. So you get organized for it to help the new crowd coming in and basically they're not interested. The basic attitude is 'If you're so smart, how come we beat you? Why do we need to take your advice? You guys lost.' There's just a disconnect there in terms of the desire on the part of the incoming party and the outgoing party in terms of how much they want to work together." The scenario Cheney sketched is one that repeats itself in most incoming administrations, if not at the senior level then with those occupying spots one notch down.

Bringing in a Team with White House Experience

Everyone we have spoken with about transitions has discussed the need to bring in people who know what they are doing, who have a sense of how the White House works, not just how the government operates in Washington. What experience buys is a better shot at a successful start because experienced hands will avoid some of the errors often made by those without such a background. Both Democrats and Republicans have a pool of experienced people around Washington to draw on, especially from the Hill, where there are many who worked in earlier administrations.

While that means having people serve who have previously worked in a White House or operated close to one, it does not exclude campaign people. They too need to be included in an executive staff, for they are the institutional memory of a campaign, which is important as they remind a team why they are there. "You need some people from the campaign involved," commented David Gergen, a White House staff member in four of the six most recent administrations. "I think there's a tendency on the policy side for recommending you keep all those campaigners out of there; it's going to wreck the place. I think that's wrong headed. I believe in having policy people sort of coming in and playing larger roles but the campaign people know what the candidate said, they know the mood of the candidate, [and] they know how the policy issues evolved in the campaign. Most of all, they know the guy. They know his rhythms; they know his demands; they know what makes him tick, what drives him crazy. You need a few people around that really know the body and are accustomed to it and how to manage it well. It's really stupid to let those people all go." Tom Griscom, who served as communications director toward the end of the Reagan administration, points out that when the Reagan White House lost all of the people from the 1980 campaign, it went off course. In the second term few remembered firsthand the 1980 campaign why Reagan was initially elected. "I do think you need people who were there almost from beginning because they do understand the fundamentals of what got the person there," he said. Once the changeover took place in the second term, "you lost that institutional memory, what were the core [policies]." That loss worked to the president's disadvantage.

Michael Deaver, who served as deputy chief of staff during the first term of the Reagan administration, discussed his recommendation to candidate Reagan that, should he win, he bring James Baker into his White House. Deaver went to Reagan in Middleburg, Virginia, three or four weeks before the election to talk to him about appointing a chief of staff. "That was the smartest thing he ever did as far as I was concerned because we got a seasoned guy who knew the ropes, knew how to deal with the Congress, knew how to deal with the media in town, was a respected political figure," said Deaver. "It wasn't like Jimmy Carter who came to town and brought all his Georgians. Reagan did bring a lot of Californians, but in the middle of all those Californians he put someone who was the first among us who was a seasoned Washingtonian, a guy who knew his way around." Deaver believed having someone heading the staff who knew Washington bought longevity for the new administration. "I don't think Ronald Reagan would have been reelected if that hadn't happened. I don't think he would have been a two-term president," he said. "He had a lot of counsel from Baker and people that Baker brought to the table who had been through other wars, who had been through fights with the Congress, who knew how to work with the Republican minority leadership and knew how you used OMB [Office of Management and Budget] and all these things that Jimmy Carter never figured out."

Retaining and Making Use of the White House Institutional Memory

Learning from predecessors also means keeping around some of those people who have made the place work for years. It is a mistake to assume that people who have served from one administration to another are likely to be partisan or instantly disloyal to a new president. Such career staff would include the executive clerk and people at OMB and the National Security Council who know the ropes. They become an important information source as new staff begin their work and want to find out how things have been previously done. The executive clerk, for example, maintains the records for legislation, executive orders, and appointments coming out of the White House. Andrew Card, who served as deputy chief of staff for Pres. George W. Bush, noted that administrations need to "be careful that everyone doesn't drain out of the White House; you want to have some institutional memory. Yes, in theory they are all there by the grace of the president." To get rid of the people in a White House with experience in performing the tasks associated with its many offices is to invite trouble on several fronts, as was the case with the Clinton administration. "As you remember, they did pull the plug on a lot of those people, and it took them some time to get back up to speed and it also invited distrust," Card commented. Two of the critical places for institutional memory are the OMB and the career staff who work in the Executive Office of the President. When in one administration a senior political staff member suggested that the deputy associate directors be fired, an OMB veteran pointed out that this "would be a catastrophically dumb idea both from the point of view of ever having OMB as an institution work very well but also from the point of view of all the institutional knowledge and skill you lose."

Develop a Strategic Plan for Policy Proposals

If much is to be accomplished in the hectic and conflicted first few months in office, it cannot be done by inadvertence; there must be a strategic plan. James Baker discussed the role of early policy preparation in the successes of President Reagan's first term. "One reason I think that the Reagan administration succeeded the first term as well as we did was that we had a really definitive, well-thought out, right-here hundred-day plan. We went back and we looked at the plans of everybody all the way back to Truman. What were their first goals, priorities, and objectives? We drafted a hundred-day plan and we stuck to it." The first and only priority was the president's economic plan, and "we did not let national security [or] foreign policy issues that were not absolutely critical get in the way of a single-minded focus on that plan."

When a president-elect and his team establish their priorities, it is important they choose their battles wisely. "So many demands are coming at you from people that it is easy to commit yourself to actions and initiatives you might regret later on," advised Harrison Wellford. "Choose the battles that you first engage very, very carefully because so much disproportionate attention is paid to those." President Carter made early attempts to eliminate water projects that made him expend a great amount of presidential time, energy, and reputation. He never did win on the issue. In the case of the Clinton transition, the gays in the military issue became a lightning rod for his early months. "I always thought there was a different way to do that that didn't make that the defining issue of the first two months because it couldn't have been more perfectly designed to get him off to the wrong start," said one person close to the process. It happened in part because there was not in place a decision-making process emphasizing close scrutiny of initiatives, including passing them through a sieve of policy advocates and those knowledgeable about governmental and public responses. Early planning allows a new team to stave off those importuning them with their agendas.

The benefits are many of having a refined agenda in place well before the president-elect takes office. "Everybody who came in knew where he stood," David Gergen said about the White House staff who came in to work for President Reagan. "There were no struggles over the soul of the administration, over the overall direction. You knew what the philosophy was; then you knew what the policy prescription was going to be at least in the domestic area." Along with the agenda, a White House needs to complement it with a communications operation capable of synthesizing and packaging a message for the administration. Robert Lipshutz, counsel to President Carter, discussed the consequences of not having this. "We never had a public relations person really thinking about the various things that would have perhaps allowed the president to do all the things that he wanted to do, or at least try, or at least have them on [the] agenda and put our best foot forward," he said. "Instead the press, you might say, and the political people outside of the administration set the tone that you're talking about rather than us setting the tone."

A crucial aspect of a successful strategic plan is a comfortable working relationship with those on the Hill. The administrations that have been successful have been ones that worked closely with Congress from its earliest point, including having people familiar with congressional operations head the team. Upon taking office, James Baker sent Kenneth Duberstein to the Hill to see the minority whip for the House of Representatives, Trent Lott, as his first assignment. Duberstein recalled: "It was a crucial interview. The president had the prerogative to appoint me anyway, but the person I was going to be working with was Trent Lott in part along with others. So you needed to run it past him." In addition, Duberstein recommended that the names of people be run by committee chairs. "Consult with your friends. Consult with your committees of jurisdiction. I don't mean consult with twenty senators but I mean with the chairman and the ranking member; I mean the Senate leader and minority leader."

Howard Baker indicated that the length of a honeymoon depends on the relationship of the president with Congress. "I decided that I was going to be Ronald Reagan's flag carrier in the Senate and worked very hard at trying to coordinate the Senate's agenda with the president's agenda. I think that was a distinctly superior arrangement. But that relationship between the congressional leadership and the White House has a great deal to do with how long that honeymoon lasts, the quality of effort." Convincing the congressional leadership to work with the new president is a task that begins early with the campaign advisers in policy areas informally discussing agendas with the leaders of their party in one or both houses. Once the election is over, the legislative affairs director sets the stage for the preliminary discussions.

Conclusion

An appearance of arrogance associated with planning for governing stops most presumptive presidential nominees from organizing their plans for the transition to power until well after the summer conventions. In fact, the greater risk lies with the absence of planning for the assumption of power. Those who have served in White House posts and know the advantages and disadvantages associated with the quality of the start an administration strongly believe early planning is associated with an effective first year in office. It is during his early months that a president staffs up his administration, lays out and marshals support for the top-priority items on his agenda, and shapes his relationships throughout the governing community. In a setting where those coming into office can anticipate vacant offices and empty drawers, their planning must be completed and their decision-making processes in place well before they come in to office. The White House is no place for on-the-job training.

Notes

1.   The interviews were conducted during 1999 and 2000 for the White House Interview Program, principally by Martha Joynt Kumar. The interviews, averaging

around two hours, were made available to the directors and deputies coming into the seven selected White House offices in 2001. Some material also was made available to the transition team. Depending upon the release conditions governing the interviews, the transcripts were made publicly available beginning in the middle of 2001 through the White House Interview Program website <www.whitehouse2001.org> and by the Office of Presidential Libraries in the National Archives. The project was developed through the board and members of the Presidency Research Group, a section of the American Political Science Association. The board of the White House Interview Program oversees the project.

    2.   The job numbers come from <www.opm.gov/fedlist/data.htm>.

Lessons from Past
Presidential Transitions
Organization, Management, and Decision Making

JOHN P. BURKE

I N ADDITION TO CAREFUL AND EARLY CONSIDERA-
tion of the key positions on the White House staff and other appointments, transitions are also a time when presidents-to-be and their
advisers need to think about how the pieces fit together into a larger
whole. Part of that effort involves crafting the decision-making processes
and the various channels of information and advice that, once in office, a
president will need to utilize in making policy choices. Another piece entails the marketing and selling of those policy proposals to the public and
Congress and otherwise bringing them to successful fruition. Still another
are the management tasks that are associated with policymaking and implementation. How are the skills and talents of a diverse range of actors—
some of whom may be newcomers not just to the White House or the executive branch but to Washington itself—successfully brought together
and coordinated? How is a sense of teamwork and commitment instilled
and conflict and tension avoided?

Beginning with the Carter effort in 1976, transitions have shared common elements:

- Transition-planning activities undertaken before the November election
- Organization of a postelection transition

- Creation of teams directed at policy planning and the crafting of a presidential agenda
- Establishment of groups concerned with gathering information on particular agencies and departments
- Attention to cabinet and subcabinet appointments
- Appointing and shaping a White House staff

Yet there has also been significant variation in how each of these transitions went about these tasks, some of which received more emphasis than others, and what was accomplished successfully and what was not.

Perhaps most significant in differentiating successful from unsuccessful transitions is the degree to which these tasks were recognized as contributors to presidential decision making and the formulation of successful policy outcomes. In the 1992 Clinton transition, for example, cabinet appointments quickly became a major preoccupation to the detriment of selecting a White House staff and figuring out how it would be organized. Clinton would not settle on the appointment of his chief of staff until mid-December, and a number of top staff members were not selected until a week before inauguration day. In the absence of staff-personnel decisions, little could be done to figure out how "people" could be organized into an effective "process" that could flesh out campaign promises into concrete and politically feasible policy proposals.

But Clinton does not stand alone in his troubles. Jimmy Carter wanted a leaner, more collegial White House staff than had been the case during the Nixon years, and he wanted a more significant role for his cabinet. Yet during his transition, little effort was made to plan for how those hopes might operate in practice. As a result, Carter ended up with a staff that became compartmentalized rather than collegial, a cabinet that never functioned effectively as a group, and he found himself overburdened in policy detail.

George H. W. Bush's broader experience placed him in a better position than "political outsiders" like Clinton and Carter in making personnel choices. Yet Bush's transition efforts would likewise backfire occasionally. Although some of his key assistants were appointed early on, the selection of the presidential assistant for domestic and economic policy was not made until early January, and some of the units that were central to the marketing and selling of the administration's proposals (the White House Political Affairs, Public Liaison, and Intergovernmental Affairs Offices) were placed at lower organizational levels in the White House staff than had been the case under his predecessors.

For Ronald Reagan, the transition provided a clearer recognition of the organizational needs that would fit with his style as a decision maker as well as more attention to decision-making processes. But it also crafted a process that left Reagan largely uninvolved in the early stages of policy formulation and demanded a high degree of trust and cooperation between those to whom much had been delegated (most notably Ed Meese, Jim Baker, and Michael Deaver).

Each of these transitions also provides positive legacies. Carter recognized, as none of his predecessors had to date, the complexity of the transition process and the scope of activities now required for that effort. What his transition broadly undertook in 1976 would set the parameters of the task for his successors. Reagan's 1980 effort illustrates the importance of a clear policy agenda, commitment to that agenda, and the creation of processes that would secure that agenda. George H. W. Bush was skilled in selecting associates who were personally loyal to him and, in some cases through Bush's own efforts years earlier, had acquired the Washington political and policy expertise that would make their own transition to new positions much smoother. For Bill Clinton, the 1992 transition saw the creation of the National Economic Council (NEC) and the appointment of an experienced economic team.

The Seeds for a Successful Transition Are Sown Early

What is accomplished before election day directly bears not only on how quickly the actual transition is up and running afterward but also on how smoothly and effectively it will operate. As Leon Panetta observed, "The sooner you start this process the better off you are in hitting the ground running if you [are] elected, as opposed to starting from scratch."[1]

The postelection period simply allows too little time to get up to speed in dealing with the hurdles that will be faced in making appointments (financial disclosure requirements and FBI background checks), setting up the physical logistics of the postelection transition (office space, equipment, and the possible division of labor between operations in Washington and the president-elect's home base), as well as decisions about top-level appointees that are normally expected soon after election day.

Andrew Card, who was a participant in the incoming 1988 Bush transition and then headed its outgoing transition in 1992, recalled, "I think it's critical to have someone thinking about personnel, but it's important that that person or someone think about the process for personnel because it's the process that gets you into trouble." Card especially counseled the Clinton team in 1992 that "it was going to take them twice as long as they realized to get people completed with their background checks and their financial checks and everything else and that they should start soonest on that."[2] An effort that is on track regarding personnel—both in planning an appointments process and in preparing for the variety of legal hurdles to be faced—will be of inestimable value to a speedy and effective postelection effort.

Transition Planners versus Campaign Staff

The practice for all of the transitions from 1976 on has been to separate any transition planning before election day from the operations of the campaign. The conventional wisdom is that the campaign must remain focused on the immediate task at hand rather than become preoccupied with planning for an administration that may not come to be. Moreover, this separation has not only been organizational but also geographical, with each group operating in different locations.

Yet even when organizationally and physically separate, tensions between the campaign staff and the transition team have often still erupted, and they present an important management challenge that needs to be addressed during the preelection period. As Harrison Wellford explained, the emergence of "conflicts, rivalries, and jealousies" can mean "that even when good work was done, it failed to find the audience that it was supposed to find because it became hostage to all these internal conflicts."[3]

Developing Trust: Leadership, Respect, and Communication

One difference among recent transitions is the degree of trust that exists between the campaign staff and the preelection transition group, particularly its leadership. In 1976 Carter's choice of Jack Watson to head his transition operation quickly generated concerns among the campaign team that Hamilton Jordan headed, and these were to spill over into the postelection period. As Landon Butler, one of Jordan's campaign deputies, recalled: "It resulted in some bad blood because there were sort of the feelings that we won the campaign and now we're going to turn it over to the smart people. It was bitter. It was very bitter at the time and that didn't go well."[4] Next to the selection of a running mate, the person the presidential candidate chooses to head any transition-planning operation will be the most important and consequential personnel decision that will be made until election day.

More generally, in Harrison Wellford's view, "you need to choose people in those jobs [campaign staff and transition planners] who have mutual respect and recognize the importance of both functions and try to keep the tension from developing by having information flow back and forth." A perception that a candidate is measuring the White House drapes before election day is a political liability, thus the tendency for secrecy about transition planning. But too great an effort to keep the transition operation "hermetically sealed off from everybody else" can leave "key campaign people [feeling] that they were not involved."[5]

Oversight

Oversight of the activities of the preelection transition operation is also a crucial part of the management task. In 1980 Ed Meese, who was director of the campaign, met almost daily with Pendleton James, the head of the preelection effort. In 1988 George Bush, Jim Baker, and John Sununu held frequent meetings with Charles "Chase" Untermeyer, who directed the pre-election effort. In both of these instances, informal linkage to the campaign was clearly established either by a key player in the campaign's operation (Meese) or at the highest levels in the case of Bush and his advisers. In 1976 and 1992, by contrast, oversight and linkage to the campaign were more tenuous. The day after his election, for example, Bill Clinton was reportedly surprised to find out that his campaign staff was upset and angry with Mickey Kantor's efforts during the preceding months. Furthermore, in both 1976 and 1992, internal struggles that had been festering broke out, delaying the business of the transition.

In Harrison Wellford's view, "A lot of it is the tone set by candidate himself." Another remedy, in his view, is (as Meese was in 1980) to make the campaign chief "very involved in setting up the planning committee . . . and making it clear that he has confidence in the people that are doing the planning and sees himself as one of the reviewers of the information before it goes to the president-elect."[6]

How Much Preelection Planning Is Enough?

The Reagan and Bush transitions also differed from those of Carter and Clinton in the scope of their efforts. Preelection planning in 1980 and 1988 was largely limited to developing a personnel operation and determining what steps needed to be taken after election day, while in 1976 and 1992 the mandate was more broadly drawn to include not just personnel but also policy planning, White House staffing and organization, and a range of matters relating to the agenda of the new administration and its first months in office. "Friendly takeovers," especially by sitting vice presidents, make the transition easier, and the scope of the preelection effort is likely more limited. But the Reagan 1980 preelection effort is also instructive: a party turnover but without the more elaborate efforts of 1976 and 1992.

Informal Decisions at the Top

The Reagan preelection effort in 1980 was not bereft of early planning in some of these areas. Rather the difference is that they occurred within the inner circle of the candidate and his advisers, not in some separate operation from which the campaign staff might have felt alienated. In 1980 Reagan and his advisers had begun to think about key positions, such as chief of staff, before election day, and they also benefited from a number of task forces, tied to the campaign rather than the transition, that had begun the process of defining policy choices.

One lesson that might be drawn here is that while a preelection transition operation may be needed, transition planning during this period need not be restricted to those formally charged with it. The presidential candidate and his or her inner circle must begin the staffing and organization process even before election returns are in. At a minimum, in David Gergen's experience: "Given the fact that the transition is only eleven weeks long—it's so compressed—you have to get as much done as possible before the transition starts and not wait for the transition. Unless you prepare well for the transition, you're going to find it much more difficult."[7]

Up and Running after Election Day: Organizing and Managing for a New Presidency

As George C. Edwards III, Martha Joynt Kumar, James Pfiffner, and Terry Sullivan have rightly noted in the previous chapter, presidents-elect must move quickly on key staff appointments following the election. Not only does this still speculation (and also an element of internal competition) about who will be appointed, but it also permits those new appointees to move with dispatch in organizing their own staffs and otherwise acquiring the information and expertise needed to "come up to speed" through contacts with their predecessors and with their opposite numbers in the incumbent administration. In 1992, although Clinton had broached the possibility of serving as his chief of staff to Thomas L. "Mack" McLarty shortly after the election, it was not until mid-December that the appointment was announced. McLarty was able to contact some of his predecessors as chief of staff, but the delay left him less time to assemble a White House staff, who in turn had little time to prepare for the tasks ahead.

Quick Movement on the Transition's Organization

The postelection transition continues to pose management challenges. One is the degree to which the president-elect is ready to move quickly in putting in place a postelection transition operation. Again, preelection planning will figure significantly in that effort. In 1988, although his mandate was quite limited, Untermeyer prepared a lengthy memo for Bush on the steps that needed to be taken, and Bush immediately took action. Jack Watson had done the same for Carter in 1976. But the tensions between Watson's operation and Hamilton Jordan's campaign team spilled over after the election, and there was almost a two-week delay before the transition's organization was fully worked out. Carter was reportedly irritated at the squabbling among his lieutenants, but he provided little personal guidance, preferring instead that they work out the differences themselves. The whole episode proved costly, and in the interim, valuable time had been lost. According to one staff member, "basically nothing was happening."[8]

A transition operation that is clearly in place shortly after election day presents a number of obvious benefits to a successful transition. In 1980, for example, not only was James Baker's appointment as chief of staff settled early, but he also was designated as deputy director of the transition and placed in charge of White House planning on November 6, two days after the election. Baker had ample time to prepare for the task ahead as well as the organizational authority and clear mandate to do so.

Having a transition operation in place also permits the appointments operation to commence, which in turn has a number of advantages. It may help dampen the uncertainties of those involved in the campaign or transition eager to learn about their jobs in the new administration. The sooner top layers of the administration are filled, moreover, the sooner second- and third-level staff positions can be determined. Early appointment also extends the time frame in which the official-designate can begin to get a handle on the new position.

Continuity in Transition Leadership?

Like the early designations of Untermeyer and C. Boyden Gray in 1988, Baker's appointment and mandate in 1980 is indicative of the benefits of making early decisions on key appointments and providing an element of continuity between the transition and the new administration. Yet, interestingly, an element of continuity has often been more difficult to achieve between the pre- and postelection leadership of the transition. In 1988, while George Bush had slotted Untermeyer to direct personnel matters, the postelection operation was codirected by Craig Fuller, his vice presidential chief of staff, and Robert Teeter, one of his principal campaign strategists. In 1992 Clinton passed over Mickey Kantor in favor of Vernon Jordan and Warren Christopher. In 1976, while Watson would emerge as the transition's "coordinator," a number of important functions (including personnel and "political coordination") were assigned to Hamilton Jordan, and a separate communications operation was instituted under the direction of Press Secretary Jody Powell. Only in 1980, when Ed Meese oversaw the preelection effort and then served as director of the postelection effort for Reagan, do we find one person who retained a central role in both the pre- and postelection periods.

While continuity may be advisable, it may not be a necessary requirement for a successful transition. Bush's postelection appointment of Fuller and Teeter indicates that presidents-elect can safely switch horses in midstream; indeed, given Untermeyer's limited mandate from the start, that may have been the intent. But if the aim is to have a more limited operation before election day and then proceed more vigorously thereafter, decisions about who will head the transition will need to be made quickly. The roughly seventy-five days on average until the inauguration leaves little time for delay or indecision.

The Problem of Transition Leaders Who May End Up in the Cabinet

Clinton's appointment of Warren Christopher to codirect his transition's postelection operation presents another important lesson about continuity, now within the transition itself. In this case, it raises the issue of entrusting transition responsibilities to someone who then is nominated to a cabinet-level position. As Christopher himself would later note, following his mid-December nomination as secretary of state, "I began to shift gears to preparing to assume leadership of the State Department."[9] In fact, Clinton would face a double-whammy in this regard: the person charged with heading up the transition's personnel operation, former governor Richard Riley of South Carolina, also was appointed to a cabinet position, secretary of education. According to one 1992 transition member: "The personnel process was a complete mess" once Riley was tapped for the cabinet; "it was just chaos . . . , there were no real people with experience running it."[10]

"Beltway," If Not Prior White House Experience, Especially Helps

Another element of a successful transition is enlisting the services of those with Washington if not prior White House experience, not just at the top but also throughout the transition organization. This presents an obvious challenge to those presidents-elect who do not have prior Washington experience, but it is not insurmountable. Ronald Reagan, while a political "outsider," could benefit from the services of those who had served in the Nixon and Ford administrations. As Harrison Wellford explained: "they knew how things worked. They were highly professional people. As a result, from day one with Reagan there was a discipline and order to the process." But the Carter and Clinton experiences were different. "Carter came in after years of Republican rule and put together an ad hoc team the way you do with very few people with much experience. . . . The people actually making the decisions were people out of state government for the most part or out of the campaign who had no experience in national life at all. . . . Clinton was much the same way. . . . So you had a sense of amateur hour with Clinton."[11] In 1992, in the view of Leon Panetta: "When it came to the White House staff it was almost like, my goodness, we're at inauguration day, we better bring in a lot of people who worked in the campaign. You cannot do that. . . . They've got to know how the White House operates. You have to have grownups."[12]

But Loyalty and Prior Association also Count: The Key Is to Blend

While Washington experience may help, personal loyalty and familiarity with the new president are also of great benefit. As David Gergen explained, the ability to blend the two were key to the success of the early Reagan presidency: "The success of the Reagan blend was he brought some people who knew him well and were extremely loyal to both his program and to his philosophy and to the man, all of whom were newcomers to Washington. . . . But he blended that with a team of experienced Washington insiders who didn't know the man as well but knew Washington well." So too with some of the campaign staff, in Gergen's view. "There is a tendency on the policy side to keep those campaigners out of there. . . . But the campaign people know what the candidate said, they know the mood of the campaign, they know how the policy issues evolved in the campaign. Most of all, they know the guy."[13]

The Advantages of Timeliness

Timeliness in organizing the transition affects the ability of the new administration to have its people in place in agencies and departments come inauguration day. This is especially needed when there is an interparty transfer of power, and at least one high-level appointee of the new administration needs to be in place on January 20. In the case of the new Clinton administration, for example, there were difficulties with the appointment of a new attorney general, and the Justice Department was headed for several weeks by a Bush administration holdover. Webb Hubbell, a Clinton confidante and Hillary Clinton's former law partner, was slated for the number-two position at Justice, but even his nomination had not yet been confirmed when the administration took office. According to Hubbell, while "the job was getting done" in those early days, "the administration couldn't get its program under way because it still had a Republican attorney general. And the media began focusing on what they called a leadership vacuum at Justice."[14]

Timing and the Policy Agenda

The president-elect's political agenda might also figure in the timing and pace of cabinet and other appointments. Early action on appointments in areas that are at top of the president's agenda permits a head start on a confirmation process that is proving to be increasingly lengthy. Early action in particular policy areas also may prove of political benefit: signals of presidential commitment and priority. Both in 1980 and in 1992, Presidents-elect Reagan and Clinton emphasized their intentions to vigorously pursue new economic policies by making early appointments and by clustering them together to convey the sense of an economic team. Early action in appointing the White House staff is also critical here. As David Demarest, Bush's communications director, observed: "You need a White House that is driving the agenda."[15]

Policy Teams

An effort at continuity might also be of value at other points during the transition. All recent transitions have created policy teams to translate campaign promises into concrete proposals. Placing members of the new administration who will have responsibility in those policy areas on those teams will likely facilitate the policy-development process in a timely way. During the 1992 transition, Sandy Berger headed up the national security policy group and became deputy national security adviser in the new administration. In domestic policy Bruce Reed served as deputy director and later became deputy director of the Domestic Policy Council. In economic affairs Robert Reich headed up the group (he would be tapped as secretary of labor), within which were also Robert Rubin (who would become head of the new National Economic Council), Laura D'Andrea Tyson (the chair of the Council of Economic Advisers), and Gene Sperling (who would become Rubin's deputy at the NEC).

Presentation of a budget message to Congress and the State of the Union address, both of which occur soon after inauguration day, especially require timely action. Although some issues may have clearly risen during the campaign, as Andrew Card has noted, "You've got to start thinking about it anew." Moreover, effective movement on the policy front is linked to other elements of a successful transition, particularly in having people in place who are adept at the art of governance rather than just successful campaigning. Again, according to Card: "Identify your White House staff early and identify a team of people that will start working on your first policy initiatives. Have them work with people in the campaign but have it be under the government types rather than the politics types."[16]

Mack McLarty later recalled that in 1992, while getting a government in place was a first priority, "the second was certainly to get an economic plan developed. The president had been elected in large measure on the economic ideas he had put forth. We needed to get ready for legislation, get it to Congress, and start debate." And like Card, McLarty also noted the difference in the task before and after election day: "Obviously you weren't governing in the campaign. You were running in the campaign."[17]

Department and Agency Teams

The teams that most transitions have created to focus on particular departments and agencies are also part of this equation. Some transitions have found these efforts useful, others less so. Landon Butler cautions that in the 1976 Carter transition, "there was a lot of wasted effort . . . in doing a department-by-department study of what the issues were and presenting [Carter] with policy books . . . that didn't turn out to be relevant."[18]

While department-focused teams may be especially necessary when there is a change in party, friendly takeovers by the same party do provide an opportunity for a leaner effort in this area. In 1988, for example, the Bush transition could rely—and with a degree of confidence—on the work and reports that were produced by the Reagan administration.

Yet attention to what is going on in the agencies and departments is useful no matter the nature of the transition. The candidate's agenda aside, the transition needs reliable information about budgets, personnel, organization, pending bills, legislation up for renewal, congressional liaison, and other matters that may be specific to only one department.

Establishing a Cordial Working Relationship with the Outgoing Administration

Not only are transitions the occasion for the president-elect to meet with the incumbent president for the traditional policy briefing and tour of the White House, but they are also times when members of the transition staff must work constructively with their counterparts in the outgoing administration. Both levels are critical. As Harrison Wellford observed: "It's very important to the success of the transition that the president-elect develop a constructive, cooperative relationship with the outgoing administration and the atmosphere of cooperation and mutual respect be communicated to the outgoing transition team and the incoming transition team. If that's not done well, then you have the potential for really big problems that can screw up the first hundred days of the new administration." In particular, transition members need to avoid the "tendency right after the election to still want to fight election battles."[19]

Likewise, the outgoing administration can smooth the way for their successors. As Landon Butler noted of the 1976 transition, "I think, by and large, we learned far more from our predecessors than we did from any written material. . . . They genuinely wanted us to be successful. . . .

I think the most important thing would be to try to make sure they talk to their predecessors and to set a tone and establish in writing: don't make this a bitter transition; don't walk out the door."[20]

Early Decisions: Not Just People but also Process

Early decisions are also advantageous in beginning to put together the processes that the president will use in developing policy and making decisions. Part of that effort will be directed at the organization and operations of the White House staff. In 1980, not only was chief of staff–designate Jim Baker able to craft a White House staff, but he and Ed Meese also early on settled on the division of labor between their respective responsibilities. In 1992, by contrast, the planned task force on the White House that had been envisioned by the preelection transition-planning effort was eliminated in the postelection effort. White House matters would be handled informally by Clinton and his top advisers in Little Rock Yet in competition with the daunting task of cabinet appointments, White House planning was delayed.

How the Cabinet Figures In

How the cabinet will play a role in policymaking is also a matter that might be profitably raised during the transition. Cabinet government—at least in the sense of some collective process involving the whole cabinet—is surely elusive. Yet cabinet members either individually or in particular policy areas will need to be involved in the process. Even if policymaking is centered in the White House, many policy issues will likely touch on areas of departmental responsibility and many will likely cross departmental boundaries. Even policies that neatly fit within the domain of a particular department may be matters of White House interest, direction, and coordination.

There is little statutory guidance here, and a new administration has a significant degree of organizational and administrative discretion.[21] What nondepartment heads will be designated members of the cabinet? Will subgroups of the cabinet be created (for example, a domestic policy council or an economic policy council of some sort)? How many cabinet councils will there be? What cabinet members will serve on them? Will cabinet members chair them (the Reagan-Bush practice) or will they be led by White House staff members (Nixon and Clinton)? How will the work of the councils be staffed? Will the White House's Office of Cabinet Affairs take the lead (the practice in the second Reagan term and under George H. W. Bush) or will White House domestic and economic policy staff play the major role (Reagan first term and Clinton)?

Institutional Memory

Institutional memory between one administration and another can be lean in a White House where, quite literally, at noon of January 20, offices are empty and papers have been carted off to await the opening of yet another presidential library.

But people with experience can fill in some of the gaps. In the 1988 Reagan-to-Bush transition, for example, David Bates, who was placed in charge of the White House cabinet affairs office, could turn to Reagan incumbent Nancy Risque (as well as Bush transition codirector Craig Fuller, who had been secretary to the cabinet duirng Reagan's first term). Jim Cicconi, the new staff secretary, could call on Richard Darman (as well as draw upon his own experience as deputy chief of staff to Jim Baker). J. Bonnie Newman, who was placed in charge of White House administration and management, could turn to Rhett Dawson, whose responsibilities overlapped with hers. C. Boyden Gray established a close working relationship with Arthur Culvahouse, the head of the Reagan legal counsel office, as did Untermeyer with Robert Tuttle in personnel.

The Bush transition also enjoyed good cooperation in assembling other information that would prove useful. It was largely able to dispense with the cumbersome teams that both the Carter and Reagan transitions had created that were directed at particular departments and agencies. In their place incumbent officials were charged by Chief of Staff Duberstein with assembling that information for them. With respect to White House organization and planning, Andrew Card (who was tapped to serve as John Sununu's deputy chief of staff) would later recall that: "I went and got every flowchart from every previous White House, and I had worked in the Reagan White House so I had a sense. . . . So we were ready to staff up on day one."[22]

The 1988 Bush transition clearly benefited from the fact that it was a transfer of power to a sitting vice president of the same party. Yet friendly takeovers are not without their problems, particularly if officials within the incumbent administration maneuver to retain their positions. On November 10, 1988, President Reagan instructed that all political appointees sub-

mit letters of resignation "effective at the pleasure of the president," an order that had been agreed upon before the election by the Reagan and Bush
camps. But, as Card would later note, "the friendly takeover was more
difficult than the hostile because in the friendly takeover there was almost
an expectation that they would stay on."[23] In David Gergen's view, "It is a
much cleaner process when you change parties. Everybody knows, if
you're on the old team, you leave and you leave with good grace."[24]

Some Final Points

Transitions are linked to subsequent presidencies in other ways. Unintended consequences may issue from them, warning signs may emerge,
and they are increasingly subject to media scrutiny.

Unintended Consequences

Presidents-elect and their transition advisers need to be attentive to the
unintended consequences of what might seem appropriate actions at the
time but that may come back to haunt them later. The pledges to cut
the White House staff that are often made during the campaign and transition are but one example. Both the Carter and Clinton White Houses, for
example, were negatively affected by that pledge. In Carter's case it led to
intramural competition and bickering about which units were to be cut.
For Clinton, the permanent White House staff would suffer, the White
House correspondence unit most notably.

  In George H. W. Bush's case the issue was not size but hierarchy. He
wanted fewer staff members with the title of "assistant to the president"
(the top White House rank just below the chief of staff). The thought was
that the number of assistants had grown over the Reagan years—"title
creep"—and that at the start of the Bush presidency there would be twelve
assistants rather than twenty or more. More assistants might be added,
moreover, at some future point as a reward for good service. But the
change had unintended consequences: the units scaled back were the
White House Political Office, Public Liaison Office, and the Intergovernmental Affairs Office—all crucial to marketing and selling this president's
programs. Moreover, "title creep" was scaled back within particular units.
As a result the White House speechwriters no longer had staff rank that
entitled them to presidential commissions, and thus they no longer had
White House mess privileges. News stories about the "demotion" of the

speechwriters quickly appeared in the press, and the inferences were drawn about the communication strategy and skills of this presidency. In addition, the speechwriters themselves were perhaps cut off from a valuable, informal setting for interaction with their counterparts on the policy side of the White House.

Heeding Warning Signs

The transition also can be a time when warning signs appear, particularly as campaign promises begin to get translated into policy commitments. In 1992 Judith Feder headed up the healthcare policy team during the transition. Her message to Clinton, as David Broder and Haynes Johnson have recounted in their book, *The System,* was that healthcare reform was going to be more costly and more difficult than anyone had imagined. Clinton reportedly grew angry at Feder, the messenger, yet it was the message that was the problem. It was an early warning sign Clinton then ignored.

Dealing with an Increasingly Attentive Media

The media are paying more attention to transitions now than in the past. Not only does this subject the transition to increasing scrutiny that must be dealt with, but additionally both positive and negative coverage can affect the administration once in office: transition successes and failures are often taken as harbingers of managerial and political competence. In 1992, for example, Clinton pledged not just to have the most ethical administration, but he also proposed the most ethical transition. Tighter rules were quickly developed than had prevailed under the Bush transition four years before. Arguably, the effort was well intended, but predictably the media began to raise questions: Would Transition Chairman Vernon Jordan step down from a number of corporate boards on which he served? What about the corporate clients of Transition Director Warren Christopher's law firm. Would Mack McLarty, the CEO of an oil and gas firm, participate in the selection of an energy secretary?

As Harrison Wellford noted, right after the election "it's honeymoon; everybody thinks the president-elect is wonderful and his team are all geniuses." But the media "has a kind of calendar in their mind about what the pace of the transition should be. . . . But very soon, very soon—surprisingly soon, within two or three weeks—if you start to slip up in your appointment process, in the relationships with Congress, in the relationship with the outgoing president, and the timing for all of this begins to slip, then all of a sudden—in your first challenge as an executive of the administration—you're beginning to be seen as wanting."[25] Drawing from his own experience in running the personnel operation during the Bush transition, Chase Untermeyer explicitly recommended that "there be one member of the Press Office assigned to handle personnel issues full time because that is such a key story. . . . I could recruit the Bush administration or take care of my own personal press but I couldn't do both.[26]

Finally, a general point by David Gergen remains valid: "it's even more important to get the transition right because the difficulty of governing and taking hold is more difficult than it used to be. You don't get the deference one could count on from the press."[27]

Transitions Are also Times to Think about the President

Although transitions largely focus on personnel, policy, and process, they are also linked to a new president, particularly in creating a new environment in which the president must function as a decision maker. As Martin Anderson observed, "you've got to set up an internal organization that is able to reflect and is sensitive to the president."[28]

What are the president-elect's capacities as a decision maker, particularly any strengths or weaknesses? How do past experiences relate to the task ahead both in what they have prepared the president for and what they have not? How is the West Wing different from Sacramento, Atlanta, or Little Rock? How is it different from the governor's office in Austin or the vice president's office down the hall? The preinauguration period is not only a time for a transition to a new administration, but it is also a time of transition for the person who will occupy that office.

Related to the president-elect's capacities as a decision maker are the people who will serve at key points in the decision-making process. How does the staff and decision-making processes need to be tailored to this *particular* president? How should the *particular roles* of key staff members be defined. Both John Sununu and Mack McLarty publicly stated that they wanted to be "honest brokers." Yet what does that mean in practice? To what extent should a chief of staff or an NSC adviser attempt to compensate for a president's weaknesses. To what extent should they be policy advocates?

In Mack McLarty's view, concerns about the president's requirements as a decision maker, the role of key staff members, and the broader process in which they would interact need each to be factored in. As for Clinton, according to McLarty, "he was not against a formal staff system. . . . But he did reject it being a clinical process where he was served up kind of pros, cons, three positions and accept, check, or defer." Clinton's preferred style: "[He] wanted a large range of opinions, to be coordinated for sure. But he is clearly an engaged person in terms of both his political style, his personality, and his policymaking style. So that was kind of the framing of it." At the same time, for the staff: "The feeling was to have the White House and certainly the chief of staff's office as an honest broker. . . . There was at least a sentiment that you should have an operation that reflected a much better flow of information to the president, a wider flow of information."[29]

Transitions Set Management Tasks

Finally, the transition period begins the process of bring people and organizations together in ways that foster an effective work environment—it is the starting point for those management tasks that will be crucial once the administration is office. It is a time for creating a sense of teamwork. As Harrison Wellford explained: "People begin to jockey for their positions in the key jobs. A lot of the camaraderie and teamwork and good feeling that you ended the election night celebration with comes to a crashing climax." Moreover, Wellford continued, success on this front it related to organizational effectiveness of the transition. "I think the more poorly organized you are, the worse that it is."[30]

Transitions thus present an opportunity for sending strong signals about expectations regarding behavior and commitment. In David Gergen's view, this recognition helped Reagan in 1981: "Everybody who came in knew where he stood. There were no struggles over the soul of the administration, over the overall direction. You knew what the philosophy was; then you knew what the policy prescription was going to be at least in the domestic area."[31] More broadly, as Clinton's second chief of staff, Leon Panetta, recently remarked in a 1999 panel discussion on transitions, "The reality is that you need to have a sense of mission, of duty, of discipline."[32] I would suggest that task is also one that must begin during the transition.

Notes

1.   Leon Panetta, interview with Martha Joynt Kumar, Monterey Bay, Calif., May 3, 2000, White House Interview Program.

2. Andrew Card Jr., interview with Martha Joynt Kumar, Washington, D.C., May 25, 1999, White House Interview Program.

3. Harrison Wellford, interview with Martha Joynt Kumar, Washington, D.C., Apr. 30, 1999, White House Interview Program.

4. Landon Butler, interview with Martha Joynt Kumar, Washington, D.C., Oct. 14, 1999, White House Interview Program.

5. Other contributors to a successful preelection transition are organization and a sense of shared mission. As Harrison Wellford explained, in contrast to the Carter effort in 1976, in the Reagan preelection planning four years earlier: "[They] were assembling key teams that did form the backbone of the transition effort well before the election and the hierarchies between them were pretty well set. . . . [F]or the most part they were well organized, had a pretty good idea of what Reagan's needs were going to be, and were ready to go after election night." Wellford interview.

6. Ibid.

7. David Gergen, interview with Martha Joynt Kumar, Arlington, Va., Aug. 26, 1999, White House Interview Program.

8. Robert Shogan, *Promises to Keep: Carter's First Hundred Days* (New York: Thomas Y. Crowell, 1977), p. 81.

9. Warren Christopher, *In the Stream of History* (Stanford, Calif.: Stanford University Press, 1998), p. 7.

10. Anonymous 1992 Clinton transition official, interview with author.

11. Wellford interview.

12. Panetta interview. Panetta goes on to note: "You can't just have a bunch of campaign types come in. By grownups I mean people that have experience, that have been around, that bring a level of stability and management to the operation so that you have a disciplined operation. Campaigns by their nature can be undisciplined. People go out and operate on their own. They're doing a lot of stuff on their own. But when you go into the White House, the amount of focus, the amount of attention that's made, you absolutely have to have a disciplined operation on your hands. That's not easy to do with campaign types."

13. Gergen interview.

14. Webb Hubbell, *Friends in High Places* (New York: William Morrow, 1997), p. 185.

15. David Demarest, interview with Martha Joynt Kumar, Washington, D.C., Dec. 7, 1999, White House Interview Program.

16. Card interview.

17. Thomas L. "Mack" McLarty, interview with Martha Joynt Kumar, Washington, D.C., Nov. 18, 1999, White House Interview Program.

18. Butler interview.

19. Wellford interview.

20. Butler interview.

21. There is more statutory guidance concerning the National Security Council, although there remains considerable discretion on how the role of the NSC adviser is defined and how the NSC staff is organized and utilized.

22. Card interview.

23. Ibid.

24. Gergen interview.

25. Wellford interview.

26. Chase Untermeyer, interview with Martha Joynt Kumar, Arlington, Va., July 6, 1999, White House Interview Program.

27. Gergen interview.

28. Martin Anderson, interview with Martha Joynt Kumar, Stanford, Calif., Aug. 12, 1999, White House Interview Program.

29. McLarty interview.

30. Wellford interview.

31. Gergen interview.

32. Leon Panetta, "Running the White House," sponsored by the Heritage Foundation, Mandate for Leadership Forum, Nov. 18, 1999.

A Tale of Two Transitions, 1980 and 1988

JOHN P. BURKE

THE 1980 REAGAN AND THE 1988 BUSH TRANSI-tions offer important case studies for understanding the challenges of presidential transitions. Although not without its shortcomings, the 1980 transition was, at least comparably, the most successful since the modern era of presidential transitions commenced with the Carter effort in 1976. The 1988 transition offers useful lessons about "friendly takeovers": the passing of power from a president to a president-elect of the same party. It is also of interest because it offers the only instance of a sitting vice president elected to the presidency since Martin Van Buren in 1836.

The 1980 Transition

The Reagan transition of 1980, while not perfect by any means, offers a number of important lessons, particularly when presidential power falls to someone from outside the Washington beltway. Its preelection effort was marked by harmonious relations between transition planners and the campaign staff, aided in no small measure by the direct and continual oversight provided by Ed Meese, the campaign's director. Pendleton James, who headed the preelection effort, also operated under a more limited mandate: a personnel-planning operation rather than the more ambitious effort Jack Watson had headed for Carter in 1976 or that Mickey Kantor would undertake for Clinton in 1992.

James operated out of the media limelight, moreover, and the Reagan inner circle worked to still any public venting of the internal workings of (and possible rifts within) the Reagan camp.

James's limited mandate meant, furthermore, that some of the activities that some preelection transition operations have undertaken would be handled elsewhere. Meese himself took on the job of organizing the post-election work. Nor was a separate policy shop set up as had occurred in 1976. There would be no "hijacking" of the policy agenda by the transition group, as some in the Carter campaign had perceived four years earlier.

Postelection Transition: Quickly Up and Running

Although some observers have viewed the postelection transition in 1980 as overorganized and cumbersome, it operated smoothly and effectively for the most part.[1] Meese's work paid off with a quick announcement of the transition's organization by President-elect Reagan at his first post-election press conference on Thursday, November 6. It was also an effort that drew not just from Reagan's California associates but also from other parts of the Republican party, including a heavy dose of those with Nixon and Ford White House experience.

Even before his appointment as chief of staff was announced, James Baker was placed in charge of White House organization and planning. His efforts in this regard are a model for how a chief of staff can effectively prepare for a new White House. By November 15, Baker had already met with Chief of Staff Jack Watson and Staff Director Al McDonald of the Carter White House, and he had set up twenty transition teams to examine each of the units in the Executive Office of the President. By the third week in November, Baker had begun a series of meetings with former chiefs of staff and other former White House officials, including Donald Rumsfeld and Richard Cheney.

In making White House staff appointments, Baker cast his net widely while including longtime Reagan associates. His efforts here are especially in contrast to the late staff appointments made by the Clinton transition in 1992 (some just days before his inauguration) as well as the quality and expertise of Baker's picks. More generally, as James Cicconi (who would serve in both the Reagan and Bush White Houses) noted, the early appointment of a chief of staff is critical: "That needs to be one of the earliest appointments a president-elect makes in large part because that organizes the president's own personal staff support for virtually all his subsequent decisions and for the vetting of those decisions, even potential cabinet appointments."[2]

Possible Fault Lines

There were developments during the 1980 transition that might have led to considerable internal turmoil, most notably the selection of Baker rather than Meese as chief of staff. Yet Baker and Meese were able to work out their differences quickly and settle on a division of labor. The internecine warfare that sometimes erupts in transitions did not develop, at least initially.

What would prove problematic, however, was the way that Baker and Meese divided their respective responsibilities. As "counselor to the president," Meese was placed in charge of both domestic and national security policy development as well as given responsibility for coordinating the input of the cabinet. For his part, Baker coordinated and supervised all White House staff functions, hired and fired all White House personnel, presided over meetings of the White House staff, coordinated the White House paper flow, and set the president's appointments and schedule.

This division of labor proved consequential. Although the media were quick to label Baker's job as "administrative," it quickly became clear that it was more than that, if not in fact "political" in some important sense. Baker controlled the liaison units, the political affairs office, and most importantly, the congressional affairs unit, each of which had important "political outreach" and liaison functions. Baker's morning staff meetings would be crucial in defining the daily agenda of the administration. The "legislative strategy group" he created would be especially important in the administration's dealings with Congress. Policymaking had been split, in a sense, from politics in the arrangement. The ability to pull them together in a coherent manner would turn on the working relations between Reagan's top aides.

Attention to Decision Making

The transition period also provided a time for planning and then activating the various channels of information and advice that Reagan would utilize once in office. This attention was directed not only at the analysis of

White House operations that Baker undertook but also to other parts of the administration's decision-making processes.

Like his predecessor, Reagan's gubernatorial experience served as the foundation for what would become his presidential decision-making processes, particularly how the cabinet would be used. But whereas Carter did not take up the issue of precisely how input from the cabinet might be structured and ended up with an ill-fitting combination of full cabinet meetings and poorly organized task forces, Reagan and his associates used the transition period to think about how the cabinet might better be brought into the administration's policymaking deliberations, and by February the cabinet council system was up and running.

Although the eventual record of the cabinet council system was somewhat mixed—some councils proved more successful than others—at the very least Reagan and his advisers had given some thought to the cabinet's role in the policy process. It was quite unlike the situation four years earlier when there was much rhetoric about cabinet government but little consideration of how it might be achieved.

The work undertaken by Meese and Baker during the transition, moreover, paved the way for Reagan's first-year success; it provides a case study for what a successful transition buys a new president. As Marlin Fitzwater observed: "I think when Reagan first started, Jim Baker and his staff were highly competent people who passed the 1981 tax cuts, which were the economic centerpiece of the whole administration. . . . They knew how to deal with the Congress. They knew how to get things done."[3]

Building Bridges to Congress

One important part of the 1980 transition was the effort undertaken to build a better relationship with Congress than had been the case four years earlier. Meese created a "congressional advisory group" as part of the transition's formal organization as well as a foreign policy commission of four senators (Democrats Henry Jackson of Washington and Richard Stone of Florida and Republicans John Tower of Texas and Howard Baker of Tennessee, the new majority leader of the Senate).

Other steps to develop better relations with Capitol Hill were also undertaken. As part of his efforts to reorganize the White House staff, James Baker moved the White House congressional affairs unit from the Old Executive Office Building (now the Eisenhower Executive Office Building) back into the White House proper. According to the administration's 1981 self-study of the 1980 transition, the move was done to "indicate the importance the Reagan administration wanted to place on relations between the Congress and the White House."[4] As part of the transition's organization, Meese also created the Office of Congressional Relations to handle relations with the Hill.

Reagan's own efforts were also an important part of the equation. According to the administration's transition study, "The biggest successes . . . were in [Reagan's] visits to the Hill, the lunches in Blair House, [and] the one-on-one visits set up with leaders early on."[5] Throughout the transition, moreover, members of the Reagan team—especially Nancy Reagan—sought to introduce themselves to "social Washington," many of whom, while Democrats, had been ignored by the Carter White House.

Strategic Planning

One innovation in the 1980 transition involved the creation of the Office of Planning and Evaluation under the direction of campaign pollster Richard Wirthlin. The efforts of Wirthlin and his staff especially focused on planning an overall strategy for the new administration. Their most important product, an "Initial Actions Report," emphasized the need to act quickly to take advantage of the honeymoon period with Congress. As Ed Meese later recalled:

> Dick [Wirthlin] put together a strategic plan that integrated our major policy issues, which we knew from campaign days were going to be economic revitalization and rebuilding the military as our two primary goals. He put that together with the communications plan that came from the communications people. . . . He put that together with the legislative plan that came to us from Tom Korologos and the people working the Hill. . . . So we had a pretty good plan on inauguration day, strategic plan of where we wanted to go, so that we didn't dilute the president's efforts and so that we integrated the various efforts of the White House in furtherance of this particular plan.[6]

Unlike Carter's laundry list four years earlier, the need for a more focused and limited agenda—largely directed at enacting the president-elect's economic program—was emphasized.

"Reaganomics" during the Transition

The one area where the Reagan transition was a bit less than crisp was in moving his budget and tax plans from campaign rhetoric to concrete proposals. The groundwork had been laid by some of the task forces organized during the campaign as well as by Reagan's own commitment to cuts in domestic spending and significant tax reductions. During the early weeks of the transition, Caspar Weinberger took the lead on budget matters, while George Shultz headed an economic coordinating group that sought to pull the pieces together, particularly in reaffirming Reagan's commitment to tax relief.

Yet the real job of finding actual cuts fell to David Stockman, whose appointment as OMB director was announced on December 3. Stockman "soon discovered," as he relates in his memoirs, that it would be up to him to "design the Reagan Revolution." He quickly found that while "everything was getting attention, nothing was getting priority."[7] Time was of the essence—a plan would have to be devised within ten to fifteen days of Reagan's inauguration.

One difficulty Stockman faced early on was obtaining accurate forecasts crucial in determining revenue estimates on the supply side and entitlement demands and cost-of-living increases on the demand side. Yet by January, 1981, no appointments had been made to the Council of Economic Advisers, the usual in-house source of such projections. Stockman attempted to muddle through, drawing on an interim forecasters group. That he had begun as early as he did enabled Stockman to grasp the difficulties of the task ahead. But his experience during the transition, particularly in getting others to take seriously the enormity of the task ahead, was a portent of future difficulties. But they forged ahead, and the seeds were sown for the mounting deficits of the Reagan and Bush years.

The 1980 Reagan transition is notable compared to what occurred before and after for the presence of a president-elect who was its centerpiece but not its driving force. While Ronald Reagan provided broad policy direction and was the reference point as some of the decision processes were cut and tailored to his needs, a presidency had been created in which much was delegated. Its test would come, first, in whether the arrangement was fundamentally sound in the way staff responsibilities had been parceled out, and second, whether President Reagan could rely on the skills and expertise of those selected and if his trust would be repaid in competence and the securing of policies to which he was so deeply committed.

The 1988 Transition

Not only was George H. W. Bush's 1988 transition to the presidency a "friendly takeover" by a sitting vice president, but it was also a passage to the presidency by a seasoned political insider whose pre-presidential experience had encompassed a variety of legislative, executive, and political roles. Not surprisingly, Bush began to prepare early for a possible presidency, enlisting the services of longtime associate Chase Untermeyer early in 1988.[8]

Untermeyer's mandate, however, was limited: "My charter was simply to prepare a plan for the transition and for a transition headquarters, but do nothing in the way of personnel," he would later recall.[9] Bush's own career preparation for the presidency, particularly his eight years as vice president, placed him in the position where he did not need the more extensive transition efforts of Carter in 1976 or Reagan in 1980. This was not a political outsider and his local entourage arriving unprepared at the White House steps.

As in 1980, oversight was crucial to the success of the preelection transition effort. In 1988, however, this was provided directly by Bush, John Sununu, and James Baker, who met a number of times with Untermeyer. Moreover, a number of crucial decisions were made during this period that would affect not only the transition but also the Bush presidency. One was Bush's decision that Untermeyer would not only head up the personnel operation during the postelection period but also serve as director of White House personnel. Another early decision was the selection of C. Boyden Gray, another key member of the Bush inner circle, to serve as the transition's legal counsel and then as White House legal counsel. As Gray would later recall: "Bush asked me to go work for him two weeks before he was elected, and he said, 'I should have asked you two months ago.' . . . The volume of paper that goes through the White House Counsel's Office is ten times that of all the other offices combined."[10]

Both of these decisions provided a crucial element of continuity to the daunting appointments process that lay ahead. As Gray observed, "Certainly the day of the election there ought to be 100 people doing nothing but filling out those forms." As to the job of White House legal counsel: "The incoming White House counsel should interview previous White House counsel and be immersed on all of the land mines that he or she is going to face. An hour and a half, three days before inauguration is not enough."[11]

Advantages of a Friendly Takeover: A Little (and Early) Help from Some Friends

In contrast to the more cautious approach prevailing within the Bush camp, the Reagan administration undertook a series of steps to prepare for an orderly transfer of power. Its efforts far exceeded those of recent outgoing administrations, and they provide important evidence of the advantages that accrue when power passes to a president-elect of the same party. As Kenneth Duberstein, the outgoing Reagan chief of staff, later observed: "Reagan wanted it seamless. Reagan wanted it the best hand-off that he could possibly get. . . . Certainly there were sensitivities. Certainly there were difficulties, but it wasn't two ships passing in the night. There were enough of us who knew each other so well that you could work things out."[12]

Chase Untermeyer recalled that his preelection meetings with Robert Tuttle, director of White House personnel, were "extremely valuable." Half of these sessions were lengthy affairs in which they proceeded "department by department, agency by agency, job by job, as to what the various positions and responsibilities were, what kind of people were there now, and candidly assessing who would be good to retain, who would be good to move to another position, or who would be good to terminate."[13]

The briefing books that Tuttle had requested his staff to prepare were extremely useful, according to Untermeyer. "Each book contained the 'authority sheets' for each presidential appointment, with the staffer's experienced judgment as to which jobs were the most important, the most difficult, the hardest to fill, etc. These books became the hour-by-hour bosom companions of my own personnel staff after the election." Untermeyer would later recall that "None of this was available to my counterpart in the Dukakis campaign, nor could it have been." Furthermore, "in a normal transition of one party to the other, all that would have been delayed until the actual transition, and even then it would have been shared grudgingly at best."[14]

Postelection Transition: An Active President-Elect

Following the 1988 election, George Bush continued to be an active force in shaping his administration, quite different from Ronald Reagan's comparative indifference to staff and organization matters and Jimmy Carter's preference in 1976 to let his fellow Georgians work out differences among themselves. Bush played a direct role in selecting both staff and cabinet members. Both John Sununu's appointment as chief of staff and Brent Scowcroft's as national security adviser were his personal calls. He was also directly involved in determining some of the organizational and decision processes of his presidency: retention of the remaining economic and domestic policy councils of the Reagan second term and naming a White House staff that had fewer "assistants to the president" at the top. Bush's staff appointments as well as his own low-key interpersonal style also dictated a somewhat different organizational culture in this White House— "fewer cowboys," as one participant would later recall.

Bush's ability to move quickly on key appointments, especially with respect to his White House staff, also was of great benefit. As James Cicconi recalled, Bush made major appointments "fairly early, and it worked pretty well. He had most of the major White House positions either named or the people were considering the offers by the end of November. Then all of us had much of December and at least three weeks in January then to prepare to assume our responsibilities."[15]

This "lead time" is an especially crucial component of a successful transition and presidency. As Marlin Fitzwater pointed out, "The one thing I learned was that a new job at the White House is never going to be what you think it is and you better learn what it is before you start changing things around because you don't get any chances to fail."[16]

At his first press conference the day after the election, Bush unveiled his transition team. As Reagan had done in 1980, Bush shifted his transition leadership. Craig Fuller, his vice presidential chief of staff, and Robert Teeter, his pollster and campaign strategist, were appointed codirectors of the transition. The choice of Fuller and Teeter alleviated some of the tension that had developed in previous transitions—most notably Carter's— between the campaign staff and those with the kind of political and governmental experience that would likely lead to a White House position. As David Bates (who would become secretary to the cabinet) explained: "Fuller had come from the vice president's office and Teeter had come from the campaign, so you had one guy representing more the governance side and the other guy representing more the campaign. I don't think the campaign felt left out. I think there was a real nice melding."[17] Almost all of the others selected for top transition positions were longtime associates of Bush in some form or another.

A Cabinet of Friends and Associates

The same pattern of prior association with George Bush also pervaded his cabinet selection. Whereas Carter or Reagan might have had a close relationship with one or at most two of those designated for the cabinet, Bush had some association with nearly all of them, either from his earlier career or from his vice presidency. That surely created stronger bonds, but it also harbored dangers. In the early months of his presidency, there was an unusual degree of "slip-ups" and "freelancing" on the part of some cabinet members, and they often compromised the administration's policy message. Bush's own penchant for more informal and free-flowing contact with his cabinet members also generated some difficulties.[18] Most cabinet members "exercised the president's invitation for direct access," Deputy Chief of Staff Andrew Card later recalled, but they "didn't necessarily respect the chain of command and wouldn't always report on it, which created tension."[19]

During the transition, Bush and his advisers also decided to continue the structure, organization, and leadership of the two-cabinet council system that had been developed during Reagan's second term. One consequence was that Treasury Secretary Nicholas Brady and Attorney General Richard Thornburgh (holdovers from the Reagan cabinet) retained leadership of, respectively, the economic and domestic policy councils. Another was that the work of the councils continued to be coordinated by the weaker Cabinet Affairs Office in the White House rather than the domestic policy staff. Although the two heads of those operations, David Bates and Roger Porter, were apparently able to develop a cordial working relationship, the experience of the first Reagan term, in which the domestic policy staff took the organizational lead, was also one in which the councils operated more effectively.[20]

A Staff Bush Knew and Could Trust

One particular benefit that can accrue from a friendly takeover is the ability to draw not only from longtime career associates who bring a degree of loyalty and trust but also, if the pre-presidential experience is Washington-based (and especially if it includes the vice president), a degree of expertise and "inside the beltway" (if not prior White House) experience.

A friendly takeover can also bridge some of the separation between campaign and governance. As Bowman Cutter noted: "Running a campaign is different from running a government. They have typically no idea about how to run an organization or a government and they spend a lot of time learning. . . . In the Clinton and Carter campaigns, the transition was pretty substantial from campaign to government, and people didn't know anything about government."[21] For George Bush, the vice presidency and his other political roles enabled him to draw on an unusually rich reservoir of talent. In particular, a number of Bush associates had served in various capacities in the Reagan White House or elsewhere during that administration.

The advantages are several. First, appointees come with a degree of experience and require less on-the-job training, especially in preparing for the "fishbowl" experience of serving in the White House. Second, they are likely to have a much better fix on what their new jobs might entail. Third, they are better positioned to develop the contacts with members of the outgoing administration during the transition period that will get them up to speed quicker come January 20. James Cicconi, who served as an assistant to Jim Baker during Reagan's first term and then as deputy chief of staff and staff secretary under George Bush, observed: "I was a hell of a lot better at my job under President Bush because I had worked in a more junior position under President Reagan. . . . I saw how it worked; I saw how White Houses work and are structured, how decisions get made. I learned the importance of speaking up and how to affect a decision, how to deal with pressure and stress in the job and balance things in your life at the same time. I was a lot better the second time around than I would have been coming in cold, a lot better."[22] But there are dangers here too. While familiarity may not breed contempt, it may generate a degree of lassitude and a lack of vigor that can handicap a new administration. A friendly takeover especially needs to establish its own record and differentiate itself somewhat from its predecessor.

Some Organizational and Personnel Difficulties Nonetheless

Like Reagan, Bush recognized that the organization of his White House staff, particularly the appointment of a chief of staff, would be an early priority of his transition. John Sununu would later tell reporters that Bush had discussed the possibility of his appointment as early as two weeks before election day.[23] In fact, Bush did not immediately announce Sununu's appointment but waited until November 17.

In the interim, Bush fended off an attempt to resurrect the "troika" of the early Reagan years, which would now cast Craig Fuller as a kind of Jim Baker, with Sununu playing Meese and pollster Robert Teeter taking on some of the Mike Deaver role. To his credit, Bush did not let the matter linger or unduly permit bickering among his top aides. But an effort to bring Teeter on board the staff did continue until early January, 1989. The failed negotiations with Teeter would have repercussions later as communications strategy and the public selling of the Bush presidency came to occupy a lesser position in the staff system—there would be no high-level Mike Deavers in this administration. Nor would there be an Ed Meese figure, with cabinet rank and counselor status, to push a Bush policy agenda at the highest (other than Sununu) levels.

Other organizational decisions made during the transition had important effects. Andrew Card recalled that, with respect to White House organization, Bush "gave pretty firm direction." He was very clear about what "decision-making funnels" he wanted reporting to him. Furthermore, he wanted fewer people at the top of the White House organizational pyramid. Yet Bush's choices here would prove consequential for his presidency: the personnel and units affected by the reduction were those in the area of public and political liaison, intergovernmental relations, and speechwriting. All of them were crucial to the "marketing and selling" of the Bush program, but they were downgraded in the White House hierarchy and placed under the assistant to the president for communications. As Bush staff secretary James Cicconi later observed: "We made the mistake of putting all those things under it [communications] and it was too much, I thought. I thought organizationally it was a very, very difficult management task. There was probably just too much there. I thought those areas functioned probably a whole lot better in the Reagan White House, where there were pretty senior people in charge of each of those offices."[24]

Crafting a Policy Agenda: A Beginning or Missed Opportunities?

As we have seen with the Reagan transition, the transition period is important not just for getting a team in place but also for translating campaign promises into policy priorities and for beginning to establish a legislative agenda. In Bush's case, this was especially necessary, given a campaign that was comparably devoid of major initiatives.

Early efforts were made in the area of foreign policy, where Bush had clearer commitments and great personal interest. Andrew Card recalled that Bush "was very active with Brent Scowcroft and Jim Baker getting up to speed as secretary of state. Brent Scowcroft is a seasoned national security person, and the president had latent interest in those areas. So there was a lot that went on in the foreign policy side."[25]

In domestic matters, Richard Darman, the director-designate of OMB, began to work on budget issues, particularly a strategy for dealing with mounting federal deficits.[26] A special group was created during the transition to begin to grapple with some solution to the savings and loan crisis. Yet, at least compared with the Carter and Reagan efforts, other domestic policy matters appeared to stall. In part, this may have been a legacy of a president-elect (especially in this case a sitting vice president) taking over from a president of his own party: less of a policy revolution, more of a policy continuation and fine-tuning. But part too may have stemmed from a delay in settling on a domestic policy adviser until early January, Bush's own predilections to favor foreign policy, and a worsening fiscal picture.

By all accounts, the 1988 transition was well organized and managed. As a "friendly takeover," Bush and his associates benefited from close cooperation with the outgoing Reagan administration. This occurred not just during the postelection transition but also before the election. That key aides such as Chase Untermeyer and C. Boyden Gray could prepare for the tasks ahead, particularly with respect to the hurdles presented by the appointment process, is no small accomplishment. Bush also benefited from a skilled pool of talent from which to make his personnel selections, especially with respect to the White House staff. The problem that "political outsiders" face in combining personal loyalty and association on the one hand with expertise and experience (especially Washington-based) on the other is surely lessened for a sitting vice president. An unusually large number of his aides not only had a longstanding personal association with him, but many had also served in the Reagan administration; Bush's "sponsorship," "career mentoring," "strategic placement" (or whatever one wants to call it), especially during the Reagan years, now paid off.

But friendly takeovers also face challenges. Some are the same issues as other transitions. Have the right persons been picked for key roles such as chief of staff and NSC adviser? (In Bush's case, one would work out— Scowcroft—while another would prove problematic—Sununu.) Is there an effort to turn campaign rhetoric into a presidential agenda? Has the staff and other parts of the decision-making process been structured to not only take advantage of the president's strengths but also compensate for any weaknesses as a decision maker?

Some challenges may be unique to friendly takeovers, especially when the successor is the vice president. How do new presidents begin to differentiate themselves from their predecessors and from an administration in which they have participated? In Bush's case it may have led to a tendency to downplay the communications functions and media presentation of his presidency, to un-Deaverize it (although Deaver was long gone) and differentiate it from the Reagan years. But with a lean domestic agenda in the first place, effective "marketing and selling" may have been especially required. The "vision thing" may have been irritating to George Bush, but ignoring its call would eventually come at a great price, especially four years later when this president and the record of his administration needed to be marketed and resold to the American public.

Notes

1.   One area often cited for criticism is the teams sent out to each department and agency. A number of Washington veterans appointed to cabinet positions, such as Alexander Haig and Caspar Weinberger, felt that their work was less than useful. Other teams, particularly those assigned to the independent regulatory agencies, encountered some resistance, particularly where team members were drawn from private sector enterprises under the agencies' regulatory domain and where possible conflict of interest questions might arise. See John P. Burke, *Presidential Transitions: From Politics to Practice* (Boulder, Colo.: Lynne Rienner, 2000), pp. 98–99.

2.   James Cicconi, interview with Martha Joynt Kumar, Washington, D.C., Nov. 29, 1999, White House Interview Program.

3.   Marlin Fitzwater, interview with Martha Joynt Kumar, Washington, D.C., Oct. 21, 1999, White House Interview Program.

4.   Draft report, "Transition of the President and the President-Elect," n.d., OA5097, Edwin Meese Files, Ronald Reagan Presidential Library, Simi Valley, Calif.

5.   Ibid.

6.   Edwin Meese, interview with Martha Joynt Kumar, Washington, D.C., Jan. 21, 2000, White House Interview Program.

7.   David Stockman, *The Triumph of Politics: How the Reagan Revolution Failed* (New York: Harper and Row, 1986), p. 75.

8.   Untermeyer first met Bush when Bush was running for Congress in 1966. He later served as his executive assistant (1981–83), deputy assistant secretary of the navy for installations and facilities (1983–84), and assistant secretary of the navy for manpower and reserve affairs (1984–88). Untermeyer's work on the transition did not begin in earnest until April, when Bush's nomination was secure. At a meeting in Kennebunkport, Maine, over the Memorial Day weekend, Bush gave the final go-ahead and notified his campaign staff that Untermeyer would be undertaking transition planning.

9.   Chase Untermeyer, correspondence with author, Dec. 9, 1998.

10.   C. Boyden Gray, interview with Martha Joynt Kumar and Nancy Kassop, Washington, D.C., Oct. 4, 1999, White House Interview Program.

11. Ibid.

12. Kenneth Duberstein, interview with Martha Joynt Kumar, Washington, D.C., Aug. 12, 1999, White House Interview Program.

13. Chase Untermeyer, "The Reagan to Bush Transition: A Miller Center Panel and Discussion," in *Presidential Transitions: The Reagan to Bush Experience,* ed. Kenneth W. Thompson (Lanham, Md.: University Press of America,1993), p. 180.

14. Untermeyer, correspondence with author, Dec. 9, 1998; Untermeyer, "Reagan to Bush Transition," p. 180.

15. Cicconi interview.

16. Fitzwater interview.

17. David Bates, interview with author, Oct. 5, 1998.

18. For further discussion, see Burke, *Presidential Transitions,* pp. 237–42.

19. Andrew Card Jr., interview with author, Sept. 17, 1998.

20. As best as I can reconstruct, the decision to continue with the council arrangement of the second term, especially with the lead role to be taken by cabinet affairs, predated Roger Porter's appointment in early January, 1989, as assistant to the president for economic and domestic policy.

21. Bowman Cutter, interview with Martha Joynt Kumar, Washington, D.C., Nov. 8, 1999, White House Interview Program.

22. Cicconi interview.

23. Gerald M. Boyd, "Sununu Answers His Critics: I Have to Be Tough Enough," *The New York Times,* Nov. 19, 1988. The day before the election, Bush recorded in his own diary that he discussed announcing Sununu's appointment as chief of staff with Jim Baker, "but that will come later." George H. W. Bush, *All the Best: My Life in Letters and Other Writings* (New York: Scribners, 1999), p. 403. Other reports indicated that on election day, Bush had privately told Craig Fuller—a possible contender for the job—and others in his inner circle that he wanted Sununu for the position. See David Hoffman, "His Political Stature Gave Sununu Edge," *Washington Post,* Nov. 18, 1988.

24. Cicconi interview.

25. Card interview.

26. Darman's efforts here are especially noteworthy since he developed a two-step approach: a first-year budget that would avoid new tax increases and force Congress to make any difficult cuts, with the issue of raising taxes postponed until the next year. With the "big fix" and the problem of finessing Bush's "read my lips" election pledge to come later, it was a decision that set the stage for the 1990 budget agreement and that would have repercussions on Bush's chances for re-election in 1992.

2

The White House Environment:
Politics, Organization, and Work Life

The Political Environment
of the White House

JOHN H. KESSEL

AN EFFECTIVE WHITE HOUSE STAFF, HOWARD BAKER tells us, is an extension of the president. Drawing on their own experience, other White House veterans explain why. Richard Cheney considered a good White House staff as absolutely essential to a president's success. "A president can do a lot based on his own personal skills, but there's a limit. His reach, his ability to guide and direct the government, to interact with the cabinet, to deal effectively with the Congress, to manage his relationship with the press . . . are all key ingredients to his success," and the presidential staff gives him these capacities.[1] David Gergen, who served in communication posts in four administrations, pointed out that the presidential staff has become "his intelligence-gathering operation, it's his media management team, it's his congressional team, it's his formulation of his policy."[2] Because of these staff contributions, W. Bowman Cutter, who held economic positions in the Carter and Clinton White Houses, added, "it maximizes the most valuable commodity you're dealing with, the time of the president."[3]

Who are the critical players in carrying out these responsibilities? Interestingly, there is a bipartisan consensus on this point. With small variations, Democrats Leon Panetta and Harrison Wellford (who worked on reorganization and administration in the Carter Office of Management and Budget [OMB]) and Republicans Roger Porter (who held economic/

domestic posts in three administrations) and Jerry Jones (staff secretary in the Nixon and Ford White Houses) listed the same positions: chief of staff, congressional relations chief, press secretary, national security assistant, economic advisor (usually including the OMB director and sometimes another source of economic guidance), chief domestic aide, and counsel. These persons give vital advice to the president and direct important staffs of their own. Whether the president is a Democrat or a Republican, he needs skilled professionals in these positions.

Returning to Howard Baker's fundamental point, how does the White House staff allow the president to extend his own governance throughout a complex political environment? Since the staff serves as intermediary between the president and all the other institutions that make up the political environment, it must be anchored at both ends. That is, presidential aides must adapt to the president's way of doing business as well as to the work styles of legislators, journalists, diplomats, economists, and all the others who inhabit the political jungle surrounding the White House. Only when the staff is secure in their relations with the president *and* all the presidential clienteles can they bring essential stability to the president's relations with his political environment.

Adaptation to Presidents

Presidents, of course, differ from one another. Clinton was different from Bush who was different from Reagan who was different from Carter and so on all the way back to Washington himself. Yet Roger Porter emphasized an important characteristic they have in common. Presidents come to office as mature individuals. "They're not in the formative stage of their life; they're not figuring out how they're going to do things. . . . Given [that and] all of the pressures that are attendant with that job, the notion that they are going to adapt is rarely the case."[4] The result, in the words of James Cicconi, a deputy of the chief of staff in the Reagan and Bush administrations, is that one usually has "to adapt the system in the White House to the president's work style rather than expect [presidents] to adapt their work style to the system."[5] Hence White House staffers must discover how each president likes to work, how he likes to make decisions, the degree of detail with which he is comfortable, what types of things he wants to see himself, and what types of things he is willing to let others handle for him.

There are other constants in adapting to presidents. One is the importance of trust. Trust is essential to full and frank exchanges and to the president's willingness to let key aides act in his name. When Leon Panetta was asked to take over as chief of staff, he went to President Clinton and said, "I have to have your full support because there are some decisions that have to be made, and I need to make sure that I have your full support and trust in that process."[6] He said the same thing to the first lady and, in fact, set up regular meetings to report to her. These lasted for about six months, by which time bonds of trust had been solidified with both President and Mrs. Clinton.

Still another constant is that some staff members must be able to take bad news to the president or insist that he attend to some task he would rather avoid. Consequently, there are times when aides must be firm with their president. Michael Deaver, a deputy chief of staff who had known Ronald Reagan for twenty years, could say to him: "Wait a minute . . . this is Michael and it is important that you don't dismiss what I am saying here. . . . It's important that you listen carefully to what I'm saying." He explained: "Sometimes you have to hit the president in the head with the proverbial 'two-by-four' to get his attention." Few people, Deaver explained, could have that kind of conversation because few were confident enough of their relationship with the president to use such blunt language. Still, Deaver continued, it was vital to have staff members who could go into the Oval Office and say, "I hate to tell you this, but this is what [other] people won't tell you."[7] Speechwriter David Demarest, who had not known George H. W. Bush nearly as long as Deaver had known Reagan, spoke about the effort needed to get President Bush to consider something he would rather dismiss. "You'd really have to get in there and say, 'Mr. President, I know you may not agree with me, but I'd appreciate it if you would just hear me out.' You could see there's a little impatience there, but you've just got to do it."[8] Roy Neel, who served as deputy chief of staff in the first year of the Clinton administration, spoke of the need to tell the president that sometimes a faithful campaign aide was not the best person to appoint to the White House staff. "It's very tough and it takes a senior staff and a chief of staff that's willing to stand up to the president . . . and say, 'No. There's a better person who is better suited to serve you in this role.'"[9]

Even at this early point, one can see two requisites of a White House staff. First, if a staff is to carry out its crucial responsibilities, those in the key positions must have a high degree of competence. Second, if a staff is to have an effective relationship with their president, there must be persons who, either out of long acquaintance or from personal capacities, can win the trust of the president and be willing to speak with complete candor. Ideally, staff members ought to have both capacities, but practically some bring a high order of professional skill and others close personal ties. It is clear, though, that both abilities must be present for a staff to be effective.

Adaptation to Political Environment

Each unit of the presidential staff works in a different segment of the political environment and, hence, must adapt in a somewhat different way. Further, sometimes the persons with whom they interact are intermediaries to those ultimately affected, as when a domestic staff member has direct contact with the Labor Department and union officials in order to gauge the reaction of blue-collar workers. And in some cases, knowledge of the environment may come from literature. This happens if the counsel's office looks up decisions in a law library or the Council of Economic Advisers analyzes recent statistics. Whatever the means of contact, though, the staff must have positive knowledge of the reaction of clientele groups in order to assure stable relations.

We cannot, of course, recount all White House contact with external actors. Therefore, we will focus on the environments in which six vital units are active: Congress, the media, foreign policy, economics, domestic policy, and the legal environment.

Congress

The need for cordial relationships with Capitol Hill is illustrated in a story told by Pendleton James, Reagan's initial personnel chief. Bryce Harlow, who handled congressional relations for both Eisenhower and Nixon, had counseled him never to appoint a congressional staffer to a regulatory job because the staffer would always be beholden to the congressional sponsor. Then Sen. Bob Packwood asked for three jobs, and James asked Chief of Staff James Baker what he wanted to do. "[Baker] looked at me like I'd just fallen off the turnip truck. He said, 'Give them to him.' . . . [Baker] was thinking politically. He knew he was going to need Packwood's vote on issues."[10]

Kenneth Duberstein, who was Reagan's head congressional liaison before he became chief of staff, spoke about vetting potential nominees before personnel decisions are made. "You consult with the chairman and ranking member, with the Senate leader and minority leader, saying, 'Here are the people we are thinking about. Do you have any sense of any of them? This is not a final decision that's going to the president. . . . Here is the short list.' The reactions vary: So and so is wonderful. I've never heard of this guy. She is very close to a senator from another state. And so on." What the legislative-liaison staff wants to do, Duberstein explains, is to identify political pitfalls. "You're saving the president problems because if in fact he goes forward with an intent to nominate and then it blows up, you are spending chips that you're going to need elsewhere."[11]

Leon Panetta recounted the decisions on priorities that are made after the major outlines are set in the budget and the State of the Union message. He used reauthorization of the elementary and secondary education act as an example. "Do you want to try to get it done before the budget process or . . . during the appropriations stuff or do you want to save it for negotiations at the end if you have gridlock on the budget and try to negotiate in to a final packet with the Congress? There are all kinds of tactical decisions that you have to make. If you're smart you try to say we want to get the budget, we obviously want to get our appropriations and priorities. On top of that we want to get elementary and secondary education done."[12]

These decisions need to be made with accurate information in hand. Howard Baker underscored the efficacy of conversations with former Senate colleagues, saying that he got better understanding from them than in any other way. "When [Dan] Inouye and Warren Rudman came down, for instance, . . . and sat down with me in the office, we knew each other, we didn't have to have any preliminaries and I got the straight scoop from them about what was possible and what was not possible. And they got the straight scoop from me on how the president would react. It didn't take fifteen minutes."[13]

Kenneth Duberstein also stressed the importance of free and open exchange of information with legislators. "You have to share information. There aren't any secrets in this town. The walls talk. Gotcha or surprises don't work when you're legislating." It is essential, Duberstein emphasized, to realize that many Hill veterans possess as much or more expertise than do White House staffers. Therefore, one should work with them even though it often takes a long time. New administrations, he said, often come in with an almost religious fervor. "It doesn't work in this town. You have to make friendships; you have to make accommodations with the other side."[14]

Finally, when working on the Hill, one needs to understand that there will be times when a representative or a senator cannot vote with the administration. Donald Rumsfeld made it quite clear he was not looking for 100-percent support. "I want someone in Congressional Relations who can get Joe two times out of [three], get Michael three times out of ten, and can get Jane four times out of ten. And we'll have floating coalitions. Now that's a way of dealing with the Congress. You don't dead-end it and say, 'By gosh, if you vote against me, you're the enemy, and I'm not going to talk to you, I'm not going to deal with you.'"[15]

The Media

The reporters who are the core of the Press Office's constituency are those accredited to the White House, especially those on the White House beat who show up every day and spend most of their time in the Executive Mansion. Pete Roussel, a longtime Bush aide who worked in the Press Office during the Ford and Reagan administrations, spoke for all White House spokesmen when he said, "you're in the middle of a giant taffy pull."[16] On the one hand, there is a voracious press corps saying tell us everything; on the other hand, the White House is saying tell them just this. The staff member is reminded of both masters by his continual contact with White House colleagues and the stack of pink slips alerting him to return reporters' phone calls.

When Gerald Warren, who had been city editor of the *San Diego Union*, was joining the Nixon White House press staff, the tenor of Nixon and Haldeman's comments was "you're working for us and not for the press." Warren said he told them he knew that, but while he recognized "you won't fill [all the press's desires] because you're working for a president, . . . [a press spokesman must] know their needs and know how [journalism] works."[17] Press Secretary Michael McCurry came to the Clinton White House after serving as the State Department spokesman. He thought the White House journalists' needs had been neglected. McCurry told the president, Mrs. Clinton, and Panetta: "You've got to have some flexibility in [the press secretary's] job to be able to wrestle with the press every day and see what they're interested in, make sure they're taken care of in addition to taking care of our agenda. . . . I'm going to have to bend over backwards to help these people out, and you're going to have to understand that."[18] Two presidents who were as defiant of the press as any were both told that their spokespersons could be effective only if they were cognizant of reporters' requirements and worked with them.

"My constituency," Ray Jenkins explained, "was the American Society of Newspaper Editors." Prior to joining the Carter Press Office, Jenkins had been editor of the *Montgomery Advertiser-Journal,* and he was to serve as liaison between the White House and editors across the country. Working through the network of contacts he had built up through the years, he would place calls saying, for example, "Look. We've got a policy initiative that we're going to announce tomorrow, and if you're going to editorialize on this, I'll be happy to set up an interview with the secretary of the Treasury, or [perhaps] a conference call with him so your editorial board can discuss it."[19] He would not make such arrangements for, say, *The New York Times* reporters who were quite capable of getting their own interviews, but on a slightly less august level, he would arrange interviews with ranking administration officials. His external journalistic contacts combined with his internal Press Office access often enabled many newspapers to write better-informed stories.

Reporters were often successful in obtaining administration action. The Reagan White House was reluctant to have presidential press conferences because the preparation required that the president's schedule be cleared for two preceding afternoons. Finally, Michael Deaver tells us, Press Secretary Larry Speakes would come in and say, "I can't take it any more. You've got to do a press conference."[20] Deaver said it always bugged him that they would be forced to respond, but they adapted to the reporters' needs.

Marlin Fitzwater, press secretary for both Reagan and Bush, found ways to use his press constituency to help him inside the White House. He asked President Bush if he would like to hear his briefings. Bush said, "Yes. I heard LBJ used to listen to briefings." So Fitzwater had a speaker placed on the president's desk and on those of key staff members as well. In that way they could all hear the questions reporters were asking and judge how well he was defending the administration. Fitzwater also used his constituency's need for information to find out things. "I could go to OMB and say 'I really need to know this.' They would say 'why; why do you need to know that?' Everybody wants to protect their information. I said, 'Hey, look. I've got fifty reporters down there that are demanding to know this.'"[21]

Foreign Policy

Members of the National Security Council (NSC) staff are recruited largely from the State Department, Defense Department, and from academic specialists in foreign policy. Since the NSC constituency consists principally of foreign political, diplomatic, and military leaders and the American agencies that deal with them, the backgrounds of the NSC staff members are congruent with those of their clientele groups.

The type of contact each person has depends on their rank and responsibilities. The assistant to the president for national security affairs has become one of the most important jobs in government. This is true whether the national security assistant is as much a magnet for publicity as Nixon's Henry Kissinger or as unassuming as Brent Scowcroft, who served both Ford and Bush. Sandy Berger, President Clinton's national security assistant, remained constantly in touch with heads of government and his own counterparts in international affairs. He was the first American sent to China after the Taiwan elections in March, 2000, at the president's side during the Israeli-Palestinian negotiations at Camp David that July, and left with him to travel to the G-8 economic summit in Okinawa.

It is less widely realized that other staff members are involved in similar activities. For instance, David Aaron, President Carter's deputy national security assistant, sat in for his boss, Zbigniew Brzezinski, at a lot of meetings and ran others himself at the subcabinet level. Because of his rank, Aaron was more adaptable. "I have a little more flexibility in some respects because I don't have any problem talking with a [State Department] desk officer or talking with a cabinet officer. I can do both. The protocol is a little more awkward for Zbig. He really can't do that."[22]

Aaron was also centrally involved in discussions during the late 1970s about whether the United States should station medium-range missiles in Western Europe. In late 1977 German chancellor Helmut Schmidt had suggested installing such weapons to counter Soviet missiles. A discussion within the U.S. government concluded that the missiles should be installed, but it should first be ascertained if European governments were willing to provide adequate support. Aaron was chosen to conduct these negotiations because he represented the president (rather than a single governmental agency). He sounded out heads of government about this during 1978 and 1979. Similarly, in 1989, when a post–Cold War vision of NATO was being previewed, and again in 1990, when a negotiating position on conventional forces in Europe was being developed, Robert Gates,

President Bush's deputy national security assistant, and Lawrence Eagleburger, the deputy secretary of state, were dispatched for talks with Prime Minister Margaret Thatcher and other European leaders.

James Thomson, a physicist detailed from the Defense Department in the late 1970s, served as a member of the Carter national security staff. His responsibilities dealt with defense and arms control related to Europe, and his activities are typical of a rank-and-file NSC staffer. When in Washington, he spent most of his time coordinating policies with colleagues on the NSC staff, the State Department, the Defense Department, and the Arms Control Agency. "I'm a twenty to thirty phone call a day guy," he said. Thomson also made a number of trips to European countries and to NATO headquarters. He made an interesting point about how foreign travel facilitated working with others in the domestic political environment. "We travel together a lot, and there's nothing like that to make personal friends. You go out and you go drinking a lot. Really, it helps business. [Back in Washington] you can call up and say, 'This is just bullshit.' Or 'Can't you get your guys to fix things?' Really, it makes things much easier."[23]

James Fetig's responsibilities were still different. A career army officer in the Clinton NSC Press Office, he quickly found that while certain topics—Israel, China/Taiwan—were very sensitive, every policy had a history that went with it, words that had been said and not said as well as other words that had unanticipated connotations. In gathering guidance the NSC Press Office "would start with the NSC policy directorates. Their job was to go to agencies . . . and get input for the day . . . and then distill those into succinct talking points that could be used by anybody that required them. They were the ones who made sure that the language, the nuances, were exactly right."[24] Working in a sensitive environment, the NSC Press Office wanted to convey accurate information, but even more they were anxious to avoid unintentional misunderstanding.

Economics

Many federal agencies have some effect on the American economy, but the most important entities through which the president works are the Treasury, the Office of Management and Budget, and the Council of Economic Advisers. Each of these has contact with flesh-and-blood humans and abstract economic data, and each deals with different aspects of the economy.

Secretaries of the Treasury tend to come from corporate or financial backgrounds. The Treasury needs to be in touch with the financial markets to carry out its responsibilities, so it requires leaders who have many contacts in this community. Clinton's Robert Rubin, cochairman of Goldman, Sachs, was typical in this respect. "What I think [Clinton] thought he was getting [by appointing Rubin] was kind of an instant stamp of adulthood from the financial community," said W. Bowman Cutter. As it happened, he got much more. Rubin had "an absolutely unique capacity to deal with people and get things done. . . . [He really had] a focus on knitting a lot of things together, international economics, what you say about the private sector, what you say about markets; [and] a knowledge from the beginning that it was important to have a good relationship with [Alan] Greenspan."[25]

For decades, the OMB has been collecting budget requests from agencies throughout Washington and compiling them into the budget the president submits to Congress. Every fall, experienced budget examiners go over each request with the agencies, and if they approve add it to the budget. By the time the budget reaches the director and the president, almost all the decisions have been made, although controversial calls are still open to appeal. The civil servants in OMB are less oriented to politics than to efficiency in the allocation of resources. "The whole matters," Cutter explained. "If we do this, . . . how does [it] affect the rest of the programs? How does this affect what else is going to happen with the budget? [Since they often oppose particular programs because of the effect elsewhere in the budget,] they are always regarded by [politically oriented members of] the White House staff as the people who for some unknown reason won't let them do what they want to do."[26] The involved process of compiling the budget means that someone who understands the myriad decisions that went into it should defend it. While chief of staff, Leon Panetta spent a lot of time negotiating on the Hill because he was familiar with the budget issues. "I would suspect," he said, "[that when I was] OMB director with McLarty [as chief of staff], McLarty basically let me do the negotiations on it because he wasn't that familiar with the issues. I think that even now, I think [Chief of Staff] John Podesta probably lets [OMB Director] Jack Lew do a lot of that."[27]

The Council of Economic Advisers (CEA) represents the views of professional economists. Over the years they have been very influential or almost totally neglected, depending on the esteem in which the president holds them. The council consists of only three economists, but the staff includes several more. Usually, the economists come from universities, and sometimes are quite distinguished. The Kennedy CEA, for instance, included one member, James Tobin, and two staff members, Kenneth Arrow and Robert Solow, who were future Nobel Prize winners. Their activities included doing economic analyses, helping members of the White House staff understand economic data, and writing a turn-of-the-year *Economic Report*. The completion of the *Economic Report,* along with the State of the Union message and budget, is an action-forcing deadline that compels each administration to set its policy direction for the coming year.

Given the separate constituencies to which these agencies are adapted and the different aspects of the economy they address, there is an obvious need for coordination. There are two formal mechanisms through which this is accomplished. Each administration creates a coordinating body. The oldest is the "troika," made up of the Treasury secretary, OMB director, and chair of the CEA. The troika can be as simple in operation as these three persons meeting for lunch. Then, other officials can be added to create "troika-plus" groups. Finally, there are elaborate councils such as Ford's Economic Policy Board and Clinton's National Economic Council.

The second mechanism is the troika's annual forecasting exercise, begun by President Kennedy. Over time, three organizational levels have been recognized as T1, T2, and T3. T1 consists of the three principals; T2 is at the deputy level, the assistant of the Treasury for tax policy, an assistant director of OMB, and a member of CEA; T3 comprises staff members from the three agencies. T1 begins by stipulating the economic assumptions. T3 then gathers data and shapes a forecast within the parameters they have been given. When they are satisfied, the forecast goes upward to T2, and when T2 is satisfied, it is passed along to T1. Ultimately, it is presented to the president as a recommended forecast.

The economic activities of any administration are determined by challenges presented by the economic environment. Although Democrats have a greater tendency to rely on governmental mechanisms and Republicans lean toward private enterprise, economist Samuel Morley and political scientist Erwin Hargrove, after interviewing ten CEA chairs, concluded "that each administration fights the problem it confronts." If any administration is faced with serious inflation, or high unemployment, or any other serious problem, it really has no choice but to deal with it as best it can.

Domestic Policy

The problem with domestic policy, according to Donald Rumsfeld, is that there are so many domestic departments that almost all issues are multi-departmental. Therefore, you need a mechanism such as the Domestic Council "to sort and sift among the departments and agencies and assign jurisdiction and coordinate decisions so you don't end up tripping over your shoelaces in dealing with the press, or with the Congress, or even have the left hand not know what the right hand is doing."[28] Accordingly, the domestic staff's constituency is a wide array of agencies and, beyond that, the various population groups these agencies represent.

Whom did the Domestic Council staff members consult? "We had a couple of professors from major law schools," recalled one Nixon staff member. "I mean it's a process of trying to get the best minds that we could to look at the problem along the way. And even before that we had a long string of meetings. We'd bring down a group of five or six people, and spend an afternoon talking about the problem."[29] A colleague of the same staff member spoke about contacts within the agencies and beyond.

> Each of us has within his area certain antennae that operate. One is people in the agencies that . . . call [in with] early warning of problems that are upcoming as well as opportunities. And each one of us has three or four relatively influential people in the agencies that we contact on a regular basis, daily. Another one, and this is one that a lot of people miss, [is that] we talk to a fantastic range of people. When we're out, maybe a speech in California, we'll talk to educators pro and con, and there are a lot of ideas that get popped into the system that way.[30]

Meetings are staples of domestic staff life. If anything, they become more exhaustive as one moves up the hierarchy. In early 1979 President Carter asked Stuart Eizenstat to head an interagency task force on energy legislation. Eizenstat "spent weeks of intensive meetings every night at five o'clock getting all the agencies together to see what the next wave of energy legislation might look like. We sat down with the agencies and talked it through. We asked them to staff it out and come back and let the other agencies see it."[31] Fifteen to twenty persons, principally assistant secretaries and assistant administrators, attended. At the same time, Eizenstat and his colleagues were in constant touch with members of Congress, committee staffs, and representatives of the trucking, rail, and airline industries. Major policy development is not done casually.

Finally, the president makes major decisions. In 1991 there was a question whether President Bush should sign or veto a civil rights bill. James

Cicconi wrote a statement recommending that Bush sign the "not very good, but not horrible" bill. Counsel Boyden Gray wrote a statement strongly recommending a veto. "They were just diametrically opposed points of view," Cicconi said. "I sent both statements to the president. . . . I recommended that he read both. I told him what the differences were and why." Bush read both, then called him saying he preferred Cicconi's view.[32]

Any policy proposal, Leon Panetta felt, should "be scrubbed the same way so that we know the numbers, what it costs, what's going to happen, are defensible and we don't blow up by just throwing an idea out there." The idea of Hope scholarships came up during some campaign sessions, but President Clinton directed that it be subject to this type of analysis. After it was reviewed by the Department of Education and OMB, Bruce Reed of the Domestic Policy Council and Gene Sperling of the National Economic Council brought the results to Panetta. In his judgment, there were three options. "We then took those issues, brought them to the president, went over it with him. He made the decision, and we then packaged it and had it ready for the speech."[33]

Legal Environment

Virtually all White House interaction with the legal environment originates in the Office of Counsel to the President. Four aspects of the counsel's position bring the office into contact with various legal institutions: chair of the War Powers Committee, chair of the Judicial Selection Committee, acting as the White House conduit to the Justice Department's Office of Legal Counsel (OLC), and as the principal defender of the president's constitutional prerogatives.

When Congress passed the War Powers Resolution in 1973, it was thought to be a check on the president's ability to deploy troops overseas. In practice it has not proved to be so, but it is still legislation to which attention must be paid. In addition to the president's counsel and the head of the OLC, the War Powers Committee included senior legal officers of the State and Defense Departments, the Joint Chiefs of Staff, the CIA, and the NSC. Meeting on an as-needed basis, this committee would determine what had, in fact, happened in some overseas situation and what action— often a notification—was needed so the White House could adapt to the events that had taken place.

The Judicial Selection Committee is a group of White House and Justice Department officials who consider possible judicial appointees. The White House is most involved when there is a Supreme Court vacancy. Peter Wallison described decision making when Antonin Scalia was chosen for the high court. President Reagan wished to consider only sitting federal judges. Two lawyers in the counsel's office and several in the Justice Department read the opinions of appeals court judges and then wrote memoranda describing the judges' philosophies. In this particular instance President Reagan was more taken by the chance to appoint the first Italian American justice than by any philosophical nuances, but Robert Bork and Anthony Kennedy, both of whom were subsequently nominated for the Supreme Court, were among the judges analyzed.

The Justice Department's Office of Legal Counsel drafts the legal opinions of the attorney general and provides opinions for all governmental agencies. With respect to the president, it responds to requests for legal opinions or oral advice from the president's counsel and reviews all executive orders and proclamations for form and legality. In adapting to each other, the relationship between the counsel's office and OLC can be mutually supportive or somewhat contentious. If the president's counsel makes a request, this may alert OLC to developments inside the White House. Their opinion, in turn, may strengthen the counsel's hand inside the White House as they provide an external statement (as opposed to the counsel's own view) that the president is constrained by statutes to act in such-and-such a way. The president's counsel, however, might be a rival to OLC if government agencies take a question to the White House rather than to OLC. In any case, the counsel's office and OLC keep each other busy.

Yet another responsibility is to serve as custodian of the rights and responsibilities of the office of the presidency. A lawyer's understanding of the durability of precedent makes counsel reluctant to agree to any diminution of power that would handicap a future president. Consequently, A. B. Culvahouse (who succeeded Wallison as counsel during Reagan's second term) explained, "you're the last and in some cases the only protector of the president's constitutional privileges. Almost everyone else is willing to give those away in part inch by inch and bit by bit in order to win the issue of the day, to achieve compromise on today's thorny issue."[34] The counsel tries to guard against any erosion of presidential authority.

Each of the counsel's activities deals with the law in some respect. But since the entire White House must consider both policy and politics, the counsel is invariably surrounded by a blend of law, policy, and politics.

Interpreting Incoming Information

The contact between the White House staff and the political environment generates a lot of information. Since the information comes from different segments of the environment, each of which has a language and a culture of its own, it needs to be interpreted as it ascends to the upper levels of the White House. Talented as the senior staffers may be, it would be unusual for the same person to understand a foreign-intelligence report about Afghanistan, a monetary analysis from the Federal Reserve Board, the interpersonal chemistry between members of a Senate committee, and so on. All of these bits of information have meaning, but someone must place them in context by providing related intelligence so the implications can be understood.

In dealing with the media, for example, Howard Baker said, "Marlin [Fitzwater] was indispensable. Marlin almost every day would tell us what the lead was going to be that night on the 6:30 news. Tom Griscom [a Baker aide who served as communications director] did that too. It was invaluable to be able to know even hours in advance what was likely to confront us in the papers or on television."[35]

Regarding breaking news, there is also a tie between the media and those responsible for policy. Pete Roussel told of a midnight phone call from Deborah Potter, then with CBS News. "She said, 'Pete, we've just had a report that 250 marines have just been killed in Lebanon. Do you know anything about that?'" When you get a call from a good reporter like that, you usually perk up." In this case Roussel had barely put the phone down when he got a call from National Security Assistant Bud McFarlane telling him of an incident in Lebanon. "Bud," Roussel replied, "CBS just called me about it. They're already on to it."[36]

When domestic proposals come in, they need to be to be routed to other agencies to determine how they affect those agencies' plans. Phillip Brady, who served as staff secretary during the Bush administration, said that when he got a request to get something on the president's desk as quickly as possible, he "would take it to Edie Holliday, the cabinet secretary, and say, 'you take care of the external vetting [outside of the White House complex] and then I'll take care of the internal vetting.'" If it were an educational issue, it might be sent to the education office in the Department of Labor or to the Justice Department to determine if the federal government had authority to take the proposed actions. "Internal vetting," Brady continued, "meant going to the Office of Policy Development, or perhaps OMB [which had a section devoted to educational issues]."[37]

Howard Baker acknowledged that at first he did not understand many of the technical terms contained in reports he was receiving from OMB. He sought help from Dan Cripman, who had been his economic adviser when Baker was Senate majority leader. "You have to come down here and . . . be my interpreter," Baker implored. "You've got to tell me what this means."[38] With Cripman's help, he reached a necessary threshold of understanding and thereafter was able to deal with OMB without difficulty.

Coordination

Given a segmented White House staff, how can media relations, congressional relations, counsel, and relevant policy activities be focused so the actions of each unit reinforce the actions of other units? A number of coordinating routines have been developed, the most important of which is a series of morning meetings. All administrations from Nixon to Clinton have held morning meetings, and those in the Reagan, Bush, and Clinton administrations have been quite similar in form.

One is a large senior-staff meeting, including all the assistants to the president. This is an informational gathering. The heads of all the offices report what their unit is doing. More importantly, the chief of staff announces decisions that have been made and tells everyone what is to be emphasized in the immediate future. As Leon Panetta explained, this meeting gave him a chance "to let the larger staff know what's happening with the president, what are the major issues so . . . they didn't feel like they were out of the loop as far as the process was concerned."[39]

The second session, sometimes held before and sometimes after this larger meeting, is often called the "real meeting." Attendance here is limited to about half a dozen people: the chief of staff and the core members of the senior staff. This is a decision-making meeting in which the pros and cons of proceeding one way or the other are frankly discussed.

After the "large meeting" and the "real meeting," each of the unit heads would hold a meeting with their own staffs. They would pass along decisions that had been made or announced at the earlier meetings and then would discuss what their unit would be doing. It is this sequence—an exchange of information in the senior-staff meetings followed by sharing the information with each individual staff—that produces close coordination of the several White House units.

At the same time the unit heads are meeting with their own staffs, the chief of staff meets with the president. He briefs the president on what has been discussed at the preceding meetings plus any other matters he wants to call to the Chief Executive's attention. In turn the president instructs the chief of staff what he wants to have done and what issues he wants to have emphasized. That meeting, in Howard Baker's words, is "really the focal point of the administration."[40]

There must be routine senior-staff meetings, Bowman Cutter argued, because "the real functions, the administration of the White House, the president's calendar, the congressional relations, the press relations, the political constituency relations do all pretty much work better when they are knitted together."[41] Richard Cheney used virtually the same metaphor. As a result of the meetings, "you'd get everybody sort of stitched together."[42] So we end as we began. Regardless of whether they are Democrats or Republicans, thoughtful White House veterans are in fundamental agreement on how the presidential staff should serve their president and their country.

Notes

1. Richard Cheney, interview with Martha Joynt Kumar, Washington, D.C., July 27, 1999, White House Interview Program.

2. David Gergen, interview with Martha Joynt Kumar, Arlington, Va., Aug. 26, 1999, White House Interview Program.

3. W. Bowman Cutter, interview with Martha Joynt Kumar, Nov. 8, 1999, White House Interview Program.

4. Roger Porter, interview with Martha Joynt Kumar, Cambridge, Mass., Oct. 22, 1999, White House Interview Program.

5. James Cicconi, interview with Martha Joynt Kumar, Washington, D.C., Nov. 29, 1999, White House Interview Program.

6. Leon Panetta, interview with Martha Joynt Kumar, Monterey Bay, Calif., May 4, 2000, White House Interview Program.

7. Michael Deaver, interview with Martha Joynt Kumar, Washington, D.C., Sept. 9, 1999, White House Interview Program.

8. David Demerest, interview with Martha Joynt Kumar, Washington, D.C., Dec. 7, 1999, White House Interview Program.

9. Roy Neel, interview with Martha Joynt Kumar, Washington, D.C., June 15, 1999, White House Interview Program.

10 E. Pendleton James, interview with Martha Joynt Kumar, New York, N.Y., Nov. 8, 1999, White House Interview Program.

11. Kenneth Duberstein, interview with Martha Joynt Kumar, Washington, D.C., Aug. 12, 1999, White House Interview Program.

12. Panetta interview.

13. Howard Baker, interview with Martha Joynt Kumar, Washington, D.C., Nov. 12, 1999, White House Interview Program.

14. Duberstein interview.

15. Donald Rumsfeld, interview with Martha Joynt Kumar, Chicago, Ill., Apr. 25, 2000, White House Interview Program.

16. Peter Roussel, interview with Martha Joynt Kumar and Terry Sullivan, Houston, Tex., Nov. 3, 1999, White House Interview Program.

17. Gerald Warren, interview with Martha Joynt Kumar, Middleburg, Va., Oct. 18, 1999, White House Interview Program.

18. Michael McCurry, interview with Martha Joynt Kumar, Washington, D.C., Mar. 27, 2000, White House Interview Program.

19. Ray Jenkins, interview with Martha Joynt Kumar, Washington, D.C., Sept. 8, 1999, White House Interview Program.

20. Deaver interview.

21. Marlin Fitzwater, interview with Martha Joynt Kumar, Deale, Md., Oct. 21, 1999, White House Interview Program.

22. Personal interview with author.

23. Personal interview with author.

24. James Fetig, interview with Martha Joynt Kumar, Rockville, Md., Feb. 5, 1999, White House Interview Program.

25. Cutter interview.

26. Ibid.

27. Panetta interview.

28. Rumsfeld interview.

29. Personal interview with author.

30. Personal interview with author.

31. Personal interview with author.

32. Cicconi interview.

33. Panetta interview.

34. A. B. Culvahouse, interview with Martha Joynt Kumar, Washington, D.C., Sept. 15, 1999, White House Interview Program.

35. Baker interview.

36. Roussel interview.

37. Phillip Brady, interview with Martha Joynt Kumar, McLean, Va., Aug. 17, 1999, White House Interview Program.

38. Baker interview.

39. Panetta interview.

40. Baker interview.

41. Cutter interview.

42. Cheney interview.

The White House Is Like City Hall

MARTHA JOYNT KUMAR

W HEN A STAFFER FOR A NEW ADMINISTRA-
tion enters a West Wing office for the first time, he or she
knows right off that they are in a world different from any
other. "When you walk into the White House at the beginning of an administration, it is empty," commented Bernard Nussbaum,
counsel to President Clinton. "All of the files are gone. Even the secretaries
are gone."[1] By the terms of the Presidential Records Act, the records of
one's predecessor are sitting in a warehouse waiting for the creation of a
new presidential library. While there may or may not be furniture in the
office, one item that assuredly will be in place is a ringing telephone. "I
think my first day I got 300 phone calls from people asking specifically for
me," related Jan Naylor Cope, who worked in the Office of Presidential
Personnel.[2] One presidential aide in the Clinton administration recalled
that he walked into his boss's office "and found that the office was empty
and that all eight of his telephone lines were ringing." He confessed: "I
didn't pick up the phone. And the reason for that was, once I said hello and
identified myself, I didn't know how to help any person who was on the
other end of the line. . . . And so I stood, not particularly knowing what to
do, with his telephone ringing off the hook."[3] Nussbaum answered his
phone, commenting on the business of the first day: "The minute you walk
into the office, the phones are ringing. It's as if the ten biggest litigation

cases in your life are going on simultaneously. I went to the office straight from the inauguration and went to work right away, doing executive orders on that first day." No records, no furniture, no support staff, no information while at the same time you face a deluge of phone calls from people asking for answers to questions for which most likely you have no response. All of this makes for a first day that is an anomaly in the prior experience of most who go to work at the White House.

In addition to the lack of institutional memory and the immediate demands for action greeting staff members, there are natural forces working against a smooth transition to power. First, a White House is organized around a president who may or may not come in with a sense of how important his staff will be to the success of his administration. Second, the White House is an artificial construct created all at once from a pool of people many of whom do not know one another. Third, it is difficult to weave together the necessary elements of campaign workers and old White House and Washington hands. Fourth, it takes every administration time to discover the knowledgeable people working within the White House and in the Office of Management and Budget (OMB). Fifth, mistakes made early make it difficult to catch up and get ahead. Sixth, too many people come into office tired and have difficulty responding to the volume and variety of work. Finally, emptying out offices in the White House and in the executive branch is a daunting task, especially if the transition does not involve a change in party.

It Takes a President Time to Appreciate the Place of Staff

Pres. Gerald Ford discussed his initial lack of appreciation for the margin a staff buys for a president. "I started out in effect not having an effective chief of staff and it didn't work. So anybody who doesn't have one and tries to run the responsibilities of the White House I think is putting too big a burden on the president himself. You need a filter, a person that you have total confidence in who works so closely with you that in effect his is almost an alter ego. I just can't imagine a president not having an effective chief of staff." The chief of staff represents both the staff and the need a president has to organize his time and his tasks. When he began his administration, Ford had an open-door policy with cabinet officers and top officials. He soon found he had little time to do anything other than meet with those who requested his time. "Traditionally, every cabinet officer wants to see the president as often as possible and other top people as well," said Ford. "The net result is there aren't that many hours in a day with all the other obligations that you have to handle on a daily basis."[4]

If the president does not choose a chief of staff, the framework for the White House staff structure is not established and filled in. President Clinton did not announce a chief of staff until mid-December, 1992. Until he named Thomas McLarty, no choices could be made on the decision-making process to be used for the chief executive, and the president-elect's relations with Congress and the news media had no permanent staff member assigned to them until right before Clinton and Gore came to Washington. The senior White House staff was appointed five days before the inauguration, which left them no time to organize before they began their jobs.

The White House as an Artificial Construct

An administration is constructed from a standing start, not gradually developed through experience. The people who come into the White House are coming into a building governed by the rules of politics and moved by its dynamics rather than a common understanding of rules of management. "The most important thing to grasp first is how much a White House itself, especially as it starts off after a change in the party occupying the White House, resembles a city hall," noted Lloyd Cutler, who served as counsel to both Presidents Carter and Clinton. "It is very, very difficult to organize. It isn't as if General Electric bought a company and sent in a management team that had worked together for twenty years and then they came to reshape this company that they bought. A new president naturally relies on the people who helped him get elected and also then seeks ethnic balance, geographic balance, leading public figures, experts in various fields."[5] Inevitably, these people do not know each other well as the administration begins. Yet they are required to gather and analyze information and then make decisions whether or not their decision-making process is in order.

At the same time a White House is pulled together from disparate sources, the president and his senior staff often have to withstand strong pressure from groups to get their people on board. One veteran White House staff member described this: "The incoming White House can't have a deaf ear or political tin ear but it must be disciplined to withstand that kind of pressure. It's always going to happen, and you have to have very diplomatic outreach teams, and you have to have people in the White

House that are open and receptive, but you cannot populate the government and the White House by quota. It just won't give you the team you have to have."[6] Thus, as office directors assemble their staffs, they need to develop strategies and mechanisms to fend off those they want to hold at arms length and not let into the building.

The Difficulty of Weaving Together a Staff Representing Five Types of Knowledge

One of the most difficult aspects of a transition into the White House is the need to accommodate in the government those who worked in the campaign while at the same time integrating into the operation those who know the president, even though they did not work in the campaign; those with White House knowledge; others with Washington experience; and people who have substantive knowledge in the areas of social, economic, and national security policy. "You want somebody who has at least served in the upper echelons of the White House staff and knows what goes on, knows how that place runs," Leon Panetta advised. "I would then say with that person you're going to assign one of your top campaign people who knows people, knows personnel, and knows the politics of the president and who they screwed and who they don't want to screw and brings a political sense to that. That's the best combination. If you can get those two in one person you're even better off."[7]

Campaign People

The problem with having campaign people come into the government is they remain to be tested on their ability to govern. Those who work in campaigns think in a short time span, see the world in black and white, and have a sense of attack. While fit for political battle, these qualities are not necessarily what one wants to emphasize in governing. "Campaigns are inevitably exercises of shifting tides and winds and expediency," observed Roger Porter, who worked in all three of the last Republican administrations of the twentieth century. "You're trying to resolve this little thing here and this little thing there and keep this group on board and what we have here. That is different than governing," he observed. During a campaign, one is living a very different life than is true when governing. "You have to build coalitions. You're not in an us-them, we've got to defeat them; we've got to destroy them. There's just a different mentality. . . .

But when you govern you've got to figure how to build a coalition and work with others because, in fact, in our system power is so widely distributed and fragmented that that's the only way you can effectively govern. Those are not necessarily the same set of skills that get illuminated during the course of a campaign."[8]

Martin Anderson explained the dynamic of bringing into the White House people who worked on the campaign. "They work so long and so hard and become so much of the team that when the candidate wins, they automatically come in. It's just the most natural thing in the world." There are several priorities for a president, including the loyalty of those serving on his staff. "They have to be competent for the job," he noted. "But given the choice of taking someone who was competent and fully agreed with Reagan and someone who was brilliant and disagreed, you took the first one. You also want loyalty, total, absolute loyalty and enthusiasm. Then if they know something about Washington, that's nice but not that critical."[9]

Those people who have not worked on a campaign are looked upon with suspicion. Gerald Warren, who worked in the Press Office and the Office of Communications in the Nixon and Ford White Houses, explained his entry and the manner in which he sought to fit in. "I walked in to the White House for the first time on January 21 early in the morning. I had come in on the red eye. I was advised by a very wise person who had been through this before to skip the inauguration festivities because I wasn't a member of the team. . . . I was a newspaper editor. I wasn't identified as a Nixon person. I had to overcome that within the staff." When asked how one overcomes the initial cool response of those who have worked with the president-elect, Warren said, "I think just by quietly going about your work and learning the ropes of the White House staff, how the White House staff works and doesn't work, which is a very difficult thing for people coming in for the first time to do."[10]

Personal Presidential Choices

In addition to choosing his own chief of staff, a president will select four or five other senior staff members. President Ford explained his picks. "The Press Secretary, I made the choice. First Jerry Ter Horst, then he left and then Ron Nessen. Those were personal choices." As a veteran of the Hill, Ford chose his legislative liaison. "I felt I had a better knowledge of the kind of a person who ought to do that, and I picked Jack Marsh, who had been in Congress with me as a southern Democrat. Then when I went as vice president, he was over at the Pentagon as legislative liaison for the Pentagon. Then when I became president, I drafted Jack to come and be my legislative liaison," he recounted. "Another is your speechwriter. In my case I felt I wanted to pick the head of speechwriting, and I picked Bob Hartmann, who had been my chief of staff when I was vice president. A speechwriter has to have an intimate relationship with the president and the president with the speechwriter," he declared. "Those are the kind of people that a president has to pick personally." They may make different choices, but presidents will select a handful of people to occupy positions they consider to be crucial to the manner in which their presidency functions.

Substantive Policy People

As a White House starts up, substantive policy people must be represented from its creation. Leon Panetta discussed some of this blending of personnel.

> You want the most qualified people in those kinds of positions because, as you go through the decision-making process, you may want to make some changes, you may want to bring some political input into it. You have got to have the substance down so you know what the hell you're getting into. . . . You want somebody in these positions whose first thought is not the politics of it but the substance of it. What's the right economic policy? What's the right national security policy? What's the right policy in terms of the counsel and the law? You want people that make straight calls on that. It's easy to make political decisions on top of that.[11]

An area in which political and substantive people clashed in the Clinton White House was economic policy and the priority to be accorded to deficit reduction. David Dreyer, who worked for Robert Rubin, discussed the conflict that can take place between political and policy people. "There are times when the political people were advising him [Rubin] he couldn't 'break a campaign promise' by underfunding or not funding a particular program where he was able to persuade them and cabinet people who represented those programs that we had to hit a particular dollar figure on deficit reduction where the financial markets would regard as credible," he said. "He got all of those people singing off of the same sheet of music about the president's priorities and the depth of the deficit reduction we were going to do, and that meant that some of our tax promises and some of our programmatic initiatives weren't going to be as fulfilled or as out front as they wanted them to be."[12]

White House Experience and Knowledge of the Rhythms of Washington

A well-functioning White House is generally a blend of people from the campaign and those with a previous tour of service in the White House as well as some who are familiar with the rhythms of the Washington community. James Cicconi, who served in the Reagan and Bush administrations, discussed the advantage of prior service. "I was a hell of a lot better at my job under President Bush because I had worked in a more junior position under President Reagan," he said. "I was able to see how Darman and others, how that job functioned, when it functioned well, when it functioned poorly, how it needed to adapt to the president's style of work. . . . I learned the importance of speaking up and how to affect a decision, how to deal with pressure and stress in the job and balance things in your life at the same time."[13]

William Galston, who worked in the Clinton White House, observed: "The only institutional memory that counts is what's in somebody's head. A database across time is no substitute for someone who's been there before and is going back."[14] James Baker discussed what one learns from being in or near a White House. His first experience with the White House was coming to meetings there during the Ford administration when he came in place of the secretary of commerce, Rogers C. B. Morton, who was ill at the time. Baker learned "[h]ow options should go to the president. How decisions should be made. The role of the honest broker. The land mines that you have to be aware of as chief of staff."[15] Once he came in as chief of staff, he found just how well his earlier experience had served him.

Those who have worked in Washington develop a sense of the rhythms of the congressional calendar and its implications for an administration, the relative strengths and weaknesses of interest groups working around town, and the needs of news organizations as they do their reporting on events in and around Washington. The issues and level of criticism a White House has to deal with varies depending upon where the president's initiatives are in the legislative process. A knowledge of interest groups and how they work is important for those running a White House, as is a familiarity with the routines of news organizations.

Discovering Knowledgeable Insiders

It takes some time before those coming into an administration appreciate the knowledge of the White House support staff, including the professional staff and those working in the Office of Management and Budget. The White House has rhythms that repeat themselves from one administration to the next. "There are certain people who have that metronome in their head and know how it's supposed to work, like the clerk downstairs in the White House," observed Warren. "There's always someone in each office, some secretary in each office, who has the key, who knows how it works. The difficult thing is to find that person and then, in the case of a Republican administration replacing a Democrat or vice versa, protecting that person and saying please help us." Invariably such people are demoted until the new staff recognizes the usefulness of those who previously served. In the case of the Press Office, for example, Connie Gerard worked for press secretaries from George Reedy through Marlin Fitzwater. "Each of us going in, in those circumstances, seems to make the same mistake," Warren said. "They move these people away as if they were [Lyndon B.] Johnson loyalists. Well, she may or may not have been but she knew how the place worked; she was willing and eager to share that with us. It took us about a week of stumbling around before we brought her back in to a prominent position in the Press Office."

There is a whole group of people in the OMB who know White House operations. William Galston, who worked on education issues during the first term of the Clinton administration, described the importance of permanent people in the executive branch. "Just think about it institutionally," he said. "There are very few people in senior staff positions in the Congress who didn't start out with junior staff positions in the Congress. There is a training process. But somehow when you get to the White House, the cycle of training and experience is broken, and it's as though you're starting over again with each administration." He observed: "Without the assistance of senior OMB people, career people, I would have been lost in the early months on my job. . . . You have to figure out that they're there and you have to figure out how to interact usefully and respectfully."[16]

Coming in Tired

If the president-elect moved directly from the campaign into transition mode, it is quite possible he failed to rest during that time period. The result is coming into the White House tired. If he is exhausted, so too will be his staff, for wherever a president is during the transition, he is certain to have staff who follow his moves. David Gergen described the problem and the Clinton example. "I do believe that the physical pacing of the president is so important. The transition time is one in which its extremely important to put him down for a while to recharge the engines. You come off a grueling campaign and everybody is exhausted. If you don't allow those people to have some time, especially the candidate, to find himself or herself again, get yourself back together, and be ready for what is going to hit in January, you're just asking for enormous problems," he said. For Reagan, it was not difficult to take time off after the election and get rested. "That was sort of his natural bent anyway," Gergen observed. "After he did a picture, he relaxed; that was his way of life. Then you get up for the next one. Clinton I saw at Renaissance Weekend in Hilton Head in late December or early January 1993. I was stunned at the pace he was trying to keep. . . . He was going on like four hours sleep. He had been doing it all through the transition."[17] The result was a president who came into office without having taken time off to make the switch from campaigning to governing.

Early Mistakes Cost Valuable Energy

Especially in the area of appointments, the early months of an administration are difficult ones replete with opportunities to go off track. Jerry Jones, who worked in the Personnel Office during the Nixon White House, told of the huge number of resumes he had to deal with that had been requested by those working in the transition. He was brought into the White House to deal with letters solicited by the personnel transition team from people whose names were in *Who's Who in America*. Transition staff had sent letters to them asking they send in names of people appropriate for jobs in the administration. They enthusiastically did so. "The EOB [Executive Office Building]'s halls on the first floor, over by the Personnel Office, were stacked with letters from these people. And then, when they didn't hear from them—which they couldn't do because there were multithousands of these letters and resumes everywhere—it simply broke the system down. . . . Then, when they didn't hear again, they started calling."

One mistake in the appointment process can draw the energy of a new administration into areas where it had not planned to go. "The John Tower confirmation, failure to confirm, that was a serious bump in the road for us," observed Andrew Card, who served as deputy chief of staff in the early part of the George H. W. Bush administration. The Tower confirmation was a problem because it was unanticipated and threatened to compromise their routines and focus. "It preoccupied senior staff attention at the White House for probably two weeks when we couldn't afford to give it the attention." They were lucky with the selection of Richard Cheney to be secretary of defense in place of John Tower. "The background check was fast because it was easy. There were no skeletons that anybody could find, and Cheney knew the process, the process knew him. So we stopped the bleeding very, very quickly." If Cheney had not been so easy to confirm, the administration could have faced serious difficulties thereafter. "If we had stumbled after the Tower problems, I think it would have taken us a long time to recover, and it would have jeopardized any momentum we had on the policy side," Card said.[18]

Emptying out the Offices

One of the difficult tasks at the end of an administration is emptying out the offices of political appointees, and for those coming in, it is making certain that task was thoroughly accomplished. Chair huggers are rampant in the White House and throughout an administration. If it is a transition involving a change in party, the White House is automatically cleared. In a transition involving the same party and where a vice president is the president-elect, the problems of clearing the desks are magnified, requiring the cancellation of White House passes and leaving people on the payroll for a short period of time. In the transition from the Reagan to the Bush administrations, one official familiar with the process said White House staff had their passes canceled a week after the inauguration but were kept on the payroll for two to three weeks.[19]

In a hostile transition, pressure is there to protect the people out in the departments and agencies, which makes it difficult for those coming into the White House to set up their administration. The rest of the executive branch is more difficult to clear out than is the White House. Traditionally, the president-elect chooses to empty out the offices under his own direction or have the incumbent president fire people just before leaving. At the request of President-elect Clinton, President Bush sent letters to people his administration appointed informing them they were terminated. A person involved in that transition said people out in the departments sought to hold on to their jobs by requesting of the Bush people: 'Don't tell them

I'm around; let them find me.' 'I've done a good job; of course, they want
me on their team.' 'They'd be foolish to replace me.'"[20] In fact, they did
clear the decks and then requested of each department head a briefing
book with the responsibilities sketched out for each of the political appointees, from the "Schedule Cs" to the department secretary.

A friendly transition has unanticipated problems. Those coming into
office believe the transition will be a smooth one and fail to take into account the two important issues they will confront: bringing in their own
people and thinking through representation of their party's coalition. One
person familiar with the transition from Presidents Reagan to Bush spoke
of these challenges. "I think the friendly takeover was more difficult than
the hostile because in the friendly takeover there was almost an expectation for the people who were left in the Reagan administration that they
would stay on and how dare you punish me and fire me. . . . At least when
you have a hostile takeover there's an expectation on those who are in
jobs that they are likely to be out of them."[21]

A friendly transition has the additional problem of taking into account
all of the factions within a party. "The other thing is, in a friendly takeover,
there's still the reality that there are different camps. When it's a hostile
takeover you don't have to worry about the different camps," said one participant. "When we came in as the Bush team, we had to worry about the
old Reagan team, we had to worry about the Bob Dole campaign workers,
the Pat Buchanan campaign workers, the Republican factions that complicated both the personnel process and the early policy-debate process."[22]
The personnel issue in a friendly transition is especially difficult because it
is unanticipated and little attention is given to it when something could be
done to ameliorate hard feelings toward the incoming team. In the case of
the transition from Presidents Reagan to Bush, the incoming people could
have insisted President Reagan fire people rather than leave the task to
them. The hard feelings felt by those asked to leave remained for years to
come.

Reducing the Slope of the Learning Curve

Those coming into the White House have strong forces lined up against
them as they set about to create a smooth-running operation. The new
staff come in at one time, they do not know one another, and they are required to make decisions of great magnitude from their first day on the job.
In addition, there is scant written information on White House operations

left behind by those who preceded them. But most often on inauguration day, there is a feeling of goodwill among the public and in the Washington community for those who begin their term in office and a willingness to give them time as they find their way. It is a period "where you want to wish the new guy well whether you voted for him or not, and you want to give him the benefit of the doubt initially," commented James Cicconi about the early months of a president's term. "So there is a period where there is almost a suspension of partisanship, a knowing suspension of it and where a sense of fair play enters in."[23] If the incoming staff makes use of information relating to the start up and operations of those in administrations preceding them, they can make even greater use of their early days in the White House. As is true of any institution, the White House is an organization that has discernable rhythms and routines associated with its operations. Perhaps the most effective resource for those accompanying the chief executive as he enters office is the group of those who previously served in the White House. Not only are the previous occupants a great source of information on where one can find the gears and levers operating the institution, but those who worked in the building also are almost uniformly eager to help. It is up to the president and his staff to find them and then to make use of their information.

Notes

1.   Bernard Nussbaum, interview with Martha Joynt Kumar and Nancy Kassop, New York City, Nov. 9, 2000, White House Interview Program.

2.   Jan Naylor Cope, interview with Martha Joynt Kumar, Washington, D.C., June 8, 2000, White House Interview Program.

3.   Background interview.

4.   Gerald Ford, interview with Martha Joynt Kumar, Oct. 10, 2000, White House Interview Program.

5.   Lloyd Cutler, interview with Martha Joynt Kumar and Nancy Kassop, Washington, D.C., July 8, 1999, White House Interview Program.

6.   Background interview.

7.   Leon Panetta, interview with Martha Joynt Kumar, Monterey Bay, Calif., May 4, 2000, White House Interview Program.

8.   Roger Porter, interview with Martha Joynt Kumar, Cambridge, Mass., Oct. 22, 1999, White House Interview Program.

9.   Martin Anderson, interview with Martha Joynt Kumar, Stanford, Calif., May 5, 2000, White House Interview Program.

10. Gerald Warren, interview with Martha Joynt Kumar, Middleburg, Va., Oct. 18, 1999, White House Interview Program.

11. Panetta interview.

12. David Dreyer, interview with Martha Joynt Kumar, Washington, D.C., Aug. 1, 1999, White House Interview Program.

13. James Cicconi, interview with Martha Joynt Kumar, Washington, D.C., Nov. 29, 1999, White House Interview Program.

14. William Galston, interview with Martha Joynt Kumar, College Park, Md., June 5, 1997.

15. James A. Baker III, interview with Martha Joynt Kumar and Terry Sullivan, Houston, Tex., Nov. 16, 1999, White House Interview Program.

16. Galston interview.

17. David Gergen, interview with Martha Joynt Kumar, Arlington, Virginia, Aug. 26, 1999, White House Interview Program.

18. Andrew Card Jr., interview with Martha Joynt Kumar, Washington, D.C., May 25, 1999, White House Interview Program.

19. Background interview.

20. Background interview.

21. Background interview.

22. Background interview.

23. James Cicconi, Andrew Card, and Phillip Brady, interview with Martha Joynt Kumar, Washington, D.C., Sept. 22, 1997.

The Pressures of
White House Work Life
"Naked in a Glass House"

MARTHA JOYNT KUMAR

"WHEN THEY COME TO THE WHITE HOUSE, there's no forty-hour week and they shouldn't expect it," said Pres. Gerald Ford. "It has to be almost a twenty-four-hour-a-day job for both the president and the staff."[1] The White House is a place where the work load is heavy, the hours long, the pressures great, and the benefits manifold. As hard as people say the work is, few would trade the time they spent working in the White House, nor is there a shortage of people wanting to work there. Donald Rumsfeld, chief of staff under President Ford, expressed the view of many that their service involved dual aspects: "In the White House you are very much at the center of things. There is an amazing flow of information. It is stimulating, because there's so much pressure. In my case, it was working with just a truly wonderful human being; a fine, decent, honorable, good person." At the same time, though, the work in the White House is staff work. You are not the principal player, the president is. That is a situation difficult for some staff members to get used to. Rumsfeld continued: "The disadvantage for me was that I had run large organizations and then I found myself back as an assistant. And I knew, as anyone in that job ought to know, that no one really cares what you think. What they really want to know when they ask you a question is what the president thinks. There-

94

fore you constantly have to answer, respond, and behave in a way that reflects what you believe to be the president's thinking and the president's best interest." Responding as the president would means staff members have to behave in a way that puts him in the foreground and themselves in a relief position. "That causes a change in how you handle yourself. You're not as natural. You're not as responsive. You're not as open because you're trying to do it in a way that serves him and his presidency. That is a very different kind of a job than running something yourself. So it has those pluses and those minuses."[2]

The Allure of the White House

The pressures of White House work life relate to the volume and variety of the assignments, the heavy commitment of hours and days, the generous amount of criticism directed toward the president and individual staff members, and the narrow margin of error allowed to those working for the chief executive. Though less numerous than the pressures, the benefits are an important component of White House work life. They revolve around the importance of the decisions made there, the interesting people and situations one confronts, the increased likelihood of having an interesting and lucrative career after leaving, and having a part in history as it is made.

"Interesting People, Interesting Situations"

Working in the White House has clear rewards, most especially because it is interesting and important work. "It's exciting," said Abner Mikva, counsel to President Clinton. "You're at the point of some very important decisions. Whether you're making them or not, you're involved in the decisional process. You're dealing with interesting people, interesting situations. There just was not a single boring moment that I had."[3] For those who live life close to the edge, the White House holds a strong appeal. Alonzo McDonald, who headed the McKinsey Company before he came to the White House to establish a management system for President Carter, found the pressure to his liking. "The benefits are: one of the most extreme lifetime challenges that one can ever have. For those of us who have always walked along the edge, whether in business or whatever, it's: How close can you walk to the edge without falling off? It's not everybody's cup of tea. . . . This was sort of the ultimate of being fully exposed. You were naked in a glass house every minute."[4]

Satisfaction comes with the work and with one's place in history as well. James Fetig, who served as the liaison to the Press Office for the National Security Council in the Clinton White House, commented: "The benefit as a citizen is to understand the glory of this republic and how it works, to have a chance to serve the American people and serve the Constitution and the highest office of the land firsthand, personally; to be there, to be part of history; to stand in places where history has been made. It's a very uplifting and motivating thing to do. When you walk through the gate of the White House every morning, you have no question of why you're at work. Getting motivated to go to work at the White House was never an issue, never a problem whatsoever. It was a delight to do no matter how frustrating it could be day by day, hour by hour."[5]

Close to the President

The importance the White House experience takes on in the lives of those who worked there can be seen in the positive views held by two men who for very different reasons had some bad memories associated with their White House tenure and the years afterward. Both H. R. Haldeman and Michael Deaver in retrospect would not have turned down the opportunity. Michael Deaver, deputy chief of staff in the Reagan White House, spoke about the conversation he had with former Nixon White House chief of staff H. R. Haldeman following Ronald Reagan's election as president. As Deaver related it, Haldeman encouraged him to go to Washington with Reagan, pointing out: "'You've got to go back. There have only been forty men [presidents], and each one of those men had a guy like you and so there's only forty people like that.' I said, 'You mean to tell me after going to federal prison and public humiliation that you would go do this again?' He said, 'In a heartbeat.'" When Deaver went to see Haldeman several years later, Haldeman took him into his office behind his house. "We walked into this place and that's all it was. It was every cartoon that had been drawn about him. Every photograph of him with everybody in the world. We sat down and he said, 'We have wonderful memories, don't we?' I said, 'Yes.'" In Deaver's case, he too has memories of his White House days in his office. "If you look in this office, I do have that picture over there of the five presidents. That's the only thing I've got because I love that picture, the way the light shines."[6]

Career Enhancement

Many former White House staff find work-related benefits follow them out of office. Michael Deaver explained this intangible package of benefits, including the effect on his post–White House employment. "I got a lot of stuff out of it. I got exactly what Bob Haldeman said. There were only forty people that were close to a president like I was. Some of them didn't even have a guy like me," he said. "So that was an incredible opportunity. I learned a lot about how the whole system works, and so it's given me a different caliber in the business I was in; calibrated me up to a different level. And I love my life and I love what I do."[7] Once people learn how the system works during their White House years, they have many opportunities to stay in Washington and work on issues related to the government operations they became familiar with during their tenure.

Wherever they go, those who served in a White House take with them the experience of working in an environment where they were constantly under multiple and intense pressures related to their assignments. Pete Roussel, deputy press secretary during the Reagan administration, explained the benefits. "I remember during the economic summit here [Houston] one day we were walking to a meeting and somebody in the car—they had all the major CEOs gathered for a meeting—[said,] 'Pete, you've got to go in to this meeting and brief the CEOs about this economic summit. Aren't you nervous?' I said, 'Are you kidding? This is fun. This is a day at the beach compared to what I've been through.' It disciplined me mentally, and I guess emotionally too, in ways that no other experience, none, in life, I don't think, could possibly do. So it was a great value to me in that way, and I commend it to anybody else that does it for that reason."[8]

For many, the benefits of White House work life translate into a lucrative career after leaving office. Those who come into the White House from a campaign as twenty-somethings living on meager earnings during the year or two preceding the election leave several years later with experience and contacts they use for the remainder of their careers as lawyers, consultants, or business people. For Clinton staff such as Rahm Emanuel, George Stephanopoulos, Dee Dee Myers, and Doug Sosnik, the White House years were followed by lucrative careers once they left the administration. Even those who work elsewhere in government find the White House experience an enriching one.

Never a Slow Day

The rush of activity in the White House is both a draw and its greatest limitation as a work place. "My advice to anybody in any future White House is there is never a slow day, even if there's a slow day," observed Pete Roussel. "It just doesn't happen there." As evidence, Roussel described a presidential golfing trip to Augusta, Georgia, which Press Secretary Larry Speakes "suggested would be quiet from a news standpoint." First, a gunman burst through the gate of the golf club and took as hostages two aides to the president and held them in the pro shop. Roussel briefed reporters throughout the day and evening on that situation.

> Finally it got to be midnight; I said what a day. I go to my room and the phone is ringing. I pick it up and it's Deborah Potter who was then a CBS reporter. . . . She said, "Pete, we've just had a report that 250 Marines have just been killed in Lebanon. Do you know anything about that?" When you get a call from a good reporter like that you usually perk up. I said, "Deborah, I don't know anything about that. Let me get back to you." I put the phone back down and it started ringing again. I didn't even have a chance to dial. I picked it up and it was Bud McFarlane, then the NSC [National Security Council] director. He said, "Pete, you need to come down to my room. We've just had an incident in Lebanon involving some Marines." I said, "Bud, CBS just called me about it. They're already on to it." It just shows you, again, for your purposes, how the life in that operation changes moment to moment.[9]

On those rare days that begin slowly, they rarely end that way. For most who serve in senior and midlevel posts, the White House is a great place to be, though for a limited amount of time.

Working in the White House: The Pressures

People who work in the White House at the senior level rarely serve out a full four-year term with the president while working in the same job. They either leave or shift from one position to another, as happened in the Clinton administration with Robert Rubin, George Stephanopoulos, Bruce Lindsey, Gene Sperling, Leon Panetta, Bruce Reed, Rahm Emanuel, and Sylvia Matthews. In fact, Matthews, Sperling, Lindsey, and Reed were still in the Clinton White House as the administration closed, though no one was in the same position he or she held in January, 1993. Most who work in the White House expect to stay two years or so and then leave for another post elsewhere. Though the benefits of working there are many, the pressures are indeed great, and the toll service in the White House takes is heavy in terms of one's time, energy, family, and personal life.

Constantly on the Job

White House working hours are long no matter what the administration or the office one works in. Alexander Haig described the heavy commitment of time he made when he worked in the White House as chief of staff for Presidents Nixon and Ford. "I usually was in by seven and I never went home before midnight seven days a week. I did that for two years." In addition to his two years with that schedule, Haig had the same hours previously during his four years serving as the deputy to National Security Adviser Henry Kissinger in the Nixon administration. In fact, Haig commented, it was worse working for Kissinger "because Henry used to have his ideas at night. He would call me at one, two o'clock in the morning, three o'clock in the morning, and I had just gotten home. He didn't sleep but four hours a night. I didn't sleep but three hours a night. And I did that for seven years. That's the kind of job it is and that's why you have to change. People do get burnout."[10]

While few worked the hours Haig observed, a normal White House day involves little time for oneself or one's family. Marlin Fitzwater, press secretary to Presidents Reagan and Bush, discussed the demands of a day and observed that one really has only about two hours to oneself when working at the White House. He broke down a typical day: "You usually leave about 7:30 or 8:00. This is the worst part. You get home at 9:00—it takes an hour to get home—have a drink, and you realize that you have to be in bed by 11:00 in order to have enough sleep to deal with the next day. So basically your entire private life is boiled down to between 9:00 and 11:00. That's tough to take. That's the part that people can't understand. People ask, what's it like to work in the White House? How many hours do you work? But the idea that there's really only two hours a day where you can deal with yourself or your family, that's the tough part."[11]

The constant pressure to be at the White House means people have little time to spend with their families. Ron Nessen, press secretary to President Ford, discussed the lack of time he had with his child. "I left home at

6:30, as I said, and I, usually because I had this thing about returning phone calls, got home at 9:30 or 10:00 or later if there was something going on. My son was eighteen months old then. I never saw him. Sometimes I'd wake him up at 11:00 to play with him because that was the only time I'd see him."[12] Phillip Brady, staff secretary during the Bush administration, talked about the illusion for young children that their father is not around. "One night I put my oldest son to bed. It was on a Sunday night. I put him to bed and he said without any sense of sarcasm, 'See you next week, Dad.' I was home all that next week; it was just that I'd leave before he got up and I got home after he went to bed. So the only time I could possibly see him was on the weekend when we weren't traveling."[13]

Even when senior White House staff are at home, their life is not their own. The White House pervades their life outside of the building as well. "The first day that I was assigned to the White House, there was a knock on the door at home and there were two guys with telephones," related Alonzo McDonald, who worked as a senior adviser to President Carter. "My wife said, 'Who are you?' and they said, 'We're from the White House. Where does he sleep?' They put one next to my bed. They said, 'Does he have a place where he sits down to read after dinner in the evening?' She said, 'Yes, right there. We need one there.'" McDonald observed from his experience: "The fact of the matter is that you're on duty twenty-four hours a day, seven days a week. You don't take time off or anything else."[14] Others at the senior level have felt the same continuing presence of their work no matter where they happen to be.

Physical Stress

White House work has a physical dimension to it. James Fetig, who was the press officer for the NSC while working with the Press Office, discussed the physical difficulties inherent in working in a White House. "The most difficult thing that anybody ought to know when they come in is going to be physical," he said. "It's the lack of sleep. The phone rings most nights and you almost never have a night of uninterrupted sleep. You start averaging four to five hours of sleep, and the rest of the time you're at work."[15]

Margita White, who headed the Office of Communications, provided an example of the physical toll of White House work. She left the White House for a seat on the Federal Communications Commission (FCC). White related how she arrived at the decision to take the FCC post.

I came back on Air Force One [at] three-thirty in the morning—I had been on Air Force One or the press plane back and forth—from a six-state trip, regional briefings, and what have you. I got home about three-thirty or four, went to bed, got up at six, knocked over a full pot of coffee on my leg, was taken in to the shower with cold water and then to the emergency room, and I had second-degree burns all the way down my leg. As they peeled off the skin and I was in the emergency room, I had a phone call from Dick Whalley, who was then the chairman of the FCC. He said I just want Margita to know what I did. He talked to my ex-husband and [Whalley] had just found out that there was going to be a vacancy on the FCC, and he had gone to the White House and said I want Margita White. When I came to, I learned about this. I thought, you know, I think I want to do that.[16]

Recognizing Burnout

There is no optimum amount of time to spend working at the White House, but burnout is a real factor. The difficulty with burnout is people rarely recognize it in themselves. Accompanying this factor is what Chase Untermeyer, personnel director for Pres. George H. W. Bush, dubbed the "White House narcotic." A person who is on the staff "should want to leave, otherwise they run a couple of risks, one of which is White House burnout. The other is sort of the opposite, which you can call the White House narcotic, the sense that this is all too wonderful, I can't possibly leave it; I can't possibly leave being in a situation in which if you walk into the White House Mess you see famous people or various cabinet secretaries; or out on the lawn: 'There are all these flags today. I wonder who's coming?' Or walking through the lobby of the West Wing: 'What movie star will I see?' All of that is wonderful to the degree of telling stories at the Thanksgiving dinner table, but from the point of view of really doing anything with your life, I think it's of limited value."[17]

People on their own rarely recognize they are reaching the point of burnout, but when they do, the president should honor their request to leave. Most often in the White House, others have to recognize it for them. "If it's your job to oversee fifteen people, if you're the chief of staff or the deputy chief of staff, you can figure out pretty quickly—there's so much happening so quick. There's so much performance going on," said one person who worked in a senior level White House position. "It doesn't take you long to evaluate it. It doesn't mean somebody makes one mistake and they're gone, but you can pick it up pretty quickly. Attitude is a big thing; energy level, enthusiasm. And you have to differentiate between success and failure. The success/failure issue as opposed to the effectiveness/energy/enthusiasm issue. There are going to be successes and failures."[18] Those at the top have to be aware of the need to recognize burnout in others as well as in themselves.

Getting It Right

Did you get it right? Is the president satisfied with what you did, if indeed your work rises to his level of attention. Don Baer, director of communications and strategic planning for the Clinton White House, described the pressure associated with "getting it right." There is "a lot of pressure and stress on you about in the meantime how did the thing that you planned a week ago play today when the president went out and did it. How did it play in the press? Did all the pieces of it fit together and go the way you had planned? How did he feel about it because you don't always have the time [to go over it] in specifics, and even if you do, he's not going to remember most of them to tell him exactly what he's doing and why he's doing it and what his place in all this is; here's what he's going to say. What did he want to say? Did it come out the way he thought it would?"[19] Those are all concerns associated with the job you are doing for the president.

Ann Lewis, who took over the communications post following Baer, indicated that in addition to the physical strain of working the number of hours one does in the White House, there is an emotional strain that comes with the consequences of one's work. "The second is the emotional strain when everything you may say and do is enormously important, is watched so closely, and has potentially the impact that a White House statement does."[20]

Jody Powell, press secretary to President Carter, discussed the stress of it all. "There's a tremendous amount of pressure to get things right, to not make a problem worse or create a new problem because you either got it wrong in terms of understanding it or you said it wrong. I didn't find that particularly onerous, but it is probably the biggest source of pressure, that you need to be careful. You have to be careful but you can't be so careful that you're not communicating either. So you're balancing those two things."[21] For a press secretary, the issue of "getting it right" and being timely in providing information is of particular importance.

In addition to accuracy and timeliness, a press secretary has to avoid the trap of the off-hand comment. Speaking on the record in public for sometimes an hour a day, the press secretary is especially vulnerable to misstep. These remarks are scrutinized throughout the world for hidden meanings, not just factual accuracy. Thus, when he or she gives in to the bon mot, it can sometimes have repercussions in other countries. Marlin Fitzwater, press secretary to Presidents Reagan and Bush, spoke of an error he made that followed him even after he left the office. "That's where I came up with this idea of saying [Mikhail] Gorbachev throws out arms-control proposals like a drugstore cowboy. And my deputy said, 'Don't do it, Marlin. It's not right; it's not accurate. It's too cute; it's too colloquial. Don't try it.' I'd say all right and every day for five days they'd talk me out of it until the sixth day I used it. . . . It was a terrible mistake. They were absolutely right."[22]

Hostile Political Climate

An added stress in the Clinton White House, which was a factor of somewhat lesser importance in the Reagan and Bush White Houses, was that associated with a plethora of lawsuits and their attendant subpoenas requiring people appear on the Hill and before grand juries. Ann Lewis indicated the need to factor these pressures when considering the stresses of White House work life. "You add to that being in, as we are, a hostile political climate in which the danger of lawsuits, special investigators, having your notes or papers sort of called in on any particular issue is ever present," she said. "I think the biggest impact is that it takes time away from positive things. You're in a defensive mode much of the day. The things that it does, which I actually think are not bad, are that you remember to think all decisions through very carefully. You have a much more structured decision-making process than I think you would if you didn't always think someone was looking over your shoulder or tomorrow you'll get a subpoena on that or you'll see it in the *Washington Post* or whatever." At the same time the process of making decisions was improved, it was accompanied by a reluctance to take risks. "I think it slowed things down tremendously and made it more difficult, and I think people were a lot more cautious sometimes than they needed to be just because it was easier to do nothing, because nothing could be criticized, than it would be to take a risk and do something even if it wasn't that much of a risk."[23]

Scrutiny

With litigation now such an important factor in White House work life, there has been something of a common understanding among staff that one limits the amount of notes one takes. "There are a lot of times when somebody would literally take out a pen and start writing something and someone would say, 'What are you writing?' And people going, 'Oh. You're right,'" said Jodie Torkelson, who served as director of the White House Office of Management and Administration. "It wasn't—yes, I think everybody just knew that writing in this administration turned out to be deadly to people and nobody wanted to get subpoenaed. I had staff that got subpoenas because they took a phone message . . . and they had to go and testify all because they wrote the guy's name down because he called about his health benefits. That's all it was. So it wasn't like it was irrational behavior; it was so silly the kinds of people that were getting dragged in to things for the dumbest of reasons that no one felt secure writing anything down. You just didn't. If you didn't want to have a legal bill, you didn't take a note."[24]

Scrutiny of those working in the White House can be so severe that even when one is saying nothing, it still indicates an answer. Ron Nessen discussed the kind of scrutiny the words of a press secretary receive from the reporters listening in the briefing.

> One time a reporter asked me about rumors that Bill Simon was going to resign as secretary of the Treasury or he was going to be fired as secretary of Treasury. And there was some discussion in the White House of whether he was going to stay or go. I knew about the discussion. The reporter said what about the rumors that Simon's going to be fired or something. I was trying to think how am I going to answer this; I don't want to lie about it. There is some talk but nothing's decided. So I just took a second to think about what I was going to say and the reporter starts scribbling down wildly because of this long pause, this long pause when I was thinking of what I was going to say. He interpreted that to mean something. There's a lot of scrutiny. You have to be careful what you don't say or how quickly you say it.[25]

No Margin for Error

Ray Jenkins, who served as a senior advisor to President Carter and handled some press matters, spoke of pressures in addition to the time one spends at the White House.

> It is a high-stress job, but it is high stress not because of the long hours but because there is absolutely no margin for error whatsoever. Now you're going to make errors and then you spend the rest of your time correcting but you just have to remember that once a problem reaches the White House basically it has no solution. If it had a solution it would have been solved at some level lower down. It's so often a roll of the dice. Sometimes you roll seven and sometimes you roll eleven. The stress is not so much from the long hours—because the hours literally are twenty-four hours a day. It doesn't matter if you're at the White House or whether you're at home or in San Francisco or where. The stress arises from the burden of the job rather than the length of the hours.[26]

Marlin Fitzwater provided an example of when a minor error by an entry-level staff member in the White House quickly turned into a presidential-level decision on whether to fire her. A young woman mixed up the contents of two envelopes, with presidential talking points ending up in an envelope marked for Sam Donaldson. "The talking points, unfortunately, were written by some legislative affairs person and it said, 'Greetings. Hello, members of Congress. Glad to have you here today. (Hold up your hand or shake hands or something).' This is really written by some guy who has never met the president probably, some kid who is trying to be thorough so he puts in all the instructions, which happens often when you're writing briefing papers. Anyway, Sam got it, ran a story on the evening news about Ronald Reagan is so dumb he doesn't even know enough to say hello and shake hands." While an innocent mistake, it caused reverberations that were felt right up to the Oval Office. "Yet it was a mistake of such magnitude and ramifications, it was on national television, the basis for a story, and the president of the United States thought she should be fired." While the discussion between the president, Chief of Staff Howard Baker, and Fitzwater resulted in the woman keeping her job, it is surprising to consider such an action rises to the presidential level and does so quickly. For Fitzwater, "it was always a great example of the risk you face and the small margin for error. That's a lot of tension. If you think of a twenty-year-old kid taking a first or second job and having to live every day with the idea that if they happen to give somebody the wrong piece of paper their career is over."[27]

The pressures may be great for those working in the White House, but these are outweighed by the benefits of being there. It is exciting for the people who do the important tasks associated with almost every level of White House work. Those who have served generally find their time to be a high point in their lives no matter what work they do afterward nor how much money they earn. At the same time, in their post–White House years, they well remember the pressure of the long days and slim margin for error. When they leave, most White House staffers are more than ready to get on with their lives with experiences, contacts, and knowledge that will serve them well for the remainder of their careers.

Notes

1.   Gerald R. Ford, interview with Martha Joynt Kumar, Palm Springs, Calif., Oct. 10, 2000, White House Interview Program.

2.   Donald Rumsfeld, interview with Martha Joynt Kumar, Chicago, Ill., Apr. 25, 1999, White House Interview Program.

3.   Abner Mikva, interview with Martha Joynt Kumar and Terry Sullivan, Chicago, Ill., Apr. 26, 2000, White House Interview Program.

4.   Alonzo McDonald, interview with Martha Joynt Kumar, Washington, D.C., Feb. 2, 2000, White House Interview Program.

5.   James Fetig, interview with Martha Joynt Kumar, Rockville, Md., Feb. 5, 1999, White House Interview Program.

6.   Michael Deaver, interview with Martha Joynt Kumar, Washington, D.C., Sept. 9, 1999, White House Interview Program.

7.   Ibid.

8.   Peter Roussel, interview with Martha Joynt Kumar and Terry Sullivan, Houston, Tex.., Nov. 3, 1999, White House Interview Program.

9.   Ibid.

10.   Alexander Haig, interview with Martha Joynt Kumar, Washington, D.C., Dec. 2, 1999, White House Interview Program.

11.   Marlin Fitzwater, interview with Martha Joynt Kumar, Deale, Md., Oct. 21, 1999, White House Interview Program.

12.   Ron Nessen, interview with Martha Joynt Kumar, Washington, D.C., Aug. 3, 1999, White House Interview Program.

13.   Phillip Brady, interview with Martha Joynt Kumar, McLean, Va., Aug. 17, 1999, White House Interview Program.

14.   McDonald interview.

15.   Fetig interview.

16. Margita White, interview with Martha Joynt Kumar, Washington, D.C., Oct. 26, 1999, White House Interview Program.

17. Chase Untermeyer, interview with Martha Joynt Kumar, Houston, Tex., July 6, 1999, White House Interview Program.

18. Background interview.

19. Donald Baer, interview with Martha Joynt Kumar, Washington, D.C., July 22, 1999.

20. Ann Lewis, interview with Martha Joynt Kumar, Washington, D.C., July 7, 1999, White House Interview Program.

21. Jody Powell, interview with Martha Joynt Kumar, Washington, D.C., Aug. 2, 2000, White House Interview Program.

22. Fitzwater interview.

23. Lewis interview.

24. Jodie Torkelson, interview with Martha Joynt Kumar, Washington, D.C., Oct. 19, 1999, White House Interview Program.

25. Nessen interview.

26. Ray Jenkins, interview with Martha Joynt Kumar, Washington, D.C., July 8, 1999, White House Interview Program.

27. Fitzwater interview.

3

White House Offices:

Seven Keys to a Successful Start

The Office of Chief of Staff

CHARLES E. WALCOTT
SHIRLEY ANNE WARSHAW
STEPHEN J. WAYNE

T HE OFFICE OF WHITE HOUSE CHIEF OF STAFF is crucial to the successful operation of the contemporary presidency. As former president Gerald Ford explained: "I started out in effect not having an effective chief of staff and it didn't work. So anybody who doesn't have one and tries to run the responsibilities of the White House I think is putting too big a burden on the president himself. You need a filter, a person that you have total confidence in who works so closely with you that in effect his is almost an alter ego. I just can't imagine a president not having an effective chief of staff."[1] Ford's second chief, Richard Cheney, elaborated on the need for effective White House organization: "Well, it's crucial in terms of how he's going to function as president, whether or not he's effective. His reach, his ability to sort of guide and direct the government, to interact with the cabinet, to deal effectively with the Congress, to manage his relationship with the press, all of those are key ingredients to his success. The White House staff structure and set up and how it functions as an organization determines whether or not he is successful in these relationships. No matter how hard he works or how smart he might be, he can't do it by himself."[2]

The job of the White House chief of staff has many common elements from one administration to the next. But there are also key differences, resulting mainly from different presidents' ideas, work styles, and beliefs about how the White House should operate. A chief of staff's understanding of the job has to arise out of close communication between the new president and chief of staff since the president defines the chief's role. But former chiefs of staff likewise stress the value of understanding the basic nature of the job, the possible variations in its performance, and above all, the pitfalls that any chief of staff must avoid. The best way to do this is to talk with those who have held the job before. A typical comment is that of Landon Butler, deputy chief of staff in the Carter administration. "I think, by and large, we learned far more from our predecessors than we did from any written material."[3] To supplement such conversations, though not to substitute for them, we present here a summary of the wisdom offered by former chiefs of staff and their top aides in extensive interviews.

Basic Elements of the Job

As recently as the beginning of the Carter administration, it was possible to argue that the White House could be run without a chief of staff. Those days are past. The complexity of the modern White House requires discipline and coordination that can only be achieved if there is a central coordinating point, someone other than the president to oversee the operation. This job is not easy. Long days, constant crises, persistent rivalries (much of them built into the institutional structure and processes), the roles of the personnel that occupy the White House, and overlapping missions and interests create a pressured, short timeframe in which to operate. Many chiefs of staff see their job as the second most important and most difficult in Washington.

Roles

Most chiefs of staff agree on the critical roles they must perform in their managerial and advisory roles.

Managerial

select the key people on the White House staff and supervise them
structure the White House staff system, including the Office of Chief of Staff
control the flow of people and paper into the Oval Office, adjusting it to the president's style of doing business

manage the flow of information and opinion to and from the president, and do so in a way that brokers honestly among differing
perspectives and recommendations

Advisory

advise the president on issues of politics, policy, and management
protect the interests of the president
negotiate with Congress, the executive branch including the Executive
Office of the President (EOP), and extragovernmental political
groups and individuals to implement the president's agenda

Operating Styles and Environments

Although they agree on the chief of staff's roles, they do not agree on a
single, "best" way to achieve them. Some of their disagreement stems from
the differing people and circumstances involved. The exact nature of the
job will depend upon such things as

presidential styles
the circumstances in which a chief of staff inherits the job
the personnel with whom they had to contend and the budget they
had to administer
partisanship (precedents and advice from earlier administrations)

Variations in the White House environment also naturally affect organizational arrangements, operational procedures, and personnel decisions. Such factors include the structure of the staff, particularly at the time
the chief of staff assumes office; coordination with other White House
units; and the patterns of day-to-day activities that must vary with the
president's style, decisional timeframe, and to some extent the administration's priorities. Moreover, a chief of staff's role is a reflection of the
president: it is always limited by the president's preferences, views, and
habits of management and leadership.

Personal Attributes, Strategies, and Tactics

In addition to role, structure, and processes, former chiefs of staff agreed
that certain personal attributes, political strategies, and operational tactics

are more likely than others to be successful. *Decisiveness, sensitivity, credibility,* and *political savvy* are deemed essential traits for the job.

Strategies based on realistic assumptions about public expectations, those that correctly anticipate elite and public reactions, and those that consider the mood of the country and are designed to work within the broad parameters of public opinion are more apt to achieve the desired goals. Similarly, tactics that incorporate the president's bully pulpit to gain political leverage, that see information as an instrument of power, are also most likely to be successful in today's media-oriented environment.

Chiefs of staff and their deputies also expressed general agreement on the dangers that may be encountered. Their warnings to future chiefs of staff echoed difficulties that tend to be intrinsic to the job.

Managerial Roles

Perhaps the core duties of any chief of staff involve establishing and operating a management system that is effective in providing both advice and implementation of decisions and is congruent with the president's working style.

Selecting and Managing White House Personnel

Ultimately, the entire White House staff, with very few if any exceptions, will report to the president through the chief of staff. At the outset of an administration, the chief of staff should and often has been primarily responsible for assembling the staff in the first place. They must ensure that no matter what personal agendas aides may have (and most aides do have them), it is the *president's* agenda they must pursue.[4] More generally, James Baker advised would-be chiefs of staff that "the people who succeed in Washington are the people who are not afraid to surround themselves with really good, strong people. . . . A strong White House staff buys the president one hell of a lot, I think."[5]

In order to exercise effective control over White House operations, chiefs of staff must be able to pick their principal deputies at the very least. They should also be given latitude for approving presidential selections. A White House observer noted his boss' latitude in staffing the first Bush administration: "When the White House staff was put together, there was very little interaction with the other part of the transition. In other words, it was basically Sununu [who] did his own thing. . . . [A]nybody that was appointed by the president, that would be an assistant to the president, deputy assistant to the president, special assistant to the president, the president was involved. But to his credit, he gave a very long leash to John Sununu."[6] Even before the administration begins to function, the chief of staff–designate should oversee the White House transition, which should be separate from the rest of the transition to government.

Two criteria deemed essential in the initial choice of top staff aides are *political savvy* and *Washington experience*. James Baker noted: "It [political credentials] gives you far more cache in policy debates and interdepartmental policy. . . . If you've been out there and fighting the political wars with the president, you are in a better position to speak to those issues that other people are not who just maybe gave some money."[7] Marlin Fitzwater likewise noted the difference between the management challenges of the White House and elsewhere and the importance of both Washington experience and personal relationships: "In terms of the people management, it's a very small group and it's always a personality kind of thing. And that's also why I think businessmen have such a difficult time . . . because they always think in line-staff structural relationships, and in business they don't have to worry about personal relationships because they have the power. They give orders; they take away your salary; they can fire you; they can give you bonuses. And in the White House all those normal management techniques go out the window. Oftentimes you can't fire people."[8] Another experienced observer similarly warned that former political executives, such as governors or cabinet members, may have a hard time adjusting to a staff role after the experience of being principals.[9]

A third factor, implicit in the advice that the chief of staff pick the top staff, is *loyalty*. Samuel Skinner noted that "there's a tendency, if loyalists [to the president] get in to the White House and they . . . don't have a duty and responsibility to the chief of staff as having put them there, the chief of staff can have them go around him very easily unless you have a president who never lets that happen. Even though you control the process, there are ways to get around it."[10]

Naturally, a chief of staff who comes in the middle of an administration usually does not have the luxury of completely cleaning house but still must have some flexibility in getting the shop in order and the right people placed. This was the problem that beset Skinner and to a lesser extent, Leon Panetta, when they took over for Sununu and Mack McLarty respectively. In the words of Henson Moore: "The president had his staff. He had been goaded, pushed, convinced into getting rid of Sununu and Card, people . . . he liked. And he wasn't going to hear of anybody else being replaced on that staff. So once that word gets out to the people who are supposed to be reporting to you and taking orders from you that you can't touch them, you have limited authority to really make things happen."[11]

Skinner concurred, noting that "the president also made it quite clear that he did not want a wholesale change in his staff." But, said Skinner, "A good friend of mine, Vernon Jordan, told me . . . you've got to have your own people in order to make anything work in Washington. I think those people have to be accountable. The only other way you're going to do that is to fire one of the president's favorites and let it be known that you've got to fire him. That's hard to do."[12]

Along the same line, James Baker noted that one does not have to fire people to move them out. When he brought his team aboard the White House in 1992, he chose to "layer" the existing staff, moving the new people to the key jobs. "They probably resented that, and rightly so. They weren't fired, but they were layered."[13] Leon Panetta did the same when he succeeded Mack McLarty.[14]

Keeping people too long, however, can be a problem, especially if personalities clash or working styles conflict with one another. Ford's chiefs of staff, Rumsfeld and Cheney, faced such a situation in dealing with long-time aide and speechwriter Robert Hartmann, whose dismissal from the White House was out of the question. Their solution to this internal problem was to circumvent Hartmann whenever possible. While sometimes temporarily effective, this approach can allow a persistent source of conflict to remain rooted in the White House. It also opens the door to end runs by people who are out of the loop but who still have access to the president and to leaks.[15]

The same kind of problem can appear when staffers experience burnout or when a president wants to replace people but is reluctant to simply let them go. This invites friction and discontent. As Howard Baker put it, "If you cut the dog's tail off, cut it all off at once."[16]

Structuring the Staff

Although the White House Office and the Office of the Chief of Staff have become substantially institutionalized across recent presidencies, there are still many possible ways to organize them. A new administration thus must make important decisions about organizational structure.

The White House Office

A chief of staff can think of structuring in three different senses. The first is constructing the organization and mission of the White House Office as a whole. Since most White House staffers report to the president through the chief of staff, the chief of staff must work with the president to set up an overall reporting and decision-making system for the White House Office. As many White House veterans have noted, this is best done as soon as possible after the election so the White House staff will be ready to function immediately after the inauguration, if not sooner.

The experience of recent presidencies indicates that there has been relatively little variation in the overall design of the White House staff in terms of offices and responsibilities. The basic model for the modern staff system dates back to the Nixon administration and has been modified, though only at the margins, since then. Thus, it is likely that the major political offices—Congressional Relations, Public Liaison, Communications and Press, and so forth—will appear in some form in any new administration, as will the key staff organizations, such as the Office of Management and Administration and the Staff Secretariat. Likewise, the basic model for the National Security Council (NSC) and its staff as well as the domestic policy staff has become stable. The Clinton White House's employment of the National Economic Council to deal specifically with economic policy continued the existence of a White House–based economic policy group, some form of which has functioned since the Ford administration.

Within this overall framework, however, there are have been important differences in operating patterns. Most generally, one can distinguish between relatively "strong" and "weak" chiefs of staff. This is, of course, an oversimplification, but it does point to a contrast in organizational strategies. The primary differences are in the degree to which the chief of staff controls information flow to the president and the extent of the chief of staff's control over the president's schedule. As previously noted, the contrast between Sununu and Skinner in the Bush administration and between McLarty and Panetta in Clinton's illustrates the strong and weak models. From these examples, it is also clear that the relative "strength" of a chief of staff is not just a matter of that officer's preference but is also dependent upon circumstances and personnel. The key point, however, is that the chief of staff is bound by the president's habits and operating style.

A further dimension of chief of staff "strength" involves the scope of the chief's control of information and access. While all chiefs of staff have sought to oversee the flow of paper and people in the areas of domestic policy and politics, they have varied in their relationship with the National Security Assistant (NSA) and the NSC staff in general. The NSA is one of the principal potential White House competitors of the chief of staff. Some chiefs of staff, such as Leon Panetta, have insisted that the NSC go through them, while others have not. This is not always the choice of the chief of staff alone. Nonetheless, it can be a fateful choice. In the first four years of the Reagan administration, for instance, the NSA did not report through Chief of Staff James Baker but through Counselor Edwin Meese. Moreover, once William Clark became NSA, his longtime relationship with the president rendered him outside staff control. In hindsight, Baker indicated that he would want his own person in the job of NSA from the start.[17]

On the whole, the "strong" model tends to be the one lauded by most of those who have served as chief of staff or deputy chief of staff. Indeed, Skinner and McLarty are the only recent chiefs of staff since Hamilton Jordan under Carter who did not clearly attempt this approach. But the chiefs of staff caution that this "strength" must be exercised within the understanding that they are not the president but a member of the White House staff, and serve only the president's agenda.

Organization of the Office of the Chief of Staff

The second structural responsibility of the chief of staff is to design his office. As Howard Baker observed, "a chief of staff and a national security advisor . . . are now so loaded with responsibility and with paper . . . that they sort of get in the same category as the president does. If they don't have somebody prompting them or watching out for them, they'll get in the same fix."[18] Recent administrations offer contrasting models of structuring the office and dividing responsibility.

General Patterns

Most Chief of Staff Offices have been relatively lean, with one or two deputies reporting directly to the chief of staff. Most Democratic administrations have had two deputies, with one assigned to handle political chores and the other to oversee White House operations. Republican White Houses have sometimes relied on just one deputy, whose job has varied among such foci as communications, administration, and congressional liaison.

In addition to the chief of staff and the deputy or deputies, there have usually been two or three assistants (variously titled "personal assistant," "executive assistant," "staff assistant," or just "secretary") to the chief of staff and one person at roughly the staff-assistant level to work under each deputy. By 1998, this number had grown to five.

Beyond that, chiefs of staff have varied with regard to the placement of additional people and duties directly within the Office of the Chief of Staff. Donald Regan, for instance, formally had three deputies (holding the rank of deputy assistant to the president), one of whom, Frederick Ryan, supervised the administration's Private Sector Initiative and with it a substantial staff.

Election season has normally brought campaign responsibilities to the chief of staff as well. This has often been reflected in the addition of people reporting to the chief of staff. Jack Watson's office at the end of the Carter administration, for example, contained several deputies, including a labor liaison and a research director. Leon Panetta's office likewise expanded, providing organizational positions for counselors and senior advisors.

When elections are not impending, a relatively lean chief-of-staff operation is still a viable option. However, the most recent trend is in the other direction. The second four years of the Clinton White House witnessed a continuation of the practice of placing senior advisors in the chief's office. Thus, the total personnel at the level of staff assistant or above within John Podesta's Office of the Chief of Staff in 1998 numbered twenty. That compares with seven under James Baker in 1992.

Division of Labor in Recent Administrations

A key issue in this organization is how the work is divided among the chief of staff and the deputies. There are clearly more demands upon the chief of staff's office than one individual can satisfy. Delegation is therefore critical.[19] Patterns have varied, depending mainly on the interests and experiences of the chief of staff and top staffers. There is no "one best way" to set things up. Depending on the background and interests of the chief of staff and the top aides, the office is frequently involved in congressional relations, communications strategies, and political liaison. For instance, former members of Congress, such as Howard Baker, Leon Panetta, and Henson Moore, were naturally drawn into that arena. Michael Deaver was deeply involved in communications planning as James Baker's deputy even before he took over the operation formally.

At the outset of the Reagan administration, James Baker explicitly

President Ronald Reagan
White House Office of Chief of Staff
1983

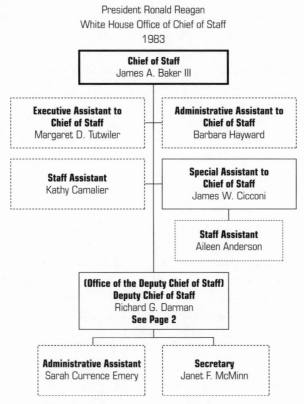

White House Interview Program (whitehouse2001.org). Based on data in *The White House Telephone Directory*, 1983, National Journal Group Inc., Washington, DC. *Key:* ———— = positions with "to the president" in their title; --------- = staff working for indicated assistant.

excluded the Chief of Staff's office from policy development, leaving that to Counselor Edwin Meese; Baker assumed responsibility for process. Michael Deaver, who had the title of assistant chief of staff, was responsible for scheduling and travel, the East Wing (the offices of the first lady and the military), and anything to do with communications.[20] When David Gergen left the White House, Deaver formally took on responsibility for communications. Richard Darman, who replaced Deaver as assistant chief of staff, did not have responsibility for scheduling, which remained with Deaver, but he did oversee management and administration. Another deputy, James Cicconi, was primarily responsible for overseeing the

Figure 4b.

President Ronald Reagan
White House Office of
the Deputy Chief of Staff
1983

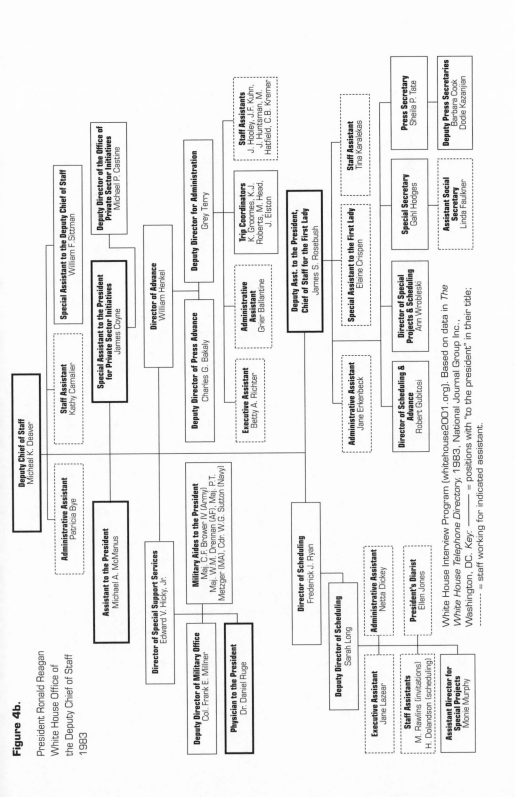

White House Interview Program (whitehouse2001.org). Based on data in *The White House Telephone Directory*, 1983, National Journal Group Inc., Washington, DC. *Key:* ——— = positions with "to the president" in their title; -------- = staff working for indicated assistant.

decision-making process.[21] When Donald Regan succeeded Baker, he put three deputies in place and allowed the Office of Chief of Staff to expand considerably. But Howard Baker, Regan's replacement, reverted to a simple model with two top assistants, one of whom specialized in decision-process management.[22] When Baker's deputy, Kenneth Duberstein, became chief of staff, the same model was retained.

Little changed under President Bush's first chief of staff, John Sununu. He had one deputy, responsible for overseeing White House operations, and with a varied portfolio beyond that. By the fall of 1991, that deputy, Andrew Card, was the only top aide in the office.[23] Under Samuel Skinner, however, the Office of the Chief of Staff returned to a deputy and a counselor, Henson Moore and Cameron Findlay, respectively. Moore dealt mainly with White House mechanics, with press, scheduling, and speechwriting reporting to him. He also became involved in congressional relations, and the job evolved beyond that to include traveling with the president.[24]

When James Baker replaced Skinner at the end of the Bush administration, he brought in his own people but kept the basic model. In fact, his deputy, Bob Zoellick, "actually ran the White House at that time," while Baker functioned mainly as chairman of the Bush re-election campaign.[25]

The Clinton chiefs of staff followed a familiar organizational pattern, with two deputies (or the equivalent) serving under the chief of staff, but Leon Panetta, in the process of strengthening the chief of staff's role, expanded his office. Initially, under Mack McLarty, the responsibilities of the deputies were defined rather loosely, as McLarty adjusted to the particular strengths of Mark Gearan and Roy Neel and to getting along without Harold Ickes, whom he had hoped to employ.[26] When Panetta succeeded McLarty, he made Ickes deputy in charge of political affairs and some oversight of substantive issues, while Erskine Bowles took charge of scheduling and management of White House personnel. Panetta also placed senior presidential advisors George Stephanopoulos and Rahm Emanuel in the Office of Chief of Staff, assuming that they would report to the president through him. Moreover, with the 1996 election impending, Panetta placed additional White House staff units—speechwriting and communications—in his now-expanded office. As chief of staff after the election, Bowles in part reverted to the earlier pattern, taking considerable scheduling responsibility himself, while speechwriting and communications were dropped from the chief of staff's office. But the office did not shrink back to the simpler model of prior administrations. Senior advisors and others stayed, and the overall staff grew, in part to coordinate the now-expanded office.

Figure 5.

President William Clinton
White House Office of Chief of Staff
Fall, 1998

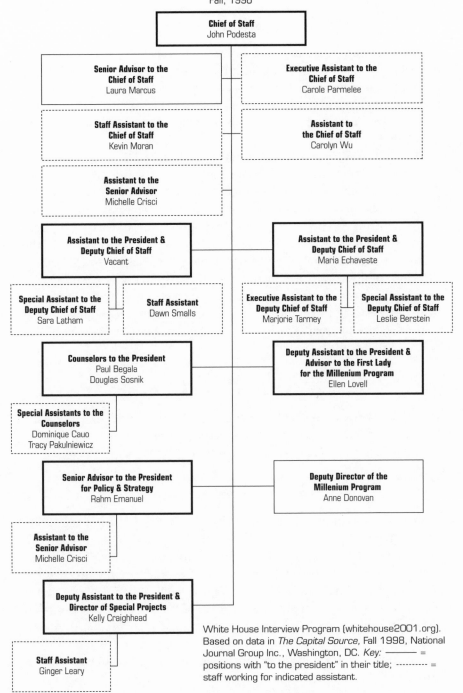

White House Interview Program (whitehouse2001.org).
Based on data in *The Capital Source,* Fall 1998, National
Journal Group Inc., Washington, DC. *Key:* ———— =
positions with "to the president" in their title; ---------- =
staff working for indicated assistant.

Not all organizational structuring—recurring, predictable activities and re-sponsibilities—is found on organization charts. Successful chiefs of staff have supplemented formal arrangements by initiating regular group meet-ings with key White House personnel. This has been an essential manage-ment tool so long as the senior-staff meetings do not get too large and unwieldy.[27]

In addition, different chiefs of staff or deputies have taken the lead in initiating meetings to plan communications strategy, brief the cabinet, plan the president's schedule, or organize task forces or "war rooms" for the pursuit of unusually important projects.[28] The extreme case of infor-mal structuring can be found in the small group Alexander Haig brought together during the waning days of the Nixon administration to handle the routine business of the White House while the president focused on his fight for political survival.[29] In any case, the desirability or need for such organizational innovations will most likely be dictated by a president's par-ticular agenda and by circumstances, such as the onset of a campaign sea-son or the development of major legislative efforts like Carter's energy plan or Clinton's healthcare initiative.

Controlling the Flow of People and Paper

The White House is inevitably a hierarchy, with the president at the apex. The chief of staff serves as gatekeeper and coordinator, assuring that the president's time and effort are most effectively employed.

Getting Control of the Paper Flow

The chief of staff must take responsibility for the operation of the White House. To do so, lines of authority must flow to and through his office to the president. No matter how White House functions are organized, the in-formation flow must be up and to the chief of staff, usually through the staff secretary, cabinet secretary, and deputy chiefs of staff. Only by moni-toring the full flow of paper to the president can a chief of staff assure that all relevant information has been received and all relevant points of view represented.

The fundamental purpose of orderly processes in the White House is to provide the basis for the best-informed decisions possible. The job of the chief of staff is to assure that all relevant voices are heard in the decision process and that choices are made in light of full information. James Baker summarized: "You have to make sure you have an orderly system, that you have a system that's fair. Otherwise, you start the leaking to the press, one against the other. You have to have a system that lets the president hear all sides. And you have to have one that, if you're going to be running the White House, you have to know what's going on."[30]

To assure such fairness, all recent White Houses have employed a decision process whereby decision memoranda are routinely circulated, usually by the staff secretary, to all officials with expertise or a stake in a presidential decision. The chief of staff must monitor the workings of this process closely, for it is here, in the framing of the decision and the description of options, that staffers may be tempted to push their own particular interests or substitute them for those of their principals. As Howard Baker said of this kind of problem: "Well, that's exactly the level of detail where it occurs, in the staffing of the memo that's going to the president, the decision memo with the options describing—that's where all the fights occur—describing what the background is, describing the discussion, describing the options. . . . We tried not to let that spill up to the president but sometimes the memos were so controversial . . . we just couldn't forge consensus about what this paper would look like."[31]

Due to the crucial position of the staff secretary in the operation of this system, it is imperative that the chief of staff pick a trustworthy person for that post. Mark Siegel, who served under Carter, noted that Hamilton Jordan, even before he became chief of staff, was careful to place his own man, Rick Hutcheson, in that position.[32]

The chief of staff or someone on his personal staff must supplement the staff secretary in the exercise of judgment as to what gets to the president and what does not. Deputy Chief of Staff Andrew Card, who had this responsibility under George H. W. Bush, contrasted the staff secretary's monitoring with his own: "He did it watching for policy or consistency of language. I did it to protect the president. Is this something the president has to have today? . . . the staff secretary job is to be pretty policy wonkish, too. This policy is inconsistent with the one we had the president say last week . . . That was more of an editorial role; mine was more of how do I protect the guy in there from wasting his time and energy."[33] Leon Panetta made a similar point: "I wanted to funnel all of the issues and decision making that ultimately had to go to the president through the chief of staff's operation. That helped a great deal because it came in kind of a vacuum in which staff people and others weren't getting decisions on issues unless they had to take it to the president. And there are a lot of decisions, frankly, that you could make that don't necessarily have to go to the president."[34]

Beyond decision memoranda, presidents also require background papers on issues. President Clinton, for instance, "would want maybe a summary with several pages of backup on a particular matter we were considering."[35] The chief of staff is often responsible for the preparation of such materials and for their thoroughness and balance. At the very least, the chief of staff must monitor what goes to the president. If the president's outbox contains material that never went through the inbox—if, in other words, people are bypassing the staff system—the chief of staff must address the problem. Whether by paper or in person, such end runs will tend to upset the balance of the decision system.

Of course, the discretion implied in these accounts is liable to abuse as well as to the perception of abuse. Although H. R. Haldeman denied that he tried to control policy in the Nixon White House, the perception that he did nevertheless was strong. Thus, it is important for the chief of staff to involve other White House staff in his decision processes and to maintain confidence in the essential accessibility of both the process and the president.[36] Sherman Adams, the first chief of staff under Eisenhower, stressed the importance of procedures to attain this result.[37]

Adjusting and Conforming to the President's Style

The president must feel comfortable with the people on the White House staff and with the way it works. Although "the chief of staff's personality dominates the way the White House works, it can only be done if it has the blessing of the president," noted one person who served in the chief of staff's office.[38]

If a president wishes to keep control of a lower-level decision or administrative matter, there is little a chief of staff can do. That such an arrangement may be ineffective needs to become obvious to a president before the system can be streamlined. Ford, Carter, and Clinton found this out the hard way at the beginning of their administrations.

Landon Butler, who worked in the Carter White House, stated: "We were a direct reflection of what the president wanted around him and what he needed. In our case, Carter played a very hands-on role in virtually every aspect of putting the White House together."[39] Mack McLarty

also set up the type of system that Clinton wanted, noting that the operation of "the White House and to some extent the administration . . . was
clearly driven by the campaign. And I think to have dramatically altered
that would have created a whole other set of dynamics and problems."[40]
A senior official familiar with the Clinton operation added: "Mack had a
very untenable situation in that regard and did the best he could with
that. . . . [H]is authority was constantly and often inadvertently or indirectly undermined by the president's willingness or indulgence" to allow
individuals who had developed a relationship with him in his campaign to
see him.[41]

Most other recent presidents have had a very different operating style
that encouraged much more staff control over their schedule, speeches,
and visitors. This has been the case for all but Carter and Ford. And, like
Clinton, Ford rather quickly abandoned the "spokes-of-the-wheel" system
of open access for a more structured system with a strong chief of staff,
even though the title was carefully eschewed. Carter, after trying to do
without a chief of staff altogether, in the style of his Democratic predecessors, ultimately turned to Hamilton Jordan, then Jack Watson, as chief of
staff, though neither was what one would call a "strong" chief.

Guarding the Door to the Oval Office

A very important aspect of the chief of staff's role is to guard the flow of
people and paper into the Oval Office. Time is an incredibly important
presidential commodity. It is up to the chief of staff to help him manage it
effectively. "You need to have discipline and order and be discriminating,"
said James Baker.[42]

Limiting access to the Oval Office serves another purpose: it saves the
president from his friends and supporters. Presidents are politicians and as
such, like to please. What they do not like to do is say no. Thus, an important function of the chief of staff is to protect their boss by eliminating or
reducing those politically embarrassing situations that put a president on
the spot. Sometimes, of course, obstructing access can be carried too far.
Donald Regan overly protected Ronald Reagan. The president's friends had
to go public to reach him. When H. R. Haldeman kept people out of the
Oval Office, however, he was following Nixon's wish to avoid special
pleadings.[43]

Among the chiefs of staff, there was also general consensus that presidents need to be protected from what James Baker called "Oh-by-the-way

discussions and decisions," that is, decisions that are made on the spur of the moment without staff consultation or consideration of consequences. "It's not in anyone's interest," stated Baker, "to get 'oh-by-the-way decisions' as a guy is leaving a meeting." One way to discourage this practice is for presidents to issue a generic warning at their first cabinet meeting that such practices will be considered out of order and not tolerated.[44]

Because the job of the staff is to run interference for the president, especially when the discussion turns from the prepared agenda, "you need to be knowledgeable about what he's [the president] telling people and what they are telling him. You need to have an understanding with him about it." In Reagan's case, he regularly informed his staff if he met with anyone without the staff being present. In Bush's case, unless the meeting was listed as private, an aide from the Chief of Staff's Office would always be in attendance.[45] Being with the president also involves traveling with him. Either the chief of staff or a designated deputy should be on all trips away from the White House.

Coordinating Presidential Appearances and Statements

The Office of the Chief of Staff must be involved in scheduling the president, which includes long-range planning (perhaps three months). The chief of staff need not be deeply involved personally, however. For instance, during the first Reagan term, James Baker delegated responsibility for scheduling (along with communications and relations with the first lady and her office) to his deputy, Michael Deaver.[46] Similarly, Henson Moore, under Samuel Skinner, had responsibility for scheduling and also had the speechwriters and the Press Office reporting to him. But whether it is the chief of staff or a deputy, all these streams—where the president will be, what the president will say, and how attention will be gained for it—must come together.

As gatekeeper, the chief of staff must review all presidential schedules, briefings, and speeches. Leon Panetta noted, "If it was a low-level speech to a particular group, I would just sometimes review it very quickly but let the people involved with the policy have the largest impact." But on high-level speeches, such as State of the Union or other major pronouncements, Panetta paid close attention.[47] Much of the friction between him and Dick Morris, Clinton's political advisor, stemmed from Morris's penchant for changing speeches that had gone through the chief of staff's clearance process.[48] So strongly did Panetta object to this end running that he threatened to quit unless it was stopped. And it was.

Managing Information and Brokering Opinions

In performing the gatekeeper's role, the chief of staff must function as an honest broker. Practically all of the chiefs of staff and their deputies interviewed considered this role essential. James Baker put it this way: "Be an honest broker. Don't use the process to impose your policy views on the president." The president needs to see all sides; he cannot be blindsided.[49] Additionally, cabinet members need to know that their position will be fairly represented, especially if they encounter difficulty in presenting it themselves. Mack McLarty noted that former chiefs of staff he talked with had "a pretty high degree of consensus about the honest-broker approach, that the chief of staff certainly needed to be viewed by cabinet members and others as someone who would not shape information in a way that would unduly affect the president's decision making."[50]

Honest brokerage does not mean having no opinions or refusing to offer them when asked by the president. It does, however, mean assuring that the decision process will include all relevant points of view without allowing the agenda or views of the chief of staff to bias or distort that process.[51] Nor is it enough to be in fact an honest broker—the chief of staff must be *perceived* as such by those seeking access, personally or for their ideas, to the president.

Although chiefs of staff disagreed on how tight personal access to the president should be, there was unanimity that it should be administered fairly and with sensitivity to the position of those who wish to gain an audience. As James Baker put it: "You walk around with a target on your chest and back. You use up your chits pretty quickly because the job of the chief of staff is to say no to people. Everybody wants something from the president, and your job is to say no or say yes, maybe, but."[52]

Being a good listener is another attribute of the honest-brokering function. According to Howard Baker: "There wasn't a day went by when, in a senior staff meeting, somebody didn't point out what I didn't know about and was not sensitive to. It was an early warning system that worked very well."[53]

As a broker, the chief of staff is also responsible for presidential briefings. The regular morning meetings between the chief and the president are a time for briefings. But for more formal briefings involving multiple participants, the chief of staff normally works with other staffers, including national security and domestic policy advisors.

Advisory Roles

Although the chief of staff is first and foremost an honest broker, it is unlikely that a staffer so close to a president would not be called upon as an advisor as well. This is particularly true in areas of the chief of staff's special interest or competence. Leon Panetta, for example, as a former OMB director, was an advisor on budgetary matters.[54] Mack McLarty, with a background in private business, advised President Clinton on his economic planning.[55]

Advising the President on Politics, Policy, and Management

One important aspect of advising is integrating policy and politics. Most other advisors, both inside and outside the White House, specialize in one or the other. But the chief of staff is expected to be conversant with both. James Baker gave an example of this in discussing the advice President Bush received concerning the economy in 1992: "I want to tell you the problem there was not so much that President Bush wasn't listening to [his advisors]. . . . But he was listening to his economic advisors, who were giving him good economic advice—*good economic advice*—but lousy political advice. This, I think, was the fault of the White House staff and organization at the time. . . . They should have been able to see that, while the economy might not have needed any action . . . , we nevertheless needed an economic or domestic policy agenda abound which to coalesce a campaign."[56] More generally, Baker described the Office of the Chief of Staff as "the place where policy and politics come together."[57]

Protecting the President's Interests

The role of the chief of staff as advisor to the president is inherently problematic, however, since as it has the potential to conflict with the role of honest broker. Nevertheless, the chief of staff is often required to advise, especially when that consists of carrying bad news or disagreement to the president. Others may want to but often find that they cannot. This role falls under the category of protecting the interests of the president. One former chief of staff spoke to this issue: "you've got to have a person who can *tell you what they think* . . . , and it's rare when you're president. Most people come up to me as chief of staff and say I'm going in and tell him it's the dumbest thing I've ever seen and he's simply got to change it. They get in there, slobber all over him, kiss his ring, tell him how wonderful he is, leave and walk out and say, gee, I really told him. I'd say that's the most groveling, sycophantic behavior I've ever seen in my life. And they say, no, I told him. . . . People just simply do not walk in, point their finger at the president, and say, look: that's wrong."[58] Henson Moore explained: "It's just something about the Oval Office, there's something about the aura of the power of a president that people just won't say what really needs to be said to a president except a very choice few people who are so close to him and were so close to him before he was president that they can overcome it, or they have such a position of trust and respect held for them by the president that they don't feel intimidated."[59]

Moore expressed his frustration that he and his boss lacked such credentials. "Sam Skinner and I were not that close to the president. We were staff and he listened to us politely, but if his initial instinct was different from mine or Sam's, he'd go with his initial instinct. We didn't have the ability to turn him from that."[60] A factor that aggravated this problem in the Bush White House was the President's decision to keep White House operations separate from his reelection campaign. This effectively kept Skinner, the chief of staff, out of the political loop and greatly limited his overall influence, even with elements of his own staff.[61]

The protection of the president's interests is perhaps most crucial during times of crisis. The Iran-Contra affair in the Reagan administration illustrated what can happen when the advisory system fails to work well. James Baker made that clear: "When [President Reagan] got in trouble was when that system broke down after I left and after Mike Deaver left, particularly. They got him to agree to some things on Iran-Contra and other things that were a mistake. Bill Casey always wanted to go in there and see the president by himself. But as long as the president would tell us, then we could act to . . . say, 'Wait a minute. Do you really want to do this or do you not?'"[62]

Mack McLarty also faced a crisis when the Whitewater accusations began to fly during the Clinton administration. Here, protection of the president's interests had more to do with coping with forces beyond the presidency. He described his approach: "The way you deal with that . . . as effectively as you can, and I think we were reasonably good at it, is to really try to segment it and separate it as much as you possibly can and isolate it. You've got to deal with it, but we did set up a task force to deal with it. Therefore, you've got people who are concentrating on this, capable, skilled, dealing with the issues, and then that allows, obviously, the agenda to go forward."[63]

Presidents may even endanger their interests themselves. H. R. Haldeman, President Nixon's chief of staff, wrote: "I soon realized that *this* president had to be protected from himself. Time and again I would receive petty vindictive orders . . . after a Senator made an anti–Vietnam War speech: 'Put a 24-hour surveillance on that bastard.' And so on and on and on. If I took no action, I would pay for it. The president never let up. He'd be on the intercom buzzing me ten minutes after such an order. . . . I'd say 'I'm working on it,' and delay and delay until Nixon would one day comment, with a sort of half-smile on his face, 'I guess you never took action on that, did you?' 'No.' 'Well, I guess it was the best thing.'"[64]

Negotiating with the Environment: Congress, the Departments, and Others

Chiefs of staff need to get around Washington. They cannot remain closeted in the White House. But one area of difference among the various chiefs of staff was how much visibility they should personally have. Howard Baker, James Baker, Richard Cheney, and Kenneth Duberstein all urged the chief of staff to stay in the background and not become the center of attention. Increasingly, however, chiefs have functioned as spokespersons, negotiators, and occasionally as go-betweens on key issues. Sununu linked the Bush White House to conservative groups, and James Baker was liaison to the Republican political establishment in 1992. McLarty developed and maintained the Clinton administration's contacts with the business community, while Panetta fostered its relations with Congress.

A key element of the role of most recent chiefs of staff has been congressional relations. Although the White House has an office that specializes in this, the chief of staff has nonetheless become a major administration spokesman, at least since the emergence of James Baker in that role during the early Reagan years. Prior to that, even a former member of Congress like Donald Rumsfeld did relatively little in that area.[65] John Tuck went so far as to say that Howard Baker "became in fact the congressional affairs guy as well as the chief of staff" because members trusted him and "knew what he said would be the policy of the administration."[66] While that will not often be the case, Andrew Card nonetheless estimated that congressional relations is "probably a good 30 percent of the responsibility" of the chief of staff.[67]

Another "external" aspect of the chief of staff job is dealing with the press. The chief of staff may be asked to play a public role as spokesperson for the administration on Sunday talk shows and the like. Beyond that, there is room for a quieter role. As James Baker pointed out: "You have to be willing to background the press. Background, not leak. There's a big difference. But one of the things Cheney told me before I took the job, he said, 'Be sure you spend a lot of time with the press giving them your spin, why you're doing these things. Talk to them. But always do it invisibly.'" Baker argued that the "on the record" public presence, attempted by Donald Regan, worked less well because "nobody wanted to hear it from the chief of staff. He wasn't elected. They wanted to hear it from the president."[68]

Leon Panetta, in contrast, met regularly with the press for both formal and informal briefings. "You met with the press in the Roosevelt Room to brief them on issues. For example, if we were putting out a budget or putting out a major issue . . . and you wanted to make sure that the press would give it the kind of emphasis that we wanted, you would do briefings. . . . Then sometimes I would do a one-on-one briefing with a reporter in the chief of staff's office. And it varied depending on what the issue was. I didn't do that for everything."[69]

The chief of staff also may become involved in cabinet relations, though this is likely to be a smaller part of the job. The White House normally has a cabinet secretary handle most of the load. Indeed, a veteran of the office noted that "there is natural tension between the chief of staff and a cabinet."[70] Presidents have varied in whether they have given the chief of staff cabinet rank.

Finally, the chief of staff must deal in some ways with interest groups, at least to the extent of scheduling the president for fundraisers. In turn, according to Panetta, the White House must be sensitive to donors: "These are the kind of big players who are always around. . . . They are constantly the people you turn to because they have the money for these events. I think, as a result of that, there is without question a greater sensitivity to the issues that they are involved with. . . . Now, does it control policy, which is the major question in the minds of the American people? Does it control policy? Not necessarily but it sure as hell has an impact as far as decisions that are made."[71]

Personal Styles and Attributes

There is no single set of characteristics that defines an ideal chief of staff. Nonetheless, there are critical interpersonal dimensions to the job, and any successful chief of staff must be sensitive to them.

The Variety of Approaches and People

Both presidents and chiefs of staff come from a variety of backgrounds; display a diversity of personal strengths, weaknesses, and operating styles; and encounter widely differing circumstances during their time in the White House.

Much of the advice relevant to this mix of factors is embedded in what has gone before. Certainly, the key is for the chief of staff to adapt to the style of the president. The hands-on approach of Jimmy Carter or Bill Clinton certainly required a different form of staff support than the hands-off approach of Ronald Reagan.[72] Likewise, the temperament of the chief executive requires adjustments. The objective is achieving the trust of the president. Leon Panetta stated: "The first and foremost quality that is essential is trust. You've got to have their trust. To some extent, you have to build that trust because you're just going in to a job, you have to prove yourself. But, ultimately, if you have that trust and you develop that trust, you can do the job."[73]

One also needs to adapt to the various other prominent actors in the White House. Mack McLarty stressed the importance of the vice president: "Another concept I felt strongly about that was not necessarily echoed from the other chiefs of staff [with whom he spoke] was that the vice president be integrated into the Office of the President. Clinton and Gore clearly ran as a team; the vice president was someone of real standing, a strong personality. And the president's wishes were to have Vice President Gore as an integral part of the team."[74]

Leon Panetta elaborated upon the importance of the first lady: "I think, if there's anything that is probably as common a trend in the White House as presidents who don't want to offend people, it's that they have very tough first ladies who have been through a lot of the battles and, just by the nature of what they've gone through, are very strong individuals." Panetta developed a weekly briefing session for Hillary Clinton for the first six or eight months of his tenure as chief of staff. After that, the necessary trust having been established, the meetings "kind of faded away."[75] Similarly, in the Reagan White House, part of Michael Deaver's value as deputy chief of staff lay in the confidence that Nancy Reagan placed in him.[76] When Deaver left, Donald Regan was unable to establish such a relationship, which helped lead to his downfall.

Chiefs of staff have come from very different backgrounds. Washington savvy, as noted above, is a desirable trait regardless of background. But there was also a suggestion that people who have been top decision-makers have a harder time adjusting to the staff role than others do, as both Governor Sununu and Treasury Secretary (and former Merrill Lynch CEO) Regan discovered. "You must realize," said one former official, "that the spotlight is not supposed to be shining on me; it is supposed to be shining on the other guy."[77]

"You Are Not the President"

James Baker, Kenneth Duberstein, and others reiterated the importance of the chief of staff never forgetting the staff component of his title. As Baker put it: "You're really powerful but every bit of that power is derivative from the president. The minute you forget that you get in trouble."[78] Duberstein made the point with a story of a "crusty Democratic congressman" who once said to him, "'Duberstein, you're smarter than 95 percent of the SOBs up here. You know it and we know it. But what you have to remember is we're elected and you ain't.' One of the best pieces of advice I ever got."[79]

Not only must chiefs of staff keep their own egos in check, but they must also be sensitive to the egos and interests of others who work in the White House. Long hours, constant pressures, and personal ambitions can produce dysfunctional behavior that undercuts a team effort. According to Henson Moore, a former member of Congress and deputy chief of staff in the first Bush administration, "The hours are very long. The pressure is very great for the president, to have him be successful. The warfare and backstabbing is more acute there than I ever saw in the department or ever saw in the Congress. If something goes wrong, you don't want to be blamed for it; you want to put the blame on somebody else. You want to have an exit strategy that you leave as a hero not as a dog."[80]

Developing a Daily Schedule

Though each White House has its own characteristic rhythms, the daily schedule of the chief of staff is likely to fall into fairly predictable patterns due to the nature of the chief's responsibilities. The day begins, typically at 7:00 A.M., in a meeting with a small group of top staff within the chief of staff's office. This meeting provides a framework for the larger meeting of all senior staff, ten to fifteen persons, most of whom carry the designation "assistant to the president." This is usually held at 7:30 or 8:00 A.M. There is a sense throughout the various administrations that only senior staff should attend, not their designees. The senior staff meetings usually begin with a discussion of the schedule of the president's day.[81] Finally, there is a private meeting between the chief of staff and the president at which the president is usually briefed on his daily schedule and on other matters that emerged in the senior-staff meeting. The chief of staff may also attend the president's national security briefing, which also occurs in the early morning.

Of course, variations on the daily schedule of the chief of staff may occur as a consequence of several factors, such as presidential travels, reelection demands, or policy emergencies. Apart from that, though, where the typical pattern has not been routinely followed, problems have arisen. Samuel Skinner, for instance, noted that this was sometimes a problem during his tenure.[82]

Conclusion

The tasks of the chief of staff are many, varied, subtle, and critically important to the success of a presidency. While there can be no simple prescription for doing the job right, certain principles do emerge from the experiences of those who have held the position. Very briefly summarized, they are:

1. *Gain control.* The White House is large and complex, and its responses to events must often be immediate. This is not an environment conducive to lengthy discussion or loose management. Successful chiefs of staff have been "strong" but not self-interested or autocratic.

2. *Adapt to the stylistic preferences and needs of the president.* Just as presidents differ, optimal approaches to working with them will also. Nothing is more important to remember than that the power of the chief of staff derives only from the president. One who forgets this precept, who acts as if he were president, will get into trouble sooner or later.

3. *Protect the president.* Adjusting to the presidential style does not preclude compensating for presidential weaknesses. H. R. Haldeman's well-

known tales of the presidential orders he did *not* carry out serve as a lesson and a warning for any chief of staff.[83] Above all, help the president avoid making what James Baker called "oh-by-the-way" decisions, where commitments are made without sufficient staffing or thoughtful consideration.[84]

4. *Choose bright, trustworthy, and loyal subordinates.* Be willing to delegate work to them in the certainty that it will get done as it should.

5. *Be an honest broker.* Arguably, this is the *most* important point of all.

6. *Run a lean shop, be flexible, and establish a rhythm.* Under most circumstances, keep the Office of Chief of Staff itself relatively lean to keep the management challenges of that office reasonable. Be sensitive for the need of informal, fluid, and often temporary organizational devices (regular meetings, war rooms, and such) to cope with particular problems and opportunities. In addition to establishing clear rhythms for normal presidential and White House days, be careful to include in discussions and decisions only those with a need and competence to be there. Be careful at the same time not to create groups that are too unwieldy to accomplish their work.

Notes

1.   Gerald R. Ford, interview with Martha Joynt Kumar, Rancho Mirage, Calif., Oct. 10, 2000, White House Interview Program.

2.   Richard Cheney, interview with Martha Joynt Kumar, Washington, D.C., July 27, 1999, White House Interview Program.

3.   Landon Butler, interview with Martha Joynt Kumar, Washington, D.C., Oct. 14, 1999, White House Interview Program.

4.   W. Henson Moore, interview with Martha Joynt Kumar, Washington, D.C., Oct. 15, 1999, White House Interview Program.

5.   James A. Baker III, interview with Martha Joynt Kumar and Terry Sullivan, Washington, D.C., Nov. 16, 1999, White House Interview Program.

6.   Background interview.

7.   James A. Baker III, interview with Martha Joynt Kumar and Terry Sullivan, Washington, D.C., July 7, 1999, White House Interview Program.

8.   Marlin Fitzwater, interview with Martha Joynt Kumar, Washington, D.C., Oct. 10, 2000, White House Interview Program.

9.   Background interview.

10. Samuel Skinner, interview with Martha Joynt Kumar, Washington, D.C., Apr. 24, 2000, White House Interview Program.

11. Moore interview.

12. Skinner interview.

13. J. Baker interview, Nov. 16, 1999.

14. Leon Panetta, interview with Martha Joynt Kumar, Washington, D.C., May 4, 2000, White House Interview Program.

15. Fitzwater interview.

16. Howard Baker and John Tuck, interview with Martha Joynt Kumar, Washington, D.C., Nov. 12, 1999.

17. Panetta interview; J. Baker interview, Nov. 16, 1999.

18. H. Baker interview.

19. See J. Baker interview, Nov. 16, 1999.

20. Michael Deaver, interview with Martha Joynt Kumar, Washington, D.C., Sept. 9, 1999, White House Interview Program.

21. James Cicconi, interview with Martha Joynt Kumar, Washington, D.C., Nov. 29, 1999, White House Interview Program.

22. H. Baker interview.

23. Andrew Card Jr., interview with Martha Joynt Kumar, Washington, D.C., May 25, 1999, White House Interview Program.

24. Moore interview.

25. J. Baker interview, Nov. 16, 1999.

26. Thomas F. "Mack" McLarty, interview with Martha Joynt Kumar, Washington, D.C., Nov. 16, 1999, White House Interview Program.

27. See Card interview, H. Baker interview.

28. Deaver interview; Moore interview.

29. Jerry Jones, interview with Martha Kumar, Washington, D.C., Apr. 11, 2000, White House Interview Program.

30. J. Baker interview, Nov. 16, 1999.

31. H. Baker interview.

32. Mark Siegel, interview with Martha Joynt Kumar, Washington, D.C., Jan. 4, 2000, White House Interview Program.

33. Card interview.

34. Panetta interview.

35. McLarty interview.

36. Panetta interview.

37. Sherman Adams, *First Hand Report* (New York: Harper and Brothers, 1961), pp. 50, 72.

38. Background interview.

39. Butler interview.

40. McLarty interview.

41. Background interview.

42. J. Baker interview, July 7, 1999.

43. Background interview.

44. J. Baker interview, July 7, 1999.

45. Moore interview.

46. Deaver interview.

47. Panetta interview.

48. Bob Woodward, *The Choice* (New York: Simon and Schuster, 1996), pp. 140–41.

49. J. Baker interview, Nov. 16, 1999.

50. McLarty interview.

51. Jones interview.

52. J. Baker interview, July 7, 1999.

53. H. Baker interview.

54. See Panetta interview.

55. McLarty interview.

56. J. Baker interview, Nov. 16, 1999.

57. J. Baker interview, July 7, 1999.

58. Background interview.

59. Moore interview.

60. Moore interview.

61. Skinner interview.

62. J. Baker interview, July 7, 1999. See also Deaver interview.

63. McLarty interview.

64. H. R. Haldeman with Joseph DiMona, *The Ends of Power* (New York: Times Books, 1978), pp. 58–59.

65. Donald Rumsfeld, interview with Martha Joynt Kumar, Chicago, Ill., Apr. 25, 2000, White House Interview Program.

66. John Tuck, in H. Baker interview.

67. Card interview.

68. J. Baker interview, Nov. 16, 1999.

69. Panetta interview.

70. Card interview.

71. Panetta interview.

72. See Butler interview; McLarty interview; J. Baker interview, July 7, 1999.

73. Panetta interview

74. McLarty interview; Roy Neel, interview with Martha Joynt Kumar, Washington, D.C., June 15, 1999, White House Interview Program.

75. Panetta interview.

76. Deaver interview.

77. Background interview; Jones interview.

78. J. Baker interview, Nov. 16, 1999.

79. Kenneth Duberstein, interview with Martha Joynt Kumar, Washington, D.C., Aug. 12, 1999.

80. Moore interview.

81. Phil Brady, interview with Martha Joynt Kumar, Washington, D.C., Aug. 17, 1999.

82. Skinner interview.

83. Jones interview.

84. J. Baker interview, July 7, 1999.

The Office of Staff Secretary

KAREN HULT
KATHRYN DUNN TENPAS

T HE SUBJECT OF WHITE HOUSE STAFFING HAS never been the centerpiece of presidency literature. However, among the times when staffing should be the primary focus is the transition period when the president-elect prepares to enter office. When one thinks of the White House, one may well envision numerous components—virtually all essential to the sitting president and most competing for the president's attention. A study of the Office of the Staff Secretary reveals that this little-known entity is indeed at the vortex of presidential action, as it determines what paperwork makes its way in and out of the Oval Office.[1] We draw on the experiences and insights of previous presidential aides to provide a "how to" manual of sorts that would be useful to incoming staff secretaries and their staffs, particularly those who enter with a new administration. Not intended to be a theoretical or an exhaustive study of the Office of the Staff Secretary, this chapter seeks to offer a more practical perspective of the inner workings of this key White House unit.

We proceed in four stages. Part one identifies the primary tasks of the staff secretary and, in the process, highlights the magnitude of the staff secretary's responsibilities. Part two explains how this office interfaces with other White House units, demonstrating that its contacts are primarily limited to others within the White House staff apparatus. Part three outlines the internal organization and operations of the Office of the Staff Secretary, paying particular attention to the subunits within the office. We conclude with advice for newcomers in part four by drawing lessons from past staff secretaries.

Main Tasks of the Staff Secretary

The primary job of the staff secretary is to control the paper flow to and from the president. James Cicconi, staff secretary for George H. W. Bush, underscored how critical this is:

> I knew that the core function of my job was being the president's inbox and outbox essentially, coordinating the decision-making process in the White House for the president, making sure that the issues were teed up for his decisions; he had the options and decisions placed in front of him, and when he made them, ensuring they were implemented; and that everybody that needed to be in the loop was, that he had the full range of advice from his advisers before he made a decision; people weren't cut out by other people, and that once he made the decision, there was a disciplined process of implementation. That's a job that is huge because you're really having to be involved with everything that passes through the president's hands for a decision.[2]

Control Paper Flowing into the President: Serve as the "Inbox"

The volume of material coming to the president is astounding. Coping with it is initially "like trying to drink out of a fire hose."[3] Such an onslaught requires an administrative staff that typically has worked two shifts and an alert staff secretary sensitive to what the president *must* see, what he *should* see to make informed decisions, and what he *prefers* to see.

The material flowing into the staff secretary's office covers a wide range: presidential decision memos, bills that Congress has passed and associated signing or veto recommendations, standard forms requiring the president's signature, the daily briefing book to prepare the president for the next day's schedule, White House guest lists, samples of personal mail from friends and colleagues, and presidential "night reading," "weekend reading," and "trip reading." In recent administrations too, the staff secretary has been at the center of the speech drafting and clearance processes.

Perhaps most important, according to George H. W. Bush's staff secretary, Phillip Brady, "the staff secretary and the staff secretary's office is responsible for making sure whatever it is that's being proposed and sent to the president is ready for primetime." He elaborated:

That means has it been legally reviewed? If it's a policy document, are the options laid out for the president? Do they truly reflect the variety of opinions in a clear fashion that senior officers want to make sure are brought to the president's attention? If it's a speech being sent in to the president, is it a speech that truly reflects administration policy, that's consistent with previous statements the president made? Has it been vetted? By that I mean if a speech comes in to the staff secretary's office from the speechwriting office, then it was our responsibility to circulate it around to those who would have a substantive interest in the speech. So it would go to the counsel's office absolutely for legal review. It would also go to the chief of staff. Perhaps if there are some national security–type issues, foreign policy issues addressed in it, it would go to Brent Scowcroft and his office to take a look at it. Significant administration policy statements would go to OMB [Office of Management and Budget], Richard Darman or Roger Porter who was the head of OPD, the Office of Policy Development. It would go to those various offices with very quick turnaround times. Sometimes speeches came in and the turnaround times were really short, so there was a lot of follow-up responsibility in getting people's comments. The comments would come back in and then the Office of the Staff Secretary had the sometimes-difficult job of reconciling comments because you'd get comments that were 180 degrees apart or really did a number on the flow of a speech.[4]

From a somewhat different vantage point, Alonzo McDonald, deputy chief of staff under President Carter, described his view of particularly effective decision memos for the president: "The stuff I thought should come in was stuff in which the issue was crisply defined, the recommendation was clear, the level of consensus related to that issue should be clear, and the key elements of evidence that swung it should be clear so that, in a short executive summary of two or three pages, one could say here's all the background we really like [it] but here's the core issue."[5]

White Houses differ as to whether national security and other highly sensitive materials are put through the "staff system" In the first Bush White House, for example, there were "National Security Council matters, some highly confidential matters that would go to the president more directly, through the national security adviser to the president. . . . Those individuals may take things directly in to the president with others, cabinet secretaries perhaps, where highly confidential matters are involved. But, by and large, the staff secretary process was observed very well. Once materials get to the staff secretary's office, the vetting might be reduced depending on the sensitivity of the material."[6]

Most staff secretaries try to prioritize the papers coming into the president. One Nixon staff secretary recalled, for instance:

Most of the stuff that went in to the president I would also classify it all into different categories, such as "for your information," "action required" if he needed to sign something, if it was a bill by Congress, if it was an important document of any kind, if it was some emergency preparation bill of one kind or another. And then I had other information—I had broken down a system of different colored folders, red, yellow, blue, manila for emergency types of things. The red folders were for immediate action. They were the CIA daily file on the progress of the Vietnam War or they were special important messages from Kissinger or Haldeman or people who sent them up. They'd filter up to me, and then several times a day, I would take them up to the president and collect what else he had and keep his office going in that way. I know it sounds [probably] like it's not workable, but it absolutely was almost failproof.[7]

James Cicconi also noted the importance of adjusting the flow of materials to a particular president's "work style."

[Y]ou needed to understand the president, how he liked to work, how he liked to make decisions, the degree of detail he was comfortable with, what types of things he wanted to see and what types of things he was willing to delegate unseen, style of work and level of involvement, level of information. You can drown a person. . . . I mean I learned trial and error with President Bush that he was a clean-desk guy, but that was a problem if you sent him a long memo that was a fairly in-depth analysis of a problem. . . . I learned that at Camp David he got up at six or seven in the morning and got his coffee and sat on the porch by himself and went through his paper. The birds are chirping and there's nobody around. . . . And I could tell because things like that memo would come back with extensive marginal notes and comments and maybe even a memo he wrote in response to it.[8]

Nixon staff secretary Jerry Jones recalled that the president "hated to get anything over a page on a decision memo, and the staff secretary couldn't send more than a few sentences" on the cover memo to the president.[9]

Follow up on Paper Flowing out of the Oval Office: Serve as the "Outbox"

Often as important are the papers coming out of the Oval Office. In most White Houses the staff secretary also has been responsible for channeling presidential decisions, questions, and comments (on, for example, the daily News Summary) to the appropriate parties. A former Nixon staff secretary remembered:

an impeccable system of tracking down the president's requests. That was, of course, part of my job because I was allowed forty-eight hours literally and oftentimes six or eight hours—to every question the president had answered, he used big yellow legal pads. He used alphabets. Haldeman was an H; Kissinger was a K. Everybody had a letter, major people in the cabinet, senior White House staff. The president, through the day and at different meetings during the day, would designate things on the yellow pad, and I would take it and implement it all. It was a remarkable follow-up system. I would take the memos, anything the president wanted done or needed done, and follow it up. If I didn't have an answer within a matter of hours, I'd send out a second alarm system.[10]

In contrast, the Clinton operation, observed one White House staff member, paid relatively little attention to implementation.

That tended to be more honor system. In other words, if the president would send something back, he would send some document back and there'd be a question on it—Bruce Reed, what about blank?—it would more be the case that we would depend on Bruce Reed sending an answer back than that we would be calling Bruce and saying what about that. I don't think that there was particularly a conceptual or a principal reason for that as much as it was just a time thing. And I think that it was a combination. There was a time thing, and that you could pretty much depend on the notion that if one of the president's senior advisers was asked a question by the president, he would think he better answer it. We constantly would get back—there were a lot of information memos, not a lot in percentage terms, but there were a lot of information memos that we would get in a given period of time or a week that would be in response to things that the president had asked. . . . We thought about trying to do a real serious tracking system, and we just ended up thinking that the cost-benefit analysis part of it didn't warrant it; there were undoubtedly some things that slipped through the cracks but not important enough to kind of do this whole time-intensive thing.[11]

Whichever path an administration follows, Jerry Jones, who served as staff secretary under both Richard Nixon and Gerald Ford, cautions that it is important not to overstate what such "implementation" responsibility involves.

The staff secretary is simply a conveyor belt for the decision. The responsibility for decision implementation goes to somebody else. So if it's a domestic policy, the decision paper comes from the Domestic Council, written by Duval if it were a transportation matter, or by [Shepard] if it was a legal matter, or by Cavanaugh if it were a Health, Education, and Welfare matter, Fairbanks if it was an environmental matter. If it were an NSC problem, it would come from one of their guys through Henry. If it were an economic matter, it would come from Shultz. The decision is made, the staff secretary conveys his decision back to the Domestic Council officer who sent the decision in, or the OMB officer . . . ; they have the implementation responsibility. Usually, they are having to coordinate two or three departments to implement a broad policy.[12]

Coordinate and Monitor the Decision-Making Process

At first glance, the staff secretary's job may seem mostly "administrative." But it is quite substantive in both policy and political terms: the staff secretary must be "in the loop" on key issues and fluent with complex questions and positions. "The staff secretary job is to be pretty policy wonkish too. This policy is inconsistent with the one we had the president say last week. Let's send it back and make sure it's consistent. Or that speechwriter is always trying to get that policy into a speech and we're not going to let him do it."[13] That means that the staff secretariat must be, in the words of Eisenhower aide Wilton Persons, "the one office in the White House that knows the most about what is going on and where it is taking place."[14]

The staff secretary guides and oversees the policy decision-making process by making sure that all appropriate sources were consulted, thereby providing the full range of advice to the president. Jerry Jones stressed that the purpose of exposing policy options to wide scrutiny is to help ensure that the president sees the views of critics as well as proponents.

> But the job of the staff secretary is to kill ideas. I know that sounds awful, but the problem with the White House is people run in with great ideas and they don't understand the consequences of this brilliant genius idea. And you have to send the genius idea to its natural enemies and test it and see if the natural enemy can kill it. If the natural enemy can't kill it, then it's worth going with. If it has a hole in it, you have to know it has a hole, and the way you know that is you send it to its enemy. So if the Domestic Council has a great idea, you send it to OMB, and they'll kill it if they can. If Treasury has a great idea, you send it to Commerce. . . . You have to do it in a hurry, you don't have a prolonged debate. . . . It may have several natural enemies. The congressional guy may absolutely go bonkers over something cute that somebody wants to do that undercuts the leadership up on the Hill. . . . Then when there's a conflict, you throw it to the president: here's a brilliant idea that somebody thinks is awful. You have to know it.[15]

Similarly, the staff secretary must check to be sure that presidential speech drafts are consistent with prior statements and have been circulated and approved ("cleared") by those with substantive interests in the speeches. Rhett Dawson, assistant to the president for operations during the Reagan administration, elaborated: "So, if the president was going to make a speech, . . . you wanted to fact-check it. You wanted to make sure it didn't take you in a new course on policy without thinking about that and identifying it. You wanted to make sure it was accurate before the president uttered it because the person who hands the president the speech actually has to know it's right and then you have to vouch for it."[16]

Rather clearly, the "routing procedures" (in the Clinton White House, for example, a "circulation cover sheet" attached to a packet of materials) are critical to rounding up relevant actors and input. Decisions about whom to include and exclude on particular memos are inevitably political, but they play an important role in the policy process. Including all senior staff on every decision is clearly not the most efficient means of obtaining feedback; rather, a grasp of the policy and political elements of the decision should assist in formulating the routing list. Jerry Jones recalled, for example:

> Almost always on any major decision there is conflict on the staff, and the president has to know the conflict. The staff secretary under the staff system is in charge of that transmission belt. What the staff secretary would do is take a paper say from the Domestic Council that recommends a decision—usually there are four or five choices and perhaps subchoices to the choices. Then the staff secretary takes that paper and he gives it to OMB and he gives it to the NSC guy, he gives it to the economic group, and anyone else he thinks ought to see it. . . . So the staff secretary has almost total authority on who that should go to. He might get guidance. The president really wants to hear what Eliot Richardson has to say about this, or he really wants to hear what someone else has to say, or he'd like to hear what somebody outside the government has to say on this. So the staff secretary then staffs that paper and he gives a deadline, I've got to have what you have to say about this COB [close of business] day after tomorrow. And people tell you. The staff secretary then writes a cover memo to the decision paper saying, "Mr. President, this has been sent to the follow[ing] people and this is what they say," boom. "This is the choice they would recommend to you," boom. And you do it in as brief a piece of paper as you can.[17]

In some cases information like polling is sensitive, and presidents and their chiefs of staff prefer to limit circulation. In the Bush White House, the president would receive the labor statistics from the Department of Labor and different financial data information. That would come to the staff secretary's office . . . , but we'd send it in a red folder to the president directly and privately. It wasn't vetted in any way, shape, or form. It was something which we were very careful of. Sometimes other documents would come in with restrictions on them, saying this should go to the president with a copy to the chief of staff and the national security adviser only. If I had some questions on the restrictions with some issues . . . , then I would get on the horn with whoever had sent it in and say, "don't you think so and so should also be aware of this? Don't you think the president would also like advice from so and so?" And we'd work it out. So those things were judgment calls. . . . [W]hat you really want to have in these various positions is people with judgment because you have to make these calls on a very expedited basis, frequently with inadequate information.[18]

Of course, assessing who gets what and when will likely be something that the staff secretary learns on the job.

Often the complexity and diversity of views lead staff secretaries (or their top deputies) to add summary memos to the material on a particular subject that goes to the president, which seek to crystallize the primary disagreements or issues to be decided. According to one former staff secretary, "you need to fairly quickly get a six- or seven-page memo, understand it, and be able to, at least as we handled the job, boil it down into a six-by-nine—generally—piece of paper, [a] short synopsis that says attached is a memo on such and such; here's the main issue; here's what you have to decide; here's where the different players in the administration stand."[19]

A key challenge in preparing such memos lies in treating all sides of the debate fairly so as not to bias the president's decision making. Many former occupants of the office have used the term "honest broker" to describe their duties. For instance, James Cicconi noted:

Your "normal" decision memo from the domestic side or the national security side generally came in draft form. It was circulated to the appropriate people by my office for their review, advice, comments. Before it went to the president, their comments came in to my office as the "honest broker" with a copy to the people that originated the memo. I was the check in making certain that whoever was the author of the memo or speech or what have you played straight on the comment process. If they didn't take a comment or accommodate a comment, I would ask them why or my staff would. If I wasn't satisfied with the answer, then I could overrule because I had the final responsibility for the paper that went to the president being full and complete and reflecting all the views of his advisers as honestly as possible.[20]

Oversee Correspondence, the Executive Clerk, and Records Management

Recent administrations typically have placed the offices of correspondence, executive clerk, and records management under the jurisdiction of the staff secretary. Of the three, the executive clerk's office and records management are run by longtime professionals with a superb working knowledge of managing and preserving presidential records. Past administrations have benefited greatly by holding over staff members in these units.

Although the Correspondence Office also has relied on numerous aides who stay from one administration to the next, typically it has been supervised by a presidential appointee. The person selected to head the office must have a strong sense of the importance to the president and the administration of responding appropriately, depending on both the author of an incoming message and the subject of the message. Bush staff secretary James Cicconi has told of his efforts to remind the correspondence staff to handle mail with care. Attached to a memo was an illustrative note: "a 1939 letter to President Franklin Roosevelt. The letter, as Cicconi recalled, was messy, crudely typed, full of cross-outs and misspellings. Its author told the president of a theory he had, by means of which an explosive device of incredible magnitude could be created. . . . It was signed: Albert Einstein."[21]

While a sizeable full-time staff works in the Correspondence Office, the unit also relies heavily on volunteers and interns. The volume of mail can be quite large. During the first Bush administration, incoming mail ranged from 35,000 to 40,000 letters per week.[22] In response to controversial legislative proposals, this number can skyrocket. After the introduction of the Clinton healthcare initiative, the White House was receiving about 48,000 pieces of mail (including faxes) per day. This flow not only varies with reactions to presidential speeches, visible events, and controversial actions but also has continued to increase from administration to administration. The expanded use of e-mail only adds to the volume. In the first six and a half years of the Clinton administration, for example, the White House received 3,876,105 e-mails.[23]

Located in the Correspondence Office as well is a presidential "comments line" that receives in excess of 300,000 calls each year. The office also houses an agency liaison unit that handles "hardship cases" culled from letters, e-mails, and the comments line.

Key Contacts

Unlike many of the offices in the White House, the staff secretary's office faces inward—most contacts will be with those inside the confines of the White House (and the Eisenhower Executive Office Building [EEOB]).

The President

Since the primary task is to control the paper flow in to and out of the Oval Office, the staff secretary's principal "client" is the president. As noted above, the key to successful performance appears to be the ability to match the president's work habits with the staff secretary's so that the latter will not bother the president with the trivial, overwhelm him with massive memos, or prevent him from receiving all points of view in a policy debate. This judgment is critical—knowing what to pass on, when, and how. According to one former staff secretary, the job requires someone who can make thoughtful decisions quickly—they need to have a demonstrated track record of wise decision making under intense pressure.

President's Personal Office

Known during the Clinton administration as Oval Office Operations, the president's personal staff also will be an almost constant contact point for those in the staff secretary's office. Indeed, the presidential aide has been called the "last quality checkpoint" for the briefing materials sent to the president.[24]

Chief of Staff

Aside from the president and the Oval Office staff, the chief of staff will likely be the staff secretary's most frequent patron. Interestingly, the proximity of the chief of staff to the staff secretary has varied over time. For instance, during the Reagan White House, Richard Darman was located in a separate staff secretary unit within Chief of Staff James Baker's office, and David Chew was lodged in a newly created White House operations office after Donald Regan departed. So, while the chief of staff has a close working relationship with the staff secretary, the placement of this individual is likely to depend on the preferences of the president and the chief of staff.

The working relationships between chiefs of staff and staff secretaries can differ with the issue and the chief of staff's management style. For example, on some matters, the staff secretary may choose to pass along information to the president after consulting with the chief of staff. In other cases, the chief of staff may only need to be informed of particular memos.

Meanwhile, the approach to management (or the "style") of the chief of staff can make a difference in the nature of the working relationship with the staff secretary. Clinton chief of staff Leon Panetta described himself as "a control freak in the sense of wanting to make sure as chief of staff that I had my finger on everything that was taking place. So I wanted to funnel all of the issues and decision making that ultimately had to go to the president through the chief of staff's operation."[25]

Another staff secretary recalled some of the similarities and differences among some of the chiefs of staff for whom he worked.

> So all of those basic operations you did whether it was [Chief 1] or [Chief 2] or [Chief 3]. At some level that didn't matter, and you were kind of flooded with correspondence and proclamations and executive orders and all that kind of stuff. You were doing all that kind of stuff anyway. . . . [U]nder [Chief 2] . . . there were more situations that I recall—I know I went to more meetings in [his] office when it was [his] office where senior advisers were pulled in to discuss their views on a given decisional issue and where the objective was to try to narrow differences or find some consensus or whatever. So I think there was clearly more of that under [Chief 2] than under [Chief 1] and probably somewhat more under [Chief 2] than under [Chief 3]. It's not a dramatic difference in your job; there just was a little bit more of that kind of involvement."[26]

Yet the cooperation and support of the chief of staff is likely always valuable. "[T]he most valuable commodity in the world is presidential time, the president of the United States' time. So that's one thing that a staff secretary in particular and a chief of staff with the staff secretary in a support-ing role wants to ensure that you protect that time and you only bring to the president's attention those things . . . that are . . . not just appropriate but timely. . . . So you're working with the chief of staff; you're having to serve as a wall in some instances, the last stop in some instances."[27]

Important Others

Other important contacts include the cabinet secretary, White House counsel, OMB director, the national security assistant, the press secretary, and the heads of units for domestic policy, economic policy, political affairs, and speechwriting. The staff secretary's office may need to ask them for in-put on an issue, prod them to complete a memo in a timely manner, or tap their knowledge for the president's daily briefing book.

Internal Organization and Operations

The units that are included in the Office of the Staff Secretary have varied somewhat both within and between administrations. Under Pres. George H. W. Bush, for example, scheduling was lodged there. The unit that has shifted in and out of the staff secretary's office most frequently is also by far the largest component: correspondence. In the first term of the Reagan administration and part of the second, for instance, correspon-dence was placed in the Office of Administration (where it had been for much of the Carter presidency); by the spring of 1987, the Office of Oper-ations in the White House lodged the staff secretary, the "White House sec-retariat," and the presidential correspondence unit. During the Bush and Clinton years, correspondence returned to the staff secretary's office.

The most common configuration of the Office of the Staff Secretary in recent administrations has consisted of four components: the staff secre-tary, executive clerk, records management, and correspondence. In 1998, for example, a total of ninety-seven staff members worked in these areas: four in the Office of the Staff Secretary, five with the executive clerk, twenty-four in records management, and sixty-four in correspondence.

Staff Secretary

In the past the staff secretary has hired one or (in the Clinton administra-tion) two deputies and two or three administrative assistants. Even though

Figure 6.

President Ronald Reagan

White House Office of Staff Secretary in the Office of Operations

Fall, 1988

(Though the Staff Secretary's Office did not exist in 1988, the Office of Operations assumed the same responsibilities)

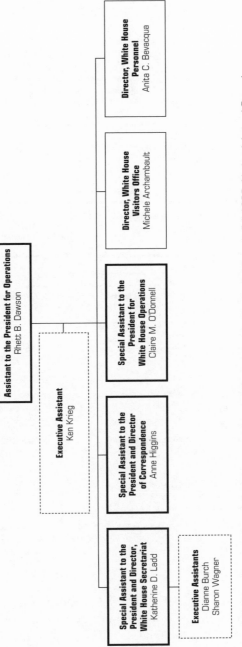

Assistant to the President for Operations
Rhett B. Dawson

Executive Assistant
Ken Krieg

Special Assistant to the President and Director, White House Secretariat
Katherine D. Ladd

Executive Assistants
Dianne Burch
Sharon Wagner

Special Assistant to the President and Director of Correspondence
Anne Higgins

Special Assistant to the President for White House Operations
Claire M. O'Donnell

Director, White House Visitors Office
Michele Archambault

Director, White House Personnel
Anita C. Bevacqua

White House Interview Program (whitehouse2001.org). Based on data in *The Capital Source*, Fall 1988, National Journal Group Inc., Washington, DC. *Key:* ⎯⎯⎯ = positions with "to the president" in their title; ------- = staff working for indicated assistant.

Figure 7.

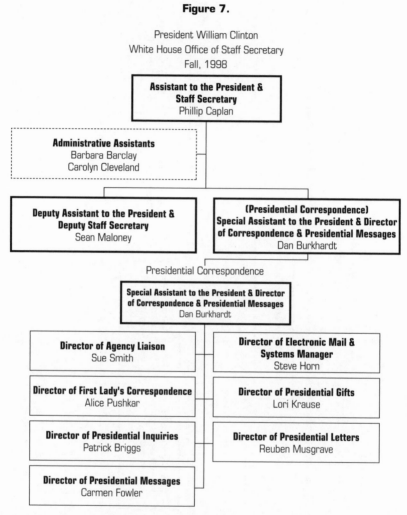

President William Clinton
White House Office of Staff Secretary
Fall, 1998

**Assistant to the President &
Staff Secretary**
Phillip Caplan

Administrative Assistants
Barbara Barclay
Carolyn Cleveland

**Deputy Assistant to the President &
Deputy Staff Secretary**
Sean Maloney

**(Presidential Correspondence)
Special Assistant to the President & Director
of Correspondence & Presidential Messages**
Dan Burkhardt

Presidential Correspondence

**Special Assistant to the President & Director
of Correspondence & Presidential Messages**
Dan Burkhardt

Director of Agency Liaison
Sue Smith

**Director of Electronic Mail &
Systems Manager**
Steve Horn

Director of First Lady's Correspondence
Alice Pushkar

Director of Presidential Gifts
Lori Krause

Director of Presidential Inquiries
Patrick Briggs

Director of Presidential Letters
Reuben Musgrave

Director of Presidential Messages
Carmen Fowler

White House Interview Program (whitehouse2001.org). Based on data in *The Capital Source*,
Fall, 1998, National Journal Group Inc., Washington, DC. *Key:* ——— = positions with "to the
president" in their title; --------- = staff working for indicated assistant.

President Nixon's staff secretary Jon Huntsman possessed all the current
staff secretary duties as well as management and administration, no recent
staff secretary has assumed such broad and varied responsibilities.

In general, it would be misleading to suggest that there is a sense of routine within the office. Although the influx of paper is constant, each day the

issues differ. Demonstrating the difficulty of attempting to create a sense of routine, one staff member recounted an attempt in which the two deputy staff secretaries tried to divide incoming mail according to foreign and domestic issues. Almost immediately, the overlap and "crisis" nature of much of the material precluded such a division of labor. The office's responsibilities vary as well depending on whether the staff secretary is traveling with the president, preparing a briefing book for an overseas trip, or gearing up for a major speech. Some memos will need to be summarized in a cover memo, others will require routing for input among interested parties, and still others will have to be returned for additional work by the author.

In short, the Office of the Staff Secretary must be prepared for whatever hits the desk. Virtually the sole certainty is that no two days will ever be identical. Indeed, almost the only routine feature of the operation appears to be the need for a seven-day workweek and long days, with two shifts of employees to receive and log in new papers. Principals must be nearby in case an important document arrives requiring the president's signature. Such an event can occur at almost any time, and someone must be present to deliver the document to the president for his signature.

Daily Schedule

The staff secretary's day often is a long and fragmented one, punctuated by meetings, phone calls, and questions from the president and chief of staff. Andrew Card has called the staff secretary position one of the "workaholic jobs. That's too much work for one person to do but you can't delegate it."[28]

The day usually begins relatively early and can end quite late. Bush staff secretary Phillip Brady remembered:

Most [days] typically [began at] 6:00. You had to leave by 6:30 to be there by 7:00. . . . After the senior-staff meeting, assignments came out of that, responsibilities came out of that. There'd be a full schedule of meetings you personally would have. It might be a scheduling meeting that Andy Card would be chairing as deputy chief of staff on upcoming events the following day. There might be a meeting on a speech the president is going to be giving in a few days where there's some disagreement between offices as to how that speech should be cast or what we recommend to the president as to how that speech should be cast. If there were disputes and issues, there'd be a meeting scheduled for that. You'd have a ton of things in your office that had come in for presidential action; those things then needed to be staffed out and reviewed. So my own in-box was quite large. There were other long-term projects you were involved in. . . . Frequently, you'd go to lunch in the White House Mess, which was actually useful from a business point of view because you were able to catch one another there and get approvals or work out disagreements. It was very much a business session most times. . . . The schedule was such—this isn't unique to the staff secretary; it's true for everyone in the White House in any administration—that you generally looked up and it was seven o'clock at night.[29]

Tenure and Background

Despite the hectic schedule, the average tenure of staff secretaries during the first Bush and the Clinton administrations was about two years. President Carter had a single staff secretary who served throughout his term. During the Clinton administration, in several cases the deputy staff secretary was promoted to staff secretary. (See the appendix for a list of staff secretaries and deputies from the Nixon through the Clinton administrations.) In both Republican and Democratic administrations, former staff secretaries moved on to become chief of staff (for example, John Podesta under Clinton) or filled other senior governmental positions in subsequent administrations (for example, Richard Darman headed OMB in the Bush administration). Given the breadth of knowledge gained by a staff secretary, it is not at all surprising that this broad perspective recommends them for more senior positions.

Staff secretaries tend to come mainly from law and business backgrounds and are recruited primarily for what many perceive as their uncommonly good judgment. While some have known the president, most gained their position through ties with the chief of staff. Given the closeness with which staff secretaries and chiefs of staff work, this makes considerable sense. Prior campaign experience is not a requirement, although some staff secretaries have paid their dues on the campaign trail. Many times, lawyers will volunteer blocks of their time rather than resigning from their positions, for example, on Hill staffs or in law firms.

Executive Clerk

This unit serves as the receptacle of the original copies of presidential documents. All documents to be signed by the president (and thereby represent public activity) are collected and researched. Researchers in the office compare documents with a statute's requirements, respond and conduct research for congressional requests, and check the authorization for a presidential nomination or appointment.

The executive clerk (or a representative from the unit) is actually best known as the individual who personally delivers presidential messages to the Hill and is permitted on the House and Senate floors to deliver veto messages.

> The executive clerk's office is also the official White House voice to the Legislative Branch. You see on TV someone coming in to the well of the House saying, "Mr. Speaker, a message from the president," and either bringing back a veto or bringing back a message of some kind from the president. That someone is from the executive clerk's office. . . .
>
> He is the one who does the announcing. He actually comes in to the well of the House. The House provides privileges to that individual office, the executive clerk's office, and that is the official communication link from the White House to the Congress.[30]

Other tasks include keeping an eye on the veto clock (for example, if the president receives a bill signed by the House and Senate and does nothing for ten days, it automatically becomes law), responding to congressional requests for reports, overseeing presidential commissions, receiving declarations of emergency from governors, and monitoring the status of every bill and every presidential communication.

Not only are these tasks integral to a smoothly functioning White House, but the clerk's office also is "a very, very important part of the administration because it is the institutional memory and is viewed by each president coming in as something that is critical; you can see what's happened in the past."[31] Christopher Hicks elaborated:

> [T]he clerk's office is the only office that has any memory in the White House office. They keep the records. The [records management] office keeps the records of the president and the staff and all

that stuff. It's kind of a central file system. But at the end of the administration, under the Presidential Records Act, all those papers go to the archives. But the executive clerk's office is really the sole repository of history. You can call the executive clerk's office and get the status of bills, the status of nominees; you can say who was the secretary of war during the Teddy Roosevelt administration and they can tell you.[32]

Records Management

The Presidential Records Act of 1978 requires the preservation of all official documents generated in the course of daily business. One former staff secretary described these documents as "the basis for every presidential library." In previous administrations staff members from the National Archives Records Administration performed these preservation tasks. Through preservation, they seek to ensure a comprehensive history of the administration. Their management of records also serves as a resource for the president or policy units should they need documents. As with the executive clerk, experienced staffers are essential.

Correspondence

This large office contains most of the employees (and numerous volunteers) under the purview of the staff secretary. It is responsible for at least acknowledging all messages sent to the White House. Some messages (for example, letters from schoolchildren; e-mail, faxes, letters, and calls mobilized by identifiable groups) can be answered fully with "stock" responses, while others are forwarded to appropriate White House or executive-branch agency officials for more substantive responses. This unit also receives, logs in, arranges for notes of thanks, judges the legality, and handles the distribution of every gift sent to the president. The Correspondence Office even has its own post office in the EEOB.

Typically, correspondence aides track the content, source, and medium (electronic mail, voice-mail, fax, U.S. mail) of the messages the office receives, reporting them to senior aides or the president on a regular (often weekly) basis. Many presidents also ask to see a regular sample of the mail and phone comments that come to the White House. For example, as Phillip Brady recalled: "President Bush put great stock in correspondence, including the phone messages that came in. He received weekly compilations of all the messages. . . . Shirley Green [head of correspondence] and her office would put together both the comments that came in on the presidential phone lines as well as a compilation of the correspondence coming in and maybe some examples of proclamations that have been issued."[33]

What Works? What Does Not?: Advice from Past Staff Secretaries

Examining the various elements of serving as the president's human "in- and outbox" reveals the breadth and complexity of the staff secretary's tasks. It is scarcely surprising that many of the office's occupants learn its importance the hard way or end up reinventing the approaches of their predecessors. This section summarizes common-sense advice from those who have "been there, done that"—reflections that may help future staffers and outside observers as they seek to uncover the mysteries of the Office of the Staff Secretary.

What Works?

Attendance at key policy meetings will enable the staff secretary to understand the intensity of the various opinions as well as the substantive issues involved.

Since the staff secretary needs to know something about everything but does not have the time to be steeped in the details, these meetings can serve as tutorials. When invited, the staff secretary should attend. Second-hand accounts of meetings often will give short shrift to heated exchanges or disagreements among staff members. As James Cicconi observed: "you really had to spend time in the various policy meetings occurring in the White House—whether it was cabinet meetings, cabinet council meetings, other policy discussions in the White House—not only because you had a voice or an influence in those decisions but also so you had a sense of the discussion, the tenor of the discussion, and the views that were being expressed."[34]

Beware of and try to counteract the tendency for staff members to mask their misgivings when asked to discuss an issue with the president.

Staff Secretary Cicconi remembered using several techniques for alerting the president to disagreements among his advisers.

I put little notes on memos I would send in to him. . . . They are usually fairly mundane. Occasionally, there will be one where I'll

say, "Mr. President, what this argument boils down to is Dick Darman thinks X, John Sununu thinks Y, and Roger Porter thinks Z,
and the arguments are attached," or something like that. On other
occasions I would say, "Mr. President, based on the discussion, Jack
Kemp has pretty strong views on this issue, which aren't fully reflected in the attached memo; you may want to give him a call."
Sometimes people in a private discussion where the president
would prompt it will be more candid than they would in front of
three or four other people, who they think may leak it to the *Washington Post*. So that's what an honest broker would do.[35]

Be a vigilant guardian of the president's time.

As Phillip Brady indicated, this is "the most valuable commodity in the
world." Protecting presidential time involves being sure that whatever
memos the president sees are "ready for primetime" (for example, they
have been cleared by the counsel's office, OMB, NSC staff, and other relevant actors; they are necessary for the president to see at a particular point
given all the other demands on his attention).

*Early on, develop a keen sense of the president's working habits. Does the president
like to read long memos or summaries?*

What about news articles? Is the president interested in policy, political, or other details? Does he want all memos also routed through the chief
of staff's office? What about personal letters? How should a cabinet member's request for secrecy be handled? What types of materials should be
handled with the president in person, and what are the best times of the
day or week to do this?

*Since the staff secretary often will need a second opinion, and the president will not
be available, try to create an "open-door policy" with the chief of staff for consultation.*

Since the chief of staff is often the eyes and ears of the president, that
person needs to know about important incoming papers just as much as
the president. For instance, Bush staff secretary Cicconi recalled: "I copied
[Chief of Staff John] Sununu on everything. I had total entrée into his
office on no notice and used it. When something would come up that was
hot or contentious or difficult, we'd talk. And I was making 100 significant
decisions a day on pretty important things, and not once in two years did
John Sununu ever second guess me or overrule me."[36]

Set up at least a sixteen-hour-a-day staffing mechanism to record incoming and out-going papers on computers.

These administrative assistants will not review documents for substantive purposes but can log and track documents.

Upon careful review of existing staff in the clerk's office, the correspondence unit, and records management, aim to retain as many as you find suitable.

Their tasks are critical to the proper functioning of the White House, and institutional memory and expertise with records management are key. Among the things Cicconi remembers counseling the incoming Clinton staffers about was to "give the career people there a chance to prove their loyalty. There were a number of them that worked directly for me in there. I said, look, they're loyal to the presidency. They work for the White House and they are loyal to the presidency. They don't impact policy. They have jobs to do and they do them very well and they help you function. They will help you function on day one even if everybody around you is still learning how to do things. They know how to do things. If you come in and fire them all, you'll set yourself back months. Give them a chance to show that they're loyal, where their loyalty is."[37]

The Clinton staff soon discovered he was right. One aide observed: "The quasi-career staff who we inherited were enormously helpful in being able to tell us what the briefing book was supposed to look like and sort of what the format was for memos and stuff like that which we could either depart from or not depart from. But it was helpful at least to kind of see how stuff was done."[38]

What Does Not Work?

Attempting to divide incoming material for the president according to subject matter rarely, if ever, works.

Many of the issues are overlapping, and such a system is bound to fall apart.

We talked a little bit about dividing things sort of according to some substantive areas so that I had an interest in foreign policy and I would do more of that. I think it was that I was going to do more on the foreign and economic side and the other deputy was going to do more on the social policy, sort of the rest of domestic policy. . . . It was more one deputy would cover one, and one deputy would cover the other, and he would sort of watch over all of it. It just didn't work out that way because the staff secretary's office, in the nature of it, it flows with the nature of what's happening so that if what's coming through—it is a quintessentially reactive office as opposed to proactive.[39]

Shielding the president from contrary opinions will prevent him from making the best-informed decisions possible.

Staff secretaries should not try to hide disagreement or controversy among staff members. Clinton aide Todd Stern noted, "It was very important that we be viewed as honest brokers—that we didn't slant things one way or another, else we would not have retained the confidence of the people who had written those papers!"[40]

Spending time in supervising on a daily basis the activities of the Correspondence Office and the other units.

This takes precious time and attention away from the *primary* task of controlling the paper flow to and from the president. During the first Bush administration, James Cicconi indicated, "I just said you know where I am if you have a problem; otherwise you're in charge and I'll back you up. So I didn't really get drowned in the management detail mainly because I think early on I set up a structure that worked without my daily involvement so that I could focus my time and energy on the things that really did matter."[41]

While the autopen may be appropriate for some letters, staffers need to know when to use it. A seemingly innocent mistake may become a diplomatic disaster.

In addition, be sure that assistants are acutely aware that the autopen should be used only with the explicit approval of the staff secretary. Cicconi underscored this point: "Well, it was [an important responsibility], and one of the first decisions I made was that nothing gets autopenned unless there is a written authorization from me to autopen it. . . . Since I'm going to be responsible, I want to be responsible, and I said I do not give verbal authorizations. It was one of those things which was a heavy responsibility, and it is the only way to protect yourself."[42]

Conclusion

No amount of training or advice can completely prepare one for working in the White House. Issues, people, and crises all change from one administration to the next—sometimes from day to day. Despite the volatility and uncertainty, being aware of the experiences, accomplishments, and difficulties of past staffers may well assist those taking their places. At the same time, such knowledge may help both temper the expectations of outside observers and provide baselines for holding presidents and their aides accountable for key aspects of their performance.

Notes

We are grateful for the comments and suggestions of Martha Joynt Kumar and Bradley Patterson and for the time and effort of the former presidential staffers who shared their experiences and insights with the White House Interview Project.

1.   Yet scholars such as John Hart and Bradley Patterson have written about the Office of Staff Secretary. See Hart, *The Presidential Branch* (Chatham, N.J.: Chatham House, 1995); and Patterson, *The White House Staff: Inside the West Wing and Beyond* (Washington, D.C.: Brookings Institution, 2000).

2.   James Cicconi, interview with Martha Joynt Kumar, Washington, D.C., Nov. 29, 1999, White House Interview Program.

3.   Jerry Jones, interview with Martha Joynt Kumar, Washington, D.C., Apr. 11, 2000, White House Interview Program.

4.   Phillip Brady, interview with Martha Joynt Kumar, Washington, D.C., Aug. 17, 1999, White House Interview Program.

5.   Alonzo McDonald, interview with Martha Joynt Kumar, Washington, D.C., Feb. 2, 2000, White House Interview Program.

6.   Brady interview.

7.   Background interview with Martha Joynt Kumar, Dec. 2, 1999.

8.   Cicconi interview.

9.   Jones interview.

10. Background interview with Martha Joynt Kumar, Feb. 25, 2000.

11. Background interview, Dec. 2, 1999.

12. Jones interview.

13. Andrew Card Jr., interview with Martha Joynt Kumar, Washington, D.C., May 25, 1999. White House Interview Program.

14. Charles E. Walcott and Karen M. Hult, *Governing the White House: From Hoover through LBJ* (Lawrence: University Press of Kansas, 1995), p. 246.

15. Jones interview.

16. Rhett Dawson, interview with Martha Joynt Kumar, Washington, D.C., Apr. 10, 2000, White House Interview Program.

17. Jones interview.

18. Brady interview.

19. Background interview, Feb. 25, 2000.

20. Cicconi interview.

21. Patterson, *White House Staff*, pp. 384–85.

22. Brady interview.

23. Patterson, *White House Staff*, pp. 383.

24. Ibid., p. 327.

25. Leon Panetta, interview with Martha Joynt Kumar, Monterey Bay, Calif., May 4, 2000, White House Interview Program.

26. Background interview, Dec. 2, 1999.

27. Brady interview.

28. Card interview.

29. Brady interview.

30. Ibid.

31. Ibid.

32. Christopher Hicks, interview with Martha Joynt Kumar and Liz Griffith, Washington, D.C., Nov. 18, 1999, White House Interview Program.

33. Brady interview.

34. Cicconi interview.

35. Ibid.

36. Ibid.

37. Ibid.

38. Background interview, Dec. 2, 1999.

39. Ibid.

40. Patterson, *White House Staff*, p. 340.

41. Cicconi interview.

42. James Cicconi, interview with Bradley Patterson, Washington, D.C., Dec. 18, 1997.

The Office of Presidential Personnel

BRADLEY H. PATTERSON, JR.
JAMES P. PFIFFNER

ONE OF THE FIRST THINGS A NOMINEE FOR president must worry about is having in place an effective personnel-recruitment operation. This function is so important that the planning for it must begin well before the election, even though there is a danger that setting up the operation may appear presumptuous if word leaks to the press. As E. Pendleton James, President Reagan's personnel recruiter in 1980–81 said: "The guys in the campaign were only worried about one thing: the election night. I was only worrying about one thing: election morning. Presidential personnel cannot wait for the election because presidential personnel has to be functional on the first day, the first minute of the first hour. . . . [But] it has to be behind-the-scenes, not part of the campaign, and certainly not known to the public."[1]

"In the period before the election, how much of the identifying of jobs can be done?" former presidential assistant Bonnie Newman was asked. Her answer, "You can do almost 100 percent of it."[2]

Scope of the Office of Presidential Personnel

The person who will serve as director of this office ideally will have been designated early, even (perhaps secretively) as soon as the nominating convention concludes, or at the latest—publicly—immediately after election day. Whenever chosen, the same question faces the Office of Presidential Personnel designee: what tasks must be done before the inauguration?

The Size and Shape of the Noncareer Universe

What categories of positions are filled by political appointment, and how many positions are there in each category?

The following table shows the three categories, seven subcategories, and the numbers in each:

Figure 8. Presidential Political Appointments

Category 1: Full-Time Positions (almost All Established by Statute) Filled by Personal Presidential Appointment

Subcategory 1-A: PAS—Presidential appointees requiring Senate confirmation (cabinet secretaries and agency heads, deputy secretaries, under secretaries and assistant secretaries, as well as members of regulatory commissions, 185 ambassadors, 94 district attorneys. 94 U.S. marshals, 15 posts in international organizations, and 4 posts in the legislative branch)	1,125
Subcategory 1-B: PA—Presidential appointees not requiring Senate confirmation	20
Subcategory 1-C: Federal judges (most have lifetime tenure)—typical number of vacancies that need to be filled during a presidential term, out of a total of 868 federal judgeships—all requiring Senate confirmation	200

Category 2: Full-time, Nonpresidential, Noncareer Positions (Appointments Made by Agency Heads only with the Sanction of the Office of Presidential Personnel)

Subcategory 2-A: Noncareer positions in the Senior Executive Service (Upper-level positions)	720
Subcategory 2-B: "Schedule C" positions (Midlevel positions)	1,428

Category 3: Part-Time Presidential Appointee Positions (Established in Statute—Members of Advisory Boards and Commissions)

Subcategory 3-A: PAS—Requiring Senate confirmation	490
Subcategory 3-B: PA—Not requiring Senate confirmation	1,859
Total of Category 1, 2, and 3 noncareer positions of concern to the Office of Presidential Personnel:	5,842

Category 4: White House Staff Positions (Only Partially Limited by Statute, no Senate Confirmation)

Subcategory 4-A: Receiving formal, signed commissions from the president (assistants to the president and deputy assistants to the president)	80
Subcategory 4-B: Appointed under presidential authority (special assistants to the president and posts below—i.e., staff members for the White House, the first lady, the vice president, and the Domestic Policy, Economic Policy, and National Security Councils—excluding civilian and military details, the Secret Service, and other professional support staffs, White House Fellows, interns, and volunteers)	556

Total noncareer positions that can be filled by the White House during a typical presidential term:	**6,478**

Source: Bradley H. Patterson Jr., *The White House Staff: Inside the West Wing and Beyond* (Washington, D.C.: Brookings Institution, 2000), 220.

Some Facts about Noncareer Positions

The "PAS" (presidential appointment requiring Senate confirmation) and "PA" (discretionary presidential appointment) positions in Category 1, including most federal judgeships and the memberships on part-time advisory boards and commissions (Category 3), are created in statute. (Ambassadorships and a few judgeships are authorized not in statute but in the Constitution itself.) The number of statutory posts can be increased or decreased only by congressional action. The president personally approves each of these appointments.

The Senior Executive Service (SES) is the corps of professional federal managers just below the level of assistant secretary. By law, up to but not more than 10 percent of the positions in the SES may be filled on a noncareer basis. A department or agency head may propose a political candidate to be appointed to such a position, but it is standard practice that each noncareer SES appointment is cleared with the director of the Office of Presidential Personnel. Once White House approval has been signaled, the Office of Personnel Management grants "noncareer appointing authority" to the agency for the placement.

"Schedule C" positions are established by departments and agencies, but each such post must first be certified by the director of the Office of Personnel Management as being "policymaking" or "confidential." Once a Schedule C job is thus authorized, the department or agency head may appoint a person to the post. It has also been standard White House practice since 1981 that the director of the Office of Presidential Personnel approves each Schedule C appointment.

While both noncareer SES and Schedule C appointees are employees of the agencies in which they work, with their service being at the pleasure of the respective agency heads, the White House cannot be oblivious to the quality, and the commitment, of these noncareer people.

The Earliest Responsibilities of the Office of Presidential Personnel

As the nominating convention closes, it might seem obvious that the most pressing personnel task for whoever is the candidate would be thinking about his future cabinet choices. Not so, for an even higher priority is to determine who will be the potential president's White House staff associates. He should be prepared, at the very outset of the transition period, immediately to announce his decisions about the senior-most positions in the White House, especially his White House chief of staff and the top assistants who will head up the national security, domestic policy, and economic policy teams. These senior White House policy officers should be on hand first to advise the president as he subsequently makes the decisions on his cabinet. Experience has shown that this sequencing will help ensure the White House/cabinet teamwork that will be so vital in the administration to come. The Office of Presidential Personnel director should be among those who are designated early, though at the beginning he or she may not be—and later will not be—involved in picking White House staff members.

Identify Departmental Positions and Qualifications

The principal focus for the advance work of the personnel director should be the PAS positions. Although the total number of posts in this category is 1,125, the actual number requiring earliest placement is much smaller: the fourteen cabinet and seventeen agency heads. Three months before election day is not too early for both the personnel director and the presidential nominee to begin thinking about possible cabinet names.

Choosing—even thinking in advance about—potential cabinet secretaries and agency heads calls forth a special judgmental art. Since they reflect on who should belong on which list, the personnel director and the presidential candidate must aim to strike the right balance among seven desiderata:

1. Loyalty to the candidate and to the policies he espouses (that is, no books or other writings to the contrary—one remembers the case of Lani Guinier)
2. Competence in the field
3. Being of political benefit to the future administration
4. Diversity
5. Ability to manage large organizations
6. Familiarity with the processes of government in the nation's capital
7. Acceptability to the Senate

No potential nominee will shine in all these respects, but the candidates must meet each of these criteria to some extent. An eighth desideratum—in fact a sine qua non for *any* candidate—will be having security, financial, and tax records (one remembers the case of Zoe Baird and the "nanny tax") as well as a personal behavioral history (one remembers the case of John Tower) that will be beyond reproach in the eyes of White House lawyers and of the Senate. (Whether or not this eighth set of standards will be met can, of course, be determined only after postelection investigations.)

Even aside from the volume, the job of presidential personnel is complex, and coming to an agreement about a final nominee is difficult. As Bob Nash, director of presidential personnel in the Clinton administration, put it: "All the things you have to consider—geography, race, sex, senatorial, congressional, outside groups, White House offices. All these things. You just have to sort of make sense out of and you've got to make what you think is the best recommendation for the president and the country and the department. That's what you've got to do. And it's tough. It's really, really, really tough."[3]

Close behind the responsibility of compiling lists of possible candidates for cabinet and agency heads is the follow-up task of identifying a further group in the PAS category: potential deputy and under secretaries and assistant secretaries. The focus here may be influenced by the candidate's or the president-elect's own priorities—coming from the campaign or from his perception of the highest needs of the nation, for example, staffing soonest the departments handling education, health care, or national security. Reagan and James identified what they called "the key eighty-seven."[4] The same sevenfold balancing calculation must be made for each, but since many of these positions will bear specialized policy responsibilities, the identification of substantive competence becomes of greater importance. For these positions, the personnel director will need to probe: what specific skills will be required?

Even if the personnel chief has been put to work early, he or she will find that some useful resources exist that can aid in assembling ideas for the kinds of candidates needed. These resources include the six *Prune Books* (a prune is an "experienced" plum) compiled by the Council for Excellence in Government, in total covering over three hundred undersecretary and assistant secretary positions. Each book covers a different set of senior appointive posts and includes four-to-eight-page descriptions (gleaned from people who actually held the job) of the duties and responsibilities of each position and a list of the previous incumbents.[5]

Every four years, the Senate Governmental Affairs Committee and the

House Government Reform and Oversight Committee take turns to pub-
lish the catalogue *Policy and Supporting Positions,* colloquially known as the
"Plum Book." This publication lists, for every agency in government, all
policy positions, both career and noncareer, by job title and type of appointment. For every noncareer position (at any grade), it lists the name
and salary level of the incumbent. The "Plum Book," however, has only
limited usefulness to a future White House personnel director. While it
identifies which positions are in which category, it is of almost no help in
matching high-level candidates with job specifications because it provides
no information at all about the duties of any of the listed jobs or about the
skills required. It also appears only at election time, too late for effective
advance staff research, but its appearance on the scene promptly generates
tens of thousands of eager inquiries.

Ideas for potential candidates can come from many sources: the presidential and vice-presidential nominees will of course have immediate
prospects of their own. Their spouses may have strong views about personnel, although one former presidential personnel director considers that
it would be a "disastrous mistake" to inject presidential spouses into the
personnel decision-making process. Other favorites will emerge from the
campaign staff, major contributors, key members of Congress, supportive
lobbyists, and friendly interest groups. Thus, even well before election, not
only can a core group of perhaps two hundred positions be described but
also a preliminary list can be compiled of those who would possess the
above-described seven elements. Reagan personnel director Pendleton
James had been tapped for the job of personnel chief a year before the election. By the time the nominating convention ended, he had very quietly
established an office in Alexandria, Virginia, and, working with Reagan
and his principal associates, had started to develop lists of possible candidates. This would be an excellent model to follow.

Immediately Following the Election

The transition begins. Transition headquarters opens. By this time the personnel director *must* be designated—not some associate in a temporary
holding position, but the person who will actually become the director of
the White House Office of Presidential Personnel. Resumes, e-mails, and
phone calls soon flood into transition headquarters by the tens of thousands; applicants in person by the hundreds. The director must assemble a
large transition personnel staff—perhaps one hundred people, including a

corps of volunteers—and must develop systems for handling the immense volume of applications.

The outgoing president will typically have made a public announcement assuring the president-elect and the new administration team that he is offering full cooperation to ensure that the transition goes smoothly. Assuming that this injunction is taken seriously, the outgoing director and staff of the Office of Presidential Personnel can be expected to offer professional assistance to the new director and his associates. The White House has a computerized data file using the software program Resumix; the names in it will obviously be subject to erasure, but the new director can expect to be briefed on how the system works. Hopefully, there will be a much more comprehensive interchange between the two directors.

Another transition phenomenon pertinent to the personnel business is likely to take place: task forces may be invited by the president-elect (with the consent of the president) to visit each of the cabinet departments and afterward make recommendations to the president-elect concerning both policy and organizational matters. Typically, the members of these task forces see themselves as potential future political appointees in the very departments they are visiting and as having a "leg up" in the appointment process. The new personnel director will be under pressure on this score—but he or she must remember to accord the incoming cabinet secretary full participation in such decisions and not ignore that seven-segment measuring rod.

Identify the Vacant Positions

If the election has brought a switch in party, the changeover in the non-career ranks will, of course, be widespread; resignations of the outgoing political officials will be routine. Except for those with term appointments, almost all of the PAS and PA positions will be vacated. It is possible that outgoing cabinet members may bring to the new personnel director's attention special cases where it would be in the nation's best interest to arrange temporary continuity in a few noncareer posts; in other instances compassionate regard might allow an appointee to remain on the payroll "another month before reaching retirement age" or if "the spouse has just been diagnosed with cancer." The normal situation is the reverse: dozens of important jobs are being vacated—they cannot be left unfilled very long after January 20 without adversely affecting the government's own work.

If there is no change of party, the noncareer personnel environment is murkier—as it was when George Bush and his associates took over from the Reagan administration. The great majority of key political officeholders in the outgoing team will gladly leave—many just worn out and eager for a different scene. A few "true-blue" party loyalists, however, may want to stay on. They love what they are doing, have spouses with jobs in the area, children in local schools, and mortgages to pay. To them, resignation may seem a less-than-necessary option: they believe that the incoming president should in fact turn to their expertise and experience. The incoming personnel director is likely to be under much pressure—perhaps under some specific instructions—to give those arguments short shrift. The result can be—it was in 1988–89—a painful period. Bush's personnel director Chase Untermeyer recalled "in lots of the departments . . . the truest believers of Ronald Reagan . . . were abused. They were not treated in a dignified and polite and politically sensitive way. . . . That one area was dreadfully handled."[6]

A special word is necessary regarding members of regulatory commissions (such as the board of governors of the Federal Reserve System, or the Federal Communications Commission). These PAS positions are, by statute, term appointments—each for a specified number of years. A post of this type becomes vacant only when the term expires (or if the incumbent retires or dies prematurely). The statutes of such commissions typically require not bipartisanship but only that members from one political party not constitute more than a simple majority. This means that a president is free to fill a vacancy with a political independent—a fact that may come as a surprise to some partisans in Congress who would pressure the president to name certain "picks" of their own choosing.

In addition, ambassadors are all in the PAS category, but the secretary of state can be expected to insist that a large proportion of the appointees be from the top cohort of the career foreign service. Typically, the White House and the secretary work out a compromise that no greater than about 30 percent of the ambassadorial contingent will be nominated from outside of the career ranks.

Finally, when a Schedule C jobholder resigns, the position itself disappears. The agency must rejustify to the Office of Personnel Management the re-creation of the position before it can again be filled.

Select and Clear New Political Appointees

When inauguration day arrives, lucky is the personnel director who will even have time to witness the inaugural parade because of the other parade—one of supplicants—into the director's White House reception room. Typically, the director's one-hundred-person team of assistants during the transition moves over to the White House too.

In the new White House itself, the director of the Office of Presidential Personnel will want to make sure that several traditional rules are reaffirmed.

No other person or office in the White House is to make personnel *commitments*. The presidential personnel specialists will likely turn to the principal domestic, economic, or national security officers for advice about the selection of candidates. The political and legislative liaison staffs will funnel in streams of additional resumes from their own respective constituencies. Other members of the new White House staff, fresh from the campaign, will feel obligated to help their erstwhile buddies find jobs in the new administration. But when it comes to decision making, there can be only one point from which the final recommendation goes to the president: the director of the Office of Presidential Personnel. Even the president must pledge not to allow himself to be personally importuned to promise a job to anyone, bypassing the office review. Such end runs will undercut the process and make the Office of Presidential Personnel less useful to the president.

Cabinet heads are to be informed that the White House is to govern the selection of the political appointees in the departments—"all the way down." Some new cabinet and agency heads likely will want to boast: "The president has given me free hand to pick 'my' departmental subordinates," but that will simply not be the case, and it is clearly in the interest of the director of the Office of Presidential Personnel to make sure of this. What is meant by "all the way down"? It means that not only does the White House make the final decision on presidential appointments within each department but also that the director of the Office of Presidential Personnel signs off on *all* political appointments that a department or agency head wishes to make—that is, on Schedule C and noncareer SES positions as well. Every one? Pres. George H. W. Bush's second presidential personnel director, Constance Horner, warned: "Absolutely—every single one. I was quite fierce about this, because I saw it as a process of building future leadership. So it mattered to me what the quality of the appointee was, and it mattered to me what their decisional level was, and what their loyalty was, and their intellectual capability."[7]

In practice, this rule means that the director will, of course, engage in negotiations with the cabinet or agency head. Usually, this will result in an (almost always) amicable agreement as to the person to be chosen, but on occasion a determined cabinet secretary will appeal an Office of Presidential Personnel decision to the chief executive. A president who yields on too many such appeals immediately weakens the credibility of his personnel director.

From the above recitation and earlier comments, it will be obvious that the first weeks and months of a new presidential personnel director's tenure will be a period of constant, supercharged pressures; sticky, tangled bargaining; making as many folks disappointed or mad as one makes appreciative or pleased; and an overall smattering of chaos. The Office of Presidential Personnel staff must be competent and energetic enough to push its way through the intricate negotiations and preparations that are needed to put the director in a position to make final recommendations to the president. In each case, all eight of the above-described sets of criteria must be applied. The White House Political Affairs Office will help in ascertaining from party headquarters how active candidates were during the campaign and how much reward is appropriate. The Legislative Affairs Office will assist with informal checks on the Hill. Outside interest groups may need to be consulted, but one former presidential personnel director cautioned that in doing so one may only be giving a hostile advocacy group the opportunity to organize a campaign against the candidate.[8] (If federal judges are being proposed, it is the counsel rather than the director of the Office of Presidential Personnel who will carry the prime responsibility for the necessary vetting of such candidates.)

In many instances, the presidential personnel director will insist on interviewing some candidates personally to satisfy himself or herself that the men and women being recommended to the president are of top quality. In the Clinton White House, Presidential Personnel Director Bob J. Nash was careful to interview every PAS recommendation he made to the president. "I always interview PASs. I will interview every full-time PAS. . . . [O]ne time the president . . . had approved this full-time PAS. He said, 'that was a great recommendation you made' on whoever. 'Didn't you like him?' I said, 'Mr. President, I didn't meet him.' He said, 'don't recommend to me anybody that you don't meet.' From that day forward . . . I interviewed every full-time PAS. It takes a lot of time."[9] The director will ask the final question: "Are there ANY skeletons in your closet? I want to know. And if you DON'T reveal them now, and leave me to make a judgment call not knowing about them, finding some way to handle them, I will STILL find out about them, and then you are out, REALLY OUT."[10]

The personnel director must ascertain from the president the answers to three procedural questions: First, does the president want a single name proposed for each position or a group of alternative candidates (with one of them recommended by the director)? Second, does the president wish to have the vice president consulted about personnel recommendations? Third, what is to be the role of the White House chief of staff on personnel matters? With respect to the third point, memoranda of Presidential Personnel Director Untermeyer to the president would begin, "The Chief of Staff and I recommend."[11]

The president's approval (initials) on a personnel memorandum is only the intermediate step in the process. Afterward come the formal clearance procedures: it is at this point that the FBI starts its security-and-suitability investigation (which could take weeks), and the candidate produces his or her financial and tax records in minute detail. It is the counsel, not the personnel director, who will scrutinize the resulting reports and then notify the presidential personnel director if there is anything negative in those findings that would affect the candidate's suitability. If a candidate's financial holdings, for instance, reveal a possible conflict of interest with the job for which he or she is destined, the counsel or the independent Office of Government Ethics will require the candidate to work out a divestiture or similar "insulating" arrangement with the ethics officer of the department involved.

During this investigative period, the position will appear to be still unfilled—and thus may continue to attract new supplicants (and their supporters). It is difficult to tell them that the job is, in fact, no longer available. A final memorandum is sent to the president recommending his signature on the nomination papers. When that happens, the papers are dispatched to the Senate and a White House press announcement is released. These actions mark the conclusion of the recruitment phase for the appointee.

The Challenges and Pressures Facing the Director of the Office of Presidential Personnel

The atmosphere of the Office of Presidential Personnel is one of high pressure, especially at the beginning of a new administration. First, the office must be organized to suit the needs of the president and the new director. Then, the office must deal with pressures for appointments from Capitol Hill and mediate the conflict between the criteria that cabinet secretaries and White House staffers use to evaluate prospective nominees.

An Early Challenge: Organizing the Office Itself

The breakdown of specific internal duties within the Office of Presidential Personnel has tended to become standardized in recent administrations, and their respective organizational structures have reflected that breakdown:

1. The director (who has the title of assistant to the president) usually has two deputy directors (deputy assistants to the president) and a chief of staff.

2. There are typically three or four associate directors (with the title of special assistant to the president), each of whom handles a related cluster of departments and full-time regulatory bodies, that is, economic/financial, national security, human resources, or natural resources and the environment.

3. There is an associate director specializing in part-time boards and commissions.

4. There is an officer specializing in clearing Schedule C appointments.

5. There may be a congressional liaison officer and a political clearance officer.

6. There is an information systems officer.

As mentioned earlier, the Office of Presidential Personnel staff, during and in the months immediately following the transition, may number as many as one hundred people, several being volunteers. Later on, the staff tends to total between twenty-five and thirty-five. The patronage-placement network is in fact larger: early in the administration, White House presidential personnel directors often arrange to locate in the top office of each of the cabinet departments a political liaison who works with the Office of Presidential Personnel on noncareer appointments in the respective departments. "Our Gauleiters," as one presidential personnel director called them, may convene collectively in the White House for coordination sessions with their office comrades.

Figure 9.

President William Clinton
White House Office of Presidential Personnel
Spring, 2000

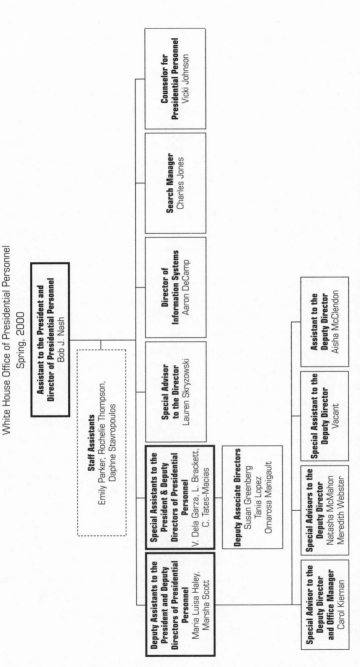

White House Interview Program (whitehouse2001.org). Based on data in *The Capital Source*, Spring, 2000, National Journal Group Inc., Washington, DC. *Key:* ——— = positions with "to the president" in their title; -------- = staff working for indicated assistant.

Bob Nash, presidential personnel director for President Clinton, felt that he could have used some additional help. Because of Clinton's promise to cut the White House staff by 25 percent, the Office of Presidential Personnel was down to twenty-five staffers late in the administration, so Nash had to depend on volunteers and interns. "I have about three volunteers who work back in the computer section because there is so much paper back there. . . . They're wonderful. We couldn't operate back there [without them]. . . . Then we have these interns. . . . I used to get about ten, eleven. Now I only get about six or seven. . . . So that's how I supplement my staff. . . . Now, if I didn't have the interns and the volunteers, I would be in trouble."[12]

Life for the Office of Presidential Personnel staffers is hectic, especially in the early months of an administration. Interviews with former members of the Presidential Personnel staff indicate that in the beginning they are often in seven days a week and that after several months things may slow down to "only" five and a half or six days a week. Workdays are often twelve to fourteen hours long at the beginning of an administration and ten to twelve after it is established. J. Bonnie Newman, associate director of the Office of Presidential Personnel in the first Bush administration, recalled running into a friend in the White House. "[H]e looked just awful. I asked what was the matter, and he said, 'I just had a call from my son on my cell phone. He was crying because he hasn't seen me in ten days. He had gotten up early but I had left earlier.' It was six thirty in the morning, so I don't know what time this poor kid got up to see his father." Newman also remembered the pressures of the job. "The entire time I worked in presidential personnel, everything you hear about having a gazillion new best friends the day you get into the job like presidential personnel is true." She had an average of 150 incoming telephone calls a day.[13] Jan Naylor Cope, her deputy director, said she herself worked "seven to seven" on weekdays and "pretty much worked every Saturday." Her first day in office, she received 300 phone calls from people asking specifically for her.[14] Douglas Bennett, director of the Office of Presidential Personnel in the Ford administration, recalled receiving 200 phone calls on a typical day and sending out 400–500 pieces of mail a day under his signature.[15] Chase Untermeyer remembered the pressure at the beginning of the Bush administration:

> I couldn't estimate [the number of phone calls each day]. At the start of the administration, it truly is ridiculously high, hundreds.

And I remember in the early days of the administration looking at my call sheets. It would be quarter of eight. . . . Here would be page after page of some of the most important people in the country, people who are used to having their calls taken immediately, let alone the same day, and here are people whose phone calls I simply could not and would not return. I was about ready to drop or I needed to eat and go home and get some sleep. There was no guarantee that I would be able to return their phone calls the next day.[16]

Some former presidential personnel directors interviewed recommended that the office have its own congressional liaison officer to help guide nominations and nominees through the Senate. "I think that having someone in presidential personnel whose sole job is to try and help shepherd people through that process would be helpful."[17] Others recommend that a press office would be helpful to handle the constant flood of press inquiries specifically about candidates and appointments. Another officer could focus on "tracking" the progress of candidates through the entire process, from recruitment to presidential nomination.

Pressures for Patronage from the Campaign and the Hill

According to Pendleton James, the pressures on the presidential personnel director are tremendous.

> There's not enough time in the day to get it done. . . . [M]y job was like drinking water from a fire hydrant. . . . There is so much volume coming at you, your mouth is only that big and the rest just sputters and spills on the floor. There just isn't enough time.
>
> . . . being the head of presidential personnel is like being a traffic cop on a four-lane freeway. You have these Mack trucks bearing down on you at sixty miles an hour. They might be influential congressmen, senators, state committee chairmen, heads of special interest groups and lobbyists, friends of the president's, all saying, 'I want Billy Smith to get that job.' Here you are knowing you can't give them all and you have to make sure that the president receives your best advice. So presidential personnel is buffeted daily and sometimes savagely because they want to kill that guy . . . because I'm standing in the way."[18]

Handling the demands for jobs for the party faithful is stressful for the president's personnel recruiter; people representing the party's campaign workers often complain that their loyal supporters are not getting enough jobs. Presidents Nixon, Carter, Reagan, and Bush were attacked publicly for not appointing enough party loyalists shortly after their elections.[19] As Pendleton James said, "presidential personnel is a mine field. Every appointment will create controversy somewhere along the line."[20]

According to Constance Horner, director of the Office of Presidential Personnel in the first Bush administration, the transition period is a particularly tension-filled time. "Anything that can reduce procedural chaos helps a lot because people are so paranoid and so atavistic during this period. It's like there's one lifeboat left and the city's in flames and everyone's trying to get on it. . . . And the degree of fear of shame that people experience—they're afraid of rejection in front of their friends and families—they are thought to be among those who might enter an administration and then time passes and they don't. People begin to ask. . . . [P]eople just go crazy."[21] Pendleton James tells this story about pressure from campaigns: "Regional political directors, none of them were getting jobs. These were advance people who worked in the campaign. They were very important people in the campaign, very important people. . . . They didn't know who Pen James was. . . . So they really rebelled against Pendleton James; [they were] very angry that none of them were being appointed to any post, mostly SESs and Schedule Cs. I tried to explain that . . . we've got to get the cabinet and subcabinet in place before we go down . . . , you'll just have to be patient. They weren't patient. They were angry and their anger was coming at me."[22] Finally, Lee Atwater, who had credibility with the campaigners, calmed them down and assured them that they would be considered for positions within the Reagan administration. The point is that the pressure for immediate action on jobs for campaigners is great, and the director of the Office of Presidential Personnel will be the focal point for that pressure.

Pressure from Congress is considerable. James said that he got some advice from the legendary Bryce Harlow, who had run congressional relations for President Eisenhower, during the Reagan transition. Harlow told him: "The secret to good government is never, ever appoint a Hill staffer to a regulatory job. That Hill staffer will never be the president's appointee. He or she will always be the appointee of that congressman or that senator who lobbied you for that job. And they will be beholden to that senator or to that congressman." After James's talk with Harlow, a senator came to talk with James and, after mentioning that sixty-four of the Reagan nominations had to go through his committee, demanded that several of his staffers be appointed to regulatory positions. Remembering Harlow's advice, James went back to the White House and asked Chief of Staff James Baker how to handle the situation. Baker said, "Give it to him."[23] Some pressures from Congress cannot be ignored.

Some friends of the president may have strong claims based on their political support but may not be qualified for high-level managerial positions. This is a predictable challenge for the presidential personnel director. But there is an art to dealing with the people who must be turned down for positions with the new administration. According to Constance Horner, one possibility is to appoint people to part-time and honorary positions.

> [F]or every person you choose, you're turning down ten, fifteen, twenty people who want the job. . . . [T]here is no way to do this and make everybody happy. . . . [T]here are numerous part-time boards and commissions that offer advice on environmental matters where people come to Washington four times a year and they discuss the issues and make recommendations. Sometimes those recommendations matter in policy outcomes, sometimes they are just a way of getting conversation going, but people will frequently be delighted to be chosen for one of those often honorary positions because what they're looking for is not really a full-time job; they're looking for service in the administration, a feeling of being part of it all, being able to insert "The Honorable" before their names.[24]

If a person is not qualified for a position of great authority, Chase Untermeyer advised, "that person can also be rewarded in other ways with advisory commissions or invitations to state dinners or other things that are within a gift of the president to do short of putting that person in charge of a chunk of the federal government."[25]

Conflict over Appointing the Subcabinet

While all PAS appointments are constitutionally the president's decision, the practical and prudential approach to subcabinet appointments (deputy, under, and assistant secretaries) is not quite so clear cut. In the 1950s and 1960s, when the White House did not have the recruitment capacity it has now, it was most often the cabinet secretary who suggested to the president the preferred nominee, and most often the president went along. In battles between the White House staff and the cabinet secretary, most often the cabinet secretary won.[26]

From the perspective of the cabinet member, the issue is one of building a management team for the department. Each person has to be chosen carefully with full consideration for how that person fits into the structure and how they will get along with the others on the team. Those in the cabinet are suspicious that the White House Office of Presidential Personnel will weigh very heavily the political service of the appointee and will neglect the expertise, managerial ability, and compatibility of the nominee with the other executives in the department.

The White House staff tends to suspect that cabinet secretaries are likely to recruit people who are loyal to the cabinet secretary but not necessarily to the president. Douglas Bennett described the process in the Ford administration: "You start at the top and then you present the cabinet officer with a list of candidates for deputy and then for the subcabinet posts within his department or her department. You don't say, 'Okay, you're a cabinet officer; you pick the rest.' That won't happen because these are all appointees of the president. They're not appointees of Secretary Jones; they're appointees of President Ford. And they understand that. Now they'll weigh in on those, which they appropriately should. So you have that at the start and it's really the dignity of the process and efficiency and logistical-operational ability."[27] From the very beginning, the Reagan administration decided to control political appointments tightly in the White House. Pendleton James explained that some earlier presidents had failed to make sure that subcabinet appointments were controlled by the White House. "Nixon, like Carter, lost the appointments process."[28] One danger is that a newly selected cabinet nominee will ask the president for the authority to appoint their own team. But agreeing to that is a big mistake. So, according to James, "We didn't make that mistake. When we appointed the cabinet member—he wasn't confirmed yet. We took him in the Oval Office; we sat down with the president. . . . And we said, 'All right . . . we want you to be a member of the cabinet, but one thing you need to know before you accept is we, the White House, are going to control the appointments. You need to know that.'"[29]

If a cabinet secretary–designate expresses annoyance at the heft of the Office of Presidential Personnel's transition shop, one former director suggested that the president-elect make a succinct speech:

I'd like to introduce you to my assistant for presidential personnel. This individual has my complete confidence. This individual has been with me many years and knows the people who helped me get elected here. PS: While you were in your condo in Palm Beach during the New Hampshire primary, these people helped me get elected so you could become a cabinet secretary. Therefore, I will depend upon the assistant for presidential personnel to help me see that those people who helped us all get here are properly rewarded. Now, cabinet secretary–designate, you may very well have people who are important to you and whom you want to bring in to the administration. I say by all means; we want to see those people. But in the event of a tie, my view as president is to help those people who helped me get here.[30]

Of course, if a member of the cabinet is a close friend of the president, that person will have more leeway in selecting his or her subordinates. Even the Reagan administration presidential personnel office did not have absolute control. But Chase Untermeyer maintained that White House control is important for political as well as constitutional reasons. When considering Schedule C appointments, one cabinet secretary asked him, "You mean I have to hire somebody just because they worked in the campaign?" Untermeyer replied, "Yes." But some kind of cooperative arrangement has to be worked out so that both the cabinet secretary and the White House staff can agree on most nominees. Untermeyer pointed out that if the White House jams somebody down the throat of a cabinet secretary, that person can be frozen out of the action at the department level and thus not be an effective appointee. "[I]f truly the White House does dictate appointees without any cooperation, give and take, with the cabinet secretary, then the appointee may well arrive in that department and walk in to his or her beautiful office but never be told about the staff meeting, or never get the key piece of paper, or not be invited to the retreat, or all the other kinds of things the cabinet secretary can do to freeze out somebody whom the cabinet secretary doesn't truly believe is one of them." Untermeyer's formula for balance between the White House and cabinet secretaries is simply: "No department or agency chief will have an appointee forced down his or her throat, that is, imposed by the White House. Conversely, every decision is a presidential decision."[31]

The Clinton administration handled subcabinet appointments by developing a list of potential nominees in the Office of Presidential Personnel and giving cabinet secretaries an opportunity to choose from among those on the list. According to Bob Nash, who worked in the transition personnel operation and later became director of presidential personnel, "we came up with a list of about ten names per PAS that were shared after going through a long arduous process. We worked seven days a week, fourteen and sixteen hours a day. Those lists would go to the president. He'd look at them and say all these are good people, share them with the secretary. The secretary would look at them, and the secretary would say 'that's the one right there I'd like to have.' That's the process."[32]

Each new administration must reach a balance between the presidential personnel and cabinet secretaries about recommending nominations to the president. What is important is that this accommodation be made explicitly and at the direction of the president rather than through drift.

Differing Definitions of Loyalty

In recruiting political appointees, the primary criterion is loyalty, but the definition of loyalty is not fixed. Some interpret it as service to the political party over the years, others see it as ideological compatibility with the president, still others as personal service to the candidate in the past or in the most recent campaign. Others argue that competence, professionalism, and the ability to manage ought to be primary criteria for appointment.

Fred Malek, the head of the White House Personnel Office for President Nixon, has argued that loyalty is certainly central in making political appointments, but construing that loyalty too narrowly might prematurely narrow the pool of talented candidates.

> Don't assume that somebody who hadn't worked for you in the past isn't loyal to you. Maybe they didn't know they could work for you. Maybe they haven't been involved in politics but there can be developed loyalty; it doesn't have to be proven loyalty. . . . Too many administrations, *too many* administrations get staffed by the campaign. The qualities that make for excellence in a campaign are not necessarily the same as make for excellence in governing. . . . To govern you need, I think, people who are of a somewhat more strategic and substantive bent than you necessarily need in a campaign. Campaigns are more tactical. . . . In governing I think you need a better sense of strategy and a better sense of management.[33]

Constance Horner agreed that there are pressures to appoint many lower-level (Schedule C) campaign workers in the government. "There are too many low-level political appointees. This really clogs up the process. . . . [T]he number of lower-level political appointees requires too much overhead and maintenance for the value to the president substantively or politically. . . . [T]hose special assistants interject themselves into the decision-making process beyond their substantive capacity because of the weight of their political influence. What that means is the other layers are created between the presidential appointee and the senior career civil service, and that weakens the utility that a president can get out of the civil service. . . . There's just too much overhead."[34]

Follow Through

The job of the Office of Presidential Personnel should not end with the nomination and appointment of presidential personnel. Further work is necessary, not only in orienting new appointees to Washington but also in evaluating their performance and providing support for spouses and families.

Orienting New Appointees

The nominees are going to wonder if the White House will help shepherd their way through the confirmation process, coach them about handling confirmation hearings, or lobby wavering senators? Unless the nominees are for cabinet-level positions or the Supreme Court, the answer—based on past experience—is no. There are hundreds of nominations, only dozens of the presidential personnel staff—and the latter are, in any case, preoccupied with the crush of still further recruitments. Unless a director can break loose some staff or hire specialists who will concentrate on being "shepherds," the new nominees will probably be left to sink or swim on Capitol Hill with little or no White House assistance. Prior to confirmation hearings, departmental "murder boards" may help grill a candidate, and departmental legislative-liaison officers may assist in smoothing the candidate's path not only for the Senate but also the House.

Fortunately, in 2001 The Presidential Appointee Initiative, an endeavor organized by Paul Light of the Brookings Institution and funded by The Pew Charitable Trusts, prepared the *Survivors Guide* for presidential appointees, with information on the nature of the process they were about to enter. The guide includes information about the ten forms that a nominee will be required to fill out—those needed by the White House for the investigative phase, and those mandated by the Senate committees that will hold the confirmation hearings. Even so equipped, the nominee is likely to have to go through the confirmation crucible pretty much alone.

Once a nominee is confirmed, a new need arises. Mirror of our contentious society, Washington is not really a friendly environment for federal executives, especially for a just-arrived, untutored senior political appointee. As one distinguished, veteran officer put it:

> Little in their experience has equipped newcomers to comprehend the complexity of government, the power of myriad special interest groups, and the level of increasingly intense scrutiny to which they will be subjected in both their public and private lives. The contemporary public policy and operational processes in government present to newcomers limitless chances for missteps and embarrassment. Many incoming appointees also have been immersed only weeks before in campaigns which have been exceedingly negative about Washington, its people, and its processes. They arrive, therefore, loath to listen to advice from either Washington career "bureaucrats" or former political appointees whom they either distrust as representing the other party, or believe have become captured by those entrenched denizens "inside the beltway."
>
> Burdened by these perceptions, these new political executives, however capable and well-intentioned, are in danger of stumbling during the first crucial months of an administration—causing grief to themselves and to the president who called them here, thereby injuring the chief executive's hard-won political capital.[35]

New appointees need orientation on how to be successful in Washington. This kind of introduction to life in the capital must come earlier and be of much wider scope than the substantive briefings that a new appointee will, of course, receive when starting on the job in his or her employing department.

It is responsibility of the Office of Presidential Personnel to supply this earlier and broader orientation—ideally in small "classes" at the White House. Congress has approved an amendment to the Presidential Transition Act authorizing orientation programs for the highest-level White House and cabinet designees during the transition period. But new appointees at the deputy, under, and assistant secretary level deserve White House orientation of this sort too, for it is in the president's own interest to have all his policy-level appointees learn to become effective federal executives. The Ford White House conducted an orientation program for its new appointees, repeating it several times during 1975 as new people joined the administration.[36]

Evaluating Performance

Except for members of regulatory commissions, and for department and agency heads personally, political executives in the executive branch report to—and presumably are evaluated by—their cabinet superiors. In the case of PAS or PA appointees below cabinet level, their performance reflects, for good or for ill, on the person who appointed them: the president. Recognizing this, the director of the Office of Presidential Personnel will look for ways to judge the effectiveness of the administration's political officials while they are on the job. A couple of examples from the recent past are instructive.

At a cabinet meeting in 1979, Carter chief of staff Hamilton Jordan handed out a two-page form. Cabinet officers were told to fill out one for each of their assistant secretaries and deputy assistant secretaries. The form contained thirty questions—for example, "How confident is this person?" "How mature?" "How stable?" "How bright?" "List 3 things about this person that have disappointed you." Unfortunately, the "White House Report Card" appeared on the front page of the *Washington Post* two days later. A month later the form was reproduced on T-shirts. The personnel chief later commented about this process, "It was very primitive."[37]

Then it was the Reagan staff's turn to be indelicate. During a White House meeting in 1984 of some two hundred midlevel appointees, the deputy director of the Office of Presidential Personnel gave a forceful talk. "You know, we are here to drain the swamp," she reminded them. "You have to keep that objective in mind. If it is not happening in the agencies where you are working, if there is foot-dragging, we need to know about it. It's getting to be report-card time!"[38]

Ford White House personnel chief Douglas Bennett remembered that cabinet officers themselves would come to the White House and ask for help in moving out noncareer underachievers. "We tried to find a soft landing for them somewhere," Bennett recalled, "Maybe in Samoa."[39] President Bush's first personnel director, Chase Untermeyer, made periodic personal visits to cabinet secretaries' offices to discuss how the PAS subordinates were performing, "just to keep the dialogue going."[40] On rare occasions, a resignation was arranged. His successor, Constance Horner, emphasized: "The OPP staff . . . depending on the interest and energy level of the staffers, rode tight herd on what was going on in the departments and agencies. And I was acutely aware of cases where failure was occurring anywhere in the [noncareer] SES level and up. I was especially aware of failure occurring at the agency-head level—and, in a couple of cases, made people move."[41]

The Clinton staff was equally informal and equally sensitive. Said Presidential Personnel Director Bob Nash: "I got a call from an office that said, 'This person is not performing.' I knew about it before; I talked to the person once before. Now, the next call is going to be, 'You've got about thirty days to look for something else.' No formal system. . . . We don't go through the system and say, 'Let's figure out . . . let's grade them all.' Don't do it."[42]

The examples from the Bush and Clinton experience add up to an important lesson: the Office of Presidential Personnel cannot avoid getting involved when it comes to taking action regarding senior political appointees who are found to be poor performers, but the actions they take must temper firmness with sensitivity.

Support to Spouses and Families

"We had a special program for families," said Bush presidential personnel director Untermeyer, who recalled a navy practice that supports families of men at sea. The Office of Presidential Personnel found a cabinet wife who was enthusiastic to help, helped her form a "presidential spouses' group," and provided lists of names and addresses of candidates being selected. "They would be able to find out about schools and houses and doctors and auto registration and which state has an income tax and who has to pay it—all those kinds of very practical matters for any prospective appointee." Spouses and families were invited to White House functions, South Lawn receptions. "It was a tremendous success," Untermeyer recalled, "critical for any administration."[43]

Conclusion

These several tasks in the area of managing the White House political personnel operation will ineluctably impend—for each presidential candidate. It is hoped that as they plan to discharge these responsibilities, presidential candidates will benefit from the experiences of presidencies of the recent past and thus aided in setting their own standards for a successful start. The following are prescriptions for success:

1. Follow the Reagan/Pendleton James example: start personnel planning early, keeping it confidential and separate from the campaign.

2. Put this planning in the hands of a person who (a) has the complete confidence of the candidate and (b) *is to be* the director of the Office of Presidential Personnel.

3. Select and announce senior White House staff first, then the cabinet.

4. Keep in the White House the right of approval for *all* cabinet and agency noncareer appointments.

5. Designate the Office of Presidential Personnel as the exclusive controller of that process; tolerate no end-runs to the president-elect/president.

6. Have an advance walk-through system that informs approved candidates what is ahead for them through clearance and nomination.

7. Provide a brief White House–sponsored orientation program for newly confirmed senior political appointees—begin one even during the transition for designees.

8. Talk with your predecessors.

According to Landon Butler, who worked on presidential personnel in the Carter administration: "There's just no substitute for the person who had your office before you telling you what it's like to be there, just what the nuts and bolts are, who to watch out for, who not to watch out for, what you can do and what you can't do, what he learned. That's the most immediate thing you can do."[44]

A presidential candidate and his director-designate of presidential personnel have to reflect on the fact that they face a daunting responsibility. Within a few short months after taking office, the winner must select, persuade, thoroughly evaluate, and install some two thousand extraordinarily capable men and women who will suddenly have to take on the management of the most complicated and demanding enterprise on earth: governing the United States. A few of them may be experienced in this endeavor; most, though, will be untutored. Many will accept financial sacrifice and leave quiet, comfortable lives only to be swallowed up in what they will rapidly discover is a roiling tempest of competition, cacophony, and contention: the environment of public life.

They will be scrutinized and criticized from all sides; pressures and demands on them will be merciless, praise and recognition meager. A few will stumble; some will become world famous. All of them, laggards and unsung heroes alike, will see themselves collectively vilified as "power-hungry Washington bureaucrats," but they must soldier on, faithfully helping execute the laws and "promote the general welfare" unto the least of their fellow citizens. They will need—and almost all of them will earn—the president's loyalty and support. In the end they will have had the opportunity—and the honor—of adding to the promise and the goodness of their country, and of the world itself. Can there be a more ennobling challenge?

Notes

1.   E. Pendleton James, interview by Martha Joynt Kumar, New York City, Nov. 8, 1999, White House Interview Program.

2.   J. Bonnie Newman, interview by Martha Joynt Kumar, Washington, D.C., Jan. 26, 2000, White House Interview Program.

3.   Bob J. Nash, interview by Martha Joynt Kumar and Terry Sullivan, Washington, D.C., Sept. 1, 2000, White House Interview Program.

4.   James interview.

5.   John H. Trattner, *The Prune Book: The 100 Toughest Management and Policy-Making Jobs in Washington* (New York: Madison, 1988); *The Prune Book: The 60 Toughest Science and Technology Jobs in Washington* (New York: Madison, 1992); and *The Prune Book* (New York: Madison, 2000).

6.   Chase Untermeyer, interview by Bradley H. Patterson, Jr., Washington, D.C., Sept. 4, 1997.

7.   Constance Horner, interview by Bradley H. Patterson, Jr., Washington, D.C., Sept. 29, 1997.

8.   Constance Horner, interview by Martha Joynt Kumar, Washington, D.C., Mar. 23, 1999, White House Interview Program.

9.   Nash interview with Kumar and Sullivan.

10.   Jay Matthews, "Are There ANY Skeletons in Your Closet," *The Washington Post,* May 2, 1995, p. D1.

11.   Bradley H. Patterson, Jr., *The White House Staff: Inside the West Wing and Beyond* (Washington, D.C.: Brookings Institution, 2000), p. 231.

12.   Nash interview with Kumar and Sullivan.

13.   Newman interview.

14.   Jan Naylor Cope, interview by Martha Joynt Kumar, Washington, D.C., June 8, 2000, White House Interview Program.

15.   Douglas Bennett, interview by Martha Joynt Kumar, Washington, D.C., Nov. 15, 1999, White House Interview Program.

16. Chase Untermeyer, interview by Martha Joynt Kumar, Houston, Tex., July 6, 1999, White House Interview Program.

17. Cope interview.

18. James interview.

19. James P. Pfiffner, (1996), *The Strategic Presidency,* p. 139; James interview.

20. James interview.

21. Horner interview with Kumar.

22. James interview.

23. Ibid.

24. Horner interview with Kumar.

25. Untermeyer interview with Kumar.

26. Pfiffner, *Strategic Presidency,* p. 66.

27. Bennett interview.

28. Pfiffner, *Strategic Presidency,* p. 67.

29. James interview.

30. Untermeyer interview with Kumar.

31. Ibid.

32. Nash interview with Kumar and Sullivan.

33. Fred Malek, interview by Martha Joynt Kumar, Washington, D.C., Nov. 23, 1999, White House Interview Program.

34. Horner interview with Kumar.

35. Dwight Ink, *Memorandum Supporting an Amendment to the Presidential Act of 1963* (Washington, D.C.,1999).

36. James P. Pfiffner, "Strangers in a Strange Land: Orienting New Presidential Appointees," in *The In-and-Outers: Presidential Appointees and Transient Government in Washington,* ed. G. Calvin Mackenzie (Baltimore: Johns Hopkins University Press, 1987), pp. 141–55.

37. Bradley H. Patterson, *Ring of Power: The White House Staff and Its Expanding Role in Government* (New York: Basic Books, 1988), p. 256.

38. Ibid.

39. Ibid.

40. Untermeyer interview with Bradley Patterson.

41. Horner, interview with Bradley Patterson.

42. Bob J. Nash, interview with Bradley Patterson, Washington, D.C., Apr. 20, 1999.

43. Untermeyer interview with Kumar.

44. Landon Butler, interview by Martha Joynt Kumar, Oct. 14, 1999, White House Interview Program. Landon Butler was deputy chief of staff for administration in the Carter administration.

Additional Sources

Mackenzie, G. Calvin. *The Politics of Presidential Appointments.* New York: Free Press, 1981.

Patterson, Bradley. Personal collection.

———. *The White House Staff: Inside the West Wing and Beyond.* Washington, D.C.: Brookings Institution, 2000.

Pfiffner, James P. *The Strategic Presidency: Hitting the Ground Running.* 2d ed. Lawrence: University Press of Kansas, 1996.

The White House Counsel's Office

MARYANNE BORRELLI
KAREN HULT
NANCY KASSOP

THE WHITE HOUSE COUNSEL'S OFFICE IS AT THE hub of virtually all presidential activity. Its mandate is to be watchful for and attentive to legal issues that may arise in policy and political contexts involving the president. To fulfill this responsibility, it monitors and coordinates the presidency's interactions with other players both in and out of government. Often called "the president's lawyer," the counsel's office serves, more accurately, as the *"presidency's* lawyer," with tasks that extend well beyond exclusively legal ones. These have developed over time, depending on the needs of different presidents, the relationship between a president and a counsel, and contemporary political conditions.

Today, the office carries out many routine tasks, such as vetting all presidential appointments and advising on the application of ethics regulations to White House staff and executive-branch officials, but it also operates as a "command center" when crises or scandals erupt. Thus, the more sharply polarized political atmosphere of recent years has led to greater responsibility, as well as heightened political pressure and visibility, for the traditionally low-profile counsel's office. The high-stakes quality of its work has led to a common sentiment among counsels and their staff that there is "zero tolerance" for error.

Law, Politics, and Policy

A helpful way to understand the counsel's office is to see it as sitting at the intersection of law, politics, and policy. Consequently, it confronts the difficult and delicate task of trying to reconcile all three without sacrificing too much of any one. The distinctive challenge confronting the counsel's office is to advise the president to take actions that are both legally sound and politically astute. For example, A. B. Culvahouse recalled his experience upon arriving at the White House as counsel and having to implement President Reagan's earlier decision to turn over his personal diaries to investigators during the Iran-Contra scandal. "Ronald Reagan's decision to turn over his diary—that sits at the core of the presidency. You're setting up precedents and ceding a little power. But politically, President Reagan wanted to get it behind him."[1] Nonetheless, Culvahouse added, the counsel is "the last and in some cases the only protector of the president's constitutional privileges. Almost everyone else is willing to give those away in part inch by inch and bit by bit in order to win the issue of the day, to achieve compromise on today's thorny issue."[2]

Indeed, Lloyd Cutler, counsel to both Presidents Carter and Clinton, observed that the most challenging part of the counsel's job is to be the one to tell the president no. Cutler noted that, in return for being "on the cutting edge of problems, the counsel needs to be someone who has his own established reputation . . . , someone who is willing to stand up to the president, to say 'No, Mr. President, you shouldn't do that for these reasons.'"[3]

One of the most essential tasks a counsel can perform for a president is to act as an "early warning system" for potential legal trouble spots before they erupt. For this role, a counsel must keep his or her "antennae" constantly attuned. Being at the right meetings at the right time and knowing which people have information or technical expertise in specific policy or legal areas are key. Lloyd Cutler noted, "the White House counsel will learn by going to the staff meetings, et cetera, that something is about to be done that has buried within it a legal issue which the people who are advocating it either haven't recognized or [have] pushed under the rug."[4]

Disaster can also strike when counsels do not make good use of the Justice Department's Office of Legal Counsel (OLC) for guidance on prevailing legal interpretations and opinions on the scope of presidential authority. The counsel must sift through the legal opinions and offer the president his or her best recommendation. Cutler described how this process works: "[OLC staffers] are where the president has to go or the president's counsel has to go to get an opinion on whether something may properly be done or not. For example, if you wish to invoke an executive privilege not to produce documents or something, the routine now is you go to the Office of Legal Counsel and you get their opinion that there is a valid basis for asserting executive privilege in this case. . . . You're able to say [to the judge who is going to examine these documents] the Office of Legal Counsel says we have a valid basis historically for asserting executive privilege here."[5]

The counsel's office is the channel through which most paper and people must pass on the way to the president and, equally, through which all outputs from the Oval Office must be monitored and evaluated. The unit exists in a fishbowl, is subject to searing public criticism when it makes the slightest misstep, and yet prompts intense loyalty among those who have served in it.

Functions of the White House Counsel's Office

Although the White House counsel's office has assumed different tasks under different presidents, the broader contours of its responsibilities began to take shape under Counsel John Dean during the Nixon administration and have been remarkably consistent since the Ford years.[6]

*Advising on the Exercise of Presidential Powers and Defending
the President's Constitutional Prerogatives*

The counsel's responsibilities associated with presidential powers are highly volatile. They involve such activities as routinely reviewing (and occasionally drafting) executive orders; reviewing pardon and commutation recommendations; approving covert action proposals; interpreting treaties and executive agreements; examining presidential statements for consistency and compliance with legal standards (and in anticipation of legal challenges); and participating in editing the State of the Union address. Tasks that have consistently related to the defense of a president's constitutional prerogatives are fewer in number. These have generally focused on issues related to executive privilege, war powers, and presidential disability or succession.

The present Washington political environment is notable for partisanship, polarization, and confrontation. Presidential actions are subject to

extraordinary scrutiny, and a twenty-four-hour news cycle accelerates the
pace of decision making, thus rendering any distinction between the "routine" and the more "crisis-laden" exercise of a president's constitutional
powers essentially artificial. As Clinton counsel Bernard Nussbaum concluded: "Small (and not so small) policy and political problems grow into
legal problems. It was my job to make sure that these political and policy
brushfires didn't become conflagrations."[7]

The counsel must therefore be well informed about political developments throughout the White House and the executive branch. Such
knowledge is crucial if a counsel is to manage the conflicts that can result
when Congress, a court, or an independent counsel exercising prosecu-
torial functions demands information from a sitting president who refuses
to accede. Despite the primacy of high-stakes politics in these stand-offs,
some political accommodation, rather than a purely legal answer, is typically the outcome. As many counsels have discovered, including Abner
Mikva, counsel to President Clinton, political considerations often over-
ride the best legal judgments about the appropriate presidential response.
"I think this president operated on the premise pretty much and I certainly
did that whatever the legal consequences or legal parameters were of executive privilege, if Congress really wanted something, politically it almost
was impossible to deny it. The more you stood on privilege, the more you
pointed to precedents, the more you showed these are the things that the
president didn't turn over, the more they could make political hay out
of it."[8]

In relative terms, the counsel's role in regard to war powers has been
less controversial. As chair of the War Powers Committee, the counsel is
responsible for notifications to Congress. In keeping with presidential
views that the War Powers Resolution is unconstitutional, however, counsels have provided Congress with a minimum of information "in the interest of comity." In the words of A. B. Culvahouse, "There is a real kabuki
dance that was done. You sent a notice up to the Hill while protesting all
the time that you're not providing notice."[9] Like a kabuki dance, the war
powers dialogue is often ceremonial, lacks a clear beginning or ending, and
reveals much about the competition for political power. Typically, precedent is followed closely, with past letters serving as models for correspondence.

Presidential disability and succession also require the counsel's attention. Culvahouse has commented on the recurring issue of temporary
presidential medical incapacity: "This is an area where the lack of an insti-

tutional memory is atrocious. The White House should not have to re-invent a process each time the POTUS [president of the United States] has surgery. We did the same thing when President Reagan had surgery (I think for skin cancer) in '87/'88."[10]

Further complicating the counsel's work as a protector of presidential powers and constitutional prerogatives is the lack of clarity associated with the counsel's responsibilities as an advocate. The White House counsel provides legal advice to the *office* of the presidency, not to the *individual* president. As such, the counsel protects the powers of the office within the constitutional order of separated powers. Determining whether the office or the individual is under attack, however, may be difficult, according to Peter Wallison.

> In fact, when I was first introduced to this job by Fred Fielding he said to me, "You are counsel to the office of the presidency. You are not counsel to the president." . . . However, in practice, it's not a very useful guide, because you really don't know—when issues like Whitewater come up—whether you're representing the president or the presidency. . . . But as soon as it becomes clear—and there's no bright line here—that this isn't just noise by political opponents, but in fact relates to the president's personal conduct, then the president should have his own lawyer.[11]

Identifying and drawing these distinctions often has generated controversy. For instance, Clinton counsel Bernard Nussbaum was widely viewed as failing to differentiate between advocacy on behalf of the office and on behalf of an individual president. For his part, Nussbaum wrote in his resignation letter that he left "as a result of controversy generated by those who do not understand, nor wish to understand, the role and obligations of a lawyer, even one acting as White House counsel."[12]

Overseeing Presidential Nominations and Appointments to the Executive and Judicial Branches

White House counsels advising about presidential nominees and appointees to the executive branch typically have focused on nominations to the top Justice Department positions and to the general counsel positions in the departments and agencies. Nussbaum bluntly stated that his office "appointed the attorney general, head of the FBI, Justice Department officials (Dellinger—I sent him over to OLC from the White House counsel's office)."[13]

White House counsels also stressed their need to appoint a counsel to the National Security Council (NSC) staff. Lloyd Cutler argued for appointing the NSC counsels to the White House counsel's office rather than to the NSC staff. C. Boyden Gray emphasized the importance of a low-key NSC observer. "We worked out a deal that I could name as [National Security Assistant Brent Scowcroft's] deputy legal advisor to the NSC, Steve Rademaker. . . . But that can be tricky. It was tricky and a huge problem in Iran-Contra. . . . Scowcroft agreed that I should never be in a situation like that. That's why he allowed me to have Rademaker in there."[14]

The extent to which the counsel's office has been involved in the judicial appointment process has differed across administrations.[15] In several recent administrations, the White House counsel oversaw the process from start to finish: the counsel chaired the Judicial Selection Committee, supervised the vetting and clearance process, and prepared the nominee for confirmation. In every administration the judicial nomination process required the careful coordination of several White House offices, consultation with the Justice Department, and extended negotiations with senators.

The selection process varies for district, circuit, and Supreme Court nominations. Senators tend to be more involved in nominations to the U.S. district courts than they are in nominations to the courts of appeal or, especially, to the U.S. Supreme Court. Partisanship, though, plays an important role in determining the amount of influence that each player will have in the process, as A. B. Culvahouse explained. "Unlike the Supreme Court, with courts of appeal and district courts you had to deal with the local Republican, in our case senators, if there were senators. If there weren't senators, the governors, congressmen, and congresswomen. District courts, I seldom got involved. . . . Courts of appeal, I would more often get involved. There would be disputes between the senators and the Justice Department. There would be disputes between maybe two Republican senators from the same state, between the governor and the more senior congressman or congresswoman."[16]

Yet over time the selection process has shifted from being centered in the Justice Department to being firmly ensconced in the White House, albeit with the status of the attorney general always a factor. Carter counsel Robert Lipshutz encountered considerable resistance from the Department of Justice when he attempted to participate in judicial selection. "[White House involvement in judicial appointments] was a struggle within the Justice Department because, number one, the White House was stepping in to what many, particularly career people, and even Griffin [Bell, the attorney general] too, felt should be strictly their prerogative, and that is helping the president pick the judges."[17] White House involvement in lower-court nominations increased during the Reagan years and had become routine by the time Bill Clinton took office. According to Nussbaum. "The judicial selection process is centered in the White House Office. A lot of other White House counsel's offices did not have the breadth and authority we had (maybe because of [Vincent W.] Foster and his access to the first lady). We had special responsibility for court of appeals and Supreme Court appointments."[18]

From the Reagan years onward, the Judicial Selection Committee, chaired by the counsel, typically included members of the White House counsel's office and the Department of Justice. In the Clinton administration it also included representatives from the first lady's office and the Office of Legislative Affairs. The selection committee's assessments have been both legal and political, weighing the potential nominee's legal philosophy and the likelihood of Senate confirmation. "Well, it's all done in conjunction with the Department of Justice and it's pretty obvious to any lawyer who the candidates are. It's not rocket science. The question is always, 'Can you get the person you really [want]?' What's the matrix of confirmability with whom you really want to go with? You can't do your ideal person, usually, because there's a confirmation problem, or there's a background problem, or there's a money problem, or there's something. So it never lines up perfectly."[19] Members of the Clinton counsel's office were invited to the personal interviews with prospective lower federal court nominees, which senior officials in the Justice Department's Office of Policy Development conducted. Counsel staff also contacted senators about possible nominees, working with senior members and staffers of the Senate Judiciary Committee.

In addition, the office's supervision of vetting and clearance (including FBI and IRS background checks and completion of Form 278 and financial disclosure forms) for all presidential nominees to the executive and judicial branches has involved the counsel in the nomination and appointment process. The time and resources consumed by such reviews are extraordinary.[20]

When the background checks were complete—or even while they were progressing—decisions had to be made about whether to proceed with the nomination or appointment. In each administration, White

House counsels noted one set of standards for appointments, another for nominations (for which standards typically varied with the visibility of the position).

> [Y]ou'd have some people that you might never send up to the Hill for confirmation, but because they were strong allies of the president, supporters and/or were people that had a lot to offer, you might appoint them to the President's Foreign Intelligence Advisory Board rather than nominate them to be undersecretary of defense because the president has unilateral appointment authority. Maybe they go to a Schedule C position in OMB [Office of Management and Budget] or DAS [deputy assistant secretary], Treasury, or whatever. You were pretty darn pure about cabinet people, deputy secretar[ies]. We were awfully pure about State, Defense, Treasury, [and] Justice.[21]

Then, when the nominations were sent to the Senate, negotiations had to be conducted about the legislators' access to the reports. "How much of the FBI files do they get to see[?] We conduct the search; we do the FBI for our benefit, not for their benefit. . . . That was subject to enormous negotiation. . . . Huge fights over that. . . . You have to negotiate them one by one."[22]

Beyond vetting the nominees, the counsel's office sometimes prepared them for the confirmation hearings. "We [the Reagan administration] did a lot of murder boards, not just for judicial nominees but for a lot of people. I probably did fifty murder boards in my twenty-two months. . . . You get a bunch of lawyers and legislative types pretending to be senators and acting like horse's rear ends. . . . What you want to do is anticipate questions, to make it more difficult for him or her than it is going to be in fact, and hit all of the areas that he or she is going to be questioned about. . . . There should be an understanding that a good enough answer is good enough. We're not striving for perfection here—we're striving for B-plus."[23]

Advising on Presidential Actions Relating to the Legislative Process

Congressional relations are a daily fact of life for the White House staff and, therefore, for the counsel's office. In recent administrations this has involved counsel aides in reviewing legislative proposals; reviewing bills presented for signature or veto, and drafting signing statements and veto messages; reviewing State and Defense Department authorizations and appropriations proposals; drafting budget rescissions and deferrals; participating in the negotiations associated with Senate treaty hearings; and joining legislative negotiations concerning policy, document requests, treaties, and nominations.

The extent to which the counsel's office has participated in policy negotiations has varied within and across administrations. The appointment of a close presidential colleague as White House counsel may allow the office to enter into more substantive policy discussions. C. Boyden Gray acknowledged, with qualifications, his influence on several key legislative negotiations.

> [Pres. George H. W. Bush] kept drawing me into the Civil Rights Bill in 1990–91. I didn't really want to do that because it was very difficult politically, but he kept yanking me back into it. . . . But I would say that civil rights was legal policy, not necessarily part of the counsel's office historically any more than the ADA [Americans with Disabilities Act] was. I did very little on the ADA act. . . . I was involved very little, maybe ten or twenty hours worth. . . . The hours I spent were very important, it turned out, but I was not involved in the day-to-day negotiation of the language or the lobbying. . . . I had to have permission to work on the Clean Air Act. I wanted to work on it because I had an interest in it but it was something that [Chief of Staff John] Sununu was wary about and the president was a little nervous about because of the time it would take from other responsibilities.[24]

At a minimum, counsels have routinely been consulted about legislative matters. The resultant advising typically has involved as much politicking as it has lawyering. For example, the Reagan and first Bush administrations seized upon signing statements, which are drafted by the counsel's office, as opportunities for statutory interpretation by the executive. These presidents used signing statements to urge courts to give the same legal weight to the executive intent of legislation as they traditionally have given to its legislative intent. Accordingly, the counsel's office became deeply involved in the associated political and policy debates.

*Educating White House Staffers about Ethics Rules
and Records Management and Monitoring for Adherence*

Perhaps the most prominent of the newer demands confronting the counsel's office is the intensified scrutiny of ethical matters. This has generated the need for a central coordinator alert to potential problems and able to take preemptive (or corrective) action. Such an emphasis involves counsel staffers in a range of activities, including distinguishing between White House expenses and campaign expenses; reviewing presidential travel; approving requests for appointments with the president and monitoring them for propriety, seemliness, legality, and executive privilege issues; responding to document requests and subpoenas directed to the president and to other White House and executive-branch officials by congressional committees and independent counsels; and serving as the ethics officers for the White House staff and executive-branch political appointees. In C. Boyden Gray's view, ethics laws "are quite complicated and obscure and overworked and ought to be deregulated."[25] Yet past counsels agree that the work is essential to a president's early success, for it allows an administration to put its own people in place, establish responsible procedures, and advance its policy initiatives.

Federal ethics statutes and regulations typically are more stringent than those enacted in the states. Likewise, the standards for the legislative and executive branches are different, creating the need for careful briefings. Counsels, therefore, have circulated a detailed ethics memo throughout the White House and also have met with aides at the beginning and end of each individual's White House service.

The need to educate and monitor staffers is particularly acute during campaign seasons, both congressional and presidential. Then, the counsel's office staff provides general briefings and memoranda about campaign activities. Changes in the associated statutes may create an even greater need for this information. Clinton counsel Abner Mikva recalled: "[W]e had two very active ethicists in the Office. One of them was Beth Nolan and the other was Cheryl Mills. . . . So the driving force was that the Hatch Act had just been amended and it had caused some changes. It now allowed people to get more involved than they had been previously."[26]

As is suggested by the counsel's role in responding to document requests and subpoenas directed to members of the White House staff and other executive-branch officials, many counsels also have had to oversee investigations. Whether conducted by independent counsels or congressional committees, these proceedings have consumed much of the counsel's resources. Lloyd Cutler remarked in this regard:

> My first job [in the Clinton administration], which occupied the bulk of my time really, was to look in to the so-called White House–Treasury relationship having to do with the RTC [Resolution Trust Corporation] in reference to the Justice Department of the whole Whitewater matter. . . . Then I had to look into the Espy case; I had to look into the Cisneros case, et cetera. . . . A lot of [developing ethics rules for the White House staff] was done in collaboration with the so-called Office of Legal Ethics, which is an independent quasi–executive branch agency, and which has the responsibility under the various ethics statutes to write regulations, give opinions as to what you can and cannot do.[27]

Bernard Nussbaum described Washington as practicing a "culture of investigation."[28] That environment is not likely to change in the near future. Although the expiration of the independent-counsel statute almost certainly will alter the investigatory process, investigations will doubtless continue with profound implications for the counsel's office.

Handling White House Contacts with the Department of Justice and the Rest of the Executive Branch

Depending on the course of politics and policy in an administration, the White House counsel routinely interacts with most executive-branch departments and agencies. Because of the nature of its responsibilities, the Department of Justice is especially important.

Department of Justice

Three factors have influenced the extent and nature of a White House counsel's contact with the Department of Justice: the scope of the president's judicial agenda, including judicial nominations; the strength of the president's relationship with the attorney general; and the relative activism of the White House counsel and the attorney general as policymakers. A larger judicial agenda creates the need for more contacts with Justice. Similarly, a strong presidential relationship with an activist attorney general may establish a line of communication that often excludes the White House counsel.

Former counsels strongly recommend that the counsel's office function as a gatekeeper for *all* contacts between the White House and the Department of Justice: "all requests for OLC opinions had to go through me, all communications with the department had to go through my office. . . . [T]here were certain exceptions, but no one could call over to the deputy attorney general and the solicitor general directly; they had to go through me. My typical point of contact was the deputy attorney general for everything except OLC opinions, then I would call the head of OLC." This oversight is designed to ensure that communications between the White House and the Justice Department are properly conducted. Any effort to influence the legal judgments of the department would generate significant difficulties for an administration. Reagan counsel Culvahouse recalled, for instance, that departmental statements of administrative policy were routinely reviewed *unless* Justice was issuing them.[29]

Attorney General

The attorney general and the White House counsel appear, at first glance, to have similar advisory roles and jurisdictions. Notwithstanding differences in accountability (for example, the attorney general is subject to Senate confirmation) and location, the distinctive contributions of the White House counsel and the attorney general more often have been negotiated through practice than by invoking abstract principles. Conflict has occurred frequently, and presidential libraries contain numerous memoranda of understanding between attorneys general and White House counsels.

Office of Legal Counsel

The resources of the OLC—including its institutional memory—render the unit an invaluable source of legal expertise for the White House counsel. Quite simply, the counsel's office cannot provide all the information and the advising that an administration needs. C. Boyden Gray elaborated:

OLC is the single most important legal office in the government. More important really in terms of scholarship and memory and research—White House counsel's office doesn't really have the staff to do all [that] and they shouldn't. It should be done in OLC. . . . [T]he White House doesn't go to court without the department. . . . OLC was a huge problem for us in the sense that they were putting on a brake. We were free to ignore their advice, but you knew you did so at your peril because if you got into trouble, you wouldn't have them there backing you up, you wouldn't have the institution backing you up. . . . When in doubt, ask them and they'll tell you where the landmines are.[30]

Several other counsels echoed Gray's description of the OLC as a formidable ally and a significant check on the White House. Precisely because of the similarities in their responsibilities, however, the relationship between the two can be highly competitive. Both are recognized as legal experts immersed in politics and policy. The consequent blurring of their jurisdictions only exacerbates tensions.

[T]he real conflict between offices, inherent conflict, is between the White House counsel's office and the Office of Legal Counsel . . . because the White House counsel's office is growing and growing and is acquiring more and more capabilities to do [the] kind of research and analysis that the Office of Legal Counsel does, and it does it for the president. The White House always wins over the agencies, always, because they're closer to the president. So they have first dibs, if you will, on any issue that comes up to the presidential level. If there's a constitutional question about the president's power, if they want, they can make that decision on their own without consulting the OLC. Whenever you get a situation like that where some group has first opportunity and doesn't even have to inform the other group, over time that first group is going to grow larger and larger and more competent and eventually freeze out completely the Office of Legal Counsel.[31]

Similarly, Gray has stressed that the ambitions of the White House counsel's office can endanger an administration. He advises reestablishing the OLC as an influential legal commentator, concluding that the advantages gained from the OLC's insights far outweigh any disadvantages resulting from its sometimes critical stance.[32]

Still, this competitive relationship does reflect differences between the units. The White House counsel is appointed by the president and does not require Senate confirmation. The members of the Justice Department include presidential appointees who are subject to Senate confirmation, nominees who need not be confirmed, and careerists. Thus, department officials have numerous and crosscutting loyalties. Further, although the president's claim to executive privilege for communications with the White House counsel has been delimited in recent years, the Reagan administration may well have sacrificed the possibility of presidents successfully making such claims about the OLC.

> [I]t had to do with a request by the Senate Judiciary Committee for all of William Rehnquist's files when he was head of the Office of Legal Counsel at the Justice Department. . . . I thought that was simply harassment, and I thought they were trying to create the kind of issue they could use to stop the nomination. I and the person who was then head of the Office of Legal Counsel in the Justice Department both felt this was a good executive privilege claim because the Office of Legal Counsel is the lawyer for the entire government, and in effect for the president, and everyone discloses everything to them to get rulings about legal issues. The whole underpinning of the attorney-client privilege, which is part of the executive privilege, is to get people to disclose all relevant information so you can give them the right advice. I thought, if there was ever a case, this was it. So I sent a memo to the president saying I thought he ought to claim executive privilege in this case, but [Attorney General Edwin] Meese did not like at all that idea. We debated it in front of the president, and the president decided he wouldn't claim it. . . . In the future if someone wants the files of the Office of Legal Counsel, they are more likely to get them because this precedent exists.[33]

Clearly, then, requesting a legal interpretation from the OLC is a strategic undertaking. If the counsel does not involve the OLC—or, having received the OLC's interpretation, sets it aside—the White House is isolated and will lack support for its actions. This is risky and even dangerous. C. Boyden Gray, for example, unequivocally concluded that the White House should never go to court without Justice's support.[34] At the same time, the OLC is staffed by experts who cannot claim executive privilege and, in any event, have allegiances that extend beyond the White House.

Other Departments and Agencies

The White House counsel's contacts throughout the rest of the executive branch are extensive. At the very least, the counsel's office communicates with the general counsels of departments and agencies and processes the paperwork associated with every presidential nominee or appointee. Indeed, with the notable exception of the Justice Department, the White House counsel typically communicates with the executive-branch departments and agencies through the general counsels.

> We used to have more or less monthly meetings of all the general counsels. . . . It's a little more difficult to meet with the general counsels of the so-called independent agencies, as you know, but we do meet even with them on some matters. . . . A lot of it has to do with the ground rules for executive privilege and turning documents over to Congress which we don't think should be turned over to Congress but which the department under the thumb of Congress always wants to turn over without ever consulting the president, whose privilege it is not to provide them.[35]

C. Boyden Gray added that exceptions to this rule occurred only when the secretary or the agency chief executive had matters to discuss with the White House counsel. Occasionally, Gray said, he would speak with the deputy secretary.[36] Again, the Justice Department was the standard exception. The White House counsel and the attorney general typically communicated with each other daily.

Principal Relationships in the White House

Within the White House Office, the counsel's principal relationship—and greatest source of influence—has been with either the president or the chief of staff. To whom the counsel reports has frequently been a product of individual counsels' past professional relationships, and this authority relationship has been established at the time of appointment. Clarity is essential here if the president wishes to avoid destructive competition between two units that are crucial to the success of the administration and its policy agenda.

The President

In electing to have the White House counsel report directly to them, presidents often have appointed individuals who were their longstanding friends or professional colleagues.[37] Even so, counsels have faced various challenges to their position and influence. The White House staff is likely to include a number of longtime presidential colleagues, all of whom may compete for access to the Oval Office.

Of course, even if the counsel is able to sustain a close relationship with the president, there is no guarantee that the president will seek or follow the advice provided. Pres. Gerald Ford's decision to pardon former president Richard Nixon, arguably the most significant legal decision of his administration, reportedly was made without any consultation. Counsel Philip Buchen provided only post hoc support and legal reasoning.

Two administrations have recruited counsels to raise the profile and significantly reestablish the counsel's office within the Washington community. Pres. Jimmy Carter appointed Lloyd Cutler to meet these needs; Pres. Bill Clinton named Cutler, former congressman and U.S. Court of Appeals judge Abner Mikva, and then former U.S. attorney and D.C. Corporation counsel Charles Ruff. Cutler, in particular, has stressed that he entered office with a promise of direct communication with the president.

> When I was asked by the president [Carter] to take this job, it was a midlife crisis of his administration, the so-called malaise period. I said, "What kind of a role do you want me to play?" I knew him, but I didn't know him that well. He said, "I want you to play sort of a Clark Clifford role." I got that in writing and, of course, Clifford was so venerable and such a great storyteller, everybody thought that Harry Truman never made a move without consulting Clark Clifford. And every time I got left out of a meeting, I would go to [Chief of Staff Hamilton] Jordan or I would go to the president and I would say, "I think that Harry Truman would have wanted Clark Clifford in this meeting." I was older than all the rest of them, so nobody could gainsay me.[38]

The White House Counsel and Presidential Privileges

The issue of confidentiality in the president's communications with the White House counsel has been a matter of intense concern. Of the various legal privileges that a president or a counsel *might* claim—executive privilege, government attorney–client privilege, work-product protection, deliberative-process protection, and common-interest doctrine—most salient are executive privilege and government attorney–client privilege.[39]

Because the White House counsel's office is in the unique position of providing *both* political and legal advice to the president, navigating the shoals of presidential privileges is an especially tricky venture. Judicial acceptance of a privilege claim is determined by many factors.[40] Varying combinations of these factors will produce different judicial outcomes, making for complex and unpredictable results.

The Clinton administration was embroiled in numerous legal controversies in which it vigorously asserted a whole host of privilege claims, and it found little comfort in the resulting federal court decisions. In contrast, most other White Houses found ways to assert such claims but ultimately chose to resolve the conflicts through compromise. In essence, the Clinton administration forced the issue into the judicial process, and the courts ruled against it, narrowing considerably any maneuverability for future claims.

Chief of Staff

The Reagan administration chose an alternative authority relationship in which the White House counsel reported to the chief of staff. Reagan's White House counsels had previously been professional colleagues of the chiefs of staff. Even so, a change in the chief of staff did not necessarily result in the appointment of a new counsel.[41] Although reporting to the president through the chief of staff might appear to be a disadvantage, Culvahouse disagreed. "[Howard Baker] is my mentor and my friend. He was my ace in the hole in the White House. I think to the extent I was an effective White House counsel [it was] because he gave me a lot of support as did the president. But people did not try to go around me or over me very frequently and never very successfully." Still, the Reagan counsels presided over an office that was widely seen as being focused more on law than on policy. "In the Reagan White House, the counsel's office was viewed as sort of an additional final check. Unlike . . . some other White House counsel's offices, we didn't really have a policy agenda. We felt like we were to be honest brokers as well as lawyers."[42] It may be that having the counsel report to the chief of staff rather than directly to the president contributed to changing the orientation of the office.

White House Staff

The White House counsel's office is in contact with virtually every unit in the White House. The consequent dialogues and negotiations add immeasurably to the office's workload. Tight deadlines compound the difficulties. "[For] everything else [apart from Iran-Contra] there were lots of cooks, lots of principals, and lots of lawyers, and sometimes just trying to reach a decision or trying to force a decision in a timely way tended to be a lot of what I did. . . . The timing was forced by your own judgment or sometimes you'd have deadlines. Sometimes you'd have the ranking Republican on the committee calling up and saying if you don't tell us what you think, the committee is going to go forward tomorrow regardless."[43]

The following are examples of the units with which the counsel's office routinely has established strong relationships.

Communications: regarding presidential speeches, travel, and campaign expenses. This relationship may be especially close during campaigns, when travel expenses and contacts are subject to strict legal standards.

Legislative Affairs: regarding legislation, nominations, and confirmations. Some White House counsels have participated directly in legislative negotiations, even communicating with senators about judicial appointments.

Personnel Office: regarding appointments and clearances. This responsibility also causes the White House counsel's office to consult regularly with the FBI and (at least through the Clinton years) the American Bar Association.

Office of Political Affairs: regarding travel and campaign expenses.

Press Office: regarding presidential press conferences. In some administrations the counsel's office also prepared presidential statements about federal court rulings that affect the presidency or the executive branch.

Office of Management and Budget: regarding budget proposals, rescissions, and deferrals.

National Security Council Staff: regarding foreign policy.

Organization and Operations

Since the 1970s, the size of the White House counsel's office has expanded from two or three attorneys to more than forty lawyers at times during the Clinton administration. Some former counsels attribute this growth to the increasingly hostile Washington environment faced by recent presidents and the mounting scrutiny of their appointees. John Tuck, an aide to Chief of Staff Howard Baker in the Reagan White House, recalled "a whole huge shadow counsel's office" that developed following the Iran-Contra revelations.[44]

Internal Division of Labor

The counsel's office has been structured internally in numerous ways. The organization charts provide two examples of the changes over time, one (Carter, 1978) relatively early in the unit's existence and the other (Clinton, spring, 2000) more recent. The growing specialization and size of the office are readily apparent. Typically, the White House counsel, as a senior presidential adviser, participates in myriad activities and issues, many of which are unplanned and unpredictable. Indeed, the counsel's time often is consumed almost completely in handling crises or unexpected demands. Thus, Reagan counsel Peter Wallison remembered: "At least politics and crises are the two things that you have to be sure [to handle]—one of the reasons you want to get a staff that is capable and has the lines of authority and lines of responsibility clear is that at some point you are going to be completely consumed with something and that means your office has to function without you. So you need a really good and capable deputy, which I had [in] Jay Stephens, and you need very good lawyers, and then they have to know what their areas of responsibility are so that they don't have to keep coming to you."[45]

Counsels, beginning with John Dean, have included at least one deputy counsel on their staffs. (See appendix.) A deputy counsel routinely serves as the primary overseer of workflow within the office as well as a substitute for the counsel. The deputy also may perform other tasks at the direction of the counsel. Abner Mikva noted: "James Castello was the deputy who really was my person and managed the staff and was at the second meeting I couldn't be at if I was at the first one. [He] probably had the most to do with the legislative agenda. He met regularly with the Legislative Office and made sure that there weren't any surprises on the Hill

Figure 10.

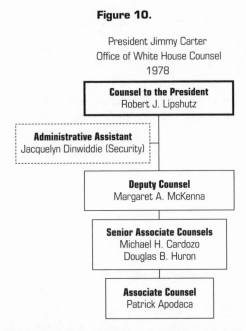

President Jimmy Carter
Office of White House Counsel
1978

Counsel to the President
Robert J. Lipshutz

Administrative Assistant
Jacquelyn Dinwiddie (Security)

Deputy Counsel
Margaret A. McKenna

Senior Associate Counsels
Michael H. Cardozo
Douglas B. Huron

Associate Counsel
Patrick Apodaca

White House Interview Program (whitehouse2001.org). Based on data in The White House Telephone Directory, 1978, National Journal Group Inc., Washington, DC. *Key:* ——— = positions with "to the president" in their title; ---------- = staff working for indicated assistant.

that the president didn't know about or what was going up as our core leg-islation didn't have any pitfalls in it."[46] Such deputies typically are charged with assuring that the counsel sees only the highest-priority items. On per-sonnel issues, for instance, Reagan counsel Culvahouse stated: "I clearly was the principal advisor to the president . . . within the White House on the vetting process, which included not only the people to be nominated by the president but also people who would be appointed by the president even if they did not require Senate confirmation as well as anyone who would get a White House staff badge. . . . I never saw their files or any-thing, unless there was a problem. So the default rule was if there was a problem certified as such by my deputy then it would be put on my desk. So I saw 10 percent of the files, roughly."[47]

In the Clinton White House, longtime presidential confidant Bruce Lindsey served for much of the administration as a "deputy counsel for special projects." According to Abner Mikva, besides a host of other activi-ties, "there was always a special project he was involved in either for the

Figure 11.

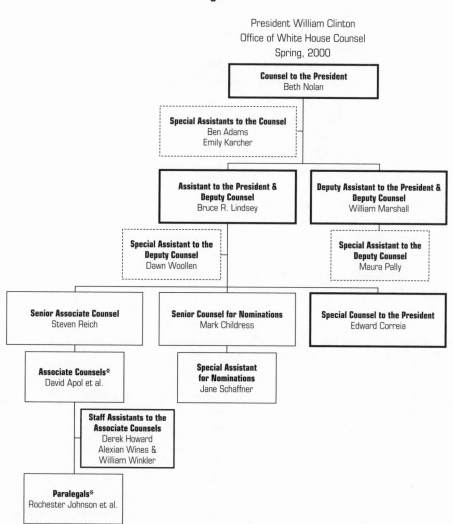

President William Clinton
Office of White House Counsel
Spring, 2000

*Associate Counsels:** David Apol, Maredith Cabe, Dawn Chirwa, Dimitri Niopakis, Michael J.
O'Connor, J. Paul Octkin, Michelle Peterson, Karl Racine, Peter Rundlet, and Sarah Wilson.
*Paralegals:** Rochester Johnson, Danela Nanau, Robin Roland, and Van-Alan Shima.
White House Interview Program (whitehouse2001.org). Based on data in *The Capital Source*, Spring,
2000, National Journal Group Inc., Washington, DC. *Key:* ——— = positions with "to the president" in
their title; ---------- = staff working for indicated assistant.

president or because the president would indicate to me or [Chief of Staff] Leon [Panetta] that he wanted somebody that could really use his clout effectively. For instance, Bruce was the point man on the baseball strike. . . . I don't think I said, 'Bruce, go do the baseball strike.' It was known that we needed somebody who could go in there and say the president really thinks this ought to be done or that ought to be done, and nobody could do that like Bruce."[48]

In addition, the counsel's immediate staff (often an administrative assistant and an executive secretary) usually is responsible for assuring that external deadlines are met and internally work is parceled out appropriately. Culvahouse, for example, reported having "three nonattorney people who worked for me: an executive assistant, an administrative assistant, and an executive secretary. The first two spent most of their time assigning out projects and making sure the work was done and the deadlines were observed."[49]

In recent White Houses, aides with the title of "special counsel" have on occasion appeared in the counsel's office. Typically, these are staffers assigned to handle short-term or "crisis" situations that may involve congressional or other investigations, such as Iran-Contra or Whitewater. Most observers attribute the swelling of the counsel's office over the course of an administration to such crises and to the heightened external scrutiny of administrations.

Moreover, given the range of diverse responsibilities that have come to be lodged in the White House counsel's office, some substantive division of labor usually appears. For instance, a deputy counsel and one or more other members of the office participated in judicial selection in the Carter, Reagan, Bush, and Clinton administrations, and this also appears to be the case in the George W. Bush White House.

Similarly, after the initial flurry of vetting for nominations and appointments at the beginning of an administration, typically one assistant or associate counsel and a security assistant (and staff) in the office handle FBI and financial disclosure reports.[50] This lawyer also is responsible for taking the confidential reports to the chairs and ranking minority members of the appropriate Senate committees, with potentially problematic allegations flagged. In the second term of the Clinton administration, a "senior counsel" was among those handling these responsibilities.

Other tasks that commonly have been assigned to particular lawyers in the counsel's office include interpreting ethics legislation and additional ethics rules issued by an administration. As noted earlier, counsels provide this advice for staffers in the White House Office and the Executive Office of the President, and, on occasion, for cabinet officials and other presidential appointees. Still other attorneys in the counsel's office focus on issues of international trade and transportation, defense and national security policy (to support the counsel's role as chair of the War Powers Committee), government regulation, and presidential travel (to determine its purpose and the appropriateness of funding sources).

Rhythms of Quadrennial Governance

Over the course of a presidential term, the activities, demands, and emphases of the counsel's office typically follow common patterns. The first year is both demanding and somewhat distinctive. After that, the work of the counsel's office—like much of the rest of the administration—to a significant extent reflects the presidency's efforts to respond to external deadlines. Still, some tasks arise more routinely throughout an administration.

First Year

A major task that begins well before inauguration day and continues through most of the first year is vetting for nominations and appointments. C. Boyden Gray remembered: "[F]or the first year that's all you do, is read FBI reports and ABA reports . . . [and] Financial disclosure reports. It's not much fun."[51]

During this early period as well, the counsel's office seeks to assure that all White House staffers and political appointees are informed of the ethics statutes, executive orders, and other administration rules under which they must work. Gray described his approach to handling the task: "My rule of thumb was: 'If it's fun, stop! If it feels good, stop! If you're having fun, you're doing something wrong!'"[52] At the outset too, the counsel's office needs to give White House staffers instructions on how to keep their files.

The initial weeks and months of a new administration also bring numerous other demands. Chief among them is the president's budget, which must be submitted by early February; the economic report is due at about the same time. The legislative agenda, congressional messages, and bills must be drafted and sent to Congress. The counsel's office is involved in all of these activities.

Annual Cycles

Especially important annual cycles are the preparation of the president's budget and the drafting of the State of the Union address and the Economic Report of the President. Although the counsel's office is not the central player, it does perform the pivotal role of ensuring that the officials involved act in accordance with prevailing legal and ethical guidelines.

Electoral Cycles

As the midterm congressional elections or a presidential re-election campaign approaches, the counsel's office faces other tasks. The office may well be besieged with requests for advice from White House aides and political appointees throughout the executive branch about the sorts of partisan and electoral activities they and their aides are legally permitted to engage in. In most administrations the counsel and staff try to anticipate such requests and related problems by sending out written guidelines and holding information sessions.

Then, as elections approach, "the president becomes more involved in direct politics, which raises questions about . . . how much of his time would be devoted to it, who pays for it, all those things. That becomes much more important every two years. Whether the president is running for election or not, usually he's out doing things, raising funds or otherwise supporting candidates, which requires you to make these kinds of allocations in the best possible way to avoid charges of various kinds."[53] Recalling the allegations of illegal fundraising preceding the 1996 presidential election, Abner Mikva regretted that "none of us saw fit to raise a warning flag for the president. . . . I had seen what goes on in state politics. I'd been a state legislator for ten years. I know governors in Illinois pick up the phone when they're sitting in the governor's office and lean on people to give money to their campaign and the party. It's just a fact of life, and I suspect it goes on in most states. . . . I think this government came in to the White House not very sensitive to the fact that the White House and the federal government is a different place. So I should have warned the president."[54]

The presidential electoral cycle also can influence submission of judicial nominations to the Senate. Former deputy Counsel Phillip Brady noted, "as you get closer and closer to presidential elections, the Senate becomes less and less receptive to confirming nominees for lifetime appointments, depending on what happens in the next presidential election."[55]

Final Year

The last year of a presidency also can be "dangerous."[56] As the final days of the Clinton presidency highlighted, this is a time when requests for pardons, commutations, executive orders, and other presidential actions may be likely to reach fever pitch. It also is a time when presidents may be especially responsive to those who have supported and worked with them for numerous years.

More Regular Tasks

Many of the other tasks handled by the counsel's office are performed throughout an administration. Reagan counsel Culvahouse recalled, for example, that this included the Judicial Selection Committee, which met "every two weeks and more frequently if—basically the idea was to get people's nominations up as soon as possible so if the FBI was able to process background checks and all the materials were in, we sometimes would meet every week."[57] Executive orders also need to be drafted throughout an administration.

In contrast, Culvahouse continued:

> Congress tends to work in fits and starts. . . . The legislative agenda can be heavy or it can be light. There were also Statements of Administration Policy that we would review. . . . Sometimes we would say, "This should not come out of the White House; the Justice Department or the State Department should issue this." Sometimes we would be involved in deciding who ought to comment on the bill, and who ought to testify. If it was going to be a Statement of Administration Policy, which is in effect attributed to the president, we would look at those carefully. Those would be in effect a letter that would say here's what the administration thinks about S-332, the omnibus such and such act.[58]

In addition, throughout an administration, new individuals must be nominated for and appointed to positions throughout the executive branch. After the first year, "the nomination process was fairly continuous. . . . So every week there would be nominations to be processed, people to be vetted, ethics agreements to be looked at."[59] Informing new hires about ethics regulations also had to continue.

Crises, Scandals, and Unexpected Events

Counsels, of course, find themselves (and their staffs) handling unexpected situations and, on occasion, crises, at least as seen from the administration's perspective. As chair of the War Powers Committee, the counsel has responsibilities whenever U.S. troops are (or may become) involved in hostilities.

A scandal of one sort or another seems likely to occur at some point during an administration. In the words of Peter Wallison: "you can always count on . . . some kind of big scandal. . . . And when I went in to that office, I assumed there was going to be a blizzard. What I didn't realize was that there would be a hundred-year snow in the form of Iran-Contra."[60]

Lloyd Cutler, who served as counsel for both Presidents Carter and Clinton, observed that the job has become more driven by scandal and congressional efforts to probe more deeply into administrations:

> We were doing executive privilege in the Carter days; we were doing it in the Clinton days. We had demands from congressional committees for White House documents and agency documents; drafts of legal opinions, for example, were so much more pervasive. Mostly, it's the difference that when I worked for Carter while we did have the Billy Carter problem and a few others, Hamilton Jordan's alleged drug violations—which turned out to be entirely untrue, while we had a couple of those, most of what I did was substantive. . . . In Clinton's time I had the same understanding that I could be in on all these things, but I had to put in so much of my own daily effort, and my staff did, on the investigations of the president, Whitewater, et cetera, that I had no time. . . . [W]orking for Carter—which was a year and a half—not more than 20 percent [of the counsel's work] was what I call playing defense. Under Clinton it was closer to 80 percent.[61]

Turnover: Counsel and Deputy Counsel

Given the demands on the counsel as well as the often unforgiving nature of Washington, it is scarcely surprising that relatively few people stay in the job for more than two years. Only Philip Buchen (Ford) and C. Boyden Gray (G. H. W. Bush) stayed through their administrations. Fred Fielding worked even longer as counsel to Ronald Reagan, serving from January, 1981, until February, 1986. (See appendix.)

In recent presidencies, counsels have departed for a variety of reasons. Some—such as John Dean—became directly involved in administration scandals. Others—J. Fred Buzhardt and Peter Wallison—departed after the president or chief of staff who brought them to the White House was forced out. Still other counsels joined the White House staff explicitly on a temporary basis to help handle political or policy crises. In Democratic administrations such figures have tended to be well respected, "old Washington hands" themselves (like Lloyd Cutler, Abner Mikva, and Charles Ruff). In the Reagan administration, by contrast, the new counsel, A. B. Culvahouse, was a trusted associate of the incoming chief of staff, Howard Baker, who himself fit the same profile.

When counsels have left the White House, in virtually all cases their deputies have departed within several months. The only exception has been Clinton aide Bruce Lindsey, who was lodged in the counsel's office from 1993 through 2000 working under multiple counsels (and always with a second deputy counsel).

In addition, turnover has been somewhat higher among deputies than among counsels. Typically, deputy counsels leave to pursue other opportunities both inside and outside the administration. From 1971 through 2000, no deputy counsel succeeded a counsel, although at least one (Cheryl Mills) turned down the job when it was offered. Clinton's sixth counsel, Beth Nolan, served as an associate counsel during the first term. Deputy counsels Cheryl Mills and William P. Marshall served as associate counsels (Mills under Nussbaum, Cutler, Mikva, and Quinn, and Marshall under Ruff) before being named deputies.

Conclusion

In sum, the counsel's office can be characterized as a monitor, a coordinator, a negotiator, a recommender, and a translator. It *monitors* ethics matters, it *coordinates* the president's message and agenda with other executive-branch units, it *negotiates* on the president's behalf with Congress and others, it *recommends* actions to the president, and it *translates* or interprets the law in its broadest context throughout the executive branch. It oversees all of the political and policy actions the president takes to ensure compliance with legal and constitutional requirements. No paper goes in or out of the president's office without the counsel's review.

The challenges for this office are daunting. The paper flow is relentless; the pressures, both time and political, are crushing; the scope of its tasks extends to every facet of the president's political and constitutional responsibilities; and the potential for disaster is as close as the next crisis. The counsel's office performs both routine and extraordinary tasks and participates in making domestic as well as foreign policy. Because its charge cuts such a wide swath and there is no time for on-the-job training, an incoming counsel must master a sharp learning curve, expect the unpredictable, and get used to making crucial decisions with incomplete information.

As a consequence of the increasing polarization and politicization of the U.S. government, there has been a greater recognition of the highly influential role the counsel's office can play. These heightened stakes have intensified the strains under which counsels operate. They must understand the "fishbowl" nature of the office, and they must be especially vigilant about reining in presidents during the last year of their administrations. Counsels must recognize as well that maintaining good relations with the Justice Department's Office of Legal Counsel is critical as an institutional check on their own instincts, despite the tensions that can arise between these two legal units.

The counsel's office sits on the edge of a precipice: it is the last line of defense for the institution of the presidency. Its ultimate role as protector of presidential privileges and prerogatives means that its advice will have profound implications for the power of the presidency for years to come.

Notes

We are grateful for the comments and suggestions of Martha Joynt Kumar and for the time and effort of the former presidential staffers who shared their experiences and insights in the White House Interview Project.

1.   Culvahouse quoted in Naftali Bendavid, "Keeping the President's Counsel," *Legal Times*, Mar. 14, 1994, p. 13.

2.   A. B. Culvahouse, interview with Martha Joynt Kumar, Washington, D.C., Sept. 15, 1999, White House Interview Program.

3.   Lloyd C. Cutler, interview with Martha Joynt Kumar and Nancy Kassop, Washington, D.C., July 8, 1999, White House Interview Program.

4.   Ibid.

5.   Ibid.

6.   John Dean established the White House counsel's office under Richard Nixon. Dean was the first counsel whose duties primarily focused on "lawyering," and he was the first as well to seek out new legal responsibilities and draw them into a separate office in the White House. Although presidents from FDR through Nixon had aides with

the titles of "special counsel" or "counsel," such staffers typically had more wide-ranging policy responsibilities. The Eisenhower White House to some extent was an exception: Gerald Morgan, as special counsel, and Edward McCabe, an associate special counsel, worked on tasks quite similar to some of those in the contemporary counsel's office. See, for example, Jeremy Rabkin, "White House Lawyering: Law, Ethics, and Political Judgments," and Michael Strine, "Counsels to the President: The Rise of Organizational Competition," in *Government Lawyers: The Federal Legal Bureaucracy and Presidential Politics,* ed. Cornell W. Clayton (Lawrence: University Press of Kansas, 1995); and Charles E. Walcott and Karen M. Hult, *Governing the White House: From Hoover through LBJ* (Lawrence: University Press of Kansas, 1995).

7.   Bernard C. Nussbaum, interview with Martha Joynt Kumar and Nancy Kassop, New York, Nov. 9, 1999, White House Interview Program.

8.   Abner Mikva, interview with Martha Joynt Kumar and Terry Sullivan, Chicago, Apr. 26, 2000, White House Interview Program.

9.   Culvahouse interview.

10.   Culvahouse, personal communication to Martha Joynt Kumar, Oct. 9, 2000.

11.   Peter Wallison, interview with Martha Joynt Kumar, Washington, D.C., Jan. 27, 2000, White House Interview Program.

12.   Nussbaum quoted in Ruth Marcus and Ann Devroy, "Nussbaum Quits White House Post," *Washington Post,* Mar. 6, 1994, p. A1.

13.   Nussbaum interview.

14.   C. Boyden Gray, interview with Martha Joynt Kumar and Nancy Kassop, Washington, D.C., Oct. 4, 1999, White House Interview Program.

15.   See, for example, Sheldon Goldman and Elliott Slotnick, "Clinton's First Term Judiciary: Many Bridges to Cross," *Judicature* 80 (May–June, 1997): 254–73; Goldman and Slotnick, "Clinton's Second Term Judiciary: Picking Judges under Fire," *Judicature* 82 (May–June, 1999): 264–84; and Goldman, Slotnick, Gerard Gryski, and Gary Zuk, "Clinton's Judges: Summing up the Legacy," *Judicature* 84 (Mar.–Apr., 2001): 228–54.

16.   Culvahouse interview.

17.   Robert Lipshutz, interview with Martha Joynt Kumar and Terry Sullivan, Washington, D.C., Sept. 1, 1999, White House Interview Program.

18.   Nussbaum interview.

19.   Gray interview.

20.   See, for example, Paul C. Light and Virginia L. Thomas, *The Merit and Reputation of an Administration: Presidential Appointees on the Appointments Process* (Washington, D.C.: Presidential Appointees Initiative, 2000); Terry Sullivan, "In Full View: The Inquiry of Presidential Nominees," Report no. 15, *White House 2001 Project,* Mar. 29, 2001 <www.whitehouse2001.org>.

21.   Culvahouse interview.

22.   Gray interview.

23.   Culvahouse interview.

24.   Gray interview.

25.   Ibid.

26.   Mikva interview.

27.   Cutler interview.

28.   Nussbaum interview.

29. Culvahouse interview.

30. Gray interview.

31. Wallison interview.

32. Gray interview.

33. Wallison interview.

34. Gray interview.

35. Cutler interview.

36. Nonetheless, communications with independent regulatory agencies were handled with special care and circumspection.

37. Most recently, Pres. George W. Bush named longtime Texas associate Alberto R. Gonzales his White House counsel.

38. Cutler interview.

39. The courts view the two as clearly distinct. Executive privilege refers to the constitutionally based protection of confidentiality of a president's communications with any government officer when the chief executive seeks advice on the exercise of official governmental duties. Its purpose is to promote candid and frank discussions between a president and his advisors. Government attorney–client privilege is a variant of the common law attorney-client privilege, but with the following crucial distinctions:

> 1. the client is the Office of the President of the United States; and
>
> 2. the advice being rendered by a government attorney to the president is "for the purpose of securing primarily either (i) an opinion on law; or (ii) legal services; or (iii) assistance in some legal proceeding." *In re Sealed Case*, 737 F. 2d at 98–99 (quoting *U.S. United Shoe Machinery Corp.*, 89 F. Supp. 357, 358–59 [D. Mass. 1950]) in *In re: Bruce Lindsey* (Grand Jury Testimony), 158 F. 3d 1263 (D.C. Cir. 1998).

40. Among those factors are whether the conversation is political or legal; whether the person is communicating with the president in a legal or political capacity; whether the request for presidential communications comes from the courts, Congress, or an independent counsel; whether the information is needed in a civil or criminal proceeding; whether the asserted public interest in confidentiality outweighs another institution's need for the information; and whether the requested information is available from an alternative source.

41. The Reagan counsels left office for a variety of personal and institutional reasons: Fred Fielding, because he "was ready to go out into the real world"; and Peter Wallison, because of pressures generated by Iran-Contra. Wallison interview. A. B. Culvahouse, the third and final Reagan counsel, served two chiefs of staff, Howard Baker and Kenneth Duberstein.

42. Culvahouse interview.

43. Ibid.

44. John Tuck, interview with Martha Joynt Kumar, Washington, D.C., Nov. 12, 1999, White House Interview Program.

45. Wallison interview.

46. Mikva interview.

47. Culvahouse interview.

48. Mikva interview.

49. Culvahouse interview.

50. See, for example, Wallison interview.

51. Gray interview.

52. Ibid.

53. Wallison interview.

54. Mikva interview.

55. Philip Brady, interview with Martha Joynt Kumar, Washington, D.C., Aug. 17, 1999, White House Interview Program.

56. A. B. Culvahouse, "Should the White House Counsel's Office Be Abolished?" (comments presented at "The Constitution under Clinton: A Critical Assessment," Duke University Law School, Durham, N.C., Sept. 23–25, 1999). In offering advice to future counsels, Culvahouse added, "You must never forget that your contribution is what you *don't* let happen in the last year of a presidency."

57. Culvahouse interview.

58. Ibid.

59. Wallison interview.

60. Ibid.

61. Cutler interview.

The Office of the Press Secretary

MARTHA JOYNT KUMAR

BEING PRESS SECRETARY INVOLVES WALKING ON a high wire and doing so daily. As the official spokesperson for an administration, he or she is the person who presents presidential information to many audiences, including the public, the president's special publics in Washington, and governments of nations around the globe. People look to the White House for comment, and it is the press secretary who most often presents it. Although the president may be seen daily in official settings making formal presentations, it is the press secretary who delivers official comment and response to events and criticism.

The press secretary represents one part of a White House communications operation. Just as the press secretary must weave together the interests of reporters and the president, he or she must also work together with a variety of administration officials in creating the portrait of the president and his policies they want to publicly deliver. As the new century begins, the function of communications pervades almost every White House office and is a central concern to three of them: the Press Office, the Office of Communications, and the chief of staff. The Press Office deals with the daily press needs of a president, manages his relationship with news organizations, and on a continuous basis throughout the day provides presidential information to reporters covering the administration. The Office of Communications deals with information as does the Press Office, but it does so in a context of persuasion and planning. Staff there design and script events illustrating the president's message. Strategy comes from the third office in the communications triumvirate, the chief of staff. It is in the chief's office where politics and policy come together with publicity. A chief of staff is responsible for pulling together the initiatives of a president and orchestrating the strategies for accomplishing their goals.[1]

The Responsibilities of the Press Secretary

There is a stability to the Press Office that is reflected in the continuity of its chief and the relatively long tenures of the press secretaries. In the seventy years we have had a press secretary, there have been twenty-two people who have served in that post. Although not all of them have had the formal title "press secretary," all were responsible for the same basic tasks and services. Over those years, four responsibilities have become regularly associated with the press secretary: information conduit, representation of his constituents, administration, and communications planning. Information responsibilities include providing presidential news to reporters on a regular basis in both formal and informal settings. Representation refers to the role the secretary plays representing the office's three constituents to one another. As the head of a unit with offices in two buildings and includes approximately thirty people, the press secretary must devote time and resources to administration. Communications planning is an important secondary task for a press secretary as he or she consults with others in the White House on future events and their staging.

Information Conduit

The press secretary's success depends upon the information he provides to reporters, to the president, and to White House staff members. Each of his three constituents assesses the quality of information through its own prism. The president wants the press secretary to use the podium to build support for himself and his programs. The White House staff wants the press secretary to take the arrows for the administration as well as to present and explain policies and actions in a favorable way. Reporters want the press secretary to provide the information they are seeking. The press secretary provides information in two face-to-face sessions with reporters and then throughout the day in a constant flow of paper to the White House press. He or she meets with reporters on an individual basis at the end of the day and talks to them on the phone throughout the day. For reporters and to some extent White House officials, how successful the press secretary is in providing information depends in large measure on that person's ability to get the correct information and news reflecting the president's thinking and responses and to provide it to reporters on a timely basis. Ron Nessen, press secretary to President Ford, discussed how similar his colleagues are in their understanding of the basic manner in which information should be distributed and the challenges they face in acquiring it. "I think most press secretaries, no matter what their background is, come to understand that the same set of rules always apply year after year, administration after administration: tell the truth, don't lie, don't cover up, put out the bad news yourself, put it out as soon as possible, put your own explanation on it, all those things. But a lot of times other members of the staff don't want to do that; they don't understand it."[2]

While the two information sessions take a great deal of energy, time, and attention from the press secretary and his staff, they are not the only venues where administration news is released during a day. The White House provides information and officials for appearances on the morning news shows, the news programs run throughout the day by cable news organizations, such as CNN, Fox, CNBC, and MSNBC, with cameras located on the North Lawn of the White House, and then in the evening for the network news programs and finally, ABC's *Nightline*. Television news organizations have at least a dozen cameras located near the driveway ready to handle their regular news spots and any breaking news. White House officials quickly learn to use the opportunities such technology provides.

Information Venues: The Gaggle and the Briefing

While a press secretary at one time informally could give reporters information in the briefing, informality has proven to be a casualty of televising the session.[3] White House information has become official and formal, yet there remain some vestiges of the informal venues where reporters and officials once regularly talked on an off-the-record basis. The "gaggle" now represents the best complement to the formal briefing, for there is still an opportunity there for reporters and officials to work through issues of mutual concern without their conversations being reported in print and on the air.[4] This session occurs most mornings when the president is in town and is held in the press secretary's office for fifteen to twenty minutes at 9:30. Then, sometime around 1:00 P.M., there is a formal televised session held in the James Brady Briefing Room, which, during busy periods in a president's term, can run from forty-five minutes to an hour.

The Gaggle

This meeting is an example of the manner in which both sides in the White House press relationship benefit from their sessions together. Held with around three-dozen wire, radio, and television reporters clustered around the press secretary's desk with tape recorders running, the session is one of mutual advantage. Reporters get some answers for their rolling deadlines to overnight and breaking events, and the White House finds out what is on reporters' minds. James Fetig, who was press representative for the National Security Council during Mike McCurry's tenure as press secretary in the middle years of the Clinton administration, explained the advantages of the session. "Out of the gaggle we would get a pretty good idea of what the stories of the day were going to be. You could tell by what they were pressing Mike on. That was the purpose of the gaggle; it was intelligence gathering for the White House and a chance to get some spin on the early news as the news developed during the day. It was a two-way street. But we'd come back from that armed with all sorts of questions that we knew we had to get answers for because they were coming right back up in the briefing."[5]

The Briefing

The briefing is a session that has several different elements to it. There are a mixture of purposes and activities served in that session, including: announcement of policy; responses to the actions of others, including the president's critics and leaders in other nations; responses to queries of reporters on subjects of their interest; and providing information on breaking news. Mike McCurry discussed the range of information found in the briefing.

> The problem with the format and the problem with the job is that you have to wear different hats at different moments. Sometimes you have to be giving a formal declaration of U.S. policy, particularly when it's a question of foreign policy, and that has to be read in just the right way and has to be communicated in a way in which it's the government speaking. There are other times when you're sort of being political and doing combat with the other team. There are other times when you're just getting raw infor-

mation in front of reporters so they can do the primal function of reporting the news. And there are other times when you're just basically trying to divert the attention or take the body blows for the president on stuff.[6]

With a large number of possible topics to be covered, a press secretary often tries to shape the tone and direction of a briefing. Marlin Fitzwater, who served as press secretary during the latter part of the Reagan and all of the first Bush administration, consciously came to the briefing with a plan of how to reduce its inherent risks. His strategy was to know five things about the big issues and to have an opening statement, even if it is a reheat of a State Department guidance statement.

One of the tricks I used to use when we had nothing else—and I hated going down there with nothing to say—I'd take a piece of State Department guidance on some issue, say Biafra hunger problems, because I knew it was absolutely spotless in terms of being correct. It had been reviewed by sixteen people at the State Department; it was absolutely safe policy. . . . I'd go down and I'd say, "I would like to read a statement this morning on behalf of the president concerning Biafra and hunger." . . . So sometimes I would do that until they got on to me and would say, "Hey, Marlin. Read us some more of that guidance from the State Department."[7]

Even the staff get into it when issues are hot or when the press secretary needs help. James Fetig discussed how he would slip information to Mike McCurry when he was briefing at the podium. He related that if a staff person was watching the briefing and noticed an error in what McCurry said, they would provide him with the correct information. "That was an interesting way of slipping so that the question could be answered in real time before the briefing closed, or if you made a mistake, they would send down the correction."[8]

Official Responses and Statements: The Paper Flow and the "Stakeout"

Throughout the day, the press secretary must issue official responses from the administration, provide background information on their initiatives, give schedules on presidential appearances and arrangements, and distribute transcripts of official information sessions. On a typical day, the Press Office issues perhaps fifteen releases relating to nominations and appointments made by the president, background information on upcoming trips and on events taking place in the White House, and transcripts of the press secretary's briefing and remarks made by the president in the Oval Office and elsewhere. When the president has an event in the East Room announcing a policy, for example, there will be paper provided reporters identifying the participants in the event and information on the groups associated with it as well as the details of what a policy initiative would do. When an event deals with a proposed policy, there are often fact sheets released providing background information on the issue. During a crisis of some order or prior to a presidential trip or visit by a head of state, one or more White House officials will come to the briefing room with background information. Those sessions are typically transcribed and then distributed for reporters to use. Since journalists need to fairly quickly use the information given in the briefing, the Press Office tries for a fast turnaround time on transcripts. Press releases remain the primary source of information for quite a few reporters covering the White House. For that reason, attention is paid to getting the information out in a way and in time for them to make the best use of it.

People involved in a presidential event, such as members of Congress, often appear at the "stakeout," approximately twenty feet from the West Wing entrance, where microphones provide reporters an opportunity to question them about their meeting with the president. This is an operation run by news organizations, not the White House. The Press Office provides sound from the stakeout through the "mult" (the multiple-feed sound system that provides audio to those in the Press Room as well as the radio and television booths], but there are no transcripts made of comments given there.

Acquiring Accurate Information: The Fitzwater Solution

Whether it is in the gaggle, the briefing, or individual sessions with reporters, providing accurate information is the greatest challenge a press secretary faces and one where he must be creative in finding ways to acquire the facts he needs and make certain the information is correct. Marlin Fitzwater spoke of the need coming in to figure out ways of confirming information. He said an important question for a press secretary to pose is:

"What is the best way for me to check out the veracity of information?" That question gets to "the most crucial job in my area, the integrity of information. I developed a very, I thought, sophisticated but at least kind of intricate beat system for putting my staff in various places around the government to check out information."[9]

For Fitzwater, getting information on specific topics meant dealing directly with the specialists in the departments. In the White House one needs information quickly and one needs trustworthy information.

> I would always ask who's the specialist on this and often would call them for specific stuff. The public affairs assistant secretary was always good at policies and what's the secretary thinking and those kinds of issues, but the kinds of information I often needed were the nuts and bolts things like, 'Okay, we've got a new education proposal here but tell me how many kids in America get Pell grants? How many new schools are there every year? . . . The one thing that departments never understand about the White House [is] . . . almost everything you need you need that day, probably within two or three hours. Departments have a terrible time responding like that because they all have clearance processes and all that business. The quickest way to circumvent that is to call up somebody and ask them specific questions.[10]

During a crisis, an effective way to get information is for the press secretary to have his staff fan out among the agencies and troll for information and to have someone from the appropriate agency come into the White House. Larry Speakes, who served in the post during the Reagan administration, described the way they did it following the U.S. action in Grenada, when the Press Office was caught without accurate information:

> We learned from that [Grenada] that when crisis occurred—the Khadafi stuff, the *Challenger*—that the minute something like [that] occurred we would send somebody from our office to the Defense Department or to NASA, whichever; they would send somebody from their office to the White House. They would come to the White House in the morning at seven o'clock and leave when we got through at night. Vice versa for our guy going there. The deal that that gave us was, first of all, someone that was fairly

knowledgeable about the subject from that department and knew the details but also knew [that], if we had a question and we couldn't answer it, they knew who to go to in the Defense Department or NASA or wherever.[11]

During some crises, the people from appropriate agencies spent several days in the Press Office answering questions. When the space shuttle *Challenger* exploded, NASA had someone there for about a week. When there was a crisis with Libya involving their shooting at U.S. naval ships, Speakes indicated the Defense Department person sent over to the Press Office was an important asset in responding to reporters queries. When reporters asked about the firepower of the ships, Speakes was able to provide knowledgeable responses. "So he's sitting there with a book of the profiles of all the foreign ships and handed it to me, and I'm able to tell them how many guns it's got on it, how much armament, how many people, length, width, and all that. It really helped to be more knowledgeable on that subject."

Presidential Information

Reporters want information about the president, and they want it from a press secretary who meets daily with the chief executive. From the media's viewpoint, daily meetings with the president are crucial because they want information reflecting presidential thinking, not that of the press secretary. Mike McCurry discussed his meeting with the president and the manner in which presidential responses fit into his briefing.

Most days, for most of the time I was at the White House, he'd have some kind of event that would be a photo opportunity, he'd get the big question on the news of the day, and [he] would have addressed it. So that was then in the can by the time of my briefing. So you had the president shaping the answer or shaping the story, and I was doing the background news around it by the time the briefing came. Occasionally, it would happen that we had practiced how he was going to answer a certain question, but it didn't come up in the photo opportunity. So when the press raised it with me, I gave the answer Clinton would have given if he had been asked. That happened a lot. That was the utility of really hearing him talk it through.[12]

Representation of Constituents

A press secretary has three constituents—the president, the White House staff, and the representatives of news organizations—and one boss, the president. Weaving together the interests of the executive and those of reporters is difficult, but a press secretary does it daily in the briefing. Marlin Fitzwater discussed the need to remember his fealty to the president. "From my standpoint, I'm trying to get the president's story out. I know [reporters are] not going to use it just the way I gave it to them, but my view is I paid the price for getting my president's position out. They listened; they took the information down, so I did my best for the president. So you try to weave that kind of fabric every time you deal with the press. If you ever get to the point where you start taking the press' role or they're asking you a question and you don't defend your president, then you're not doing your job for him."[13]

In any relationship where each side has a great stake in its outcomes, the partners will be wary of one another. Because many people coming into work in the White House do not have experience dealing with news organizations and their representatives, the Press Office sometimes has to work on behalf of the media with White House staff members reluctant to answer the queries of reporters. Throughout an administration, journalists will need Press Office staff either to cajole the people working with sensitive information or in offices under particular scrutiny to talk with them or to get their information and make it safely available to the media. It is the Press Office staff that makes the judgment calls on what information is appropriate to release. At the same time, there is pressure on the press secretary resulting from all of the unauthorized contacts staff have with reporters and the resulting information leaks. Presidents almost uniformly get upset when information the administration does not want released comes out in the open. With President Ford as the recent exception, other presidents have tried tracking down such leaks.[14]

Building a Relationship of Mutual Trust

Perhaps the most important factor characterizing the environment within which the Press Office functions is the cooperative character of the relationship between reporters and White House officials.[15] Their public grumbling and complaining may mask it, but reporters and officials cooperate with one another as they search for and disseminate information.

At the heart of cooperation is establishing a relationship of trust. Reporters need to believe in the information the White House is providing them and have confidence in the officials who provide it. Roman Popadiuk, who served as deputy press secretary in the Bush White House, described the relationship he developed with reporters. "I operated under the personal notion of full disclosure, to have the reporter have, without giving away state secrets or things of that nature, as much information as possible because I felt that made a better story for us, built a trust by the reporter and me personally and in my office, and as a result of that gave me more credibility in the future with that reporter; if I needed something deleted I could argue."[16] Fruitful cooperation for the press secretary means knowing the needs of reporters as well as those of the White House. One wants to get the right information to reporters at times when they need it. "I tried to make it my business to understand how the press worked, what they needed, when they needed it and to get our order in early if we had something to get in that first lineup of stories," Larry Speakes stated.[17]

The better the relationship a Press Office staff member has with reporters on a daily basis, the better he can serve White House staff when trouble comes. A reporter might bring a story to a Press Office staffer to pass it by for authenticity. The staff person would not offer things to add to the story but could suggest working on that second paragraph or searching around a little more on that paragraph. "That's exactly how we would say it sometimes," said Popadiuk. "You could either add to a story, which I didn't mind at times, saying you forgot some points here or your story would be fuller, or negative saying this is really off the wall and I'll tell you why."[18]

In addition to meeting their information needs, it serves the interest of the White House to have a strong relationship with reporters, for they represent an important source of intelligence about the political undercurrents in Washington. Larry Speakes said one needs to "establish that two-way street between the press—because you learned a lot from the press. They called you and said I hear this is going on, you were getting information that was valuable inside the White House, something is brewing out there that you needed to prepare for."[19]

Administration

The administrative operation has several components associated with it; the delivery of information, the logistics associated with event and White House coverage, and selecting and coordinating with the public informa-

tion officers in the departments and agencies. The press secretary's role as
an administrator involves the four daily meetings with Press Office staff
and those as the representative of the office and its interests. The press
secretary is responsible for the delivery of information to reporters and the
arrangements for covering the president at the White House as well as during travels. Reporters are circumscribed in their movements around the
West Wing. The Press Office establishes the pool of journalists coming into
the Oval Office or the Roosevelt Room, where only a small number can be
accommodated. In the Clinton White House, the press secretary had a staff
of around thirty people, including those in the Office of Media Affairs,
spread out among offices in the West Wing and in the Eisenhower Executive Office Building.

One of the first administrative issues a press secretary must deal with
is the lack of control over the office's budget, the salaries of its staff, and the
number of slots assigned to the office. Shaping an executive unit while
lacking such controls is a difficult task. If a person comes into the office in
midterm, the situation can make the organization of the operation difficult
indeed. Mike McCurry had problems bringing in a team because the salaries assigned to the office were so low. "If you're not starting from scratch
or building an office as part of a transition, you just basically are confined
by the arrangements of your predecessor," he said. "I found when I went
to the White House in 1995 I was very hampered by the budget that
Dee Dee [Myers, President Clinton's first press secretary] had negotiated,
and that was the existing budget for that staff." With George Stephanopoulos, Clinton's communications director, who was interested in a strong
media affairs operation, under Jeff Eller, the West Wing Press Office ended
up with people of a fairly low-pay grade. "Dee Dee had sort of frozen in a
budget that paid all these young kids that had worked on the campaign the
best salaries they had ever had in their life, but they weren't the salary of
a Senate press secretary or someone from a PR [public relations] company
that had experience, so you couldn't go recruit people with a lot of talent."
McCurry could not recruit a staff coming from outside or structure the office until he had created his own base of authority and could leave behind
the decisions associated with his predecessor.[20]

Communications Planning: Selecting and Staging Events

While James Hagerty, who served as President Eisenhower's press secretary, was the person who established the function of communications

planning within the White House, the press secretary no longer is the primary staff member responsible for it. There are two reasons for the press secretary's reduced role in this. First, the demands of gathering and delivering information to reporters has become a daunting task, with the twenty-four-hour news day requiring a fairly constant flow of information from the White House. Just making arrangements for reporters takes a great deal of staff time as does the need to deliver information to specialty reporters assigned to the White House, such as trade information for the Dow Jones news wire or budget information for the Bureau of National Affairs. The growing transparent quality of the White House and of a presidency requires that much more information be made available daily, which takes a great deal of time and resources. Second, there are many White House officials now involved in communications planning, and the press secretary defers to them to take the lead while remaining very important in a secondary role.

Increasingly in recent years, the function of persuasion has come into the portfolio of the press secretary through the function of communications planning and staging. "Now there is a persuasion function that is located in the office too, and that is the one I'm increasingly ambivalent about, [it] is part of the job of that office to participate in the selling of the program," McCurry said. "I think that's where you drift over to spin and you drift over to argumentation and opinion-based communicating. I think that's a little more problematic. I'm not sure that's a legitimate function of [the Press Office]."[21] The problem of bringing persuasion into the Press Office is that it raises questions about the authenticity of information provided by the press secretary and his staff.

Press Office Organization and Functions: West Wing and Eisenhower Executive Office Building Operations

During the period since Eisenhower organized the modern White House, the Press Office has been perhaps the most consistent unit in terms of the tasks it performs no matter which party controls the White House or who is president. Since it has developed and retained the same clearly defined constituencies, expectations have remained fairly similar in terms of what the Press Office provides to each. Handling the needs of the White House press corps is at the core of the organization. The West Wing operation, designed to meet the information needs of the press corps, has varied little over time. What has varied are the additions related to the out-of-town press and the electronic media found in the Office of Media Affairs, located in the Eisenhower Executive Office Building.

Press Office tasks can be divided along the lines of information development operations and units targeted to perform services for particular segments of the news organizations. The West Wing operations are defined by their tasks of dealing with current information, relating to the White House press corps, and support work for the press secretary. The offices and staff in the Eisenhower Executive Office Building work with specialized groups in the news media, including the out-of-town press. Operations designed to facilitate television and radio coverage as well as plan advance work for the press corps are housed there too.

Two recent organizational schemes demonstrate the choices a press secretary has in shaping the contours of the office. The office had a broad reach under Press Secretary Mike McCurry, who controlled Media Affairs as well as the routine aspects of the office. Under Marlin Fitzwater, there were fewer organizational parts, though his position was a strong one.

Who Works in the Press Office?

During the final year of the Clinton administration, the Press Office had approximately thirty people working in its two building locations. There were around thirteen people who worked in the West Wing operation and another seventeen in the Eisenhower Executive Office Building. It had a hierarchical organizational structure topped by persons serving as deputy press secretaries or assistant press secretaries. Of those working in the Press Office, eight were people who held titles reflecting their status of appointees of the president; their titles included the phrase "to the president." These included the press secretary, three deputy press secretaries, and four assistant press secretaries or people serving as director of a unit in the Press Office. There were a total of nine staff who directed units within the Press Office and four who held the title "assistant press secretary," including one whose title included "to the president." In addition to its paid staff, the Press Office had slots for five unpaid interns, who rotated in on a schedule of three times a year. It was not an office using short- or long-term volunteers who were specialists in particular tasks, as was the practice in other White House offices, such as the Office of Presidential Personnel.

Figure 12.

President William Clinton
White House Press Office
Spring, 1997

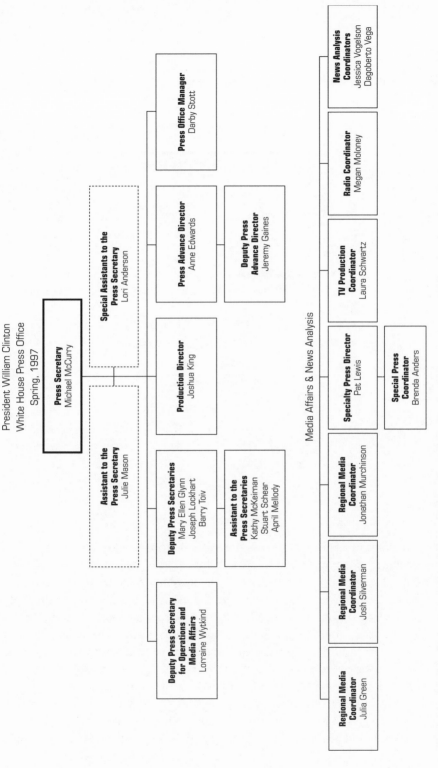

Press Secretary
Michael McCurry

Special Assistants to the Press Secretary
Lori Anderson

Press Office Manager
Darby Stott

Press Advance Director
Anne Edwards

Deputy Press Advance Director
Jeremy Gaines

Production Director
Joshua King

Assistant to the Press Secretary
Julie Mason

Deputy Press Secretaries
Mary Ellen Glynn
Joseph Lockhart
Barry Toiv

Assistant to the Press Secretaries
Kathy McKeirnan
Stuart Schear
April Mellody

Deputy Press Secretary for Operations and Media Affairs
Lorraine Wybkind

Media Affairs & News Analysis

Regional Media Coordinator
Julia Green

Regional Media Coordinator
Josh Silverman

Regional Media Coordinator
Jonathan Murchinson

Specialty Press Director
Pat Lewis

Special Press Coordinator
Brenda Anders

TV Production Coordinator
Laura Schwartz

Radio Coordinator
Megan Moloney

News Analysis Coordinators
Jessica Vogelson
Dagoberto Vega

White House Interview Program (whitehouse2001.org). Based on data in *The Capital Source*, Spring, 1997, National Journal Group Inc., Washington, DC. *Key:* ———
= positions with "to the president" in their title; --------- = staff working for indicated assistant.

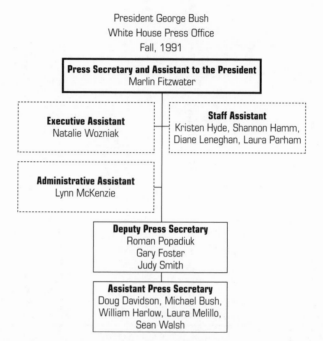

Figure 13.

President George Bush
White House Press Office
Fall, 1991

Press Secretary and Assistant to the President
Marlin Fitzwater

Executive Assistant
Natalie Wozniak

Staff Assistant
Kristen Hyde, Shannon Hamm,
Diane Leneghan, Laura Parham

Administrative Assistant
Lynn McKenzie

Deputy Press Secretary
Roman Popadiuk
Gary Foster
Judy Smith

Assistant Press Secretary
Doug Davidson, Michael Bush,
William Harlow, Laura Melillo,
Sean Walsh

White House Interview Program (whitehouse2001.org). Based on data in *The Capital Source*, Fall, 1991, National Journal Group Inc., Washington, DC. *Key:* ———— = positions with "to the president" in their title; ---------- = staff working for indicated assistant.

West Wing Operation

The heart of the Press Office is the West Wing operation handling the basic daily information needs of the White House press corps posted in the building and others who call in from outside. While there are sixty reporters who have assigned space in various Press Room warrens, there are perhaps thirty-five who use that space on a regular basis, with the others calling in or coming over when the need arises (such as for an interview or to take a reading of a presidential appearance). Whether they are calling from outside or coming into the Lower Press Office, reporters expect to have their information needs met within a very short period of time.

In addition to information, reporters also have logistical needs for their coverage. For those news organizations with staff regularly covering a president and committed to reporting both inside and outside the building, there is a structured pooling operation with rotating assignments for reporters covering the president wherever he goes within the Washington area. At the end of the Clinton administration, the pool had within it thirty-two print-news organizations as well as others representing the wires, television, and radio. In addition to the individual reporters from each news organization, there are cameras as well. Once an event occurs and a print reporter in the pool writes up a description to share with other reporters, the White House copies and distributes the reports in information-release bins, which are located in a narrow hallway behind the Briefing Room.

Upper Press Office: Staff

- Press secretary
- Deputy press secretary for operations
- Deputy assistant to the chief of staff
- Three assistants to the press secretary
- Two interns

Upper Press Office: Functions

- Manage Press Office
- Manage Media Affairs
- Coordinate key White House offices and officials
- Gather information for press briefings
- Schedule the press secretary
- Schedule interviews and facilitate requests by reporters to others on the staff
- Arrange interviews for reporters with the president
- Arrange weekly meeting for the press secretary with three news magazines: *Time, U.S. News and World Report,* and *Newsweek*
- Conduct briefings
- Maintain a briefing book for presidential press conferences
- Prepare for press conferences
- Work with the White House Correspondents Association on seat assignments in the Briefing Room and on issues related to press coverage of the president and the White House staff
- Maintain liaison with the bureau chiefs of the television networks
- Coordinate with departmental public information officers and take part in their selection

The press secretary's office is located down the hall from the Oval Office and across a narrow hall from the Roosevelt Room. He is close to those with whom he must talk every day, especially the president. During the Clinton administration, housed with the press secretary in those quarters were the deputy press secretary for operations, an aide to the chief of staff, and three assistants to the press secretary. The deputy press secretary for operations at that time was in charge of Media Affairs as well as managing the office operations in the West Wing. He or she also represented the press secretary in various White House staff meetings, including scheduling, as well as occasionally responding in an official capacity to press inquiries. The deputy handling operations also coordinated with the public information officers.

Lower Press Office: Staff

- Two deputy press secretaries
- Two assistant press secretaries
- Office manager
- Press assistant
- Five interns per semester

Lower Press Office: Functions

- Provide deputy press secretaries' official responses for the White House twenty-four hours a day
- Serve as traveling press secretaries when the president is on the road and the press secretary remains in Washington
- Organize pools to cover events in the Oval Office, Roosevelt Room, and around Washington
- Arrange setup of events, including lighting setup and laying cable for events "open press" (usually located in the East Room, the Rose Garden, and the South Lawn)
- Arrange for officials meeting with the president to come to the stakeout to speak with reporters
- Arrange for events and speeches to be transmitted to reporters through the "mult"
- Escort reporters to White House events outside of the Press Room
- Provide credentials for reporters covering the White House, including dealing with their news organizations on the number of slots per

organization and the processing of information to go to the Secret Service for clearance
- Clear reporters coming into the White House for an event
- Produce and release official statements, transcripts, and releases
- Contact reporters with updated presidential information on schedules and events
- Provide daily updates of the president's schedule on the recorded message maintained by the Press Office for White House reporters
- Copy pool reports and distribute them to reporters
- Provide responses to events and statements
- Make maintenance calls to the General Services Administration for problems with the Briefing Room and to the physical plant concerning areas where reporters are housed

The Lower Press Office is the first line of defense in dealing with reporters coming in throughout the day posing queries ranging from policy positions to requests for statements, transcripts, and schedules. There are two deputies located in the space as well as two assistant press secretaries, a press assistant, and an office manager.

Much of the work in the unit deals with servicing the media who come in and those who call in. Calls and pages to reporters on the timing of briefings, events, pool arrangements, and the setup for events all come from these staff members. They record the message for the Press Office phone line so reporters can call in for updates on the schedule for the day and information on which news organizations are pool representatives that day. This staff also sends out information updates on the electronic pagers reporters carry in order to keep up to date on changes in the presidential schedule. Staff in the Lower Press Office also work on credentialing the seventeen hundred reporters who cover the White House on a sufficiently regular basis to qualify for "hard passes." (The seventeen hundred figure was a number existing during the Reagan White House and is a limit the Press Office has sought to maintain over the years.) The hard passes allow reporters to come into the White House by sweeping their pass over the admittance mechanism controlled by the Secret Service at the northwest gate. Credentialing reporters involves getting them and their news organizations to fill out information that is then sent to the Secret Service for clearance. For those reporters who do not have clearance and who want to come into the White House for an event or an interview, arrangements are made in the Lower Press Office.

Eisenhower Executive Office Building Operation

The service operations for the press and the organization handling relations with out-of-town media are housed in the Old Executive Building, recently renamed the Eisenhower Executive Office Building. The most significant of the units found there is Media Affairs, a shop that provides a White House line to numerous news organizations outside of Washington. Under Clinton administration press secretaries Mike McCurry, Joe Lockhart, and Jake Siewert, the heart of the Eisenhower operation was the Office of Media Affairs. While in most administrations the office is an independent unit, it was not between 1997 and 2001. In the Clinton White House, it was subsumed under the Press Office and directed by the deputy press secretary for operations.

Staff

- Director, media operations
- Three assistant press secretaries working on regional operations
- Director, television news
- Director, radio services
- Director, Internet news
- Director, television operations
- Director, specialty press
- Director, press advance

Functions

- Schedule White House staff appearances on television shows
- Organize radio services, including sessions with White House senior staff for the radio "tong" and individual reporters
- Arrange weekly radio address
- Prepare news summary
- Update Internet site with official White House releases, including the daily press briefing, presidential statements, and speeches
- E-mail information to selected groups of reporters, depending on their specialty and needs

- Maintain and arrange for the use of the television studio located in the Eisenhower Executive Office Building
- Arrange public service announcements and special radio or television addresses
- Provide information to regional and local news organizations, including responses to their queries
- Brief specialized press coming in from out of town
- Arrange interviews and coverage for regional and local press when they come into the White House for an event
- Deal with the specialty press, including those writing books or representatives of news organizations with a particular specialty, such as ethnic and religious press
- Arrange satellite hookups for certain interviews
- Arrange the television setup for interviews with the president and White House officials, including television documentaries and special programming
- Provide press advance work for trips

Operating Units

Office of Media Affairs

This unit makes arrangements for out-of-town press covering an event at the White House featuring local people as well as provides information to regional and local news organizations about presidential events and actions. In addition, Media Affairs responds to queries from reporters outside of Washington as well as to specialty press. The news organizations falling under the "specialty" category are magazines other than the high-profile weeklies (such as *Time, Newsweek,* and *U.S. News and World Report*) that have regular West Wing access; those organizations have regular access to the press secretary and his deputies. The ethnic press and professional publications are dealt with by people in Media Affairs.

While the Office of Communications was established in part as a perch for Herbert Klein, a longtime press associate of Richard Nixon, it fit in with Nixon's interest in establishing a communications planning operation and a media contact organization for the nation's news outlets. Those functions have remained in a White House, but often they have been dispersed. As the years have gone by, with new technologies added and refined, Media Affairs has picked up these responsibilities, including developing and maintaining a television studio in the Eisenhower Executive Office Building, creating phone lines with cuts from presidential speeches for radio reporters, and developing Internet links to provide a steady stream of White House information on their official website.

Regional Press Contacts

"The regional desks are basically spokespeople for those regions, they are on the record," said Lorrie McHugh, who supervised their operation as deputy press secretary for operations and media affairs in the mid-Clinton years. They are the point of contact with people at the regional and local level and are available when the president travels. In addition, the regional desks provide media advisories to news organizations located outside of Washington and those with no regular White House correspondent. McHugh described the advisories. "Every event on the president's schedule, for the most part, has a media adviser attached to it. Our two radio people deal with all the radio, book interviews. The deputy director for specialty press deals with all the religious, ethnic, publications." If any of the organizations assigned to Media Affairs wants to arrange an interview with the president or with any of the senior staff, they go through this staff.

News Summary and Analysis

The news summary unit in the Clinton administration prepared the daily compilation of news articles sent to the president and to senior White House staff. The news summary began in the Nixon administration as a document describing and quoting from articles in newspapers and on television. It reflected the administration's interest in how they were covered, including providing a sense of what the major news stories were on any given day. In the Clinton White House, the news summary was a compilation of stories copied from the major newspapers, including *The New York Times* and *Washington Post*. In a sense, the news summary has been transformed and downgraded in importance by the advent of newspapers found on the Internet. While in earlier times the White House would send someone down to the *Post* for the early, or "Bull Dog," edition released late at night, today the staff view stories online. In the administration of Pres. George W. Bush, the news summary has been outsourced to a private contractor working out of Fredericksburg, Virginia.

Press Advance

When the president travels outside of Washington, the Press Office makes arrangements for the media accompanying him. While news organizations pay for their reporters' travel, it is the White House that makes the arrangements for their coverage of events and for their lodging. The press-advance unit goes to a country or state prior to a presidential visit and searches for sites meeting the needs of both reporters and the president. On a major foreign visit, the press has a representative who is involved in choosing sites and writing a detailed report for representatives of news organizations. Once they return to the White House, the Press Office distributes that report.

Public Affairs

When it is used in a White House, public affairs is a unit designed to coordinate with the White House information from the departments and agencies in the executive branch. The governmental institutions regularly provide information useful to the White House for inclusion in presidential appearances. The staff here make certain to round up information for cabinet secretaries and others who appear on television and on the road representing the administration. In the Reagan White House, surrogates were given statistics to use drawing a favorable portrait of the administration's record and told what topics to stay clear of in their appearances.

Internet Link

During the Clinton administration, the Internet came of age. The White House maintains a website where information can be released in lieu of the previous system observed by the Press Office, in which transcripts have to be ferried all over town and sent out to the regional and local press. Briefings, statements, and releases are fairly swiftly put on the website, and the Press Office staff can refer reporters to them. In addition, there are several e-mail listings of reporters interested in particular subject areas who automatically receive information concerning their interests. In Clinton's last year he had interviews designed primarily for websites with audio and video capability.

Lessons Learned

Those who have served in the office have some common observations about White House learning. No matter whether they are Democrats or

Republicans, liberals or conservatives, or come in at the beginning or middle of an administration, those who have worked in the Press Office as its head or as a deputy agreed on quite a few matters relating to the operation of the office.

Talk to Your Predecessors

Press secretaries indicated they learned a great deal from those who preceded them. Jody Powell, press secretary to President Carter, expressed the sentiment of the group. "The former press secretaries were very helpful in talking to me about the importance and difficulty of gathering the information that you need to be able to deal with questions in a briefing every day and so forth and ideas on how you organize to do that." From them a press secretary learns: "You can't do it all yourself; different ways to handle presidential approval on what you need to take to him, [and about] what you [don't]."[22]

Do Not Reduce Reporters' Opportunities or Venues for Receiving Information

You can add to what information reporters are given and opportunities there are to receive it, but you cannot subtract from it without paying a heavy cost. When the Clinton Press Office shut off to reporters entry to the pathway they traditionally used to query the press secretary, resentment from the press was swift and strong. That fight was about information, not real estate. With information routines well established, a press secretary courts trouble when altering the forums where information is delivered or reducing opportunities for reporters to acquire information about the president and his administration.

Ninety Percent of the Information You Are Dealing with Comes from the Press

While it is natural to think the information one is dealing with in a White House is exclusively held, the contrary is true. The White House staff, like everyone else in town, discovers in the press most of the information they have to deal with about a given issue and what is happening on it around town. It is important for a press secretary and his or her deputies to read *The New York Times*, the *Washington Post*, and *The Wall Street Journal* prior to the morning staff meetings. Mike McCurry said, "Ninety percent of the information about a given thing was coming from the press, not coming from inside the government."[23] Thus, one has to thoroughly read the papers and news summary. That is particularly true of foreign-policy news.

Do Not Hire People You Do Not Know

Marlin Fitzwater indicated he did not hire people he did not know because time is short and risk is high. "One lesson of management that I found in the White House was never hire somebody on the basis of interviews and paper. If you don't know them from some previous existence, it's too high a risk. You don't have time to train them; you don't have time to make it work; you don't have time to fail. You can't afford a failure. And it's really high risk hiring people that you don't know."[24]

An Inquisitive Press Corps Can Work in the Favor of the White House

While the White House spends a great deal of its energy trying to stop stories it does not like as well as redirecting reporters to stories they want covered, it can come to haunt a president and his staff. McCurry spoke of the consequences of not having been asked about the fundraising events taking place in the White House in 1996, an issue that later was to cause them difficulty. "I never got asked the question, so I never stopped to get any answers about what is that all about. I honestly do believe, if we had gotten pressed early in 1995 and the press had started raising the issue of what are all these political events you're doing in the White House, I think we would have had to get on top of it and have the answers, we probably would have checked out a little more thoroughly what can you and can you not do with respect to fundraising activities."[25]

Do Not Sandbag the Press

Ray Jenkins, who worked in the Carter White House as an assistant to the president serving in the Press Office, spoke of the importance of not playing games with reporters with their deadlines. "Now you didn't try to sandbag the press. This was something we were very careful not to do, was to play tricks with them. You didn't announce something, a very important initiative, at 5:30 in the afternoon, and say, 'Okay. Take it now and put it on the television or put it in the paper tomorrow.' You did try to respect their need for familiarizing themselves, getting the background for it, or even helping them get that insofar as possible."[26]

There Are Many Ways to Say "I Don't Know"

All reporters really want is to be able to get the information they need and have it right when they get it. To speak authoritatively when one does not have an answer rather than admit one's lack of knowledge is a serious error. Pete Roussel, who served as deputy press secretary in the Reagan administration, described a typical situation where a press officer struck an evasive note when talking with reporters. A front-page story in the *Washington Post* indicated that there was a plan to switch positions for some of President Reagan's senior aides. Not knowing if such was the case, Roussel decided the "best thing for me to say is it serves no useful purpose for me to comment on speculative stories like that. . . . As you know, that's an answer where I'm neither confirming nor denying it because I didn't know; maybe there was something afoot.[27]

Lying Compromises Your Credibility

Providing reporters with misinformation is a cardinal sin no matter whether it is willful or unintentional. When a press secretary does not get the story straight and causes a reporter to air or write an inaccurate story, reporters will not trust the information provided to them and search around the White House for other sources. Pete Roussel stated the importance he attached to not misleading reporters and why. "The one thing you have to offer in that job in my view is your credibility, your honesty, your word, your bond. The first time you tarnish that either by misleading or knowingly lying, that press corps will be on you in a second, and it will get around pretty quick. You're probably toast then."[28]

Be Wary of Adopting the Role of Persuader

The Press Office is the setting where official information is released, not a place where persuasion is the central task. Mike McCurry discussed the problem of using the briefing for persuasion rather than as a location to disseminate administration information. "In retrospect, [I] think the whole spin, the propaganda, the looking like you're trying to spin the politically attractive side of the argument . . . is very unsettling. I think it also diminishes the authority that you need to have in that process so people understand this is good information they're getting. It needs to be more of a session in which you just communicate basically factual information so people can get their work done and leave the argumentation elsewhere. I think there's too much argumentation in the process now."[29]

Combining the Functions of Communications and Public Liaison with the Press Office

More is not better. A press secretary cannot control the strategic-planning function at the same time he is handling the requirements associated with providing reporters presidential information on a constant basis. Ron Nessen talked about the need to combine communications and press and the impossibility of doing so. "[T]he problem is that the communications director's job ought to combine all the things that the press secretary does. The problem is that it takes the press secretary so long to get ready for the daily briefing, to make sure he knows everything, attend the meetings so he can soak up all the information plus all the logistics stuff—there's a trip coming up; getting ready for the trip and making sure—there's an enormous amount of reading matter. One person can't do those two jobs and it should be one person."[30]

Personality Needs

Certain people work well as press secretaries, while others do not. A cool temperament works somewhat better than a hot-tempered person. Ron Nessen explained his own situation: "I think my personality wasn't exactly the right one for the White House. I had a temper; I was thin-skinned. I liked Ford as a person; I tended to be overly protective of him and those things." Mike McCurry spoke of the importance of using humor to cool down a hot briefing room. Marlin Fitzwater spoke of the need for tolerance and patience. "In terms of personality traits and character traits, I think patience and tolerance are pretty important. . . . [Y]ou have to listen to the requests of sixty or seventy people with different agendas, different publications, different needs for information, and to give them credit for deserving that information requires an amazing amount of patience."[31]

Even if a press secretary or his or her deputies have patience and tolerance, success is hard to achieve in running the Press Office. As in all offices, though, the more one knows coming in about the rhythms and patterns of the office, the better off one is in getting purchase on the nature of the job and of the White House as an institution.

Notes

1. For a discussion of the manner in which these offices interact with one another, see the chapter "The Office of Communications." See also "Presidential Publicity in the Clinton Era: The White House Communications Quartet" (paper presented to the Midwest Political Science Association convention, Apr., 1998). The information contained in that paper will be included in the forthcoming book, *Wired for Sound and Pictures: The President and White House Communications Operations* (Johns Hopkins University Press).

2. Ron Nessen, interview with Martha Joynt Kumar, Washington, D.C., Aug. 3, 1999, White House Interview Program.

3. For a discussion of the gaggle and the briefing, see "The Daily White House Press Briefings: A Reflection of the Enduring Elements of a Relationship" (paper presented to the Joan Shorenstein Center on the Press and Politics at the John F. Kennedy School of Government, Harvard University, spring, 1999).

4. The "gaggle," referring to the sound of geese, takes its name from military sessions where commanders offer up information to subordinates.

5. James Fetig, interview with Martha Joynt Kumar, Rockville, Md., Feb. 5, 1999, White House Interview Program.

6. Michael McCurry, interview with Martha Joynt Kumar, Washington, D.C., Mar. 27, 2000, White House Interview Program.

7. Marlin Fitzwater, interview with Martha Joynt Kumar, Deale, Md., Oct. 21, 1999, White House Interview Program.

8. Fetig interview.

9. Fitzwater interview.

10. Ibid.

11. Larry Speakes, interview with Martha Joynt Kumar, Washington, D.C., June 28, 1999, White House Interview Program.

12. McCurry interview.

13. Fitzwater interview.

14. See Martha Joynt Kumar, "The President and the News Media," in *Guide to the Presidency,* ed. Michael Nelson (Washington, D.C.: Congressional Quarterly, 1996), pp. 875–76.

15. For a discussion of the nature of this relationship, see Michael Baruch Grossman and Martha Joynt Kumar, *Portraying the President: The White House and the News Media* (Baltimore: Johns Hopkins University Press, 1981).

16. Roman Popadiuk, interview with Martha Joynt Kumar, College Station, Tex., Nov. 2, 1999, White House Interview Program.

17. Speakes interview.

18. Popadiuk interview.

19. Speakes interview.

20. McCurry interview.

21. Ibid.

22. Jody Powell, interview with Martha Joynt Kumar, Washington, D.C., Aug. 2, 2000, White House Interview Program.

23. McCurry interview.

24. Fitzwater interview.

25. McCurry interview.

26. Ray Jenkins, interview with Martha Joynt Kumar, Washington, D.C., Sept. 8, 1999, White House Interview Program.

27. Peter Roussel, interview with Martha Joynt Kumar and Terry Sullivan, Houston, Tex., Nov. 3, 1999, White House Interview Program.

28. Ibid.

29. McCurry interview.

30. Nessen interview.

31. Fitzwater interview.

The Office of Communications

MARTHA JOYNT KUMAR

THE OFFICE OF COMMUNICATIONS IS ONE OF several institutions crucial to the startup of an administration because of the central place of effective communications in a successful presidency.[1] Of the four presidents elected to a second term in the post–World War II period, each one had an effective communications operation in addition to being a personally successful communicator. What an effective communications organization bought them was the opportunity to display publicly, in terms of their choosing, the issues they wanted to focus on and to develop strategies designed to achieve the president's personal, policy, and electoral goals. The components of effective communications for Presidents Eisenhower, Nixon, Reagan, and Clinton included personal attributes and a communications operation that incorporated daily press operations and an organization or, in the case of President Eisenhower, an individual (Press Secretary James Hagerty), capable of planning ahead for presidential and administration-wide publicity. From Eisenhower's administration to the present, successful communications has evolved into a system where organization plays a key role in strategic planning for the coordination of people, programs, and institutions. The Office of Communications is front and center in the campaigns waged on behalf of a president and his programs. The coordination and production roles of the director of the office and of those who serve in it are central to successful White House publicity.

While the Office of Communications is vital to the communications of an effective presidency no matter who serves as chief executive, the position of communications director has proved to be a volatile one. Since 1969 when the office was created, there have been twenty-two people at its helm, an average of less than a year and a half for each director. There have been approximately the same number of press secretaries, but that position has existed since 1929, forty years longer than the Office of Communications. The turnover rate of communications directors reflects the difficult environment incumbents operate in as well as the multiple and sometimes conflicting demands placed on them.[2] George Stephanopoulos, who held that post for the first four months of the Clinton administration, observed that his being relieved of the job was not a surprise. "By definition, if the president isn't doing well, it's a communications problem. That's always going to be a natural place to make a change."[3] The communications director is held responsible for how a president is doing, yet has little in the way of resources to affect the outcomes that form the basis for judging presidential performance. For that reason, his or her chair is the White House hot seat.

The Environment within Which the Office of Communications Functions

The important place of presidential communications can be seen in the manner in which the topic drives the agenda of daily staff meetings, the large commitment of White House and administration resources and people, and the way its function has insinuated itself into the operations of almost every White House office.

Presidential communications relates directly to what it is a president does in office and how effectively the White House can use its organizational resources to publicize their goals and achievements. "A successful communications strategy is only one aspect of a successful presidency," observed Mike McCurry, press secretary to President Clinton. "You have to have a good solid sense of priority and where you're going and mission, and everything is supportive of that. That involves good leadership from the chief of staff, good policy planning, good legislative relations on the Hill. It's all part of a seamless whole. That's what makes for a good presidency."[4]

A Position Defined by Its Relationships

The communications director is an official whose position is defined by his relationships with officials inside the White House and political people outside of that building. His work is defined by those he serves.

The President

The most important relationships for the communications director are those with the president and with the chief of staff. Michael Deaver, who served as deputy chief of staff in the Reagan White House, said his work was defined by his relationships with the president and first lady. "And I really sort of gained whatever control or power I had simply by my relationship. But I overlapped with a lot of [Chief of Staff James] Baker," Deaver said. "Baker basically gave me free rein. I spent most of my time on schedule and travel and the military office and all of the East Wing, which included the first lady and the military. Then [I] had sort of an ad hoc seat on anything dealing with communications. When [David] Gergen left, I took over officially the communications role."[5]

For David Demarest, who served as communications director for Pres. George H. W. Bush, communications had a smaller scope to it than was true of the part played by Deaver. Demarest described the role President Bush wanted him to assume as his communications director: "I think the president saw me more as the guy that ran his speeches and his events. I don't think he saw that in terms of a communications message. I think that he saw the press as the vehicle for the communications message through [Press Secretary] Marlin [Fitzwater] and through his own interactions with the press."[6] For Demarest, the job was more an administrative post than it was one in which he developed communications strategies for the president. When Bush decided he wanted Fitzwater to do communications as well as his press relations, Fitzwater did so for a short period of time despite his own misgivings of combining the two jobs.

The Chief of Staff

The chief of staff is a key White House figure in communications. Effective communications comes through coordination of people and offices with the integration of policy and political information. That process must be directed out of the Office of the Chief of Staff. Either the chief of staff does such coordination himself, as Leon Panetta and James Baker did for Presidents Clinton and Reagan respectively, or it is done by deputies. When Erskine Bowles was chief of staff under Clinton, for example, his deputy, John Podesta, took charge of communications and, following the senior-staff meeting, held a meeting each morning devoted to publicity issues.

In addition to his role coordinating publicity with policy, the chief of staff can come into the communications process as an on-camera or background presence. When James Baker was chief of staff, he spent a great deal of time explaining administration policy to reporters on a background basis. "Talk to the press a lot; stay in touch with the press. Always do it on background. Just remember, you weren't elected to anything, and people don't want to read your name in the paper. But it's important for you to keep the press informed about what it is you're trying to do and continually spend time with them."[7]

Today the chief of staff is expected to be a regular presence on the Sunday television talk programs and sometimes on the morning shows as well. Beginning with Leon Panetta, who was very used to appearing on such programs when he was chairman of the House Budget Committee, the chief of staff became a television presence explaining administration policies. Erskine Bowles eschewed such appearances when he was chief of staff, but John Podesta observed the Panetta model. In the early days of the administration of Pres. George W. Bush, Chief of Staff Andrew Card has followed the Panetta and Podesta examples more so than those of Bowles.

The Press Secretary

The responsibilities of the communications director are considered in light of those exercised by the press secretary. Of the eleven people who have served as press secretary, two of them have exercised the communications function and exercised both responsibilities. In the Carter White House, for example, the only time there was a communications director was when Gerald Rafshoon was on the staff around the time leading up to the 1976 election. Press Secretary Jody Powell was expected to take the lead in the whole of the public-relations area. Marlin Fitzwater took over the communications job for a period of a few months during the first Bush administration, but it was against his wishes and did not last long. But there is one instance when the press secretary reported to communications. That configuration was the case when President Clinton's first press secretary, Dee Dee Myers, reported to Communications Director George Stephanopoulos. Most often, though, the relationship between the two officials is one of close contact about issues of mutual interest and responsibility but no organizational connection where one reports to the other.

Other White House Relationships

The communications director regularly works with other White House offices and other federal agencies and departments as they setup events with an effect on the partners to the events. In an instance of White House–agency coordination, Don Baer worked with the Intergovernmental Affairs Office on setting up an event associated with a presidential appearance at the National Governors Association. "Intergovernmental affairs knows that the National Governors Association is meeting," he began. "What does he want to say to the NGA? It's a big, high profile event opportunity. So you'd have to have a lot of work and negotiation with them over what the governors were willing to hear from him versus what we wanted to do and say there, all those kinds of things. It was complicated."[8]

Communications Discussions Initiate the White House Work Day

Communications is central to the modern presidency, and its position is reflected in what it is the White House senior staff do every day. This is true for Republicans and Democrats alike. In the Reagan and Bush administrations, the day began with communications as an important item on the agenda. In his days in the Reagan and Bush White Houses, for example, Press Secretary Marlin Fitzwater wrote up a memo for senior staff that served as an indicator to them of the press issues for the day. "My role at the staff meeting would be always the same: 'Marlin, what do we have to deal with today?' Everybody's got my memo around the table. 'These are the issues. If any of you want to add anything to any of these or give me any advice come do it as soon as possible because I'm going to have to come up with answers.'" In the period from President Nixon forward, communications was featured as an important factor in how the day began.

For Democrats as well, press coverage of their administrations and how they should respond to news stories drives a day. The early morning meeting convened by Chief of Staff Leon Panetta was fairly consistent in its subject matter to similar sessions held in Republican White Houses. Panetta described his meetings with core White House staff, dubbed the "Managers Meeting." Its members included the national security adviser, national economic council director, the press secretary, the vice president's chief of staff, the first lady's chief of staff, the Office of Management and Budget (OMB) director, and the communications director. "The first thing was to ask [Press Secretary Mike] McCurry and George Stephanopoulos what's playing in the news that day, what's happening that day, what do they think are the big issues." As the staff discussed issues, they made decisions on what would be done during the day and who would be involved. Communications decisions were among them. "What's the best place to stage that for the president, the Rose Garden? Is it the Press Room? Is it to wait until the press goes in on an event and expect the question to be asked there? Those kinds of decisions don't have to go to the president of the United States. They're staging issues that you can make decisions on."[9]

A Calendar to Work With

There are rhythms to a year, a month, a week, and an administration. Knowing what events take place on the policy side in Washington, a president can plan out some of the opportunities he has during the year to focus on his issues in a manner of his choosing. The presidential calendar, he and his staff soon find out, comprises fixed events, most especially those associated with the congressional schedule. Two of the most important are the congressional schedule and the budget deadlines. Those are significant for the pace of policy initiatives as well as the consideration of appointments. The State of the Union message is held at the end of January; the first part of the congressional session goes from early January to the Easter recess. In the spring, commencement addresses offer an opportunity to set themes for defense and other issues a president chooses, such as technology and foreign policy; Clinton used them for all of these areas. Foreign policy comes to the forefront with the G-7 economic conference, the APAC conference on Asian economic issues, and in September with the opening session of the United Nations. In the fall Congress again comes to the forefront, with negotiations over the budget and bargaining on policies then in the committee and floor stages of consideration.

Congressional Session

Each congressional session makes a great deal of difference to the manner in which the White House functions and the shape of their agenda. Communications Director Ann Lewis commented on the link between the

White House agenda and the congressional calendar. "When Congress is in and you're close to the legislative session, you're working on budget and legislation and that's going to drive your day. Earlier in the year you have more freedom to sort of initiate and set the agenda. You try to get out most of the issues you want to make the case for early if you can." Lewis believed the congressional calendar more than any other is the cycle influencing White House actions. "I think we are sort of like the moon and the tides in that way." "At the beginning of the year we spend our time laying out our agenda and you know that by the fall we will be in the season where there will be action on it. In between we try, whenever possible, to call attention to the agenda and to get interest in it and action on it."[10]

State of the Union

Each year the calendar presents the administration with an opportunity to present its policy priorities and to do so in a setting that commands substantial public attention. The communications director is most often the official coordinating the publicity side of these fixed events. The State of the Union message is the most important regularly scheduled speech of the year. It brings together policy, politics, and publicity to focus on the president's policy agenda and how they are going to get it through.

The Clinton administration added to the importance of the speech by casting it as a series of events that began once Congress left town in November or December and the president's congressional opponents fanned out to their hometowns across the country. Left with approximately six weeks without congressional opposition, the Clinton team described the ideas to be showcased in the State of the Union message. They left a couple of items to be announced in the speech itself, but for the other policy proposals, there were stories focusing on the particulars of what the president would offer in the address and surrogates in the administration who elaborated on the need for Clinton's initiatives.

Television Is Central to Communications Operations

Other than the Press Office, there is no place in the White House where television is so central to what an office does. In an era where people demonstrate little interest in national politics, the first order of business is to get their attention. Ann Lewis discussed where television comes into their events. "What you've got to do every day proactively is figure out how do you talk to people about what you're doing and why. Left to itself, the political system talks to itself. So my goal is every day, how do I reach that audience. What do we know about them? They're busy. They've got a lot going on in their lives. They've got two jobs, two kids, two cars; they're worried about Johnny in school. . . . We are never going to be as important to them as they are to us. We've got to reach them wherever they are and whatever else they're doing."[11]

The White House does not leave to chance the images people receive about what the president is doing nor their interpretation. In the Clinton White House, the Communications Office developed banners to accompany each of the events they staged. By using a sign in this way, the White House was less dependent on the television network correspondents to mention the message in their remarks accompanying the video.

> We give you the opening paragraph, we give you the closing story, and we even give you the headline. That signage is our headline. But it's all because we're talking to an audience where we're in heavy competition for their attention, and we need to use every possible means to break through. Newspapers are where insiders and people who really care about issues read about them in depth. Insiders include members of Congress and policymakers, so they're very important. And they're also where a lot of television stories come from. So I'm not knocking newspaper stories, but they reach a smaller audience, especially the stories that are covered on A-17.[12]

The public learns what is happening in the political system through television news, but getting to people means grabbing their interest while they are paying only limited attention to the television. That is a daily challenge the White House faces. The communications director is tasked with figuring out how to break through to the public with the president's messages.

The Work of the Communications Director

More than is true for most of the offices in the White House, the Communications Office is fairly unique in the degree to which its organization is dependent upon who the director is. There is substantial variation in what communications advisers emphasize as their basic role. The Clinton White House provided an example of the various ways in which communications can be organized. There were seven people who exercised this function, though only five of them held the title of communications director. Among them, there were at least three ways of managing the job: as an advocate with the press, as a strategist and planner, and as an events coordinator. While directors may perform all of these roles, they tend to emphasize one of them. Among the Clinton communications directors, George Stephanopoulos and Mark Gearan were primarily advocates with the press, Don Baer was a strategist and planner, and Ann Lewis and Loretta Ucelli emphasized the events planning.

The Three Models of Communications Directors: Advocate with the Press, Strategist and Planner, and Events Coordinator

The group representing the advocates with news organizations, composed of George Stephanopoulos and Mark Gearan, spent a great deal of time working with the press, including appearing on television and speaking with reporters for print organizations. Don Baer explained the work done in the early years and how the emphasis of the job changed. "Everybody, whether they were called communications director or press secretary, basically thought their job was to be press secretary and not to really be a communications director in any sense of laying down strategy, helping the various output arms of the public face of the White House to know what their role would be in the context of the larger strategy for public communications. What most people spent their time doing was the care and feeding of the press rather than thinking about the strategic communications objectives of the White House and how best to push those out."[13]

When Baer came in during the early phase of the 1996 reelection campaign, he took the communications job with the title of director of strategy and planning. The strategy he worked on had as its goal President Clinton winning reelection in 1996. All of their strategies focused either directly or indirectly on an electoral victory. Once the election was over and Baer left the White House, Ann Lewis took the post. She used it to focus on staging events to showcase the president's policies, as did her successor, Loretta Ucelli. Both Lewis and Ucelli held the title of communications director. Neither of them was regarded as a spokesperson for the White House in the same sense that Stephanopoulos and Gearan were. Lewis did appear as a defender of the president during the early stages of the Monica Lewinsky scandal, but Press Secretary Mike McCurry was the central spokesperson. Loretta Ucelli did not appear publicly on behalf of the administration. Baer commented of the period: "I was succeeded by Ann Lewis, and Ann was succeeded by Loretta Ucelli, and Loretta reverted to the title of director of communications, which is what the office is now known as. So when I left, it stopped being the director of strategic planning and communications. And it's important, I think, to note that every one of those people has treated the job somewhat differently in terms of where they fit within the overall operation and function of the White House and things that they emphasized."[14]

The duties performed by the communications director in the Clinton White House depended upon who else was working on communications, including David Gergen, who had served in several administrations as a communications specialist; the closeness to the reelection campaign; and the people who held the post as well as the desires of the president. These same roles can be found in earlier administrations. The press-advocate role was exercised by Herb Klein and Ken Clawson in the Nixon administration, Gerald Warren in the Ford administration, and Patrick Buchanan in the Reagan administration. The strategist role was performed by communications directors in office during presidential reelection campaigns, including David Gergen in the Ford and Reagan administrations, Gerald Rafshoon in the Carter administration, and Thomas Griscom in the Reagan administration. The role of event planner was emphasized by Margita White in the Ford administration, Mari Maseng in the Reagan administration, and David Demarest in the first Bush administration.

The Responsibilities of the Communications Director

While the job of the communications director has varied as much as has its title, there are basic responsibilities performed by the director and those who work in the office no matter whether the incumbent works as a press advocate, a strategist and planner, or an events manager. The minimum the job entails is events management while the greater role is defining the message of a particular presidency with a strategic plan to match.

Strategic Communications

Message is central to the communications operation in terms of developing messages for the president and others to deliver. In addition the tasks of coordination and amplification come in as well. The quality, strength, and the direction of the message depend upon the ability of the president and his team to focus on their agenda and not let the entreaties of others overshadow their own interests. "Strategic communications is a balancing act," Don Baer said. "There are different pressing constituencies who want this, that or the other." The press secretary might want a press conference "because he's got the press corps beating down his door. Your people, different interest groups or different folks who want your president to come and speak to them about their things or their issues. What you have to keep in mind is what you are trying to get done for the sake of the president and for the presidency and for your objectives and not for all of their objectives. It's a balancing act at all times." He continued: "That's what strategic communications is about is sort of balancing all that, the use of the available tools and resources to be able to keep getting that message out in a coherent way that's your way, not their way."[15]

Message Development

Message development begins with the most important resource a White House has: the president's time. A part of every scheduled event for a president is the message attached to it. Don Baer described the process of insinuating a message into events. "What happened was folks came to be trained to look to the communications operation for decisions, at least first-line decisions, recommendations that would go up then to the chief of staff and eventually the president for what the schedule would be, what the message aspects of each of the scheduled events would be; how those scheduled events once they then got scheduled would be implemented or executed."[16]

The State of the Union is an example of the development of a message that resonates throughout the year. Ideally, it has all of the major elements of the president's policy agenda for a year. "I think it's true that two or three years ago we realized that there is so much in the State of the Union that, rather than save everything for the State of the Union, we could roll out some of the individual events leading up to it," said Ann Lewis. "And we've done that ever since. And it's really important because you may have twenty-five or thirty good ideas in the State of the Union. There's no way that they're all going to get attention otherwise. So this has worked out really well."[17] Often it takes the major portion of the year to work through the items mentioned in the address.

Don Baer spoke of message development as encompassing the larger message about the influence, importance, and purpose of the presidency. "To me, the job very much was about helping to form and develop both the larger message for what the impact and the importance and the purpose of the presidency was at any given moment, that's a larger message. Then the specific messages and strategic messages for public-consumption purposes that came out of what that message and themes and purposes of the White House were, and to make sure that every office or every entity that had some role in conveying what that message and image was publicly, communicating that image and message and strategy publicly, that each one of them understood what their role was in doing that and in many cases working very directly and operationally with them to ensure that those messages, themes, and strategies were in fact being conveyed."[18]

Message Coordination

There is coordination that needs to be done within the White House, as with the Intergovernmental Affairs Office. The communications director coordinates with every office that has some role in conveying the message and works with them to make sure they do so. He or she coordinates people, events, and information, then coordinates with departments on which policies to put forward, when to do so, in what sequence, and how to present them. Don Baer described the constellation of offices he dealt with inside and outside of the White House: "Speechwriting. Scheduling. Advance. I dealt a lot with the National Security Council, and within the National Security Council particular offices like the office that really ran the operational side of the NSC. But that would be about which trips are we going to take; what do we want to schedule when we're there."[19]

Ann Lewis discussed the coordination involved in event planning under her watch. Those in the room included all of the White House shops. "It's the policy shop that comes up with the ideas; they come to tell you what you need to do; scheduling and advance, for literally what the timing will be of the day. Intergovernmental because they're going to talk to their constituents; political so people know what you're doing, and cabinet affairs because there's always a cabinet officer. And legislative. You are literally going to have every shop sitting in that room if you do it right so that everybody walks out of that meeting knowing what you want to achieve, what their responsibility is to make it work, and what they're going to say to their folks."[20]

No matter who serves as communications director, coordinating the message with department secretaries can be a problem. Don Baer spoke of the difficulties presented by Labor Secretary Robert Reich when he conceived and delivered his messages without consulting the White House at any stage of development. "The president was in Hawaii for the fiftieth anniversary of V-J Day," Baer related about a particular event. "Reich, without really clearing anything with anybody I knew of in the White House, gave a speech, and his whole perspective on the news that weekend as he rolled himself out was one of pessimism basically, that we're not doing enough for the poor; people are anxious and scared and nervous; middle-class squeeze. The old message, which many of us thought was not the right message for the labor secretary of an incumbent president to be delivering three months before the beginning of the year when you're going to be running for reelection." Rather than describe the progress made during their years in office, Reich emphasized the campaign message of 1991–92, that "we're not preparing ourselves for the new economy and the people who are working the hardest, the middle class, are the ones who are not getting ahead in this new economy. Well, first off, it did not comport with statistical reality and the direction of the country." Reining in Reich never got any easier for the communications director or other members of the White House staff who wanted to see him follow White House direction.[21]

Message Amplification

Ann Lewis discussed another aspect of coordination, amplification. "The role is really take whatever the president is doing today and get it to the largest number of people. Again, maybe that's through intergovernmental, through state and local elected officials; maybe it's back to a cabinet agency like HHS [Health and Human Services]. But it's every other way of communicating the message other than the press. The press has its own operation." Some of the coordinating work is accomplished through the Office of Cabinet Affairs. "I think they do a lot of it. But it's usually done either through cabinet affairs or in conjunction with cabinet affairs, put packages together, and sometimes for intergovernmental. But a lot of work is done to be sure. Thanks to our web site, for example, we get talking points up every day. We call it 'The White House at Work,' which is something we started. So if you're going out as a surrogate, you can just pull down what the president has done for the last week or two weeks and it's there." During the time she served as communications director, Lewis added a person to the office to work on amplification. "The second person I added was an amplification staffer whose role is to get the message back out once it's been done. How do we let everyone know it's happened: get talking points out; maybe the local government might get more information on this so they in turn can spread it; taking the information, taking the president's remarks and communicating them back out."[22]

Create and Administer Units Carrying out Communications Functions

One of the clues to the varied nature of communications director is the lack of certainty of what units are within his or her domain. Don Baer described the extent of his realm when he held the position of assistant to the president for strategic planning and communications. "What's interesting is that the people who were in my direct management line or indirect management line would not be an accurate reflection of what I had to be responsible for because a lot of those didn't report to me, but I would have to be responsible for what came out of their shops. Directly or indirectly, definitely on any kind of a flow chart would have been thirty or forty people. Indirectly, if you throw in scheduling and advance—certainly the advance world in terms of what you saw on television and all that kind of stuff—another fifty or sixty people that I had to deal with."[23] Ann Lewis indicated that under her watch there were approximately twenty-five in the office. "That included speech writing (domestic), research, events— which is a small suboffice—and after that, sort of individuals. I will tell you, that is pretty much the structure as I found it, and probably the only thing I did that changed while I was here was I built up our capacity on events because I thought that was the single most important way we proactively got our message out, events at which the president, in his own voice, was going to be delivering a message."[24]

Two recent configurations demonstrate the variety of tasks and units coming under the office. When George Stephanopoulos headed the office for the Clinton White House in spring, 1993, it contained media affairs as well as the traditional units. In the final years of the administration, the office had fewer parts.

In the descriptions below, the latest organizational configuration of each office was used to provide information on how many people worked in the office and what their job titles were. For most, the date used was fall, 2000, but several, such as the Office of Media Affairs, have not existed as a separate unit for some years. For the Office of Media Affairs, the date used is spring, 1995, which was at a time when it was a strong unit within the Press Office.[25]

Figure 14.

President William Clinton
White House Office of Communications
Fall, 1993

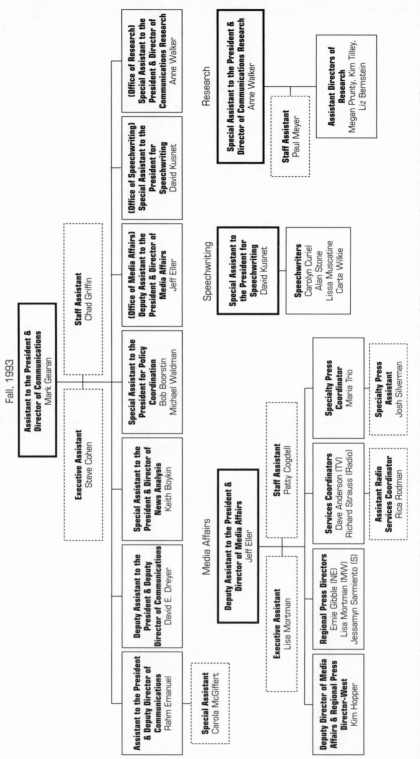

White House Interview Program (whitehouse2001.org). Based on data in *The Capital Source*, Fall, 1993, National Journal Group Inc., Washington, DC. *Key:* ———— = positions with "to the president" in their title; --------- = staff working for indicated assistant.

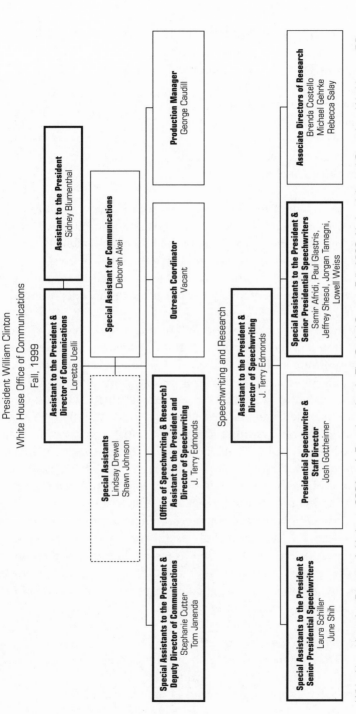

Figure 15.

President William Clinton
White House Office of Communications
Fall, 1999

Assistant to the President
Sidney Blumenthal

**Assistant to the President &
Director of Communications**
Loretta Ucelli

**Special Assistants to the President &
Deputy Director of Communications**
Stephanie Cutter
Tom Janenda

Special Assistants
Lindsay Drewel
Shawn Johnson

Special Assistant for Communications
Deborah Akei

Production Manager
George Caudill

Outreach Coordinator
Vacant

**(Office of Speechwriting & Research)
Assistant to the President and
Director of Speechwriting**
J. Terry Edmonds

Speechwriting and Research

**Assistant to the President &
Director of Speechwriting**
J. Terry Edmonds

**Presidential Speechwriter &
Staff Director**
Josh Gottheimer

**Special Assistants to the President &
Senior Presidential Speechwriters**
Samir Afridi, Paul Glastris,
Jeffrey Shesol, Jorgan Tamagni,
Lowell Weiss

Associate Directors of Research
Brenda Costello
Michael Gehrke
Rebecca Salay

**Special Assistants to the President &
Senior Presidential Speechwriters**
Laura Schiller
June Shih

White House Interview Program (whitehouse2001.org). Based on data in *The Capital Source,* Fall, 1999, National Journal Group Inc., Washington, DC.
Key: ――――― = positions with "to the president" in their title; --------- = staff working for indicated assistant.

Office of Media Affairs, Spring, 1995
- Director of media affairs
- Regional projects coordinator and specialty press director
- Specialty press assistant
- Two regional coordinators
- Television services coordinator
- Radio services coordinator
- Deputy radio services coordinator
- Two news analysis coordinators

Media affairs is an office that demonstrates the manner in which a division can be bounced around among White House units.[26] At the same time, it gives an example of the method by which publicity units are tied together, with a common element being the staff's interest in reaching an audience outside of Washington through a planned and organized effort to send information favorable to the president to those reporting across the country.

In looking through the location of the office in recent White Houses under the various chiefs of staff, press secretaries, and directors of the Communications Office and the Office of Public Liaison, one can see that the unit is most associated with a general communications or publicity effort. Only in the Carter years and in the latter part of the Clinton administration has media affairs been seen as a division of the regular press operation. At no time during the Reagan or Bush years was the unit found within the Press Office. That is because it is by nature a planning operation, and recent Republican administrations have viewed that as an element of the communications operation, which has often been associated with the chief of staff's office. With the capacity of the unit to disseminate information outside of Washington and to coordinate information within the federal government, it is particularly useful as a resource of persuasion. With the interest of the Clinton White House in bringing persuasion into the Press Office, the placement of that unit there is telling. In the Carter White House the opposite was true: media affairs was housed in the Press Office because they had no communications operation.

Speechwriting and Research, Fall, 2000
- Assistant to the president and director of speechwriting
- Deputy director of speechwriting
- Special assistant to the director of speechwriting

- Special assistant to the president and senior speechwriter
- Four presidential speechwriters
- Two senior speechwriters
- Director of research
- Three associate directors of research

The communications director has a role in what the president says, where he gives a speech, and who the audience is. All of that is part of the speechwriting process, not just the words. It is the picture as well. It also means determining which press people to talk to about the speech. He controls the content of the speech and the selling of it as well. If the communications director has control of speeches, his recommendations go to the chief of staff on the scheduling of speeches, the message aspects, and how they should be implemented or executed. Communications chiefs have sought control over speechwriting, for control over the message is critical to effective communications. Authority over speechwriting does not come with the job, it comes by assignment.

Speechwriting is both an offensive and a defensive enterprise. If an administration is not careful, it can end up dictating policy rather than describing it. Often speeches do dictate policy. "I used to think before I went to the White House, for example, that you made policy decisions and then you wrote a speech to describe the policy," observed a former chief of staff. "Oftentimes it doesn't work that way. Oftentimes, the fact of scheduling the speech drives policy because you don't get to the point where decisions get made until the president's going to be on the tube at nine o'clock tomorrow night to talk specifically about his tax policy. Your guys still haven't resolved this question of what we're going to do on capital gains or whatever it might be. It's the fact of having scheduled a time, a locale where he's going to talk about a certain issue that forces the policymakers in the administration, including the president himself, to make decisions. So speeches drive policy oftentimes rather than the other way around."[27] Don Baer spoke about the same thing happening during the first year of the Clinton administration. They would have an event scheduled and then would call the group the president was appearing before and ask what they wanted to hear.

Scheduling and Advance, Fall, 2000

Scheduling
- Assistant to the president and director of presidential scheduling
- Senior deputy director of presidential scheduling
- Deputy director of presidential scheduling
- Associate director of presidential scheduling
- Special assistant to the director
- Three deputy directors of presidential scheduling
- Presidential scheduling coordinators
- Director of presidential scheduling correspondence
- Presidential diarist
- Director of scheduling and advance for the first lady
- Two schedulers
- Staff assistant

Advance
- Assistant to the president and director of advance
- Deputy director of advance
- Two trip directors
- Eight associate directors of presidential advance
- Assistant director of advance

The communications director must have some control over the scheduling process, in order to be effective in his or her job, and also the process of advancing presidential trips, to make certain he will appear in the right place to emphasize the message he and his staff want to communicate. Michael Deaver indicated he had control over scheduling President Reagan, which was critical to his notion of presidential communications. It was first and foremost a way of protecting the president. "By the time that you took care of getting that schedule going and keeping him on schedule and protecting him, as I saw my responsibility, for whatever people were going to do or say, I had a full time job with that."[28] Ann Lewis discussed the scheduling meetings that were held once or twice a week in the Clinton White House. Those sessions involved a "significant number of people. The director of communications, now Loretta Ucelli; scheduling; head of scheduling—who walks us through what's available and what's doable— and then representatives from all the policy shops."[29] Political affairs was involved as well. Their planning is short and medium range, not long range. Lewis indicated that as interested as people are in long-range planning, it is difficult to bring it about. In the Reagan White House, however, the Blair House Group, a mixture of senior aides who met across the street from the White House on Fridays, provided them with the capacity to plan several months out. They did so during the first term and then returned to such planning later in the second term when Thomas Griscom served as the communications director.

Office of Public Liaison, Fall, 2000
- Assistant to the president and director of public liaison
- Three special assistants to the director
- Deputy director of public liaison
- Assistant to the deputy director
- Eight associate directors of public liaison
- Chief of staff
- Events coordinator
- Director of women's initiatives and outreach

The Office of Public Liaison was created in 1974 during President Ford's first month in office. Its genesis is found in the Nixon White House, where people in the Office of Communications performed the function of contacting groups to provide them with information about administration achievements. Public liaison is responsible for contacting groups with information the president and his staff want them to have, but it is also a main contact for groups wanting to get in touch with government officials. The office is divided, with associates responsible for portfolios of groups important to the president's electoral and governing coalitions.

While the first director was a man, William Baroody, and another, David Demarest, served for a short period at the end of the Bush administration, all of the other directors of public liaison have been women. There were two directors in the Carter White House, five in the Reagan White House, two in the Bush White House (including Demarest), and five in the Clinton years. Of the fourteen directors serving from 1977 onward, a man served for only a part of one year in the twenty-four-year period.

During the first Bush administration, the Office of Public Liaison was lodged under the Communications Office for some portion of the time. As the communications director, David Demarest was responsible for several units, including public liaison, speechwriting, media relations, and public affairs. Public liaison was responsible for regular dealings with interest group representatives in an effort to build coalitions and to respond to their needs. The Office of Public Liaison at the end of the Reagan administration contained several of the communications functions, including speechwriting and research, public affairs, and media and broadcast relations. While the Reagan and Bush administrations combined public liaison and communications, the same was not true in the Carter and Clinton administrations.

Public Affairs, Spring, 1991
- Assistant to the president for public affairs
- Director
- Two associate directors
- Staff assistant

Public affairs is a unit of the Communications Office that was tasked in the Reagan administration with coordinating those speaking for the administration to reporters and appearing on television or radio. In the first Bush administration, the office created and maintained a television studio in the Old (now Eisenhower) Executive Office Building down the hall from the auditorium where presidents and their surrogates often appeared for press events, including press conferences. The studio is used to tape presidential greetings to various groups he cannot meet in person, often those meeting in conventions in cities other than Washington. The studio is occasionally used as well by the first lady to do similar tapings. Even senior staff have used the studio to do interviews with the anchors of local television stations.

The unit also provides surrogates with information on what topics to speak about and which ones to avoid. For Communication Director David Demarest, the office served as an "interagency coordinating group."[30] The unit was responsible for ensuring that television appearances were coordinated and that those appearing on the media had information about the administration's achievements and recent good news. If, for example, there were some new good economic numbers, the office would let people know prior to their media appearances.

Political Coordination and Planning

Gradually, as the political resources of the White House have included regular polling and consultants who take the president's political temperature, the communications director has become a link of the chief of staff to the outside political world. Don Baer took that position during the Clinton reelection campaign. To some extent, the duties of the communications director depend upon the time in the administration when the person is in the post. Beginning in the midpoint of the first term of a president, an important aspect of the job is to run the White House communications angle of the reelection campaign. If the communications director serves during the latter part of the second term, his or her job involves yet another effort: the "Legacy Campaign."

Presidential Reelection Campaign

The influence of the communications director is at its height in the White House during the early period before the campaign begins, for at that point there is no campaign manager, the message is important, and the communications director is the person who coordinates the message, people, events, and institutions. That officer has an important role in the campaign, as demonstrated by just about every one of them in office during an election; David Gergen worked as a link to the campaign of President Ford in 1976, Don Baer for President Clinton in 1996, and Michael Deaver for President Reagan in 1984.

In addition to staging White House events for the president during the campaign, the communications chief works on coordinating the message with the campaign and with its pollsters and consultants. During the Clinton reelection campaign, Don Baer had the role of coordinating the campaign with the governing operation. His duties included smoothing over problems in the White House that swept in from the campaign, such as the aggressive role in White House activities played by President Clinton's political consultant, Dick Morris. A good example of the volatile nature of the communications director's position is the way that Don Baer was caught between Dick Morris and Leon Panetta.

The Legacy Campaign

Beginning with President Eisenhower's press secretary James Hagerty, who carried out the functions of a communications director without having the title, the person in the White House responsible for communications also takes on the responsibility of designing and implementing the "Legacy Campaign." The point of the campaign is to showcase what the president has accomplished during his term and wrap the administration tight at the end with high public-approval ratings for the president and his handling of his job. During Reagan's second term, Communications Director Thomas Griscom, and then his successor, Mari Maseng, worked on pulling together information on the accomplishments of the president and his administration. They prepared briefing materials and held events emphasizing their policy work. Griscom described how he organized the legacy effort. "I started by asking people, 'Those of you who were there in the first days of the Reagan administration, I want to see the documents you put together because you defined what this presidency was all about.' So I started that way and working back."[31] Gradually during the last year, the Reagan communications team released information on the president's efforts in both domestic and foreign policy. While there was some effort in President Clinton's final year to think about his legacy, such efforts were put aside as Clinton wanted to remain active until his final days.

Planning and Staging Events

Strategic planning lay at the heart of the President Reagan's communications operation. Michael Deaver discussed how they were able to get ahead of events by setting out time where they did long-range planning. Most White Houses find it difficult to do, but their experience was that it paid off handsomely.

> You have to [plan long term] because you're judged every day on what kind of job you're doing. When I set up the Blair House Group, it was probably the smartest thing I did. It was [Richard] Darman [director, Office of Management and Budget] and [Craig] Fuller [chief of staff for Vice President Bush] and the scheduling guy, Fred Ryan, and [Kenneth] Duberstein, I think. We met uninterrupted for about three hours every Friday afternoon at the Blair House. We would take the three-month schedule and we would plan every day for three months. Then we'd take it for the next two weeks and we'd plan every hour. Then I'd take it back and give it to [Howard] Baker to be sure he was okay with it. Then I'd give it to Reagan and be sure he was okay with it.

The Reagan group had a strategic plan that had as its goal shaping the manner in which the news was delivered through newspapers and on television. Deaver observed: "So we had a strategic plan. It was many times going to bed knowing what the *Washington Post* and, hopefully, having written the *Washington Post* headline by what we had done."[32]

Putting on planned events involves coordination of featured players and the staging of the occasion. It is the Communications Office that stitches together events, combining the resources and people of the White House with cabinet secretaries, members of Congress, and groups involved in issues featured at those occasions staged at the White House. And the communications director is a manager because he or she stages events. Ann Lewis created a small unit that dealt with events management. Following the decision to schedule an event is the decision of where it will be held and whether the president will take part. "My working principle was the most valuable resource we have is the president's time, and we'll never have enough of it. . . . If we've got an hour and a half of the president's time, we better make the most of it. So everything from where it's held to what's the signage to what's the picture to what's the language, the goal is to decide all of that to strengthen the message."[33]

Policy is the focus of events, but how it is presented depends on what stage of the process the policy is at and whether Congress is in session. Ann Lewis observed of planning these events:

> The [organization] meeting would last about an hour, and the number of events to be discussed may depend on how many days we have to fill. We can look at a month and have five message opportunities; we can look at a month and have three. It depends on what else is there. The president is going to be in Europe for eight days, and three days are already filled in; you don't have much time left. Or you can have a lot. The second thing that makes it difficult is how much competition there is, how many of the policy shops have announcements that they are trying to put on the schedule. Actually, you're a little more likely to do policy announcements when [Congress is] out of session because there's a little more space but you react to policy when they're in session.[34]

Working the Press

An important aspect of staging events is to work the press. Coverage is what they want. In addition to bringing in television, the White House uses the wire services as the tie to the local community, as Lewis explained. "Sometimes the afternoon before you might give the wires—for example, if we're going out with the story on community policing and here's what it's going to mean state by state, you can give that to the wires, and they will run in each of their regions a story about what it means for this community."[35]

Newspapers are not as hard to deal with as cameras in Lewis's view. "I don't have to sit and plot how to do an event in order to get the attention of a newspaper." She continued: "You can sit down and give a newspaper a story, work with them on the story, have the president give a speech. The reason I pay attention to events and the kind of setting I talked about is pictures for cameras. It's a different strategy in reaching newspapers. [Press Secretary] Joe Lockhart's briefing the day of an event, in which he says the president's going to speak and sort of walks people through what it's going to be about, will reach the newspapers. The combination of the president's speech and a Lockhart or [Gene] Sperling [National Economic Council director] or somebody coming in and briefing on the issues, that reaches the newspapers."[36]

Measuring Success

A final duty of the communications director is to measure the success of their operations. That is most often done through a combination of anecdotes and press clippings. Polling counts here as well. Ann Lewis spoke about measuring success. "It's a little bit more anecdotal than I'd like, but you try to test—there's a lot of public poll data available, and how well people think you're doing and what they know about what you're doing, that's useful. But the other is you can get clippings; is it being used? Is it appearing? Do people know what you're doing?"[37]

In addition to anecdotal information, polling is a way of measuring success for an administration. When asked what polls tell the White House, Lewis observed, "Like most institutions, polls can tell you, if you read them right, what people know about what you're doing, what they may not know, and you want to work harder to get the message out."[38] Knowing the public's assessment of what they were doing worked in favor of the Clinton White House as they designed strategy to move policy with a communications plan to accompany it.

Summary

The Communications Office is an important White House unit for a president, and its director is vital to him as well, for communications is closely linked with a successful presidency. Formed in 1969, this office has served for thirty-two years as a nuts-and-bolts operation, delivering information beyond the White House environs as well as staging events in Washington and serving as a center where communications strategies are developed and executed. The communications operation provides a president with the opportunity and the resources to coordinate the publicity for his administration and to shape his statements and explanations in a manner that will achieve his personal, policy, and electoral goals. While there are those who would characterize such operations as presidential fluff, the reality is that, of presidents who were reelected in the post–World War II period, all had state-of-the-art communications operations. Presidents Eisenhower, Nixon, Reagan, and Clinton had people and organizations who helped their presidents coordinate information in the executive branch, develop targeted messages aimed at identified publics, and then amplify those messages in a manner capable of cutting through the fog that so often shrouds the public's view of Washington politics and the president. For these reasons, the Communications Office is a valued operation for the president and his White House staff.

Notes

1.   For a thorough treatment of the establishment and operation of the Office of Communications, see John Maltese, *Spin Control: The White House Office of Communications and the Management of Presidential News*, 2d ed. (Chapel Hill: University of North Carolina Press, 1994).

2.   See Martha Joynt Kumar and Terry Sullivan, "The White House Communications Director: Presidential Fire-Walker" (paper delivered to the Midwest Political Science Association, Apr., 1996).

3.   George Stephanopoulos, interview with Martha Joynt Kumar, Washington, D.C., Sept., 1995.

4.   Michael McCurry, interview with Martha Joynt Kumar, Washington, D.C., Mar. 27, 1999, White House Interview Program.

5.   Michael Deaver, interview with Martha Joynt Kumar, Washington, D.C., Sept. 9, 1999, White House Interview Program.

6.   David Demarest, interview with Martha Joynt Kumar, Washington, D.C., Dec. 7, 1999, White House Interview Program.

7.   James A. Baker III, interview with Martha Joynt Kumar and Terry Sullivan, Houston, Tex., July 7, 1999, White House Interview Program.

8.   Donald Baer, interview with Martha Joynt Kumar, July 22, 1999, Washington, D.C., White House Interview Program.

9.   Leon Panetta, interview with Martha Joynt Kumar, Monterey Bay, Calif., May 4, 2000, White House Interview Program.

10. Ann Lewis, interview with Martha Joynt Kumar, Washington, D.C., July 9, 1999, White House Interview Program.

11. Ibid.

12. Ibid.

13. Baer interview.

14. Ibid.

15. Ibid.

16. Ibid.

17. Lewis interview, July 9, 1999.

18. Baer interview.

19. Ibid.

20. Ann Lewis, interview with Martha Joynt Kumar, Washington, D.C., June 17, 1999, White House Interview Program.

21. Baer interview.

22. Lewis interview, June 17, 1999.

23. Baer interview.

24. Lewis interview, June 17, 1999.

25. The office organization descriptions are based on *National Journal*'s *The Capital Source*. It has been published twice a year since fall, 1987. Prior to that, *National Journal* published a *White House Phone Directory.*

26. For a discussion of the Office of Media Affairs, see the earlier chapter on the Press Office.

27. Background interview.

28. Deaver interview.

29. Lewis interview, June 17, 1999.

30. Demarest interview.

31. Thomas Griscom, interview with Martha Joynt Kumar, Washington, D.C., July 17, 1999, White House Interview Program.

32. Deaver interview.

33. Lewis interview, June 17, 1999.

34. Ibid.

35. Ibid.

36. Ibid.

37. Ibid.

38. Ibid.

The Office of Management and Administration

BRADLEY H. PATTERSON, JR.

CHARLES E. WALCOTT

T HE OFFICE OF MANAGEMENT AND ADMINIS-
tration is a relatively recent addition to the White House staff. Its
roots date back to Pres. Jimmy Carter's 1977 Reorganization
Plan No. 1 and its accompanying Executive Order 12028, which
created the Office of Administration, centralizing into one unit the administrative and overhead operations for the several offices of the Executive
Office of the President. There was a subtext to Carter's action; it made his
White House staff appear slimmer.

An operations office remained in the White House, however, independent of the Office of Administration. In the administration of Pres.
George H. W. Bush, it was elevated and retitled as the Office of Management and Administration, with its head becoming an assistant to the president. It was important to maintain formal organizational independence for
some White House operations, separate from the units of the Executive Office, because White House actions and papers are shielded from Freedom
of Information Act requests, while most Executive Office units are not similarly shielded. It was thus necessary to maintain the White House administrative operation as a distinct element under the directorship of a White
House officer: the assistant for management and administration.

As with all White House units, the Office of Management and Admin-

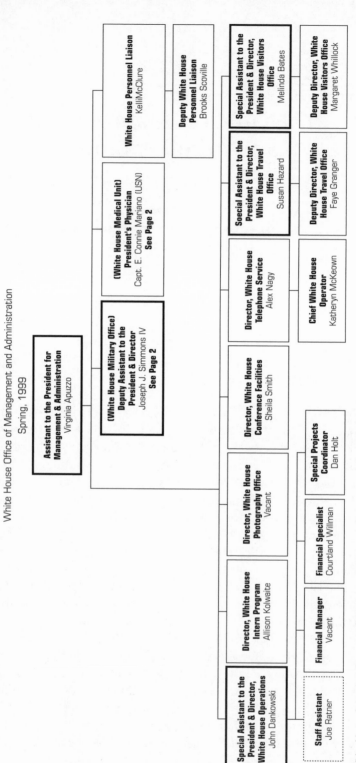

Figure 16a.

President William Clinton
White House Office of Management and Administration
Spring, 1999

Assistant to the President for Management & Administration
Virginia Apuzzo

(White House Military Office) Deputy Assistant to the President & Director
Joseph J. Simmons IV
See Page 2

(White House Medical Unit) President's Physician
Capt. E. Connie Mariano (USN)
See Page 2

White House Personnel Liaison
KelliMcClure

Deputy White House Personnel Liaison
Brooks Scoville

Special Assistant to the President & Director, White House Operations
John Dankowski

Director, White House Intern Program
Allison Kolwaite

Director, White House Photography Office
Vacant

Director, White House Conference Facilities
Sheila Smith

Director, White House Telephone Service
Alex Nagy

Special Assistant to the President & Director, White House Travel Office
Susan Hazard

Special Assistant to the President & Director, White House Visitors Office
Melinda Bates

Staff Assistant
Joe Ratner

Financial Manager
Vacant

Financial Specialist
Courtland Willman

Special Projects Coordinator
Dan Holt

Chief White House Operator
Katheryn McKeown

Deputy Director, White House Travel Office
Faye Granger

Deputy Director, White House Visitors Office
Margaret Whillock

White House Interview Program (whitehouse2001.org). Based on data in *The Capital Source*, Spring, 1999, National Journal Group Inc., Washington, DC.
Key: ———— = positions with "to the president" in their title; --------- = staff working for indicated assistant.

Figure 16b.

President William Clinton
White House Office of Management and Administration
Spring, 1999

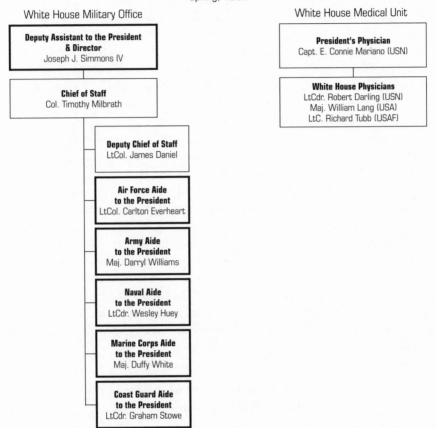

White House Military Office

Deputy Assistant to the President & Director
Joseph J. Simmons IV

Chief of Staff
Col. Timothy Milbrath

Deputy Chief of Staff
LtCol. James Daniel

Air Force Aide to the President
LtCol. Carlton Everheart

Army Aide to the President
Maj. Darryl Williams

Naval Aide to the President
LtCdr. Wesley Huey

Marine Corps Aide to the President
Maj. Duffy White

Coast Guard Aide to the President
LtCdr. Graham Stowe

White House Medical Unit

President's Physician
Capt. E. Connie Mariano (USN)

White House Physicians
LtCdr. Robert Darling (USN)
Maj. William Lang (USA)
LtC. Richard Tubb (USAF)

White House Interview Program (whitehouse2001.org). Based on data in *The Capital Source*, Spring, 1999, National Journal Group, Inc., Washington, DC. *Key:* ——— = positions with "to the president" in their title; ---------- = staff working for indicated assistant.

istration's structure, functions, and personnel are subject to presidential discretion. However, incoming presidents and their transition teams are unlikely to have a full sense of this office's importance until they have experienced its operations.

Jodie Torkelson, Clinton's assistant for management and administration, warned that the office is easily overlooked during a presidential transition. She observed that in the 1992–93 transition, the Office of Management and Administration was not "on the radar screen" and was considered "a technical organization, not necessary to cover."

The Office of Management and Administration, however, is the administrative backbone of the White House staff. In Torkelson's words: "It's an organization that has all the cats and dogs. It's the nonpolicy shop. If it's not policy, it fits in there."[1] The White House community of approximately six thousand people, including volunteers, is diverse and fluid. Careful and effective administration is necessary to knit it together. Because it is responsible for allocating critical resources to all the other White House offices, the Office of Management and Administration must be prepared to function effectively from the very outset of a presidential term.

Torkelson described her initial task as bringing order to the chaos she found regarding salary inequities, office budgets, the distribution of White House privileges, and staff support. Realizing the lack of order and rules in the Office of Management and Administration, she said: "I started asking, 'Don't you have a policy on mess and carpool privileges or who has blue badges to get in the West Wing?' No. So we started really at the basics."[2]

Clinton assistant for management and administration Virginia Apuzzo inaugurated a management system that viewed the White House as a single entity. In contrast to past approaches, which were more a matter of "stovepipe" management where each office and each function was budgeted and staffed independently. By contrast, Apuzzo saw White House and Executive Office budget and personnel lines as fungible resources managed through her office.

The Specific Responsibilities of the Assistant for Management and Administration

The Office of Management and Administration operates similarly even in different presidencies. Like every office in the White House, it must fit with the operating style of each president, but its patterns of responsibilities are likely to continue from one White House to the next. These responsibilities can be grouped into six broad categories, each involving numerous specific tasks to be performed and issues addressed.

Personnel Administration

In addition to the several hundred staff in the White House Office, the Management and Administration Office is responsible for overseeing perhaps "several thousand people, if you include interns, volunteers, . . . [and] detailees."[3] The White House community includes a broad range of staff both inside and outside of the formal White House compound.

WHITE HOUSE STAFF COMMUNITY IN 2000

1. The president and the White House Office   462
(including the Office of the First Lady, the AIDS Policy Office,
the Millennium Council, the Y2K assistant, the President's Initiative
for One America, the Office of Environmental Issues, and the
special envoy to the Americas)

2. Office of Policy Development   62
(that is, the Domestic Policy Council, the Economic Policy
Council, and the Office of National AIDS Policy)

3. Office of the Vice President   144
(including the staff of the spouse of the vice president and
the sixty-member "reinventing government" team; excluding the
vice president's campaign staff)

4. The National Security Council   190

5. The Executive Residence (including the curator)   96

6. Fifty percent of the Office of Administration   101

7. The Military Office   2,200
(including its eleven constituent units, each of which is
made up principally of Department of Defense personnel who
directly support the president)

8. Secret Service   1,200[4]
(Washington-based presidential and vice-presidential
protective units, including the Protective Research, Technical
Security, and Uniformed Divisions and part of the James J.
Rowley Training Center)

9. The White House Liaison Office of the National Park Service   100

10. The White House Service Delivery Team   133
(part of the General Services Administration [GSA])

11. U.S. Postal Service White House Branch   21

12. President's Commission on White House Fellowships   6

13. White House interns   200
(as of the fall semester, 1999)

14. Volunteers at the White House   1,000
(Total available pool)

TOTAL WHITE HOUSE STAFF COMMUNITY   5,915

Decisions on how many of the various kinds of people the White House will have, and how they will be allocated among various offices and tasks, must be made early. The best guide at the outset, according to Reagan/Bush assistant Christopher Hicks, is simply to look at the patterns established by the previous administration or administrations.[5]

Whom to Hire

For some, but definitely not all of the White House universe, the Management and Administration Assistant, backed up by accountants in the Office of Administration, controls numbers of staff and their payroll. Former Bush assistant Christopher Hicks was firm:

> What I tried to do in the Reagan/Bush transition was: "Let's clear the decks. Let's start from scratch. We have this many appropriated positions. This many are taken up by the career people. So now we have this many left. What offices, [Mr.] Chief of Staff and [Mr.] President, do you want to have? You have to have a counsel; you have to have a chief of staff; you have to have a press office. What are the [other] ones you have to have? Public liaison? What are the ones that the last administration had that you might not need? . . . Who are the people you want to head . . . these offices?" Then give it to somebody like me and say, "Figure out how many bodies I get and then make a recommendation to the chief of staff." He can talk about it with the president if he wants and then have each of the offices argue it out with the chief of staff and the president. But it shouldn't be a free-for-all where everybody is walking in to the president and saying, "My office is the most important office and therefore I need fifty people."[6]

As the months roll on, the assistant's watchfulness must never be relaxed:

> The offices within the White House Office . . . can't get away with too much of padding their own budget with people. Everybody else can. So the main role is to watch the other people, the other agencies. . . . [T]he way you watch them is not only by keeping your eyes open, but [also watching] passes, parking requests, Christmas card lists, and that kind of stuff. The other things you

have to watch in that role, though, are the agencies that you don't
have any control over, no budget authority or nothing, that aren't
part of the office of the president but operate on the eighteen acres
of the White House complex, such as the Secret Service, Park Service, GSA, and the residence staff.[7]

Whom to Keep

Reagan management and administration assistant John Rogers remembered:

When we came in, there were some people who wanted to dismiss
every single person who was on the White House payroll. Now the
president certainly has the authority . . . to do so, but there had been
a time-honored group of career people within the White House who
basically live from president to president, serve the presidency, were
proud of that association, but kept things working. The White House
telephone operators are a perfect example of that. And yet there
were some in our transition who said, "Let's get rid of the White
House operators." I fought those actions and the president
agreed. . . . We were successful in preventing inexperienced people
from the campaign from coming over to the White House and getting jobs that might embarrass the White House or the president.[8]

President Bush's assistant, Bonnie Newman, added: "They were con-
summate professionals; they weren't partisan people. They weren't Democrats or Republicans. . . . But those are the folks that keep things going and
[who], if you're willing to listen to them, can give you very wide and sage
counsel on how things need to be done. They'll spot the hotshots a mile
away, and they'll be able to tell you the first week or so who you need to
keep an eye on and who maybe is pumping too much adrenaline. You
have to be willing to listen to them. You can't be so concerned about who
carries or who doesn't carry a certain title."[9]

But Jodie Torkelson sounded a cautionary—even dissenting—note
about the continuing professional staff:

I'm not sure that I would . . . have more people around who had
been in previous administrations. I think it is a very difficult thing
for them. . . . The White House Office is such a personal office to

the president. . . . [P]eople who have been there for a number of years—they develop loyalties and friendships with the people they worked with previously. . . . At the very beginning they see things being done slightly different than they were in the previous administration, and it's a little bit of "They're changing what we worked on; they don't appreciate us." I think every administration has to sort of set its own mark. It's harder to do when you have a lot of people around who are saying, "That was never done this way before." In some ways I think it would be much better if there was a written process of procedures and record.[10]

Christopher Hicks emphasized: "The thing I think the Clinton administration made the mistake in doing was coming in and saying, 'Well, we're cutting the staff.' That's stupid . . . You don't want to shoot yourself in the foot by coming in and making some political gesture and getting rid of employees that you really need." Carter had made the same promise. "What happened," the assistant recalled, "they 'cut' the staff and then went out to the departments and just refilled it with people assigned from the departments."[11]

Whom to Borrow

Controlling the use of detailees is an issue bedeviling every management and administration assistant, as Hicks recalled: "It's real easy to abuse detailees. The chief of staff is going to call up the secretary of whatever and say, 'Can you detail somebody over here to help us out on this?' What's the secretary going to say? 'Of course.' And it's just going to accumulate. . . . The budget says the White House Office is 200 people, when in fact there may be . . . 600 people working."[12] The figure for the White House office for the fiscal year 2001 budget was 400, but detailees remain a feature of White House operations.

The law now requires that the White House annually send a written notification to Congress listing the number (and the total compensation) of employees and consultants who, in the previous fiscal year, worked in the White House offices and the number of detailees who worked there for more than thirty days. A separate statute requires an annual report to Congress giving the names, titles, and salaries of all White House employees and detailees. It is the management and administration assistant who signs the transmittal letters for each of these reports. Does even this administrator really know how many people work at the White House? Not by counting offices; not even by counting telephones. Concluded Christopher Hicks: "You know the best way to find out how many people are there is, about this time of year, you send out a memo to every office saying, 'How many invitations do you need to the White House Christmas Party?' Just all sorts of people start crawling out of the woodwork."[13]

Hicks recommended that, for reasons of budgetary honesty and fairness across government departments, the use of detailees be minimal.

> When I was in the Bush transition what I tried to convince Sununu and Andy Card and others like that to do is, no detailees, start out with no detailees. Then as . . . the administration goes on, if you really don't have a slot for someone and you can justify it, you wouldn't be embarrassed by going up and testifying to the appropriations (committees) saying this is why we supplemented our budget by bringing over this person from wherever. But detailees can be a real abuse. . . .
>
> And it's just going to accumulate.[14]

What Salary Levels to Pay

A Reagan management and administration assistant remembered: "There was a problem in the Reagan administration where each office would determine what their secretaries were getting paid. . . . So you would have some secretaries that were making $20,000 and some were doing the same job in a different office making $35,000. I tried to reconcile all that."[15]

One of the first things Torkelson noticed when she arrived to head the Office of Management and Administration was inequities in staff salaries. She recalled that when she joined the Clinton White House, "The salary range for an assistant to the president was supposed to be $110,000 to $125,000; every assistant came in at $125,000. Deputy assistants . . . were between . . . $80,000 and $110,000; the majority were at $110,000. . . . Then we had these 'special assistants to the president' which were all over the place, and they ranged anywhere from $45,000 to—the title came to mean absolutely anything—it was used so widely. . . . It was ridiculous."[16]

In part, this was caused because of an earlier practice of bringing people in too close to the top of their salary range, giving them the same salaries as their more experienced predecessors. Another problem was the use of the title "special assistant to the president" to mean such a wide variety of things that there were eighty-five to ninety "special assistants" with widely varying duties and salaries. Torkelson tried to regularize the use of titles and the assignment of salaries as well as the size of the various White House offices: "But you set the salary ranges. I really stuck to my guns to make sure that people were brought in within those ranges. I also gave offices budgets . . . ; they had to live within their budget. If they tried to bring someone in at a slightly higher rate, as long as it fit within the salary range that was fine, but then it meant they might have to do away with one person or somebody else would have a lot less salary."[17]

With respect to resource allocation, she also stressed the element of fairness: "I met with everybody, and that was the biggest thing. No one believed me when I first said, 'It's going to be fair; you'll have your budget; you can know what everybody else's budget is; I don't care; we share information.' Everybody is very suspicious because that's not how it had been."[18]

Budgeting the Total White House

In the management and administration department of any large organization, it is the budget that is a principal control mechanism. But does this hold true for the White House? "Remember," counseled Pres. George H. W. Bush's management and administration assistant Bonnie Newman, "there are several budgets involved. You've got the White House [Office] budget [separately including the residence], the Executive Office of the President budget [that is, the vice president, Office of Policy Development, the National Security Council, and the Office of Administration]. Then the [very large part of the] Department of Defense budget—as far as it involves the White House Military Office . . . , a significant support segment for the White House."[19] For most of those offices that Newman mentioned, the management and administration assistant is the control point.

In her summary, however, Newman did not mention the parts of the budgets of the Department of State related to White House international functions, the Secret Service part of the Department of the Treasury, the National Park Service White House Liaison part of the Department of the Interior, the White House Service Delivery Team part of the General Services Administration, the White House Postal Unit part of the Postal Service, the presidential support allocation of the National Archives and

Records Administration, and the President's Commission on White House Fellows. Using the best available research and making conservative estimates, Bradley Patterson has added up the costs of all of these units and has compiled what may have been the total White House budget for FY 2001; it was $730,500,000.[20] But this compilation of costs does not appear in any official public document. Patterson suspects nobody has yet put it together in such a complete form, even in the White House, but it should be so assembled. The accurate and complete budget of any institution is a vital control lever for whoever is the institution's principal assistant for management and administration.

Supervision of the White House Military Office

A key responsibility of the Office of Management and Administration under Presidents Bush and Clinton has been the management of the White House Military Office. With its 2,200 professionals, this is the largest unit in the White House. It has eleven components, most of them rendering absolutely vital services for the presidency.

The Director

The director who heads the office is a civilian, but it is considered essential that this officer have had military experience. The director has the rank of deputy assistant to the president and is aided by an active-duty military chief of staff. (Under Pres. George H. W. Bush, the director was a retired lieutenant general; under President Clinton, a retired colonel with thirty years of military service.)

One of the director's functions is to review promotion recommendations from the armed services and forward them to the president for approval. The assistant for management and administration may pay little attention to these under most circumstances. Jodie Torkelson, for instance, left virtually all military reviews and approvals to the Military Office, electing to review only the appointments of "the military aides, the little football guys, and the social aides and the top tier of the White House Military Office, who got to be the pilot of *Air Force One* and who ran *Marine One;* the people that the president would actually come into contact with, his pilot, his stewards, those were the folks I worried about."[21]

In contrast, Bush assistant Timothy McBride reported reviewing promotion recommendations in instances where there was a potential for embarrassment, such as having any connection to the Tailhook episode: "It's easy for the Military Office to say these guys are our pals; they're good guys. . . . But somebody has to be worried about the political implications for the president. That's the sort of thing that I was responsible for."[22]

The White House Communications Agency

The largest segment of the Military Office is the White House Communications Agency (WHCA). Wherever the president may be—in Moscow or Beijing, in the air, in a speedboat or a motorcade, on a raft or a horse—the nine hundred electronic wizards of WHCA and their forty-six thousand pieces of state-of-the-art encryption and transmitting equipment enable their commander in chief to be instantly linked to his panoply of diplomatic, intelligence, and military command centers and to be connected with any foreign chief of state with whom he wants to converse (something modern presidents do routinely). Bonnie Newman recalled one illustrative incident: "I remember when we were in Aspen. . . . Both President Bush and Margaret Thatcher were speaking at the anniversary of the Aspen Institute. Our communications were set up in a leased Winnebago. All of a sudden, Saddam Hussein goes into Kuwait, and the roof comes off. We have two heads of state, both of whom need to be communicating with their respective governments and other heads of state, and we're managing it out of a Winnebago parked halfway up a mountain. It was wild."[23]

The White House Communications Agency also runs the radio net and paging system for the staff, provides audiovisual equipment for the president's public appearances, and makes audio and video recordings of all White House events.

Camp David

Camp David, with its 221 acres and forty-nine buildings, is a military facility managed by the navy. It is a favorite hideaway retreat for the first family and is now often used as the site for international summit conclaves.

Air Force One

Air Force One and its huge hangar at Andrew Air Force Base are operated by the U.S. Air Force. It is the world's most important airplane, requiring the most meticulous care and maintenance. The management and administration assistant will often have the unpleasant task of deciding who gets to ride in it.

The USAF also manages the 89th Air Force Wing, a fleet of planes that can be used by cabinet members and senior White House staff when they undertake vital presidential missions and when other flight options are unavailable or inappropriate. But when is this the case, and who decides? Jodie Torkelson made it clear:

> You have a lot of people who come to work in places like the White House who are so bright—but they never really manage much; they can't say "No!" to anybody over anything. So the [White House] cabinet secretary would rubberstamp [the cabinet requests] . . . and send them along to the National Security Council, and the National Security Council would rubberstamp them and send them to me, and then I would say "Ugh!"
> [Interviewer]: Would several of them get appealed?
> [Torkelson]: Every week—all of them get appealed.
> [Interviewer]: But you got upheld.
> [Torkelson]: Yeah.[24]

Marine Helicopter Squadron One

Marine Helicopter Squadron One (HMX-1), of two hundred Marines, flies some ten helicopters, including the president's *Marine One*. The squadron is based at Quantico, Virginia, but *Marine One* flies out of the Anacostia Naval Air Station in southeast Washington, landing on a mobile "heliport" on the White House South Lawn.

The White House Transportation Agency

This unit consists of fifty military chauffeurs who drive White House staff members on official business in cars with special communications equipment. The former privilege of home-to-office transportation is now rarely, if ever, provided, but the question as to which staffers are eligible for this daytime perquisite is in the hands of the assistant for management and administration. That area of decision can add up to headaches. McBride recalled the choices that have to be made: "We ran the motor pool. . . . It doesn't seem like much, but you've got vehicles that have to transport staff to the Hill, to Andrews Air Force Base. And whenever you have folks who are very important and think they need a car available to them whenever they want one, you're dealing with egos. But you're dealing with a limited number of resources. . . . A lot of it centered around . . . maintaining an appropriate level of usage of military assets and government assets which support the president and his staff. Unless you've got somebody who is willing to say no, is willing to appreciate the opportunities for abuse, there will be abuse."[25]

The Military Aides

There are five White House military aides, one from each service (including the Coast Guard)—career officers at the lieutenant-colonel grade—who take turns carrying the "football," the case containing vital war codes. (The military social aides, who help out at formal state functions, are a responsibility of the Social Office.)

The Presidential Contingency Program

This military-program unit is charged with developing contingency plans for the continuity of government by the president in dire military or quasi-military emergencies. The assistant to the president for management and administration is briefed on these programs and is responsible for seeing to it that this planning is given the importance it merits.

The White House Medical Unit

The White House Medical Unit is headed by the president's personal physician and is made up of some twenty doctors and assistants from the armed services. It serves the president, vice president, and their families. Staff members can use the unit's help in emergencies (even a White House tourist who is experiencing chest pains may be assisted). The Medical Unit must be prepared for every possible medical emergency, especially when the president is traveling.

The White House Mess

The navy runs the White House Staff Mess, with its three adjacent dining rooms. Cabinet members and senior White House staffers are eligible to eat there—but the decision as to who is sufficiently "senior" to enjoy this privilege is a sometimes-painful task of the management and administration chief.

The Ceremonies Coordinator

The Ceremonies Coordinator makes arrangements with the armed services and the Military District of Washington to have the appropriate military units, such as honor guards, bands, the herald trumpets, or other musical ensembles, on hand at presidential functions.

It is clear that these eleven military outfits—all of them part of the responsibility of the Office of Management and Administration—perform services, some of them highly classified, that are absolutely vital for the functioning of the presidency.

The men and women of the White House Military Office are not only at the acme of competence but also are imbued with a sense of loyal service—so much so that their alacrity may sometimes have to be controlled. As Torkelson put it: "The White House Military Office is like every office in the White House: the president wants; oh my gosh, somebody says the president wants, and they all just fall over themselves trying to help. It's good on the one hand, but on the other hand, you can get your boss in a lot of trouble if you don't pay attention to what is legal or whatever just [because] you're trying to be helpful. . . . If the president walks around Camp David and says 'I'd like to have a huge golf course here,' before you could blink an eye they'd probably knock all the trees down and ruin the entire forest to build it because he said he wanted one." As Timothy McBride said, the most successful directors of the Military Office "probably had an appreciation for the potential abuse of the assets and the resources." If such problems are not caught at that level, they become issues for the Office of Management and Administration. In fact, the Office of Management and Administration must act as a kind of "reality check" on the Military Office and, indeed, the White House as a whole.[26]

Allocation of Office Space

Office space, especially in the West Wing, is at a premium and is apt to be avidly sought and hotly contested. Well before inauguration, Bonnie Newman, an especially prescient management and administration assistant, drew up a color-coded map of the White House and of the Eisenhower Executive Office Building, where most staff actually work. She was aiming at efficiency as a criterion for determining which White House of-fices should be located. Observed another director, similarly: "Why do the speechwriters have this office space? It's really impractical to have the speechwriters in this best . . . space. These are people who need to be up near the library." Efficiency, however, tends to be overwhelmed by tradi-tion: the chief of staff, the counsel, the press secretary, the national secu-rity adviser, the domestic, the economic, the speechwriting, and the sched-uling groups have occupied certain West Wing quarters for years; the incoming denizens stake their claims a priori on them. In one less-orderly White House, staffers ran in early and commandeered favorite locations. Another former management and administration assistant discovered, only too late, that the National Security Council folks over one weekend ducked into a part of their Eisenhower office space that had twenty-foot-high ceilings and "condominiumized [it] with little spiral staircases, so they were able to put twice as many people in the space they had. Then they would just call up Defense or State and Coast Guard and have all these people in there."[27]

White House units always battle for space. John Rogers noted the strains that can accompany such decisions: "Well, it can be intense and things can also be very emotional. People had a tendency to be emotional. Little things in life become very serious to them. You start with office space. People will take a closet to say they're in the West Wing rather than take a wonderful office in the Old Executive Office Building."[28]

The elegant old townhouses along Jackson Place row are also White House office space; temporary outfits like presidential commissions or the first lady's Millennium Council strenuously vie to be occupants. It is the management and administration assistant who must make the tough calls here too. But one of them reflected: "What I would suggest . . . to some-body coming in is that you have a third party go in and make some recom-mendations . . . and then present that to the group, as opposed to having everybody going in trying to figure out what piece they want, and the people that know more about it going in and grabbing up the good space."[29] Said another: "The president has to get his hair cut. Where are you going to do it?"[30]

Allocation of Parking Space, Passes, and Other Items

Like mess privileges, parking spaces become objects of contention. The same applies to motor-pool privileges, cell phones, West Wing passes, computer upgrades, and other perks. As Rogers put it, "These reach fever pitches and people get very emotional about it . . . I think because the place lends itself to these (as) indicators of status."[31] At the beginning of the first Bush administration, Management and Administration Assistant Christopher Hicks was assigning parking spaces along West Executive Avenue. He recalled: "There are [some] fifteen parking spaces there right next to the West Wing. So I put all the new assistants to the president . . . there so they had the best parking spaces. . . . I had one guy . . . , [he] found me literally . . . outside the Oval Office . . . on inauguration morning and started screaming at me for, (1) I hadn't gotten artwork hung up in his office, and (2) I had the audacity to put him at the end of that line of parking spaces. He didn't want to be number fifteen, closest to Pennsylvania Avenue; he wanted to be number one. . . . All that kind of bullshit—it's real petty stuff."[32]

Another issue is passes. Outsiders do not have passes; to enter, they need clearance from someone on the inside. In one administration the National Security Council devised a system for evading the personnel ceilings: they got a detailee from the Coast Guard but, explained the management and administration assistant, "they would not come to me for the pass because they knew I'd say no to the new detailee . . . , so they'd just repeatedly clear him in. . . . [T]here was literally a guy . . . who got cleared in daily for about a year."[33] Now a computer system identifies people who are cleared in overly frequently.

Every management and administration assistant also has the problem of determining internal access: "Who does get a blue pass to go into the West Wing? Everybody doesn't need to have a blue pass just because they want to walk around the halls. . . . Obviously, anybody who worked in the West Wing needed to have one. That took care of fifty people. Now how about the other thousand people in the complex that all want a blue pass? How do you make the determination? We actually set up criteria based on frequency of having to go over there. . . . We set up caps on numbers of passes per office . . . , putting some limits on managers.[34]

At that time it seemed possible to acquire these privileges by virtue of association with the campaign or by dropping the name of the president or first lady. Torkelson responded by developing general criteria to be applied fairly to all staff, dealing straightforwardly with complaints of unfairness and thus, in her view, contributing to better morale. In order to succeed in doing this, Torkelson noted, the support of Chief of Staff Leon Panetta was absolutely necessary.[35]

Supervision of Other Staff Operations

The Office of Management and Administration oversees a number of administrative operations that, while routine, in the White House environment can swiftly become very damaging if mismanaged.

Security

This is an especially sensitive part of the Office of Management and Administration operations. In the Clinton administration, for example, it was damaged by the mishandling of FBI files. What had been the White House Security Group was later merged into the Office of Management and Administration's existing Security Office. Torkelson explained that it worked out well because the career staff constitutes a strong workforce. "That's why I say, in the Executive Office of the President . . . , that the career staff really pull their weight. It is not a 9 to 5 kind of crew. They can't be, there are so few. Everybody's got so much to do. I think people love the fact that they work for the presidency and enjoy being there, and they know that they're someplace special."[36]

Telephone Service

Similar praise is heaped upon the professionalism of the White House Telephone Service. Jodie Torkelson declared, "I still to this day think the telephone operators are some of the best people in the business." Timothy McBride agreed, wondering at President Clinton's early efforts to cut that staff and at that administration's suspicion of careerists in other capacities as well. The White House careerists, in his view, "would serve the Office of the President and the institution with great respect." A task of Torkelson's in the area of phone service was to see to it that the operators got adequate computer support.[37]

Interns and Volunteers

The White House hired unpaid summer interns as early as the Ford administration, the Reagan White House followed suit, and the first Bush White House expanded the program to be year-round. Under President Clinton the program exploded—at its beginning, one thousand college-age students, in four groups of two hundred fifty each, were recruited into three-month service. The Intern Office is directly supervised by the White House operations chief, who reports to the assistant for management and administration. The interns are given minimum orientation about security and conduct and are then assigned to the offices requesting them. Questions arose about access to sensitive areas of the White House and about dress. (The Management and Administration Office was once dubbed the "hemline police.")

A thousand volunteers are also part of the White House staff community; offices like correspondence and social simply cannot function without them. While the Volunteer Office itself is in the staff secretary's bailiwick, the Management and Administration Office recognizes that this indispensable cohort is inextricably woven into the total White House staff family.[38]

Information Systems and Data

Information systems management is, in fact, a major area of responsibility within the Office of Management and Administration. McBride recalled the difficulty of getting money from Congress to upgrade computer and phone systems. "And we were under a great deal of pressure . . . from the House oversight folks . . . who [were] quick to define just about everything that existed over there as perks of the White House."[39] Where money is concerned, even routine management tasks can become "political" issues.

When the Clinton administration moved in, they discovered that there were more than two dozen different name-and-address files totaling 300,000 names but maintained in separate White House offices: correspondence, social, intergovernmental affairs, and public liaison. Who had attended a White House social event, been sent a letter from the president, was on the Christmas card list? The files were not cross-referenced, were not compatible, and some were not even computerized. The Clinton Management and Administration Office arranged to have these files consolidated into a single, central database but found that it had to maintain tight control over it in the central management office—and even then had to enlist the counsel's help to abort a plan to integrate the White House database with that of the Democratic National Committee.

The Photography Office

A small staff of White House photographers makes a visual record of every official activity of the president or the first lady—at home and abroad. They shoot over a thousand rolls of film each year, supplying, in effect, the visual component of the presidential archives.

The Travel Office

It is the responsibility of this unit to arrange for the official travel of White House staff and (on a reimbursable basis) to charter air and ground transportation for the press that moves with the president on trips out of Washington. Some of these arrangements involve large amounts of money and have to be made on extremely short notice—requiring experienced staff working at a rapid pace.

The Visitors Office

The White House residence is the only home of a head of state anywhere in the world that is regularly open to the public free of charge. While the National Park Service manages a visitor center (located in the Commerce Department Building) for individual public admissions, the Visitors Office in the East Wing handles group tours, including congressionally sponsored visitors and other groups proposed by civic, political, and similar associations. Questions about the processes for these approvals, and sometimes individual requests themselves, may have to be referred to the Office of Management and Administration.

The White House Conference Center

Meeting space is so short in the White House that President Clinton had five conference rooms constructed at 726 Jackson Place. A special unit in the White House Operations Office makes the reservations for these rooms.

Building Maintenance

The management and administration assistant is also building manager for the White House. Will the budget allow for a new roof for the Eisenhower Executive Office Building? Can cables be installed in the floor or in the historic walls of the East Room so it is wired for sound and video? A special event requires filling the Roosevelt Room with chairs; can the huge table there be temporarily moved out? There is a leak in the roof of the Situation Room—which is underground, under the lawn. Is it possible to fix it without destroying the park service's treasured lawn and gardens on top? To accommodate extra staff, may a cubicle be built by chopping up the domestic policy chief's venerable, beautifully paneled office? Is there money for refurbishing the vice president's residence? What about shutting down East Executive Avenue and building a park there? People routinely steal the historic doorknobs from the Eisenhower Executive Office Building—most of the original ones have now disappeared. How can this be stopped? These and a hundred other problems and projects must be evaluated.

Producing the Staff Manual

The management and administration assistants in the Clinton White House recognized the need for a written set of White House administrative processes and wrote a 131-page booklet of the "rules of the road" for White House employees. It lists services available to employees, gives instructions about procedures to be followed, presents samples of forms to be used, and includes a map of the White House neighborhood. A detailed annex lays out the legal and ethical regulations that apply to White House employees, and the manual even concludes with a directory of commonly used White House acronyms, for example, POTUS (*President of the United States*).

Fitting the Secret Service into the Mix

Besides discharging its direct bodyguard duties around the person of the president, the Secret Service has a broad protective mission: designing and constructing the physical White House environment to meet challenges, as the service sees them, to presidential security. The service insisted on building a new northwest gate, installing ballistic glass in the residence windows, placing bollards along the avenue sidewalks, and closing off

Pennsylvania Avenue in front of the White House. Measures of this sort affect many other offices in the whole White House community; some are of wide public concern. The management and administration assistant is a bridge between that total community and the leadership of the service. It is a difficult bridge, however.

Former management and administration assistants warn that the Secret Service, in its zeal to protect the president, may be hard to control, even when they might be seen as going to extremes. The closing of Pennsylvania Avenue in front of the White House, for instance, may enhance presidential security but also has its costs. As John Rogers stated, "You start building barricades around barricades around barricades [and] you send a message to the people about the nature of the institution."[40] The important key to working effectively with the Secret Service is to try to assure that they at least check with the Office of Management and Administration before acting.

Overseeing the Office of Administration

De jure, the Office of Administration is a separate unit of the Executive Office, reporting to the president. De facto, it is the institutional backstop for, and takes its instructions from, the assistant to the president for management and administration. Since Office of Administration's original executive order specifies that it "shall, upon request, assist the White House Office by performing its role of providing those administrative services which are primarily in direct support of the president," half of the Office of Administration staff of 202 persons can be counted as part of the White House staff community itself.[41] The director of the Office of Administration is appointed by the president but is not confirmed by the Senate.

In addition to its direct help to the White House, the Office of Administration supports several other agencies of the Executive Office. For these collective purposes, it has divisions for Facilities Management (including preservation of the Eisenhower Executive Office Building, which is a national historic site and sponsoring Saturday public tours there), Financial Management, General Services (printing, messengers, procurement, and property management), Human Resources Management, Information Systems and Technology (telephones, computers, and software), Security, and Library and Research Services. Carter management and administration assistant Richard Harden recalled the beginnings of the White House Library.

I asked to see the White House Library. I got this funny look and they said, "Fine." So we go down to the basement of the Old Executive Office Building, down this hall, and finally come to two rooms. One room is full of old law books and whatnot that looked like they had been there forever. The other had magazines. . . . There were two nice old ladies there. I said, "What do you all do?" They said, "Basically, when someone calls and asks for something, we call up the Library of Congress and have them send it down." That was "the White House Library." . . . What we did was move it up to the third floor, where it is now. We hired a professional librarian to come in and manage it.[42]

The three Office of Administration–managed libraries now have over sixty-five thousand volumes and one thousand journal titles.

The director of the Office of Administration is an official representing the Executive Office of the President, not the White House. Since White House assistants do not testify before congressional committees, it is the director of the Office of Administration, rather than the assistant to the president, who testifies about and defends the "White House" budget on the Hill. To be technically precise, the Office of Administration director appears before the House Appropriations Subcommittee on Treasury, Post Office, and General Government (and its Senate counterpart) to present and defend nine budget accounts: Compensation of the President, White House Office, Special Assistance to the President (meaning the vice president's office), Official Residence of the Vice President, Office of Policy Development (the domestic and economic policy staffs), National Security Council, Unanticipated Needs, the Office of Administration itself, and the Council of Economic Advisors. The first seven, and half of the eighth, can collectively be termed "White House." Since the chief usher is a White House staff officer and thus a nontestifier, the National Park Service defends the budget of the residence. Defense, Secret Service, State, GSA, and National Archives separately defend their own budgets, including those parts that support the presidential office.

Implementing the Comprehensive Design Plan for the White House and President's Park

On December 2, 1998, after three years of careful consultation among eleven cooperating federal agencies and organizations, the National Park Service released a 408-page proposal for major upgrading and renovations of the White House neighborhood. To eliminate surface parking and limit vehicular traffic, a large parking garage would be built under the Ellipse and a smaller one, for presidential motorcade and other VIP cars, would be built underneath Pennsylvania Avenue. Efficient new underground meeting and conference facilities—including a much upgraded area for the press—would be constructed under West Executive Avenue. The visitor center in the Commerce Building would be transformed into a museum with four video theaters, and then an underground corridor/moving sidewalk, which would move tourists into the White House, would be installed.

Whether and how quickly to initiate this impressive multiagency program and how to preserve the administrative capacities of the presidency in the face of the accompanying massive construction activities is currently on the agenda of the assistant for management and administration.

Desirable Qualifications for an Assistant for Management and Administration

The Executive Office of the President, and the White House offices within it, are organizationally complex and multipurposed. Those units will serve the president optimally only if their everyday administrative operations are managed efficiently, responsibly, and not least, quietly. As Clinton management and administration assistant Jodie Torkelson observed, "If I was doing a good job, [the president] shouldn't even have to think about it."[43] Good management not only makes the machine run smoothly; but also it is crucial for establishing the administration's reputation for competence and integrity in the minds of the Washington community and the public.

Because the tasks of allocating scarce and valuable resources and overseeing sensitive activities are potentially controversial, the head of management and administration must have the political sophistication to understand the ways the office's work affects status considerations within the White House orbit. Additionally, the assistant must be fully familiar with the oversight role of Congress to enable him or her to deal with congressional requests for information about specific White House activities. Here are some requirements:

The assistant for management and administration should be a person with Washington experience, an understanding of White House operations, and knowledge of congressional operations and oversight.

New assistants in this office must distinguish between units staffed by long-term White House employees and those positions that are properly political appointments of the new administration. While sometimes referred to as "career," these professional White House employees do not have civil service status or tenure, but they are traditionally invited to stay from administration to administration. They serve at the president's discretion in generally nonpolicy but vital supporting roles. Most of these employees work under the umbrella of the Office of Management and Administration. In their interviews former directors have testified to the efficiency and loyalty of these continuing employees. The assistant for management and administration must represent the importance of these continuing employees to the new administration.

Many of the Office of Management and Administration's responsibilities require that the office's supervisory staff be knowledgeable about matters such as personnel and compensation, management, purchasing, space allocation, and information systems—which require management expertise rather than, or in addition to, political experience.

Routine administrative activities of the White House and Executive Office of the President should be understood as protecting the administration. They should not be newsworthy and only will become so when failures occur.

A theme Jodie Torkelson sounded that applies to any assistant for management and administration is that she understood an important part of her job description to be maintenance of administrative efficiency and accountability. She observed that when she arrived on the job, "The White House Office [and Office of Administration] . . . needed to have a little more attention paid to the books and tracking things and policy and procedures put in place. Bills sometimes weren't being paid; vendors were calling months later and hadn't gotten paid. There didn't seem to be a tracking system for a lot of stuff. That was a big piece in all of this: accountability and how did you monitor and track."[44]

Where Close Relationships Are Needed

The management and administration assistant's relationships are on three levels. First, the assistant supervises the units, described above, that are part of the office. Here, he or she is responding to the needs of the president, seeking efficiency in the operation of the presidency.

A second level of relationships is with the other coequal offices of the

White House. The Office of Management and Administration provides administrative support to those units and deals with their many requests to meet what each perceives as its special needs. These relationships can become combative, given the sensitivity of the perquisites involved. The National Security Council, for instance—a vital element in the White House—requires space and highly specialized computer and communications facilities, such as its twenty-four-hour Situation Room.

A third level of relationships comprises those he or she has with two of the most senior White House staff. Whatever the presidency, the assistant depends upon close support from the chief of staff and from the White House counsel. The chief of staff is an enforcer in the White House world. Invariably, there are staffers in the White House and the Executive Office who will balk at, and appeal, the decisions of the management and administration assistant. Jodie Torkelson noted she could rely on backing by White House Chief of Staff Leon Panetta: "We . . . had an unspoken rule, which was I'll be the bad guy . . . but you can't overrule me and make it hard to do the job"[45]

The necessity of this particularly trusting relationship ought to be considered in the initial choices of White House personnel during the transition. In Torkelson's case, she had worked for Panetta in the Office of Management and Budget. The strong professional bond that carried over from that period made her a particularly apt choice as assistant for management and administration during Panetta's time as chief of staff.

Another crucial senior-staff level relationship for the assistant for management and administration is with the White House counsel. The assistant can obtain legal advice from within the Office of Administration, but he or she deals with an extremely sensitive range of issues that demand close, supportive cooperation from the counsel's office.

Reciprocally, the Office of Management and Administration serves the counsel's needs. In the unending requests from courts, grand juries, the independent counsel, and congressional committees for material from the Clinton White House, Jodie Torkelson reported that her office served as the counsel's "one-stop shop. They could call and say can you get this; what about this, can we get that, because most of the stuff that occurred had something to do with my operations."[46]

Conclusion

While illustrations and examples are given here, this chapter only hints at the stew of administrative, legal, security, military, financial, and personnel issues that must be superintended by whomever is the assistant to the president for management and administration. As George H. W. Bush's management and administration assistant Christopher Hicks observed: "If I saw something I didn't think was proper, I would go to the chief of staff. It's the chief of staff's decision, then, if he wants to pick a fight or not. . . . More inspector generaling is needed . . . [and] it's the person in my position. . . . The infrastructure of the White House as a place to work and support the president—whichever one happens to be sitting in the Oval Office—[became] a better place, and he, the president, [was] better supported, because the office of the president—from an administrative standpoint—worked better. And it can always use improvement.[47]

What are the qualities most needed in an effective management and administration assistant? Clinton assistant Torkelson summed them up: "I think the most important quality is always to be able to be an honest broker, because you can find yourself in positions where it's very easy to just have your one opinion rule a day, but you really have to fairly present all sides, so that even if you are the ultimate decision-maker, people understand how you got to that decision point. I think . . . a lot of times people disagreed with what I did, but I would always sit down and say, 'This is why,' and they could at least see my train of thought. [What's important?] Being as much of an honest broker as you can and not using the office for your own swollen-head purposes—because I think that's when people make the biggest mistakes."[48]

And the element that in the end is sine qua non is noninterference by the president. Torkelson made that clear too: "The president never stepped in once in all of my time at the White House. . . . Never once did he overrule me, did he question what I had done, did he step in and say, 'Did you think about this again?' Not once. I know that there were a lot of people who were very close to him who sometimes didn't like a lot of things that I did because it limited some of their perks. . . . I knew that they talked to him but . . . [he] never once interfered. . . . I think even with my relationship with [Chief of Staff] Panetta, as strong as it was, he could have undermined that so easily, and never once did."[49]

"Somebody once said," observed Hicks, "that my job—when I was head of administration—is like being captain of a minesweeper. As long as you're doing your job, nobody knows you're there. You make one mistake, and there's a hell of an explosion."[50] New Office of Management and Administration chiefs often do not have good communication with their predecessors. In addition, Hicks noted, the value of the longtime employees and the extent to which they might actually have things under control tends to be underestimated at first. Finally, and perhaps most importantly, he noted that the office is so complex and atomized that any director is forced to focus on only a part of it. Most likely, this focus will be upon those elements that seem to be the most problematic or troublesome at the time. The sheer diversity of its elements almost guarantees that the office as a whole will be unstable in some respect at any point and thus will present problems that need to be solved. Attention to those problems will at the same time compel other matters to be relatively neglected, creating new problems for the next incumbent.[51] The nature of the Office of Management and Administration makes it resistant to any solution to these problems. But the better incoming administrators understand the challenges they confront, the better they will be able to prioritize their own limited resources and those of their staff.

Notes

1. Jodie Torkelson, interview with Martha Joynt Kumar, Washington, D.C., Oct. 19, 1999, White House Interview Program.
2. Ibid.
3. Christopher Hicks, interview with Martha Joynt Kumar, Washington, D.C., Nov. 18, 1999, White House Interview Program.
4. The Secret Service does not make public any figures for its protective functions. This figure is Bradley Patterson's personal estimate of the number of those Secret Service personnel based in Washington who directly handle presidential protection. It includes the Uniformed Division (i.e., the White House Police), the technical security and protective research units, part of its Beltsville training staff, and the presidential and vice-presidential details. These details are, of course, augmented when the protectees are traveling. In 2000, additional protective details (beyond this estimate) were constituted to cover major presidential candidates.
5. Hicks interview, Nov. 18, 1999.
6. Ibid.
7. Ibid.
8. John Rogers, interview with Martha Joynt Kumar, Washington, D.C., Nov. 10, 1999, White House Interview Program.
9. J. Bonnie Newman, interview with Martha Joynt Kumar, Washington, D.C., Jan. 26, 2000, White House Interview Program.
10. Torkelson interview.

11. Hicks interview, Nov. 18, 1999.

12. Ibid.

13. Ibid.

14. Ibid.

15. Torkelson interview.

16. Ibid.

17. Ibid.

18. Ibid.

19. Newman interview.

20. See Bradley Patterson, *The White House Staff: Inside the West Wing and Beyond* (Washington, D.C.: Brookings Institution, 2000), pp. 342–45.

21. Torkelson interview.

22. Timothy McBride, interview with Martha Joynt Kumar, Washington, D.C., Aug. 16, 1999, White House Interview Program.

23. Newman interview.

24. Torkelson interview.

25. McBride interview.

26. Ibid.

27. Hicks interview, Nov. 18, 1999.

28. Rogers interview.

29. Richard Harden, interview with Martha Joynt Kumar, Washington, D.C., Jan. 20, 2000, White House Interview Program.

30. McBride interview.

31. Rogers interview.

32. Hicks interview, Nov. 18, 1999.

33. Ibid.

34. Torkelson interview.

35. Ibid.

36. Ibid.

37. Ibid.

38. For a full discussion of the intern and volunteer programs see, Patterson, *White House Staff*, pt. 3.

39. McBride interview.

40. Rogers interview.

41. Executive Order 12028, Dec. 12, 1977, sec. 3(a).

42. Harden interview.

43. Torkelson interview.

44. Ibid.

45. Ibid.

46. Ibid.

47. Hicks interview, Nov. 18, 1999.

48. Torkelson interview.

49. Ibid.

50. Hicks interview, Nov. 18, 1999.

51. Christopher Hicks, interview with Martha Joynt Kumar, Washington, D.C., Dec. 11, 2000, White House Interview Program.

4

George W. Bush Makes His Transition
into Office and into the White House

The 2000–2001 Presidential Transition
Planning, Goals, and Reality

CLAY JOHNSON III

THE CIRCUMSTANCES OF THE 2000–2001 PRESIdential transition will never be repeated, or at least I hope not for the sake of all concerned. Nevertheless, what we planned and what actually happened are highly relevant to future efforts. Most observers agree that the Bush-Cheney administration got off to a strong start in large part because it made good use of the time available to it during the abbreviated transition period. How this came to be can help future presidents-elect plan their own transitions.

Transition Planning

In the spring of 1999, I was Gov. George W. Bush's appointments director, in charge of a small group that helped the governor appoint about four thousand people to different state boards and commissions and full-time positions. When the governor decided to run for president, he asked me to succeed his chief of staff, who was leaving to direct the campaign. He also asked me to develop a plan for setting up his new administration, or as he put it, "develop a plan for what we should do after we win."

The first thing I did was read all that I could on the subject of presidential transitions. The Clinton transition difficulties had prompted a number

311

of books, articles, and studies on the topic, so there were some good historical comparisons and analyses to digest. In the spring of 2000, I also began
to visit with the likes of James Baker, George Shultz, and Edwin Meese,
who had been involved in setting up and guiding previous administrations
at the highest levels. I thought the most important conclusions from all this
input were as follows:

- Campaign leaders should not be in charge of the transition. Campaigns are about winning, whereas transitions are about preparing to govern. By necessity, campaign leaders are unlikely to have
  any time to work on the transition before the election. Also transition leadership cannot work long hours to set up a new administration if they are also recovering from the election ordeal.
- The cabinet and subcabinet selection process needs to be most effective most quickly and more than a discussion about who has
  earned serious consideration just because of their political involvement. It is important to identify desired qualities and
  prospective candidates before the discussions with the principals
  begin.
- While one should identify the cabinet secretaries by mid-December
  so they can be prepared for confirmation hearings prior to inauguration day, it is more important to select senior White House
  staff by this time. Cabinet officers can only receive clear direction
  from the White House if there are senior staff in place to do so.
  Also, it is said that the primary focus of the White House is to
  maximize the value of the president's time and voice: if the senior
  staff is not in place when the president is inaugurated, the value
  of his time and voice during the most critical "launch phase" of
  the administration is likely not to be maximized.
- The American public pays a lot of attention to how a president-elect
  acts prior to his or her inauguration, for they want to begin to
  understand what kind of president he or she will be.
- Congress and the career executives pay a lot of attention to how a
  new administration reaches out to and communicates with them.
  They hope for a lot of collaboration but fear an adversarial relationship.
- Incoming job seekers and advice givers can overwhelm a transition effort, causing the entire effort to be reactive instead of
  proactive.

Additionally, beyond these transition-specific matters, past administration officials noted that in any organization, but especially one that has to accomplish a lot in a short period of time, it is important to have accountability and clarity. Everybody had to know who was supposed to do what, with whom, and by when.

Transition Goals

Based on this review of past efforts, our transition team laid out the following goals for ourselves to prepare to assume all executive-branch responsibilities on inauguration day:

- Clearly communicate that we are aggressively preparing to govern, that we are operating without hubris or triumphant partisanship, that we are experienced and not neophytes, that we are ethical, and that we understand the president-elect is not the president until noon on January 20.
- Select the senior White House staff, an organizational structure, and a decision-making process by mid-December.
- Select the cabinet secretaries by Christmas and have them briefed and ready for confirmation hearings by January 8. Also have in place by inauguration day an organization capable of identifying, clearing, and nominating 165 or more people by April 30, which is as many as any recent administration has sent to the Senate by the one hundredth day.
- Summarize all cabinet department priorities, issues, facts, and campaign promises related to each in order to prepare the new secretaries for assuming responsibility for their departments.
- Prepare to reach out to Congress, supporters, trade associations, well wishers, and job seekers in order to show our interest in them and to connect with them in a manner of our choosing and according to our timetable. We especially wanted to establish a strong working relationship with Congress.
- Develop a preliminary 20-day, 100-day, and 180-day schedule for the president to guide the initial focus for his energies and time.
- Prepare to present the new administration's proposed budget changes by mid-February.
- Review the executive-order and regulatory issues requiring immediate attention by the new administration.

These goals were agreed to by Governor Bush and senior campaign officials around June, 2000, and with running-mate Richard Cheney in August. No one working on the campaign wanted to or really could focus on transition issues, so those discussions were to be brief or discussed over lunch.

In pursuit of these goals, before the election, we did the following:

- Committed to take in job-applicant information by means of the Internet and a special website (instead of scanning resumes as the Clinton administration had decided to do, to their consternation, as we learned). We also committed to the development of the site and related software in August.
- Estimated that the transition would cost about $8.5 million, which was about what the Clinton administration had spent eight years earlier and over $4 million more than was to be provided by the U.S. government to support the effort. Hence we alerted the finance people about the need to field a direct-mail fundraising effort right after the election.
- Drafted letters and e-mails to be sent at the start of the transition to donors, supporters, congressmen, senators, governors, and mayors about how to apply for or to recommend someone for an appointment, how to provide policy input, and how to volunteer.
- Determined that we wanted only small teams to prepare briefing books for, and interact with, each cabinet department rather than assemble larger "transition teams" that might include lobbyists and job seekers. After the transition started, we decided we did want to involve trade associations, lobbyists, and the like, though only as advisors. We then put together large advisory groups and let them advise the department policy teams as they saw fit but did not let them interface directly with the departments.

Additionally, I talked to policy people and senior officials from previous administrations about the types of people we should be looking at for the different cabinet secretary positions and specific people we might consider. I did not contact anyone to express our interest or determine theirs, but I collected about two hundred names with which to begin discussions with the president- and vice president–elect when appropriate.

In August, Governor Bush asked Cheney to head up the transition because no one knew Washington better, had more credibility with Congress, or could better represent or communicate our preparedness for the responsibilities at hand. The governor also came to understand the importance of having his chief of staff-designate on the ground working to put the senior White House staff together the day after the election, so he turned his attention away from the campaign long enough to offer the position to Andrew Card a couple of weeks before the election.

The Transition Itself: Reality

The election was held and, as everyone knows, it just would not end. The legal maneuverings and chad-counting in Florida occupied most everyone in Austin the first few weeks after election day. Andy Card, though, began to formulate his thoughts about the senior White House staff and organization structure, with input from Governor Bush, Cheney, and campaign and governor's office officials. At least once per week, we held brainstorming sessions about possible candidates for different cabinet positions. No candidate was contacted, but starting with the suggestions I had compiled before the election, we put together a short list of people to consider most seriously once the election was decided. I talked to a few campaign and governor's office people about the prospect of joining the Office of Presidential Personnel but felt it premature to talk to anybody from Washington who could add D.C. savvy to our operation. We finalized the transition website and prepared to produce the letters and e-mails that would be sent out to supporters of all kinds about how to most effectively interact with the transition once (and if) it officially began.

When the count in Florida was certified by the Florida secretary of state, Vice President–elect Cheney pushed to open a privately funded transition office in McLean, Virginia. He assembled a small group to secure space, furniture, and computers and had a longtime associate put together a congressional liaison group. The finance people set out to raise the necessary funds. A dozen or so of us flew up from Texas to set up the Presidential Personnel and Press Offices and to organize the department policy teams. We stayed in twice-daily contact with the president-elect, campaign leadership, and Andy Card in Austin. Everything was happening at warp speed. Within a week or so, with the invaluable assistance of the miracle workers who set up the office, we were effectively pursuing our outreach, press, department policy, and personnel goals.

Al Gore conceded the election on December 13. Within ten days, the entire McLean operation moved downtown to the government space at

1800 G Street N.W. We turned on the transition website to answer commonly asked questions and to receive applications—about forty thousand in a few weeks time, as it turned out. We also sent out e-mails and letters to tell supporters how to connect with us. We were effectively managing the incoming flow of advice, requests, and job seeking from the beginning.

Within days of the concession to Governor Bush, Andy Card began to formally designate members of the White House senior staff, which was only about a week later than would have been hoped for in a normal transition. Andy had conference calls or meetings with this senior staff group, twice per day up to the Inauguration, to get the group used to working together to maximize the value of the president-elect's time and voice, as they would once he was president.

We contacted cabinet secretary prospects and considered different combinations of people. The selection process went quickly because Bush and Cheney are decisive people; we had talked about the kinds of people we were looking for, and we had already edited down an initial list of prospects. Once a finalist was selected for a position, we were quickly able to assess any potential conflicts or clearance issues by having them talk to Fred Fielding, President Reagan's first White House counsel and the person who oversaw the clearance process at the start of that administration. Fred's experience allowed us to go public with our choices very quickly after selection, sometimes in a matter of hours, with only one clearance problem developing during this period.

A volunteer confirmation "shepherd" was assigned to each secretary-designate to introduce them to the relevant senators, help them with their confirmation paperwork, and prepare them for their hearings. All these "shepherds" had successfully managed the confirmation process for high-level appointees in previous administrations.

We also assigned a presidential-personnel person to each prospective secretary and made it very clear that we intended to put their subcabinet together in collaboration with them: we were going to do it *with* them, not *to* them, and vice versa. We explained our wish to talk about desired qualities for each position before we talked about specific candidates. It took us from a few days to a month or so to establish an effective personnel selection process with each of the secretaries, but in the end each subcabinet selection was a person about whom both the president and the secretary felt very good.

The secretary-designates spent a lot of time in Washington during the last few weeks of the transition. We set aside offices for them in an area we called "Secretaries Row," with the benefit being that they got to interact a little with one another before the administration began.

The department briefing books were put together with a minimum amount of disruption to the departments because of the small transition teams utilized. A fiscal "SWAT team" was put together to help the new Office of Management and Budget director-designate start to put the Bush-Cheney imprint on the federal budget. Additionally, separate people were charged to put together tentative postinaugural presidential schedules and to review existing executive orders and pending regulations for possible modification.

Throughout the transition, the president-elect met with legislators and individual groups, such as farmers, educators, and technology executives, who were interested in his priorities. The vice president–elect and the transition congressional-liaison group spent a lot of time interacting with legislators, welcoming their input, answering their questions, and keeping them updated. The reality and the message were that this new administration was working hard with Congress to follow through on the promises that had been made during the campaign.

In all, we engaged about eight hundred people in the transition effort and spent about what we had budgeted, $8.5 million. We involved fewer people than either the Reagan or Clinton transitions utilized, but we spent money on things that no one could have anticipated, like a couple of weeks of transition infrastructure, before the election was actually finalized.

Conclusions

As the election went on and on and on, and the amount of time to transition to a new administration became less and less, we kept reviewing the goals we had identified for the transition to see if there was anything we should drop because there was not enough time to get it done. Everything on the list seemed doable and relevant to assuming the responsibilities of the executive branch on January 20. So we just made sure it all got done.

We did not get as much work done on the subcabinet selections during the transition as we had planned originally, but we caught up about a month into the administration. We had a successful transition overall, though, because we were focused and prepared to act. It was very, very intense. Grown people cried during this transition, male and female, sometimes on the way home from work, sometimes in the office late at night. But as I understand it, grown people cry during a normal presidential transition too.

The Bush 2000 Transition:
The Historical Context

JOHN P. BURKE

A T ONE LEVEL, GEORGE W. BUSH'S TRANSITION to the presidency was unique and without much precedent as a guide. Unlike the situation facing his modern predecessors, Bush's "official" postelection transition did not begin until December 14 (the day after Al Gore's concession speech), when the General Services Administration (GSA) finally handed over the keys to transition headquarters in downtown Washington. Roughly half the time of a "normal" transition had been lost as the controversy over the Florida vote dragged on.

The reality, of course, was that transition planning had been well underway in the Bush camp. Vice Pres. Richard Cheney was at the helm of a not-quite-official (but clearly operational) Bush transition since the day after the election, and he would open a privately funded transition headquarters in Virginia on November 27, the day after Florida secretary of state Katherine Harris "certified" Bush's victory. Andrew Card had also operated as de facto chief of staff since election day (his appointment—as well as several others—would be announced on November 27 following certification). And Governor Bush himself faced the delicate task of appearing to be the victor but without presuming quite yet to being president-elect.[1]

But here too, modern presidential history presented no guide. Throughout the period from November 8 through December 13, Bush and his advisers faced the unique challenge of preparing for a new presidency but within their own context of an unsettled election outcome; the nearest historical reference was the far reach of the Hayes and Tilden contest in 1876.

That said, however, the Bush transition offers the best example of an effort that was aware of the experiences of its predecessors, recognized the value of the lessons to be learned, and generally was prepared to reap the positive benefits of its predecessors' experiences while avoiding the pitfalls.

Before November

As has been the case for all transitions since 1976, Bush began early to plan for his presidency. When Clay Johnson became his gubernatorial chief of staff in spring, 1999, Governor Bush also asked him to think about planning for a possible Bush presidency.[2] "I would like you to figure out what we need to do starting the day after the election," Bush told him. "Come up with a plan—talk to people who have done this before, read what you can get your hands on, confer with people, pick their brains, and come up with a plan."[3] Johnson recalled that George W. Bush, "as was his custom," had charged him to "put together a plan for the transition; what should our goals be; how do we organize; how do we accomplish those goals and so forth."[4]

The selection of Johnson, a longtime friend and trusted associate, to lead the effort followed the pattern of the more successful transitions. Like Edwin Meese in 1980 and Chase Untermeyer in 1988, he was a member of the president-elect's inner circle. His selection for the task was not likely to generate jealousy and in-fighting, as had been the case in 1976 and 1992. Johnson also knew his principal, George W. Bush, as a chief executive with a particular leadership and decision-making style, and he knew the Bush policy agenda.

Johnson, moreover, proceeded with discretion. There was little media attention about his work until shortly before election day. That was in marked contrast to 1992, when a number of stories appeared about the Clinton pre-election effort, much to the consternation of the campaign war room, and that led in turn to some counterproductive internal battles that spilled out after election day and delayed his transition.

Johnson did his homework. He immersed himself in the literature on past transitions and sought to learn their lessons especially, so that past mistakes would not be repeated. In an interview he gave to the *Washington Post* in late December, he laid out those lessons:

—proceed with hiring based on the new administration's policy priorities
—pick your chief of staff early
—have a clear understanding of what qualities you are looking for in personnel to counterbalance the political pressure to make certain appointments
—develop a clear set of policy goals, otherwise "you will have your goals set for you"[5]

For his part, George W. Bush was willing to put those lessons into practice. The selection of Andrew Card as chief of staff was settled before election day. In addition, the decision was made right after the Republican convention that Cheney would serve as the transition's chairman, presuming a Bush victory. Both Card and Cheney came well equipped for the task at hand. Both had served in key White House positions, both had headed cabinet departments, and both had been in charge of outgoing transitions for the administrations in which they served (Cheney for Ford in 1976, Card for Bush Sr. in 1992). Clay Johnson's postelection appointment as executive director of the transition rounded out the top team.[6] Their collective knowledge and experience surpassed their counterparts in earlier transitions: Jack Watson and Hamilton Jordan in 1976, Ed Meese in 1980, Robert Teeter and Craig Fuller in 1988, and Warren Christopher and Vernon Jordan in 1992.

Cheney's selection to lead the transition effort and Johnson's assignment as executive director (with heavy responsibilities in the personnel area, among others) also avoided a problem that plagued the Clinton effort in 1992: transition principals who then become slated to head cabinet departments. Their counterparts in 1992, Warren Christopher and William Riley, were picked to head cabinet departments, drawing them away to an extent from their transition assignments.

Card's selection as chief of staff before election day was especially crucial. As Clay Johnson later recalled, "One of the primary things we did in the transition—and [it] has borne fruit during the first 100 days—we got the president to do what most people running for the presidency do not want to do, [and that is] to decide who their chief of staff is to be and ask him to be the chief of staff before the election. It was critically important that Andy Card had been asked and accepted and was on the ground prior to the election and beginning to have conversations with Governor Bush."[7]

Throughout the pre-election period, Johnson would confer periodically with Bush, the latter often offering advice about whom to talk to regarding a variety of matters that might soon confront the candidate. Bush was very clear about what kind of chief of staff he wanted, and it was his call that led to Card's selection as chief of staff. As Johnson observed: "[Bush] did not want someone to be chief of staff who was overterritorial, or was a control freak, or felt like they had to control the content or the recommendations that flowed to the president. He wanted somebody who was more a facilitator, an orchestrator, and a tiebreaker; as they say an honest broker. . . . The president's knowledge about the way he likes to work led him to choose Andy Card."[8]

The Postelection Transition

By January 2, Bush had finished up with the selection of his cabinet.[9] That date placed him only about a week behind Clinton's schedule in 1992. More notable, in fact, President-elect Bush was actually well ahead of Clinton in naming his White House staff. In 1992, Clinton's press secretary, White House legal counsel, congressional liaison, and domestic policy adviser were not announced until the last week before his inauguration.

All of these positions in the Bush White House were unveiled earlier, in some cases much earlier. Andrew Card's selection as chief of staff had been settled two weeks before election day.[10] In 1992, by contrast, Clinton's chief of staff, Thomas "Mack" McLarty, was appointed on December 12. Al Gonzales, the Bush White House counsel, and Karen Hughes, the communications director, were tapped on December 17, weeks before their Clinton counterparts. As Johnson would later recall, by the time of Gore's concession on December 13, "Andy Card had made, with the president's consent, almost all of the senior White House personnel decisions. It was decided who was going to go where."[11]

In so doing, the Bush transition followed one of the key lessons of prior transitions. Early staff appointments enable those selected not only to get a leg up on their own jobs but also enable the transition to move on to other levels of staff positions. In Clinton's case, he and his advisers were essentially still stuck at the top layer of the White House a few days before he was sworn in to office. By contrast, the seemingly truncated Bush transition had already moved on to second- and, in some cases, third-level White House positions.

Two of the positions that Bush filled early—White House legal counsel and the head of the White House Personnel Office (Al Gonzales and Clay Johnson respectively)—were especially critical because they are so integrally involved in the appointment and vetting process for all presidential appointees. Swift appointments in these two areas, moreover, may have been an important lesson taken from the Bush Sr. 1988 transition. Both Boyden Gray, White House legal counsel, and Chase Untermeyer, who directed personnel, were also early appointments—the day after the election of George Herbert Walker Bush, in fact. Both contributed greatly to that earlier smooth transition to power.

The appointment of Karl Rove as senior adviser to the president and Karen Hughes as counselor to the president may also have reflected some lessons learned from the Bush Sr. presidency as well as finding places in the administration for two longtime Bush aides. Both participants and observers of the Bush Sr. White House have noted that too much was delegated to the chief of staff alone and that its communications and political affairs units were poorly organized and utilized. Those errors were not repeated.

Rove's efforts also drew on the 1980 Reagan transition, particularly the work of David Gergen and Richard Wirthlin in developing a long-range strategic plan. According to one account, Rove was placed in charge of "drawing up a detailed action plan for the first 180 days of the Bush administration. Rove's task: to take items in the agenda Bush campaigned on, turn them into pieces of actual legislation, and then choreograph their rollout for maximum political benefit. The best antidote to the public's lingering qualms about Bush's legitimacy, says an adviser, is to 'show that we're very busy doing things that real people want. We have to get some things done—fast. . . . Rove has laid out a plan—in a series of memos and calendars—for the boss's first four weeks.'"[12]

Like the successful legislative strategy group that James Baker developed as chief of staff under Reagan, Rove and Card also created a number of White House staff groups designed to further the Bush policy agenda. One was the Office of Strategic Initiatives, under Rove's direction, designed to emphasize long-range planning and provide input to meetings of senior White House aides. Other groups were created to deal with long-range scheduling, communications, and congressional liaison.[13]

The transition also was a time to instill a particular "organizational culture" that Bush valued. According to one account, transition advisers "said Bush insists that loyalty can flower in an institution known for distractions and back-stabbing."[14] James Barnes of the *National Journal* later observed that while "the Clinton White House was more of a coalition—with aides from all parts of the Democratic Party," the Bush White was more cohesive. "Because so many people on the Bush White House staff worked together either on the campaign or, even before that, in Austin, they've not only demonstrated their fidelity to Bush, they've operated as a team and formed bonds with each other, which may diminish prospects for internecine warfare." In Karl Rove's view, "Bush has tended to surround himself with people he's taken the measure of."[15]

The final days of the transition even saw what Clay Johnson termed "practicing to be in the White House," which Andrew Card had instigated: "The senior staff of the White House had begun to meet for the last ten days to two weeks of the transition, twice a day, to get in the habit of meeting with each other, communicating with each other, and to begin to talk about the president's schedule as if we were in the White House." In sum, in Johnson's view, "a lot of planning, a lot of focus, a lot of rigor and discipline. On the agenda, a commitment to do a few things very well, that was [a] mark of the transition."[16]

A Cautionary Note

Although the Bush transition understood the lessons of past transitions, it also illustrates some of the limits of transition planning and what an even well-crafted transition can bring to a new presidency. In this respect too, its experiences were somewhat unique and lacked a historical context upon which to draw. Unlike its predecessors, the new administration almost immediately confronted a number of challenges that either had not been anticipated or could not have been anticipated. Looming over all would be the economic downturn of 2001, which would put in jeopardy its tax, budgetary, and policy agendas and force harder choices than had been expected or prepared for. But the administration also faced an energy crisis in California that would force it, initially against its own wishes, to quickly develop a comprehensive energy program under Vice President Cheney's direction. It had to grapple with the moral (and political) complexities of stem cell research. The outgoing Clinton administration presented it with a variety of last-minute executive orders and regulatory rulings, particularly in environmental policy, to which it needed to respond. Politics too intervened in a hard way with the defection of Sen. Jim Jeffords from the GOP and the shift of the Senate to Democratic control. Political time had dealt the Bush presidency a new but less favorable political hand.

Finally, the events of September 11, 2001, would shock and outrage the nation, presenting the Bush administration with the gravest challenge any modern president immediately and unexpectedly would face. It marked not a transition but a transformation—not just in this presidency but also in the course of the national experience. While Bush and his associates may have drawn well on the lessons of past transitions in assuming office, what past historical context could now serve as a ready and reliable guide?

Notes

1.   In fact, the Florida delay may have had a positive aspect: it enabled Bush and his advisers to do transition planning without the media spotlight and other pressures that normally occur.

2.   Clay Johnson, telephone interview with author, Sept. 20, 2001.

3.   James Bennet, "The Bush Years: CEO, USA," *New York Times Magazine,* Jan. 14, 2001.

4.   Clay Johnson, panel discussion on "President Bush's First 100 Days," Kennedy School of Government, Harvard University, May 2, 2001.

5.   Dana Milbank, "Tome for the Holidays: A Transition Reading List," *Washington Post,* Dec. 19, 2000.

6.   Johnson interview. Cheney also enlisted the services of Fred Fielding, a transition veteran and President Reagan's first White House legal counsel, to serve as counsel for the transition's clearance process. According to Clay Johnson, "We were very knowledgeable once clearance became something we had to deal with because Fred was there, and he was an invaluable resource and a big part of our transition operation."

7.   Johnson, "Bush's First 100 Days."

8.   Johnson interview.

9.   Linda Chavez's nomination as labor secretary was withdrawn on January 9 following revelations about her assistance to an illegal immigrant. She was quickly replaced by Elaine Chao on January 11. Although the episode indicated some weaknesses in the vetting process, the Bush transition dealt with the matter with more dispatch than had the Clinton transition with its attorney general nominees.

10.   Johnson interview.

11.   Johnson, "Bush's First 100 Days."

12.   James Carney and John F. Dickerson, "Rolling Back Clinton," *Time,* Jan. 29, 2001.

13. Dana Milbank, "Serious Strategery," *Washington Post,* Apr. 22, 2001.

14. Mike Allen, "A Team Built on Conservative Discipline," *Washington Post,* Jan. 3, 2001.

15. James A. Barnes, "Bush's Insiders," *National Journal,* June 23, 2001, p. 1869.

16. Johnson, "Bush's First 100 Days."

The Real Invisible Hand

*Presidential Appointees in the Administration
of George W. Bush*

G. CALVIN MACKENZIE

IT WAS TO BE THE SINGLE MOST VISIBLE DECISION
of George W. Bush's first year in office, inspiring even a rare primetime
televised address to announce and explain it to the American people.
For weeks, the White House press office told of the president's wide-
ranging search for advice: the meetings with ethicists and scientists, with
interest-group representatives, and with dozens of ordinary citizens.

But Bush's wide search for advice did not include consultations with
the director of the White House Office of Science and Technology Policy,
the president's chief science adviser, nor with the director of the National
Institutes of Health, the government's leader in health research. And the
simple reason why George W. Bush did not consult with his appointees in
those positions is that there were none. President Bush was making decisions that affected the health and concerned the moral values of millions
of Americans without the support of scores of important players in his administration.

In fact, many of the five hundred top positions in the executive branch
that required Senate confirmation were not filled in the first nine months
of his term in office. (See figure 17 for the month-by-month progress
through September, 2001.)

Many of those who voted for George W. Bush wanted decisive action
on the new education approaches he had promised. But until the end of

**Figure 17. Pace of Completed Appointments in Top 500 Positions
in the Executive Branch, 2001.**

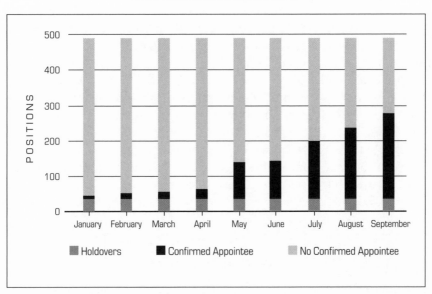

Note: Prepared by the author from data calculated from official sources by Michael Hafken of the Presidential Appointee Initiative of the Brookings Institution.

May, Education Secretary Rod Paige was the only confirmed appointee at work in that department. Around the government, the story was much the same: No one but the secretary was confirmed at Energy until May 24; the same at Interior until June 29. On September 1, eight of the fourteen cabinet departments had no confirmed chief financial officer. And when terrorists struck a brutal blow to the country on September 11, there was no confirmed U.N. ambassador, no commissioner of customs, no director of the U.S. Marshals, and no undersecretaries for the army or air force.

In 1993 the Clinton transition had broken every record for the slowest ever. But the most recent transition surpassed—if that's the right word—the painfully slow pace of its predecessor.

These are not measures of human failure, of the inability of new presidents and their aides to master the task of staffing an administration. There are some breakdowns and false starts in every transition, of course. But the starker reality is that the presidential-appointments process has become a monster that quickly overwhelms the capacity of any new administration to tame it. The problem is systemic, and it grows with each new election.

Embedded in all mainstream theories of democracy is the notion that elections are critically important navigational devices. They point political leaders in certain directions and away from others. They supply new leaders determined to pursue the goals that citizens choose with their votes. Democratic citizens rely on the assumption that, once chosen, elected leaders will do as they are bid.

But in a complex democracy, that can only occur when elected leaders have teams of experts and administrators in place to help them refine policy options, build support for their initiatives among the people and the legislature, and then implement them. Nowhere in all of democratic theory is there provision for a lag of six months, nine months, or even a year between the time the people speak and the essential administrative appointees are in place to act on their instructions.

And yet, that consistently has been the practice in the United States over the past decade.

Historical Perspective

Experienced observers of presidential transitions found little surprising in the difficulty confronted by George W. Bush in his efforts to staff the first new presidential administration of the twenty-first century. Despite the days of uncertainty following the vote in November, 2000, Governor Bush pushed forward with the essentials of transition planning. Clay Johnson, an old friend of the new president and an experienced hand in helping Bush staff his administration in Austin, had begun to plan for this personnel recruitment and selection task long before it began. He knew the magnitude of the task and the pitfalls he would encounter.[1] But knowing what lies ahead only takes away some of the surprise when you get there. It does not guarantee easy negotiation of the obstacles.

The modern appointments process is a morass of forms and questionnaires, of background checks and investigations, of redundancy and complexity. Every nominee is subjected to a scrutiny so thorough, so invasive, so tediously picayune that some nominees spend almost as much time getting through the appointments process as they do in office.

It has not always been so. For most of the twentieth century, the appointments process flowed smoothly through the routines of government. A vacancy occurred, a suitable candidate was identified (often by the managers of the president's political party), a few questions were asked to ensure that the candidate was in agreement with most of the president's program, the nomination was announced, and a quick review and confirmation by the Senate soon followed.

That description still fit the appointments process as recently as the late 1960s. One useful measure of the pace of the appointments process is the length of time that passes between inauguration and confirmation for the average nominee in an administration. The average for the Kennedy administration was 2.38 months.[2] Nixon in the late 1960s was only slightly slower, 3.39 months. Even Carter, a near total stranger to Washington, managed to get his appointees in place in an average of 4.55 months.

But then real changes began to occur as law and process caught up with the post-Watergate cynicism about public servants. The Ethics in Government Act of 1978 was the major monument to those concerns. But it was amended and its interpretation expanded often in subsequent years to seek to prevent every form of misbehavior the mind could imagine.

By the time of the Reagan transition, a noticeable change had appeared in the appointments process, and it is clearly revealed in our measure. The average Reagan appointee was confirmed in 5.3 months, more than twice as long as the average Kennedy appointee twenty years earlier. But then by the end of the 1980s, the modern appointments process was fully in place. Confirmation for the appointees of the first President Bush took 8.13 months on average, and for President Clinton four years later, 8.53 months. While it is too soon to calculate the final average for the second President Bush in 2001, it is the slowest transition in American history. (See figure 18 for the progress of Bush administration appointments through September 30, 2001.)

"It's The Process, Stupid"

What explains the very long time that it has taken to staff the new Bush administration in 2001? Not a lack of diligence or concern on the part of the new president. He was calling for changes in the appointments process months before his election. Not the people to whom President Bush delegated the task of managing the process. They worked as hard and with as much competence as any presidential-personnel advisers ever had. The answer is the process itself. Staffing a new administration in the twenty-first century has become a task too large, burdened by procedures too dense and resistance too potent.

Figure 18. Number of Bush Nominees Announced, Nominated, and Confirmed by Month, 2001.

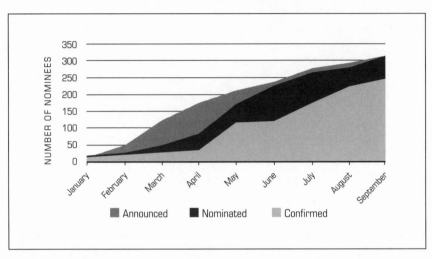

Note: Prepared by the author from data calculated from official sources by Michael Hafken of the Presidential Appointee Initiative of the Brookings Institution.

Too Many Appointees

Without any blueprint or defining theory, the number of positions filled by presidential appointees has grown steadily over recent decades, expanding outward with the creation of new departments and agencies, expanding downward as positions once filled by senior civil servants have been converted to political appointments. President Bush had nearly 3,300 positions subject to his appointment, more than any president could hope to fill in timely fashion even with an appointments process far more efficient than the one under which we currently labor. In 2001, thoughtful members of Congress had begun to call for a substantial reduction in the number of presidential appointments, perhaps as many as one-third of the current total.

Some people oppose this reduction, arguing that it will undercut the president's ability to control and lead the government.[3] Others argue that every one of the positions currently filled by appointment is critical to good management. Perhaps. But there is a heavy and unmet burden of proof on those who make this argument; it is called the facts. We have never succeeded in developing an appointments process that could adequately meet the staffing burden this many positions imposes. As a consequence, it now takes nearly a quarter of a presidential term to get an administration staffed. It is hard to sustain the case for so many appointed positions when it is so long and arduous a task to fill them.

Too Thick a Process

The Bush appointees in 2001 were expected to complete forms and questionnaires that asked more than two hundred questions.[4] Their taxes were reviewed by the IRS. Law enforcement authorities across the country were solicited for any relevant files. The FBI conducted a complete full-field investigation on them. They were subject to intensive questioning by the Office of Presidential Personnel, by vetters, and by the White House counsel.

The Office of Government Ethics and lawyers in the White House and at the agency where they would serve scrutinized every detail of nominees' personal finances, often requiring that they divest assets or alter their portfolios to avoid potential conflicts of interest. Their policy views, their public record, and all of their writings and public statements were combed for any material that might undermine their nomination or embarrass the president. When the candidates were done with all of this, if they ever were, then they endured largely duplicative inquiries and investigations at the hands of Senate committee staffs.

That it can take many months to accomplish all of this, especially at the outset of a new administration when all the systems are in overload, is no surprise. But those unfortunate nominees who are unfamiliar with the appointment process when they enter it are shocked as the months pass to discover just how hard it has become to serve one's country.

Too Fragmented a Senate

The Senate has an important role in the appointments process, and the framers of the Constitution were astute in recognizing that personnel evaluations often must rely on personal judgments. In substantial part that is why the appointments process, as they invented it, was so uncluttered with rules, constraints, standards, and specifications.

But the framers could not have envisioned the effects of a long period of divided government. The intensifying partisanship of contemporary legislative-executive conflict has invaded the appointments process and altered it substantially. For most of our history, the dominant Senate view was that the president was entitled to staff his administration with persons of his own choosing and that the Senate would object to the president's choices only when there was overwhelming necessity. That view prevails now only rhetorically. In practice the modern Senate regards itself as a co-equal participant in the appointments process. Individual senators have come to regard this process as fertile ground for their own efforts to shape the ideology of the administration, to fight for their own policy initiatives, to settle old scores, and to second-guess administrative decisions.

The most effective device at their disposal is the "hold," an arcane Senate tradition that allows an individual senator to place a hold on a nomination for whatever reasons and for however long he or she may choose. During the time a hold is in place, the nomination is dead in the water. Holds reached epidemic proportions during the final years of the Clinton presidency. Some observers assumed that this was simply a consequence of bad relations between a Democratic president and a Republican-controlled Senate, that things would change when one party controlled both houses.

But the habits of divided government die hard, and even in the few months before Sen. Jim Jeffords undercut the Republican majority in the Senate, holds were being imposed by senators of both parties. For example, Jesse Helms, the Senate's leading holder, had no reservations about putting a five-month hold on Kenneth Dam, Bush's nominee for deputy Treasury secretary. The practice of holds, combined with the much more thorough investigations that Senate committees conduct of nominees, the growing burden of scheduling hearings for nominees to so many positions, and the benefits of delay that come to those who dislike a nominee or the nominee's policy views have changed the Senate's role from that of ultimate quality check on nominees to a place where nominations often go and disappear for months at a time (as figure 19 indicates).

Conclusion

So it was business as usual for the new Bush administration in 2001, a lousy business. Staffing the highest levels of government has become a nightmare for contemporary presidents. And for friends of democracy who believe that those who win elections ought to be able to govern, the deep flaws in the presidential-appointments process are more than arcane matters of public management. They are central concerns that pose serious

**Figure 19. Average and Median Number of Days Between Senate Receipt of
Nomination and Confirmation of Executive Branch Appointees, 1998–1999.**

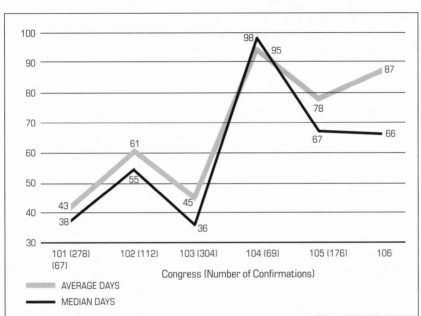

Notes: Constructed from data in Burdett Loomis, "The Senate: An 'Obstacle Cource'?" in
Innocent until Nominated: The Breakdown of the Presidential Appointments Process, ed. G. Calvin
Mackenzie (Washington, D.C.: Brookings Institution, 2001), p. 165. Data for the 106th Congress
are for 1999 only. The confirmation process for judicial appointments has similarly lengthened
over the past decade. See Sarah Binder, "Lessons Learned from Judicial Appointments," in
Mackenzie, ed., *Innocent until Nominated,* p. 185.

questions about what democracy can be and what it has become in the
United States at the beginning of the twenty-first century.

Notes

Much of the research reported here was made possible by the generous support of The
Pew Charitable Trusts for the Brookings Presidential Appointee Initiative (www.
appointee.brookings.edu).

1. Clay Johnson III, interview by author, Washington, D.C., Feb. 23, 2001.

2. Calculations for this and the presidential averages reported in subsequent
paragraphs were done by the author from data reported in *Congressional Quarterly Al-
manacs* for 1961, 1969, 1981, and 1989. The average for the Clinton administration was
calculated from reports prepared by Rogelio Garcia for the Congressional Research Service.

3.   Robert Moranto and Robert Moffett, "Keep 'Em Coming: In Defense of Political Appointees," *Washington Times,* May 2, 2001.

4.   See the detailed analysis of these forms in Terry Sullivan, "Repetitiveness, Redundancy, and Reform: Rationalizing the Inquiry of Presidential Appointees," in *Innocent until Nominated: The Breakdown of the Presidential Appointments Process,* ed. G. Calvin Mackenzie (Washington, D.C.: Brookings Institution, 2001), pp. 196–230.

Already Buried and Sinking Fast
Presidential Nominees and Inquiry

TERRY SULLIVAN

NOTHING CHALLENGES A NEW PRESIDENT'S team more than its need to fill out the executive-branch offices. The White House 2001 Project played a significant role in this aspect of the presidential transition. Its White House Interview Program provided useful information gleaned from the rarified ranks of personnel staff, while its *Nomination Forms Online* program detailed for the first time the exact particulars of the inquiry process. Already well under way by the time the Bush team began planning in 1999, the White House 2001 Project provided the Bush staff with details about two of the five great transition challenges affecting personnel: scale and complexity.[1] Scale would present the Bush people with an organizational challenge—how to cope with the numbers of applications flooding in? Complexity presented them with a managerial problem—how could they govern the process, especially its burdensome and intrusive inquiry—rather than the reverse?

The Bush team responded to these challenges, principally in managing the inquiries received. During 2001, managing inquiry has become the object of reform efforts: several reforms of the inquiry process have surfaced, including two separate changes taken up by the White House and at least one attempt to modify statutes.[2]

Scale

The Texas Governor's Appointments Office maintains a database on potential nominees. As the country's second largest state, Texas has an operation that represents something as close to the "major leagues" as governing goes in the states. According to Clay Johnson, a former appointments director, that database carried fifteen thousand names. In the twenty-four-hour period following a presidential election day, the president-elect's team typically receives ten thousand applications for presidential appointments: in one day, almost the total Texas volume. By the end of its truncated transition period, the George W. Bush White House carried some sixty thousand applications—*four* times their previous experience.

To handle this scale, the Bush planners focused on candidate assessment. In particular, early on in the transition planning and well in advance of the Republican convention, they decided on new technologies for handling the staggering flow. The Clinton transition team had relied on a "labor intensive" plan, recruiting hordes of professional headhunters working as volunteers and backed up by a sizable support staff. These volunteers recruited and then vetted candidates, relying on a record-keeping system that depended on scanning hardcopy resumes. That operation did not translate into the White House, for the sizable transition staff shrank to the small number of staff permitted by federal law. In addition, relying on the untried technology of transforming optical images into text, the Clinton team fell hopelessly behind, at one point in the transition simply throwing out three thousand applications sitting in its backlog in a frustrated effort to "catch up."

The Bush team opted for a more capital-intensive effort, relying on applicants entering initial resumes on a website that automatically fed the transition team's database. This approach reduced the need for a large transition staff, relying instead on a staff similar in size to that they would have in office. This easily accumulated database also allowed them to ignore patrons and references in some instances, searching instead for characteristics like race, region, education, or special skills. According to Clay Johnson, the director of presidential personnel, the Bush White House has used this database to fill some jobs by simply searching for appropriate candidates from those applications that have "come in over the transom." This electronic and capital-intensive approach has produced a database of around seventy thousand entries. As such, it constitutes a genuinely effective effort at addressing scale.[3]

Complexity

Quickly after beginning their work in late 1999, the Bush transition planners began to appreciate the difficulties facing presidential nominees. Of course, the Clinton nominations had suffered through a wide variety of obstacles documented by observers. Through further study and through discussions with White House 2001 Project, the Bush team became more familiar with the problems. While some seemed unavoidable, such as exposure to corrosive Washington partisanship, which slowed confirmation, others, such as the irrational complexity of nominee inquiry, appeared repairable. Consider, for example, the sheer number of inquiries presidential nominees must face. They start with four separate forms. The first originates with the White House. Called the "Personal Data Statement" (PDS), it covers some twenty-three questions. The second form comes from the FBI. Standard Form (SF) 86, commonly called the "FBI background check," develops information for national security clearances. The SF86 contains three forms: the standard questionnaire covering some seventy-nine questions, a "supplemental questionnaire" that repackages previous questions into ten broader topic areas, and the "immigration addendum" presenting an additional twenty-six questions about each non-American born person in the nominee's household or family. SF278, which comes from the Office of Government Ethics [OGE], gathers information for financial disclosure. For many nominees, a fourth form comes from the Senate committee with appropriate jurisdiction.

In filing forms, nominees must provide information on several topics. The inquiries involved unnecessarily invade a nominee's privacy and often require information that plays no significant role in determining a nominee's qualifications. Two of the most recent studies on the appointments process, from the Century Fund's Task Force and from the Presidential Appointees Initiative, have called for finding ways to restrain the intrusiveness and diminish the burdens of inquiry.

The problem of intrusive inquiry seems obvious.[4] Take the situation involving information on property. The government asks nominees not only to reveal the general value of properties but also to report those values with unnecessary precision, specifying values in one of *eleven* ranges. (See Table 1.) A nominee's inventory must draw a distinction between properties worth $99,999 or $100,010, for example, as if the change from the previous category to the next reflects a definable increase in conflicts of interest. This approach clearly reflects an assumption that disclosure of

Table 1. Asset Values Found on SF278 Financial Disclosure Statement

Place a value on assets owned by spouse or dependent children up to "over $1,000,000." For assets owned by the nominee, place value on asset up through "over $50,000,000."	• $1,001–$15,000 • $15,001–$50,000 • $50,001–$100,000 • $100,001–$250,000 • $250,001–$500,000 • $500,001–$1,000,000 • Over $1,000,000 • $1,000,001–$5,000,000 • $5,000,001–$25,000,000 • $25,000,001–$50,000,000 • Over $50,000,000

these specific values will provide useful information with which to discern an appropriate remedy for any apparent conflicts. On its face, this regulatory assumption seems flawed.[5]

The degree of burden on nominees generated by repetitive questions seems harder to fathom. The principal burden comes from the fact that the executive and Congress request a wide variety of information, all in drastically different formats. For example, all observers will assay the nominee's real property when considering conflicts of interest. The subsequent inquiry presents nominees with a blizzard of questions covering the same topic but requiring tedious reshaping of information from one answer to the next. On real property alone, nominees must muster information over four forms, in three different time periods, designating three separate classes of owners, sorting on at least two separate types of transactions, and (in some cases) indicating values across the eleven distinct values mentioned earlier. No wonder nominees consider this part of the process "embarrassing," "confusing," or at best "a necessary evil."

Developed by the White House 2001 Project's *Nomination Forms Online Program,* Table 2 details this burden. It distributes inquiries into three categories defined by how much common information they require. Questions inquiring into the same subject and requiring the same information constitute "identical," or "redundant," inquiries (for example, "last name"). Those questions concerned with the same subject but that vary information along at least one dimension constitute "similar," or "repetitive," questions. Those questions seeking distinct information represent "nonrepetitive," or "unique," questions.[6]

Among the four questionnaires the table summarizes, including a representative Senate committee questionnaire,[7] Clinton nominees re-

Table 2. Repetitiveness among Inquiries*

Administration	Clinton**		G. W. Bush	
Type of Inquiry Across Forms	Number	Percent	Number	Percent
Identical (redundant)	19	8	23	14
Similar (repetitive)	99	42	40	24
Nonrepetitive (unique)	120	50	104	62
Totals	238		167	$\lambda=29.83$

* Compiled by author from four executive-branch forms and supplements plus a representative Senate committee of jursidiction.

**Clinton numbers do not include SF86—the Immigration Addendum added in October, 2000.

sponded to approximately 238 inquiries. They answered 120 unique questions (those without an analog) and another 99 repetitive questions (those with analogs), regularly repeating the answers to about 20 redundant questions. Thus, by these estimates, nearly half of the questions Clinton nominees answered have some analog elsewhere, while the other half have no analog anywhere.

For current nominees, some recent changes have modified the situation somewhat. Because the Bush White House changed the PDS, nominees now answer nearly 30 percent fewer inquiries. They respond to more identical questions (23), fewer repetitive questions (40), and fewer unique questions (104). Thus, the Bush nominees answer only 167 inquiries. These changes appear similar to those recommended by the White House 2001 Project to the Bush planners in August, 2000, which emphasized reducing the amount of repetitiveness in favor of improved redundancy, generating a total reduction of around 31 percent.[8]

Reforming Inquiry

While effective, the Bush White House changes to the PDS constitute only one of several modifications in the process the White House 2001 Project and others recommended. Two of these changes seem worth noting. First, further reducing the burden on nominees will require that the government develop more redundant inquiries particularly covering financial disclosure and legal entanglements—the two subjects areas in which questions trend toward repetitiveness. One simple, effective change would substitute the SF278 report for the net worth statement required by almost all Senate committees. While net worth provides information that identifies insolvency, that condition constitutes only one potential conflict of interest compared to the many more clearly captured on SF278.

Second, under a statutory mandate, the OGE has recommended changes for the executive's financial-disclosure system.[9] Based on their study *Report on the Financial Disclosure Process,* their proposal included a number of recommendations, among them one affording OGE more leeway in setting standards and another collapsing almost all the financial reporting categories. If enacted by Congress, the reporting recommendations would reduce intrusiveness. The failure of OGE to support further reforms (for example, substitution of SF278 for net worth or a unified Senate questionnaire) underscores the need for the White House to take a more active role in easing the nominee's situation.

Moreover, Congress should enact similar legislation instructing the FBI and the White House to report on reducing the amount of useless inquiry in the legal arena and on adopting a single form for the executive branch, respectively. Planned improvements in redundancy across all executive forms, particularly reducing the numbers of unique questions about law enforcement, seem appropriate.

Notes

1.   The five transition challenges are pace, scale, complexity, scrutiny, and focus.

2.   See Terry Sullivan, "Repetitiveness, Redundancy, and Reform—Rationalizing the Inquiry of Presidential Nominees," in *Innocent until Nominated: The Breakdown of the Presidential Appointments Process,* ed. G. Calvin Mackenzie (Washington, D.C.: Brookings Institution, 2001), pp. 196–230; Terry Sullivan, "In Full View—The Inquiry of Presidential Nominees," *White House 2001 Project, Nomination Forms Online Program,* Report 15 (Apr., 2001); testimony, U.S. Senate Committee on Governmental Affairs, May 5, 2001 (see www.whitehouse2001.org); and Terry Sullivan, "Fabulous Formless Darkness—Presidential Nominees and the Morass of Inquiry," *The Brookings Review* 12, no. 2 (spring, 2001): 22–27.

3.   Clay Johnson, interview with author, Washington, D.C., Sept. 26, 2001.

4.   Paul C. Light and Virginia Thomas, *The Merit and Reputation of an Administration: Presidential Appointees on the Appointments Process* (Washington, D.C.: Presidential Appointees Initiative, Apr., 2000), p. 10.

5.   For SF278's statutory basis, see *U.S. Code,* vol. 5, appendix §102(a)(1)-(3). Using narrowly defined amounts rests on a "principal/agent" theory of control inherent to the legislative branch. An elected representative avoids conflicts of interests by anticipating the adverse reaction of an aroused and informed public, who must, in turn, judge and vote on the representative's qualifications. Disclosing with such precision, therefore, acts as a deterrent to potentially undesirable behavior.

Yet presidential nominees face a different situation. They come into government from the private world, where they may not have lived their lives in anticipation of governing. They cannot set their past behavior in response to future restrictions they could not properly anticipate. Thus, they enter public service with likely conflicts of interests inadvertently acquired. In response, the government must find a resolution rather than a deterrent for these extant conflicts. For the purposes of resolution, then, detailed figures provide no particular guidance because they do not necessarily provide any useful information about the nature of potential resolutions. See Sullivan, "In Full View."

6.   The typical distinction relies on analysis developed in programming the *Nomination Forms Online* software. It uses the degree to which a question either required no changes (redundant) or minor changes (repetitive) in common information or if it required to information that had no connections to other questions (unique). See Terry Sullivan, "A Guide to Inquiry," *White House 2001 Project, Nomination Forms Online Program*, Report 7, <www.whitehouse2001.org>.

7.   The analysis used the Commerce Committee during the Clinton administration and the Select Committee on Intelligence during the Bush administration.

8.   See Terry Sullivan, "Refining the White House Personal Data Statement," *White House 2001 Project, Nomination Forms Online Program*, Report 14 (released Mar., 2001), <www.whitehouse2001.org>. Drastic reductions among the unique questions seems unlikely, for nearly 60 percent of the unique questions come from SF86.

9. Issued pursuant to Public Law 106-293, *Transition Act of 2000*, 106th Cong., 2d sess., Oct. 12, 2000.

Strategic Choices and the Early Bush Legislative Agenda

GEORGE C. EDWARDS III

THE EARLY MONTHS OF A NEW PRESIDENCY REP-
resent the most important period for establishing the tone and
character of the White House's relationship with Congress. It is
the time of closest scrutiny and the greatest vulnerability to
making major mistakes. Taking the right steps early and avoiding errors
can lay the foundation for a productive working relationship. Actions
taken early create lasting impressions.

George W. Bush took office after one of the closest elections in American history. The highly unusual, protracted denouement and the truncated transition period of only thirty-eight days—about half the normal
time for a shift in power—had the potential to turn the transition into a
circus and undermine the new president's chances of legislative success.
The Bush White House had to handle four key strategic elements in its relations with Congress during its early months in office. Although there is
no official demarcation of a presidential transition, a point at about six
months in office is a reasonable period for evaluation. There is no doubt
that the tragic events of September 11 moved the administration into a
new phase of the Bush presidency.

Evaluating Strategic Position

The first step a new administration should take to ensure success with Congress is to assess accurately its strategic position so it understands the potential for change. Presidents must largely play the hands that the public deals them through its electoral decisions on the presidency and Congress and its evaluations of the chief executive's handling of his job. Presidents are rarely in a position to augment substantially their political capital, especially when just taking office.

The early periods of new administrations that are most clearly etched on our memories as notable successes are those in which presidents properly identified and exploited conditions for change. When Congress first met in special session in March, 1933, after Franklin D. Roosevelt's inauguration, it rapidly passed the new president's request for bills to control the resumption of banking, repeal Prohibition, and effect government economies. This is all FDR originally planned for Congress to do; he expected to reassemble the legislature when permanent and more constructive legislation was ready. Yet the president found a situation ripe for change, and he decided to exploit this favorable environment and strike repeatedly with hastily drawn legislation before sending Congress home. This period of intense activity came to be known as the Hundred Days.

Lyndon Johnson also knew that his personal leadership could not sustain congressional support for his policies. He realized that the assassination of Pres. John F. Kennedy and the election of 1964 provided him a unique chance to pass his Great Society legislation and moved immediately to exploit it. Similarly, the Reagan administration recognized that the perceptions of a mandate and the dramatic elevation of Republicans to majority status in the Senate provided it with a window of opportunity to effect major changes in public policy but that it had to concentrate its focus and move quickly before the environment became less favorable. Moreover, within a week of the assassination attempt against Reagan on March 30, 1981, Michael Deaver convened a meeting of other high-ranking aides at the White House to determine how best to take advantage of the new political capital the shooting had created.

If the White House misreads its strategic positions, the president may begin his tenure with embarrassing failures in dealing with Congress. Moreover, the greater the breadth and complexity of the policy change a president proposes, the more opposition it is likely to engender—and thus the stronger the president's strategic position must be to succeed. In an era when a few opponents can effectively tie up bills, the odds are clearly against the White House.

Bill Clinton overestimated the extent of change that a president elected with a minority of the vote could make, especially when the public is dubious and well-organized interest groups are fervently opposed. Nevertheless, the president proposed, without Republican support, perhaps the most sweeping, complex prescriptions for controlling the conduct of state governments, employers, drug manufacturers, doctors, hospitals, and individuals in American history. There was insufficient foundation for change of this magnitude. The consequences of the bill's failure were greater than disappointment, however. Because Clinton declared health-care reform to be the cornerstone of his efforts to change public policy, his handling of the bill became a key indicator of administration's competency at governing. The bill's death throes occurred only a few months before the 1994 elections, the greatest midterm electoral disaster for the Democrats since the Truman administration.

The unusual nature of George W. Bush's election had a substantial potential to weaken the start of his presidency. Receiving neither a majority nor even a plurality of the vote, Bush became the first candidate since 1888 to be elected with fewer popular votes than his principal opponent. Many (mostly Democrats) saw his victory as illegitimate because he received more than a half-million fewer votes than Al Gore and because of the peculiar circumstances surrounding the determination of the winner of Florida's electoral votes.

In light of the election results, the new president could not credibly claim a mandate from the people. Moreover, the Republicans lost seats in both houses of Congress, undermining any claim to presidential coattails. After the election, Republicans found themselves with only a very narrow majority in the House and required the vice president to break a fifty-fifty split in the Senate. It is not difficult to imagine a president elected in such circumstances to move cautiously, seeking first to increase his legitimacy with the majority of the public who did not support him for president. Some commentators saw the potential for paralysis in Washington, and others (again, mostly Democrats) urged the president to act as if he were indeed paralyzed, proposing only policies that enjoyed bipartisan support.

Bush was not intimidated by the narrowness of his election or the nature of its resolution, however. Although his tone was one of reconciliation, he ignored those who urged him to strike a bipartisan posture and hold off on his major initiatives. The White House correctly understood that the one policy that both unified and energized Republicans was tax cuts. Although most congressional Democrats would oppose the cuts, a majority of the public, including independents and even some Democrats, would support or at least tolerate them. Equally important, tax cuts, unlike most other major policies, could be considered under rules that prohibited a filibuster. Thus, a united, although slender, majority could prevail.

Choosing a Strategy for Governing

Having evaluated his strategic position, the president must choose a strategy for governing within the context in which he finds himself. One approach is to seek to pass legislation through relatively quiet negotiations with congressional leaders. The president's father, George H. W. Bush, provided an example with his administration's efforts regarding environmental, education, and budget policy. An alternative strategy is to take the case to the people, counting on public opinion to move Congress to support the president. The second President Bush, surprisingly to some, chose the latter course.

Soon after taking office, the president launched a massive public-relations campaign on behalf of his priority initiatives. At the core of this effort was the most extensive domestic travel schedule of any new president in American history. Bush spoke in twenty-nine states by the end of May, often more than once.

The White House employs a "rolling" announcement format in which it alerts the press that it will be making an announcement about a legislative initiative in coming days, sparking stories on the upcoming news. Then it makes the announcement, generating yet additional stories. Finally, the president travels around the country repeating the announcement he just made, obtaining both local and network coverage of his media events.

It is one thing to go public, it is something quite different to succeed in moving public opinion. Table 1 shows responses to Gallup poll questions on the president's tax-cut proposal. The results show that public opinion did not change in response to the president's efforts.

Also valuable for the president is demonstrating preexisting public support within the constituencies of members of Congress who are potential swing votes. Often, Bush's travels seemed motivated more by demonstrating his support in states where he ran well in the election than in convincing more-skeptical voters of the soundness of his proposals—he did

Table 1. Public Support for Bush Tax Cut

Poll Date	Favor (%)	Oppose (&)	No Opinion (&)
Feb. 9–11, 2001	56	34	10
Feb. 19–21, 2001	53	30	17
March 5–7, 2001	56	34	10
April 20–22, 2001	56	35	9

Source: Gallup poll, "Based on what you have read or heard, do you favor or oppose the federal income tax cuts George W. Bush has proposed?"

not travel to California until May 29 and visited New York even later. Instead, the White House gave priority to states that Bush had won and that were represented by Democratic senators, including Georgia, Louisiana, Arkansas, Missouri, North and South Dakota, Montana, and North Carolina.

Whatever the president's motivations, he obtained the support of only one Senate Democrat (Zell Miller of Georgia, who announced his support of the tax cut before Bush was inaugurated) on the April 4 bellwether vote for his full tax cut.

The president faced similar frustrations in increasing his public support with his two nationally televised addresses. His approval went up only one percentage point in the Gallup poll following his address to a joint session of Congress on February 27, 2001, and only two percentage points following his address on August 9, 2001, regarding his decision on federal funding of stem cell research.

There are many potential explanations for failing to move the public, but part of the reason for the modest response to Bush's addresses may be that he drew equally modest audiences. For example, only 39.8 million viewers saw at least part of his address on February 27 compared to 67 million viewers for Bill Clinton's first nationally televised address in 1993. Moreover, there was a substantial fall-off in viewership during the president's speech.[1]

Bush compensated for the increased difficulty of obtaining time on television for presidential speeches and of gaining an audience when television provides coverage, by his extensive traveling around the country. The question is whether the increase in local appearances led to an increase in news coverage for the president and his policies. Early indications are that it did not. Figure 22 shows that a study of the news coverage of the first sixty days of the Clinton and George W. Bush presidencies found that there was

Figure 23. Media Coverage of the President in the First Sixty Days

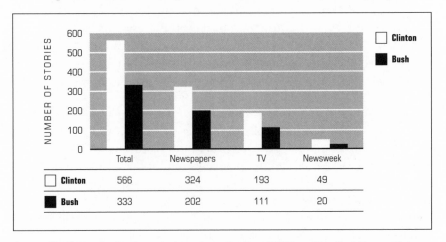

	Total	Newspapers	TV	Newsweek
☐ Clinton	566	324	193	49
■ Bush	333	202	111	20

Source: The Project for Excellence in Journalism, *The First 100 Days: How Bush Versus Clinton Fared in the Press.*

a dramatic across-the-board drop-off in coverage on television, newspapers, and news weeklies. Network television coverage was down 42 percent and newspaper coverage (*The New York Times* and *Washington Post*) was off 38 percent. *Newsweek* magazine had 59 percent fewer stories about Bush in its pages than it carried about Clinton eight years earlier. Although the president was still a dominant figure on op-ed and editorial pages, he was less visible in the front pages, newscasts, and financial pages.[2] This lower profile was unlikely to be an asset in advancing the president's agenda.

Setting Priorities

New presidents are wise to resist the temptations to try to deliver on all their campaign promises immediately following their elections and to accede to the many demands that are made on a new administration. Instead, it is important to establish priorities among legislative proposals. In addition, because the Washington community pays disproportionate attention to the first major legislative initiatives, it is especially critical to choose early battles wisely.

If the president is not able to focus Congress's attention on his priority programs, they may become lost in the complex and overloaded legislative process. Congress needs time to digest what the president sends, to engage in independent analyses, and to schedule hearings and markups. Unless the president clarifies his priorities, Congress may put the proposals in a queue.

Setting priorities is also important because presidents and their staff can lobby effectively for only a few bills at a time. The president's political capital is inevitably limited, and it is sensible to focus on the issues he cares about most. Setting priorities early also can reduce intra-administration warfare over the essence of the administration.

President Carter was widely criticized for failing to set legislative priorities, especially in light of the scale, diversity, complexity, and controversial nature of his initial legislative program. Conversely, the Reagan administration knew it lacked the political capital to pass a broad program that would include divisive social issues. Thus, it enforced a rigorous focus on the president's economic plan, its priority legislation. By focusing its resources on its priorities, the administration succeeded in using the budget to pass sweeping changes in taxation and defense policy.

Karl Rove, the president's wide-ranging senior adviser, maintained that Bush campaigned on six key issues: tax cuts, education standards, military upgrades and a missile defense shield, federal support for faith-based charities, partial privatization of Social Security, and Medicare reforms and prescription-drug coverage for seniors.[3] If these were Bush's priorities, he did a good job of focusing on them.

First, the Bush White House made a clear choice of a large income-tax cut as its highest legislative priority. This made good sense for a conservative administration. The president and his advisors felt that the notable victory of enacting a major tax cut early in the administration would signal the administration's competence in governing while unifying the Republican party for the more difficult issues ahead. Equally important, by severely limiting the government's resources, cutting taxes would set the terms of debate for nearly all the policy debates that would follow and restrain the Democrats' ability to use the budget surplus for expansion of social-welfare policies.

It remains an open question whether the tax cut has also undermined the administration's ability to fund its own initiatives, such as a defensive missile shield, or to respond to demands for popular programs, such as a prescription-drug program under Medicare. Similarly, it is unclear whether engaging in a highly partisan fight over taxes early in the administration while seeking bipartisan support on other issues had counterproductive consequences for future coalition building.

Tax cuts were not the administration's only priorities, of course. Education reform, an overhaul of defense policy, and greater federal support for faith-based social welfare programs were also high on the list. The president not only spoke extensively about each initiative but also went to considerable lengths to focus attention on each proposal in the early weeks of the administration. The faith-based initiative received attention in the week after the inauguration, followed in successive weeks by education, tax cuts, and defense.

Not surprisingly, a study of the first sixty days of news coverage of the Bush and Clinton administrations found that Bush was more successful than Clinton in controlling his message. Each of the five major stories about Bush was on his priority initiatives, amounting to more than a third of all stories.[4]

Setting priorities in the early weeks of a new administration is also important because, during the first months in office, the president has the greatest latitude in focusing on priority legislation. After the transition period, other interests have more influence on the White House agenda. Congress is quite capable of setting its own agenda and is unlikely to defer to the president for long. In addition, ongoing policies continually force decisions to the president's desk.

The Bush presidency is no exception to the challenge of controlling the national agenda. At the same time that the president was seeking support for his priority items, he had to engage in legislative battles on important issues such as campaign finance reform and a patients' bill of rights and make a highly visible decision on stem cell research. In fact, he had to devote one of only two nationally televised addresses (scarce presidential resources) of his first seven months in office to the latter. Bush also inevitably became embroiled in the issue of navy practice bombings in Vieques, Puerto Rico.

More damaging were his responses to the unexpected energy shortage in California and potential environmental regulations, many of which were proposed by his predecessor. His and Vice President Cheney's energy plan was widely viewed as a sop to the oil and gas industry the two served, and many people saw the administration as having a weak commitment to environmental protection.

Responding to the terrorist attacks of September 11 immediately dominated the president's agenda. The emphasis on national unity in the weeks that followed the tragedy and the inevitable focus of the president's energies on national security limited the opportunities for him to push hard for his most contentious proposals.

Moving Rapidly

Presidents must do more than recognize the opportunities in their environment, devise a strategy for governing, and set priorities. To succeed with Congress, they must also move rapidly to exploit those opportunities. First-year proposals have a better chance of passing Congress than do those sent to the Hill later in an administration. Thus, the White House should be ready to send its priority legislation to Capitol Hill.

The failure to be ready to propose priority legislation may be costly. A policy vacuum existed in the approximately ten months between Bill Clinton's inauguration and the arrival of a complete healthcare reform proposal on the Hill. In this vacuum, issues of relatively low priority, such as the gays in the military, received disproportionate attention in the press and may have cost the administration vital goodwill that it would need in its search for support for its cornerstone policy. In addition, the president was forced to raise healthcare reform in the context of major expenditures of political capital in battles on behalf of his budget and the North American Free Trade Area Treaty (NAFTA).

Despite a severely truncated transition, George W. Bush lost no time in sending priority bills to Congress. Proposals for a large cut in income taxes, education reform, and increased support for faith-based charities went to the Hill in short order. Specific changes in defense policy would take longer, requiring an extensive review of the massive U.S. national security programs.

The administration was not ready with proposals for all its priority issues, however. Two very important items on the "big six" list were deferred for another year. Social Security reform was delegated to a commission. Medicare and prescription drugs were postponed. Given the disappearance of the general-revenue budget surplus, the lack of consensus on these issues, and the president's limited political capital, the delays appear to be sensible strategic choices rather than evidence of disorganization or lethargy.

Conclusion

The George W. Bush administration commenced under difficult circumstances. There was never a possibility it could move a large, contentious agenda through a closely divided Congress. Within this context, the White House made a number of smart strategic choices to increase the probability of advancing its proposals. First, it made an accurate evaluation of its strategic position. It was neither intimidated by the closeness of the election or its polarizing resolution nor was it prone to overreaching. For example, when Bush saw that school vouchers were not going to pass, he expended little political capital on their behalf. The administration set priorities and focused on them. The president moved quickly on his highest-priority legislation, getting most of what he wanted in the $1.35 trillion tax cut—the largest since 1981.

All was not smooth sailing, however. Most policies had less saliency and thus brought less unity to Republicans than tax cuts. Although the president effectively exploited the opportunities in his environment, he was unable to increase his political capital. Going public did not move the public, and Sen. James Jeffords of Vermont left the Republican party, shifting the majority in the Senate to the Democrats (and eclipsing the president's success on the tax cut). Bush inevitably had to become involved in lower-priority policies and had to make substantial compromises on core items on his agenda dealing with education and the faith-based charities. The administration seemed headed for similar compromises on defense spending until the terrorist attacks of September 11 dramatically increased its salience.

Notes

1.   *Washington Post,* March 1, 2001, p. C1.

2.   The Project for Excellence in Journalism, *The First 100 Days: How Bush Versus Clinton Fared in the Press* (2001).

3.   Alexis Simendinger, "The Report Card They Asked For," *National Journal,* July 21, 2001, p. 2335.

4.   Project for Excellence in Journalism, *First 100 Days.*

Relations with Congress

NORMAN ORNSTEIN
JOHN FORTIER

EVEN BEFORE THE THIRTY-SIX-DAY FANDANGO FOL-
lowing the election, George W. Bush and his team were focused
both on the presidential transition and the initial days of the presidency. Bush and chief political adviser Karl Rove had read history,
examining how previous modern presidents had handled their initial
phase in transition and in office, and early on Rove cautioned reporters
and analysts to watch, not the first 100 days, but the first 180 days for an
early measure of the president's capacity and success.

Bush and Rove recognized that one of the major challenges of any new
administration is its relationship with Congress—and that the relationship
can make or break a new president's reputation and ability to get things
done. Given the election controversy and the close margins in both cham-
bers, Bush's challenge was extraordinary. Overall, Bush gets high marks
for picking exactly two legislative priorities—tax cuts and education reform—and staying focused on moving them through Congress. But for
reasons partly beyond his control—but only partly—the legislative successes he achieved did not fully redound to his credit. The defection of Sen.
James Jeffords and the loss of Republican control of the Senate four
months into the new administration deprived Bush of momentum and
leverage, leaving him temporarily grasping for new ways to advance his
goals.

Bush's early success surprised his critics not only because it happened but also by the ways he achieved it. Bush maintained perfect discipline in the ranks of his own party in the House on his top priority, the tax cut, giving him the leverage he needed to get the bulk of his plan through the Senate. At the same time, he was less successful in courting Democratic support than he had been in Texas. With early enactment of a sweeping multiyear tax cut, passage by both houses of versions of the president's education plan, and an ability to counter potentially embarrassing Democratic initiatives like patients' rights, campaign finance reform, and minimum wage, Bush's initial record with Congress was reasonably solid. And even this moderate success looks good compared to many of his recent predecessors, who stumbled badly in this area.

Of course, extrapolating from the first 100 or first 180 days to the future success or failure of the Bush presidency became a shaky exercise after the events of September 11, 2001. The political world turned upside down in ways that dramatically strengthen Bush's hand with Congress—and have already seemed to change his relationship with Congress's Democratic leaders. Not only did the crisis create bipartisan backing of the president, but it also gave Bush a focus that is often lacking for presidents after their initial honeymoon. However, his father's experience with the Gulf War and its aftermath underscore for Bush and scholars alike that high levels of support can be fleeting.

Agenda Setting

In setting a manageable legislative agenda and sticking to it, Bush was more successful than most recent presidents other than Ronald Reagan. Bush had two clear priorities: tax cuts and education. These were his top priorities in the campaign, throughout the transition period, and during his first six months in office. While energy policy, campaign finance, a patients' bill of rights, and faith-based initiatives were taken up, Bush did not dilute his message by focusing his time and energy on these other initiatives.

Bush had shown discipline in sticking to a manageable agenda before. In his first gubernatorial term, Bush maintained a laser-beam focus on four agenda items. When asked by a reporter to list a fifth item, he famously replied: "Sure. Pass the first four things."[1] President Bush's two-priority strategy avoided a problem that plagued the Carter administration, too many proposals competing with one another for public attention, congressional support, and space on the agenda (with most up for considera-

GEORGE W. BUSH MAKES HIS TRANSITION

tion before the same committees). Bush's administration could work both initiatives because the players were different in each policy area and because their momentum would not be diluted by other issues.

In addition, Bush exhibited good political judgment in choosing two complementary issues. The tax cut was a partisan issue that excited his base. It required a fight, and while it generated some negative publicity, the conflict raised the profile of the president, and the subsequent victory enhanced his reputation as a winner. The education reform package, however, was bipartisan, cutting across ideological lines and having a good chance of passage with 80 percent support in both houses. It reinforced Bush's image as a compassionate conservative and appealed to moderate voters. If all had gone according to plan, Bush could have had the double boost coming from passage of a large tax cut very similar to his original proposal over intense Democratic opposition, followed by a Rose Garden signing ceremony of an education reform bill, with the president flanked by Tom DeLay and Ted Kennedy.

Bush was more or less on target to achieve these twin goals, but the historic Jeffords defection changed everything. A midstream change of party control of the Senate had not been completely unexpected, although most observers had morbidly anticipated that the change would result from the death of one of the older senators, not from a single senator renouncing his lifelong affiliation with the Republican party. Both the manner of Jeffords switch and its timing on the eve of passage of the tax cut were particularly unhelpful to the Bush agenda. Instead of chronicling Bush's first major legislative victory on the tax cut, media accounts underscored the tension between the conservative and moderate wings of the party.

The longer-term consequences of the Jeffords switch also affected the Bush agenda. The membership of the Senate did not change, but majority status means control over the timing and substance of the policy agenda, and Democrats quickly took advantage of that power, scheduling votes on issues like patients' rights that the White House wanted to delay. But it was also true that, once Democrats gained control over a branch of government in Washington, they took on a new responsibility for governing, giving Bush some opportunity to cajole them into bipartisan agreements or face the prospect of being blamed successfully for gridlock.

There were several issues on the congressional agenda aside from the two major priorities. Bush addressed energy policy and faith-based initiatives but ultimately did not expend the political capital that he did on education and taxes. Energy policy vaulted upward on the priority list after the electricity crisis in California. But many of the Bush measures were seen as anti-environment, which spawned a backlash, and the energy crisis cooled as quickly as it had heated up. Bush also brought faith-based initiatives onto the national stage. His idea of involving religious charities in providing government services had bipartisan support, but questions of implementation and constitutionality hampered the passage of legislation. It was reported that the administration was considering making faith-based initiatives the next big legislative item after the tax cuts and education, but because of the difficulty of maintaining a coalition and the resignation of Director John DiIulio, the White House began to look at smaller, discrete initiatives that could be done administratively rather than a large legislative package.

Finally, there were two issues—campaign finance reform and patients' rights—that Bush would have preferred not to be on the legislative agenda in his first six months in office. Both were pushed by his campaign rival, Sen. John McCain, and both had more support from Democrats than Republicans. Bush did not control the legislative agenda on these items, but he managed skillfully to avoid ending up on the losing side of the issues. On campaign finance, Bush announced early on that he would sign a bill but would not actively participate in the congressional deliberations. This had two consequences. First, Republicans opposed to campaign finance would have to kill the bill in the House or Senate, or they would have to pass a bill they could live with. Second, the no-veto promise meant that Bush was largely absent from the debate. Negative publicity focused on the opponents of campaign finance reform in Congress, not on him. His rival McCain did steal the spotlight, but Bush avoided directly opposing him. On patients' rights, Bush had hoped to delay action until after the first six months and ultimately pass a more business-friendly version of the measure. His hand was forced when the Senate switched to Democratic control. Again, McCain was his nemesis as he allied with Democrats. In this case Bush did issue a veto ultimatum: he would oppose a bill without sufficient limits on employer liability. For a time in the summer, it looked as if Bush would be forced to take the unpopular step of vetoing a patients' bill of rights passed by both houses. But at the last moment, he persuaded the key House Republican patients' advocate, Charlie Norwood, to agree to a compromise, and he was able to stake out the position that he supported a version of patients' rights.

Despite the Jeffords switch and the subsequent shift in control of the congressional agenda, Bush's legislative agenda was more focused than those of most recent presidents. Carter had too many priorities, most of which involved action by the Finance and Ways and Means Committees. The disjointed agenda was confusing for the American people and nearly impossible to pass through Congress. Most presidential observers view Reagan's transition into office as a model. His agenda was controversial but clear. His large tax cut was passed after a strenuous fight. He propelled his agenda forward after his recovery from the assassination attempt on March 30, 1981. The clarity of Reagan's aims and his victory over opposition increased his stature as president and prepared the way for future initiatives. George H. W. Bush suffered from a lack of an initial agenda. He proposed smallish initiatives on child care, ethics reform, and Latin America, and he was viewed on the Hill as reacting to events rather than driving an agenda. In fact, his son was reportedly very sensitive to that experience and made a conscious effort in Texas and in Washington not to repeat his father's mistakes. Clinton's start, like Carter's, suffered from too many priorities. He passed the family-leave bill early on and managed to pass his budget by a narrow margin, but his economic-stimulus bill was defeated, and he became mired in issues such as gays in the military and several controversial nominations. His introduction of an education plan and his pledges for sweeping reform of welfare and healthcare also crowded the early agenda.

Overall, Bush's legislative focus on tax cuts and education helped his presidency. Some have argued that Bush should not have been aggressive on his conservative priorities but should have reflected the divided electorate's wishes and steered a more moderate course. But the likely outcome of such a strategy would have been to weaken Bush in the eyes of his adversaries while alienating his base. Bush's agenda had two prongs, the tax cut for the right and education for the center, so there was already some balancing of the agenda. It is debatable whether Bush's agenda strayed too far to the right, but a legislative agenda that completely ignored his conservative base would have put the president in the backseat, with either Democrats or conservative critics driving the car.

Relations with Republicans and Democrats in Congress

Upon assuming office, Bush faced an unusual congressional landscape. On the one hand, for the first time in over forty years, a Republican president served with his own party in control of both houses of Congress. On the other hand, the margins were razor thin in both houses, and Bush had no coattails. In fact, his party had lost seats in both houses, including four seats in the Senate. The evenly divided Senate that ensued was governed by an unprecedented party-sharing agreement that gave Democrats parity with Republicans on committees.

Conventional wisdom held that Bush might be reasonably successful in reaching out to Democrats but would likely have problems holding together Republicans. Neither assumption proved entirely accurate. Bush had been remarkably able in practicing bipartisan politics in Texas. His relationship with the late Democratic lieutenant governor Bob Bullock is well known, but Bush also had warm working relationships with a large number of Texas Democrats in the legislature, and they were essential to his success. At the start of Bush's first term as governor, Democrats controlled both houses of the state legislature. Republicans eventually won the state senate, but that body required a two-thirds vote for action. So Bush could not have accomplished anything without Democratic support. However, his success with Texas Democrats did not necessarily imply comparable success in Washington; it was no secret that Texas Democrats are much more conservative than their congressional counterparts.

Before Bush took office, he made serious overtures toward Congress. He had promised during the campaign that he would not engage in the partisan bickering that had characterized Washington in the years before his arrival. This message served Bush well politically, for he could tap into sentiment for change and stand above politics. But the promise was not merely rhetorical; Bush did make an effort to reach out and meet with Congress in a more substantial way than his predecessors. He met with Republican and Democratic members for business and for social visits (for example, screening the movie *Thirteen Days* with the Kennedys), even giving many of them nicknames. The White House went so far as to count the number of members he had met with,[2] noting at various times that Bush "has met with more members of Congress than any President in modern history."[3] While Democrats expressed some receptivity to these overtures, many were unhappy, believing that the president was unyielding on his tax cut, consulted mostly with Republicans, and paid lip service to bipartisanship without dealing with Democrats on substantive matters. Early on, the precedent was set that Bush would get the House to pass his version of a bill, usually by a narrow partisan margin, and then he would strike a deal with the Senate. This left House Democrats out of the loop. Even Blue Dog Texas Democrat Charlie Stenholm, who had backed the Reagan tax cuts, voted against Bush on key early tax-cut votes.[4]

As for his relationship with congressional leaders, Bush did not start with particularly close ties with the two from Texas, House Majority Leader Dick Armey and Majority Whip Tom DeLay, who had reserved and somewhat tense relations with the president. But the strong collective desire of congressional Republicans, after eight unhappy years of dealing with Bill Clinton, to make their president a success motivated all GOP leaders to work hard for him and his priorities. Bush made only token efforts to develop close personal ties to Democratic leaders Dick Gephardt and Tom Daschle, and the tension levels between the Democrats and Bush were quite high early on. The September 11 attacks changed those dynamics, as witnessed by the warm hugs the president exchanged with both Democratic leaders following his address to Congress and the nation on September 20.

One novel strategy that Bush employed deserves note. He visited states where he had received strong electoral support but whose senators were wavering in their support. He appealed directly to local media, hoping to exert pressure on their home-state senators and prevail upon them to support his tax package. None of these individual techniques were new, but the sum of the techniques was. Presidential candidates often seek out local media, whom they view as more positive in their coverage. Presidents often leave Washington to spread a message and demonstrate popular strength. But no new president traveled to so many states so early, and no new president used this explicit strategy of appealing over the heads of particular senators in order to affect their votes in Washington.[5] It is not clear, however, that this technique worked. Some members were annoyed by the visits, and while Bush did pick up Democrats on each of the key votes on his tax-cut package, the trips to the states were probably not the decisive factor.

September 11 and Beyond

The return of Congress after the August recess usually marks the end of the transition period for presidents. The honeymoon is over, and the public no longer views the new occupant of the White House as a president-in-training. It is often hard for even a successful president to figure out what to do and how to get another wave of initiatives through Congress. For George W. Bush, the end of his transition was more starkly noted—September 11.

If the terrorist attacks had not occurred, the fall agenda would have been troublesome for Bush. It was likely that he could have forged an agreement on education reform, but even this became more difficult after the Jeffords switch and the passage of time. Most of the rest of the agenda, however, would have been unappealing to him. Campaign finance reform promised to resurface in the House. A patients' bill-of-rights fight loomed. And the main debate would likely have been over the budget and whether Bush's tax cuts were dipping into the Social Security trust fund.

September 11 changed everything. Bush stated that the war on terrorism would be the focus of his administration. The nation united, and bipartisanship became the watchword in the Congress. Most partisan initiatives were dropped and differences muted as Congress focused on providing relief to victims, affected industries, the military, and the reform of security and transportation procedures. Bush's approval ratings reached 90 percent.

The near universal support for the president will undoubtedly fade. One should not forget that Bush's father once commanded such heights— and then was soundly defeated for re-election. In addition, the nature of the war on terrorism is that it is more open ended than conventional warfare, which may undermine Bush's standing. Nonetheless, the magnitude of the events on September 11 will likely mark the beginning of a vastly different presidency and relationship with Congress.

Notes

1.   Sam Howe Verhovek, "Texas Governor Succeeds, without the Flash," *The New York Times,* June 7, 1995, p. A1.

2.   Anne Kornblut, "Bush Outreach Runs on Persistence, Charm: He Emphasizes Working Together," *Boston Globe,* Feb. 3, 2001, p. A8.

3.   Helen Kennedy, "GOP Defector Blasts Party on Power-grab Spin," *New York Daily News,* May 26, 2001, p. 6.

4.   Christopher Lee, "Why Bush Didn't Collar Blue Dogs from the Get-go Conservative Democrats, Texans Seen as Key to his Bipartisan Efforts," *Dallas Morning News,* May 27, 2001, p. 10A.

5.   On March 28, reported *The New York Times,* Bush "had traveled to 25 states and spent nearly 30 days away from the White House."

Recruiting and Organizing the White House Staff

MARTHA JOYNT KUMAR

URING HIS FIRST WEEKS AND IN LATER MONTHS, Pres. George W. Bush has received high marks from Democrats as well as Republicans for the seasoned team he assembled to guide his administration. "If you add their years in Washington," commented Democratic senator Byron Dorgan, "you get a century's worth of experience."[1] Ten months later, Democrats continued to credit Bush for the wisdom of his cabinet choices and for his ability to make effective use of all of his administrative resources, including his White House staff. Richard Berke of *The New York Times* interviewed political figures who had supported Al Gore for president and reported that "not one of more than fifteen prominent Gore loyalists interviewed said their candidate would have done a better job."[2]

Even though all presidents can benefit from a successful start to their administrations, few accomplish it. How did George W. Bush achieve what is broadly viewed as an exceptionally smooth start? Given the circumstances of the election and its subsequent truncated transition, few observers would have predicted such a beginning. This final chapter examines some elements of an answer to that question. Five critical decisions were made during the transition and in the early days of the administration. These stood the administration in good stead as they started out.

Months later during the crisis of September 11, these choices shaped their responses. The transition team's crucial decisions relating to the White House were: start early assembling a staff; focus on the White House as the integrating institution on policy, politics, and publicity; recruit a balanced staff representing five types of knowledge; establish White House control over five key departmental positions; and maintain the fundamental organizational structure of White House offices.

Start Early Assembling a White House Staff

Beginning with our essay "Meeting the Freight Train Head On" and including those of John Burke and Clay Johnson, the authors of our transition and White House essays have argued here that experience demonstrates that an administration benefits from the early organization of a White House staff. The Bush presidency demonstrates the benefits such a start yields in terms of getting personnel in place and an agenda assembled.

Despite the delayed transition, Governor Bush began soon after the November 7 election, but before his certification on December 14, to assemble his top White House team. Beginning with the public announcement of Andrew Card Jr. to be his chief of staff on November 26, the organizational structure of the White House and the identification of the members of the team were in place by early December, according to Clay Johnson, executive director of the Bush-Cheney transition.[3] In addition to getting their operation on its way, the president-elect and his staff sent a message of contrast with the Clinton administration, which delayed the announcement of Thomas "Mack" McLarty as chief of staff until December 15, 1992, and the remainder of the White House senior staff until January 15, 1993. As the public announcement dates of White House staff (found in figure 24) demonstrate, many of the directors of key White House offices were named before the end of the year, with others designated in the first days of the new year. With several weeks between their selection and the start of the administration, staff members learned about their jobs by reading materials provided to them by the transition team and talked to their predecessors.

Focus on the White House as the Institution Integrating Policy, Politics, and Publicity

Governor Bush decided early in his transition planning that his White House operation would serve as an organizational core for his presidency. While the president-elect made clear during the transition that he planned to provide his cabinet members with leeway in managing their departments, signature policy issues for Bush would come from the White House, especially in domestic policy. The first four weeks of the administration focused on White House–driven policy issues. Among them were several domestic issues: education, faith-based initiatives, a tax cut, and patients' rights. The exposition of policies—for instance, educational testing—focused on White House leadership on the issue. During the ensuing months, policy continued to be worked out of the White House, including negotiations with the House and Senate. For example, Sandy Kress, a White House aide to Domestic Policy Council Chair Margaret La Montagne Spellings, and not people from the Department of Education, conducted negotiations on the Hill.[4] When the White House decided not to fight for school vouchers, it was Chief of Staff Andrew Card, not the education secretary, who sent the signal.[5]

Balance the White House with Five Types of Knowledge

Setting up the White House was the task of Andrew Card Jr., the person who would become chief of staff. What Card accomplished was a staff that blended the types of knowledge needed in a successful White House: knowledge of the president, the campaign, the substance of policy, past White House operations, and the Washington community.[6]

Knowledge of the President

Knowing the president's rhythms is important to understanding what information he wants to get, in what form, and when he wants to receive it. Senior aides need to have that sense; thus, people who were involved in the president's political life prior to coming into the presidency need to be included. Three people exercised that role in the early months of the Bush administration: Karl Rove, Karen Hughes, and Clay Johnson. An example of how this knowledge pays off occurred early in the transition. Card spoke to Clay Johnson about the president-elect's ideas about senior staff.

Figure 24. White House Senior Staff, 2001
Five Types of Background Knowledge

Office/Individual/Appointment Date	Policy	White House	Campaign	President	Washington • Departments & agencies • Congress • Lobbying/legal community • Party politics • News media • Think tank
Chief of Staff					
Andrew Card Jr. 11/26/2000		•	•	•	Transportation Department
Joseph Hagin II 12/28/2000		•	•	•	National party politics
Joshua Bolten 12/28/2000	•	•	•	•	USTR counsel; Congress Senate Finance Committee
Oval Office Operations					
Linda Gambatesa	•				
Senior Advisor to the President: Strategic Initiatives					
Karl Rove 01/04/2001			•	•	National party politics
Counselor to the President, Strategic Planning, Communications, & Speechwriting					
Karen P. Hughes 12/17/2000			•	•	
Communications					
Dan Bartlett 01/09/2001			•	•	
Media Affairs					
Tucker Eskew 01/09/2001			•	•	
Speechwriting					Congress—Sen. Dan Coates
Michael Gerson			•	•	National party politics
Press Office					
Ari Fleischer 12/28/2000			•		Congress—House Ways and Means, Rep. Norman Lent and Sen. Pete Domenici; news media—press secretary to Rep. Bill Archer
Deputy					
Scott McClellan 01/08/2001			•	•	
Claire Buchan					Treasury Department; USTR

Figure 24. continued

Office/ Individual/ Appointment Date	Policy	White House	Campaign	President	Washington • Departments & agencies • Congress • Lobbying/legal community • Party politics • News media • Think tank
Cabinet Affairs					
Albert Hawkins 01/05/2001	●		●	●	
Counsel to the President					
Alberto R. Gonzales 12/17/2000	●			●	
Timothy Flanigan	●				Justice Department
Intergovernmental Affairs					
Reuben Barrales		●		●	
Legislative Affairs					
Nicholas Calio 01/04/2001		●			Lobbying; legal community
Deputy Director					
Jack Howard		●			Congress—Sen. Trent Lott, Rep. Newt Gingrich, Rep. Dennis Hastert
Management & Administration					
Hector Irastorza Jr. 01/08/2001		●			National party politics
Political Affairs					
Kenneth Mehlman 01/09/2001			●		Legal community; Congress— Rep. Kay Granger
Presidential Personnel: Director, & Deputy to Chief of Staff					
Clay Johnson III 12/29/2000				●	
Ronald Bellamy				●	
Public Liaison					
Lezlee Westine			●		
Scheduling					
Bradley Blakeman 01/08/2001		●	●		
Advance					
Brian Montgomery 01/08/2001		●	●		

Figure 24. continued

Office/ Individual/ Appointment Date	Policy	White House	Campaign	President	Washington • Departments & agencies • Congress • Lobbying/legal community • Party politics • News media • Think tank
Staff Secretary					
Harriet Miers				•	
01/05/2001					
Domestic Policy **Council**					
Margaret La Montagne	•		•	•	
01/05/2001					
Deputy Director					
John Bridgeland	•	•			Congress—Rep. Rob
01/09/2001					Portman
Anne Phelps	•				Congress—Senate Health, Education, Labor, Pensions Committee; National Institutes of Health
National Economic **Council**					
Lawrence Lindsey	•	•	•	•	Think tank—American
01/03/2001					Enterprise Institute
National Security **Council: Assistant** **to the President**					
Condoleezza Rice	•	•	•	•	
12/17/2000					
Deputy Assistant					
Stephen Hadley	•				
12/21/2000					
Office of Faith-Based **and Community** **Initiatives**					
John Dilulio Jr.	•				Think tank—
01/29/2001					Brookings Institution
Office of the Vice **President: Chief of Staff** **and Assistant** **for National Security** **Affairs**					
Lewis Libby					State, Defense Departments;
12/28/2000					Congress-Cox Committee; legal community

Figure 24. continued

Office/ Individual/ Appointment Date	Policy	White House	Campaign	President	Washington • Departments & agencies • Congress • Lobbying/legal community • Party politics • News media • Think tank
Counsel to the Vice President					
David Addington 12/28/2000					Congress—House and Senate Committees on Intelligence; Defense Department; legal community
Assistant to the President and Counselor to the Vice President					
Mary Matalin 01/05/2001					National Party Polititics News media—CNN
Mrs. Bush's Office					
Chief of Staff to the First Lady					
Andrea Ball		•		•	

Note: The categories of information follow: *Policy*—people with a substantive policy specialty brought in to work primarily on policy; *White House*—those who have worked in the White House in a prior administration; *Campaign*— people who worked on the 2000 Bush presidential campaign for a substantial period; *President*—those who worked for the president or who knew him well prior to coming into the White House; *Washington*—people with experience working in the Washington community and with knowledge of Congress, departments and agencies, or national Republican party politics; Washington law firms; think tanks; or knowledge of the routines of news organizations.

Dates are included for those people whose appointments were publicly announced. The information in this chart was assembled from several sources, including interviews with reporters who covered the campaign and the White House as well as people who work in the White House. Valuable sources of information include issues of *National Journal's White House Phone Book,* published occasionally from 1981 to 1985, and *The Capital Source,* from 1985 to 1992 for the names of those working in the Reagan and Bush White Houses, and *National Journal's The Decision Makers,* June 23, 2001, no. 25. Also *Bureau of National Affairs' White House Phone Directory* for the current White House. Issues of the *Washington Post* and *The New York Times* contain dates for the announcements of appointments.

"Andy's first reaction," Johnson recalled, "was, 'the president wants to have multiple deputy chiefs of staff.' He said, 'it's really not a very good idea.' My thinking was, 'Then go back to him. He's not one that gets locked in.'" In the end, Card followed the pattern of his predecessor and had two deputies rather than multiple ones. As someone who had known Bush a long time, Johnson spent time among the staff "encouraging people to 'push back.' He's [Bush] interested in good ideas," Johnson observed, "and to give people confidence to have a dialogue with him, to have that exchange of ideas and difference of opinion."[7]

Campaign Memory and Policy Experience

Getting a staff balanced between those with campaign versus those with governing experience is always difficult to achieve for a new administration, especially at the highest level. Like most administrations, the Bush White House has a large number of people who spent time in the campaign. A *National Journal* survey of White House and administration personnel found that over 80 percent of the top staff, or "decision makers," they studied "were either paid or volunteer workers during his presidential bid."[8] No matter how long people worked in the campaign or whether they worked full time, campaign experience of any kind is important, for those who were there know the issues central to the president. In leading the White House staff, for example, a chief of staff is strengthened by campaign service. "I do think, if you can, it is important to have some campaign experience with the president you're going to serve, because your political bona fides are not subject to challenge there," remarked James Baker, who served as chief of staff in the Reagan White House and spent time on the Reagan 1980 campaign. "It gives you far more cachet in policy debates and interdepartmental policy."[9]

While an administration can have the departments and agencies play a crucial role in developing items on the president's policy agenda, the chief executive needs to have among his White House staff those who know the substance of the issues, the president's previously stated commitments, and the realities of getting particular items through the process. Those in the White House involved at the beginning of the administration in recommending specific policy choices most often are people who worked on the campaign and were responsible for shaping the president's proposals before coming into the White House. He needs close to him those who have a sense of how to knit together proposals reflecting his needs and the political realities of their policymaking environment.

White House and Washington Experience

Having Richard Cheney, a man so well known and respected around town, as the incoming vice president and selecting him as the titular head of the transition established the right note within Washington and especially with Congress, where he had been a member of the Republican leadership.

Andrew Card's White House staff structure reflected a careful balance, with a substantial number of people who know the rhythms of the Washington community as well as the organizational patterns of the White House. Having served under or worked with seven previous chiefs of staff in the administrations of Presidents Ronald Reagan and George H. W. Bush, Card had learned the value of Washington experience and knew several people with White House and Washington expertise. Two units requiring leadership from among those who know White House operations are the Office of Legislative Affairs and the Office of Management and Administration. Card brought in Nicholas Calio and Jack Howard to serve as the director and deputy of legislative affairs, where they had served in the administration of the first President Bush. Hector Irastorza, director of management and administration, also served in that office during the earlier Bush administration.

Establish White House Control over Five Key Departmental Positions

In most transitions, early efforts at filling the administration involve somewhere around one hundred positions the staff will focus on as crucial to governing. In the Reagan transition, Pendleton James, who handled personnel issues, indicated they focused on eighty-seven positions related to the economy since economic issues were crucial as they came into office.[10] The current Bush White House focused on around seventy-five positions that together would help the administration speak with one voice and interact in a coordinated manner with other departments and agencies. "First of all, I made sure our communications team is not just a team in the White House," said Andrew Card. "It is a communications team for the executive branch of government. Our legal team is a legal team for the government."[11]

In each department, the White House coordinated the selection of five positions: secretary, deputy secretary, general counsel, legislative liaison, and press spokesperson. By controlling those positions, they could manage how the department presented itself and its policies to the outside world and enhance the possibility that department officials would focus primarily on the president's agenda, not that of their respective cabinet secretary should a conflict arise. This responsibility was distributed among three senior White House staff members: Counselor Karen Hughes for public-affairs people, Nick Calio for the legislative liaisons, and Alberto Gonzales for departmental and agency counsels.[12] In addition, their White House counterparts regularly speak with those in the selected department positions. "There is a call every morning with the communications teams from all of the cabinet departments," said Card. "I know Josh [Bolten] keeps in touch with their policy wonk types and [White House Counsel] Al Gonzales with the lawyers and White House liaison people are very important too."[13]

The people they chose for these key spots were well known through their work in the campaigns of George W. Bush, their work in the earlier Bush and Reagan administrations, and the time they spent working in Congress for members of both houses. In the key departments of State, Treasury, Defense, and Justice, for example, two press officers, Mindy Tucker at Justice and Torie Clarke at defense, have a history of working for Bush campaigns.

Maintain Basic White House Units

A change in party control provides a reminder that the White House staff is malleable. The incoming administration has little political incentive to maintain the structure of the previous staff and can develop its operation according to its own political, policy, and organizational demands. Yet the switch from the Clinton to the Bush White House has brought little change in the basic organization of White House units. All of the units in the Bush White House (listed in figure 24) were found in the Clinton White House organization except for two: the additions of the Office of Strategic Initiatives and the Office of Faith-based and Community Initiatives.

What most administrations eventually discover is that no matter what their political ideology or party, there are certain tasks that have to be carried out, and the new people have little choice but to perform them. During the transition, Andrew Card suggested they would not have a White House Office of Intergovernmental Affairs. Card soon felt heat from officials around the country who wanted the office to remain, for it is an important channel for mayors, governors, and others wanting to communicate with the administration. A month and a half after Card's plans for intergovernmental affairs were carried in the *Washington Post*, the White House announced Reuben Barrales would head the unit.[14] Card found out what other White Houses have learned: there are tasks that have become integral to presenting the president and his policies to his various publics, and each office has developed its own constituents.

Where organizational flexibility lies is in the relationships those at the senior level have with one another, not in the tasks performed by the organization as a whole. Both Karl Rove and Karen Hughes have standard task-oriented offices within their jurisdictions even though their titles may be new. Rove heads the Office of Strategic Initiatives, which has within it the longstanding Offices of Political Affairs and Public Liaison. The units traditionally assigned the communications and press functions provide a good example of the manner in which the organization can be structured. Within Hughes's purview are all of the four offices regarded as having a communications function: Press Office, Office of Communications, Office of Media Affairs, and speechwriting. The number of people performing similar press and communications functions for Bush are remarkably similar to the numbers for the Clinton administration (as well as for Reagan).[15] There are forty-four people working in Hughes's office and in the four within her purview. In the Clinton White House in 1996, the number for the same functions was forty-two. The difference lay in the number assigned to the Press Office, which has eleven people in the Bush White House but had twenty-four under Clinton.

Karen Hughes assigned staff resources to those operations carrying out the communications functions related to persuasion and setting up events relaying the administration's message, while the Clinton White House focused somewhat more on day-to-day press operations. "The fact of the matter is that in the White House, no matter what the issue is on any given day, something will lead the nightly news, something will be on the front page of the nation's papers, something will be terribly important," observed Press Secretary Ari Fleischer. "Either the White House is structured to deal well with information of any consequence or it is not." The communications operations of both administrations stressed adaptability to changing circumstances. In the case of the Clinton administration, it was adjusting to a twenty-four-hour news day, with the addition of several cable news organizations operating live near the West Wing doors. The Bush White House went one step further when it created the Coalition Information Centers to provide responses to news coming out of the Middle East and South Asia after September 11, 2001. The centers are a "recognition for the first time realizing that, with the modern media, it is not enough to get your message out to your own country anymore," commented Fleischer.[16]

What is a new mix under Bush is a White House system with a chief of staff having so many different people at the most senior level deal with those in Congress and in outside institutions. In the Reagan administration there was talk of a division of authority at the top, with a troika comprising Chief of Staff James Baker, Communications Adviser Michael Deaver, and Counselor Edwin Meese. In reality it was not a confusing division of authority, for Baker represented the president to Congress and others outside the White House. In this administration, while Andrew Card serves as traffic cop, people on his staff and in other offices are negotiating on the Hill, including the vice president, who early on was actively representing the administration to Congress, and Karl Rove, who deals with a select group of conservatives. As unusual as it is for a Republican administration to have a loose structure at the top of its organizational hierarchy, administrations do start with campaign people in top positions who often disappear as the staff structure settles with one strong voice at the top, that of the chief of staff.

After the Transition

The Bush White House staff has proven capable of handling issues the president wanted emphasized in its early weeks as well as navigating the policy process with the departments and Congress once the terrorism crisis began. When hijacked airliners struck the World Trade Center and the Pentagon on September 11, 2001, President Bush's responses in the following days and weeks reflected the choices he had made earlier, in information and decision-making channels established well before he entered the White House. The organizational work undertaken during the transition and the people he brought into his administration shaped the structure he relied upon to respond to the attack. While transitions matter to the quality of the start of an administration and its ability to make effective use of early goodwill, they are even more significant for how the administration operates. The organizational work undertaken during the early months of 2000 paid off in well-ordered relationships between the president and his cabinet members and staff work well done during a time of crisis.

Those choices also guided the manner in which the administration reacted in other ways. For example, the White House retained its basic organizational structure, with time carved out of the president's basic work day for decision making on issues related to the campaign against terrorism. "Everything we had to do on September 10 still needed to be done while we addressed the issues that bubbled up on September 11," observed Card.

"We know [the president is] going to give two to three hours a day to the war effort and that two or three hours came out of a day that had already been scheduled prior to September 11, with him dealing with education, faith-based, budget, appropriations." In order to carve out that time for the president and within the White House decision-making structure, they grafted some new operations onto their standards: For example, they created external "Coalition Information Centers" and brought together the domestic and economic policy groups into one "Domestic Consequences" group. What did not change was the role of the chief of staff in managing time and personnel. "I try to manage the issues and the personnel to accommodate the time that is available for the president to make decisions," Card said.[17]

The administration's earlier investment in a White House focus played an important role in how they managed the unfolding crisis. Soon after September 11, the White House had the secretaries or the spokespeople of the Departments of State, Defense, and Justice regularly brief reporters and the public on the conduct of the defense, foreign policy, and security aspects of the campaign. Sometimes the secretaries briefed along with agency heads within their department, such as the FBI. The White House comfort level with most of the departmental appointees goes back to the manner in which they chose the secretaries and their deputies. When the anthrax attacks began, though, a different set of people came to the fore, most of whom the White House was not as comfortable with. Given that unfamiliarity, the senior staff chose to bring the issue into the White House briefing rooms, where Tom Ridge could speak for the administration accompanied by these health and security experts from the agencies. After an initially confused handling of the issue at the department and agency level, the White House soon took control. Instead of leadership from the departments controlling the issue, White House officials, chiefly Karen Hughes and Karl Rove, were involved in setting up communications strategies, including who should speak and what the message should be.

The White House staff has proven capable of handling issues George W. Bush wanted emphasized in the early weeks as well as navigating the policy process with the departments and Congress once the terrorism crisis began. The organizational work undertaken during the early months of 2000 paid off during 2001. What remains unclear is whether President Bush will be able to maintain his strong coalition of support if the war on terrorism proves protracted and the economy goes into a prolonged slump.

Notes

1.   Richard L. Berke, "Bush Transition Largely a Success All Sides Suggest," *The New York Times,* Jan. 28, 2001.

2.   Richard L. Berke, "Bush Winning Gore Backers' High Praise," *The New York Times,* Oct. 20, 2001. Bush's strong start resonated with the public as well and earned him their support. Even though he was the first president in 112 years to come into office with fewer popular votes than his chief opponent, when George W. Bush became president he established and maintained favorable ratings for his job performance, with well over 50 percent of the sample surveyed by the Gallup organization. In the twenty-one Gallup samples taken between February 1 and September 7–10, 2001, President Bush's favorable rating for his job performance ranged between a low of 51 percent and a high of 63 percent. For a comparable period, Pres. Bill Clinton's job performance ratings varied between a low of 37 percent and a high of 58 percent. Gallup polls for both Bush and Clinton can be found at <www.gallup.com>. The question asked was: "Do you approve or disapprove of the way George W. Bush [or Bill Clinton] is handling his job as president?"

3.   Clay Johnson III, interview with Martha Joynt Kumar, Washington, D.C., Sept. 8, 2001.

4.   Dana Milbank, "Bush Cabinet Takes Back Seat in Driving Policy," *Washington Post,* Sept. 5, 2001.

5.   Lizette Alvarez, "Bush's Education Plan Taps an Unlikely Source, Lieberman," *The New York Times,* Jan. 23, 2001.

6.   The latter includes: the routines and rhythms of Congress, the executive-branch departments and agencies, interest groups, the legal community, and the news media. See also chapter 5 for a more thorough description of each of the five types of knowledge.

7.   Johnson interview.

8.   *The Decision Makers,* special issue of *National Journal,* vol. 33, no. 25, June 23, 2001, p. 1868.

9.   James A. Baker III, interview with Martha Joynt Kumar and Terry Sullivan, Houston, Tex., July 7, 1999, White House Interview Program.

10. E. Pendleton James, interview with Martha Joynt Kumar, New York City, Nov. 8, 1999, White House Interview Program.

11. Andrew Card Jr., interview with Martha Joynt Kumar, Washington, D.C., Nov. 30, 2001.

12. *The Decision Makers,* p. 1871.

13. Card interview.

14. Dana Milbank, "Bush Names Rove Political Strategist; Choice Completes Troika of White House Advisors," *Washington Post,* Jan. 5, 2001.

15. The Bureau of National Affairs annually publishes the internal White House phone book.

16. Ari Fleischer, interview with Martha Joynt Kumar, Washington, D.C., Nov. 30, 2001.

17. Card interview.

Appendices

White House Chief of Staff's Office: 1969–2001

ADMINISTRATION	CHIEF OF STAFF	DATES	DEPUTY (Served during some part or all of term of chief of staff shown at left.)	DATES
CLINTON	**John D. Podesta**	1999–2001	**Karen Tramontano**— Assistant to the President and Counselor to the Chief of Staff	1999–2001
			Ann Lewis— Counselor to the President	1999
			Maria Echaveste, Stephen J. Richetti— both Assistants to the President and Deputy Chiefs of Staff	1998–99
			Douglas Sosnik— Senior Adviser to the President for Policy and Strategy	1997–99
	Erskine B. Bowles	1997–98	**John B. Podesta**	1997–98
			Sylvia M. Mathews— Assistants to the President and Deputy Chiefs of Staff	1998–99
			Victoria Radd— Assistant to the President and Chief of Staff to the Chief of Staff	1997–98
			Erskine Bowles— Deputy Chief of Staff for White House Operations	1996
	Leon E. Panetta	1994–96	**Evelyn Lieberman**— Assistant to the President & Deputy Chief of Staff for White House Operations	1995–96
			Harold Ickes— Deputy Chief of Staff for Policy and Political Affairs	1994–96
			Erskine B. Bowles— Assistant to the President and Deputy Chief of Staff for Operations	1994–95
			Charles William Burton— Deputy Assistant to the President and Director of Policy and Staff for the Chief of Staff	1993–95

ADMINISTRATION	CHIEF OF STAFF	DATES	DEPUTY (Served during some part or all of term of chief of staff shown at left.)	DATES
	Thomas M. "Mack" McLarty III	1993–94	**Philip Lader**, **Harold Ickes**— both Assistants to the President and Deputy Chiefs of Staff	1994–94
			Roy Neel— Assistant to the President and Deputy Chief of Staff	1993
			Mark Gearan— Assistant to the President and Deputy Chief of Staff	1993
BUSH	**James A. Baker III**	1992–93	**Robert Zoellick**— Assistant to the President and Deputy Chief of Staff	Aug. 23, 1992– Jan., 1993
	Samuel K. Skinner (Assistant to the President, Aug. 22– 29, 1992)	Dec. 16, 1991– Aug. 22, 1992	**W. Henson Moore**— Deputy Chief of Staff to the President	Feb. 02– Aug. 22, 1992
	John H. Sununu (Counselor to the President, Dec. 16, 1991– Feb. 28, 1992)	Jan. 21, 1989– Dec. 16, 1991	**Andrew A. Card Jr.**— Assistant to the President and Deputy to the Chief of Staff	Jan. 21, 1989– Mar. 03, 1991
			James W. Cicconi— Assistant to the President and Deputy to the Chief of Staff	Jan. 21, 1989– Dec. 28, 1990
REAGAN	**Kenneth Duberstein** (Chief of Staff to the President)	1988–89	**John C. Tuck**— Special Assistant to the President & Director, Office of the Chief of Staff	1987–89
	Howard H. Baker Jr. (Chief of Staff to the President)	1987–88	**M. B. Oglesby**— Deputy Chief of Staff	1988–89
			Kenneth Duberstein— Deputy Chief of Staff	1987–88
	Donald T. Regan (Chief of Staff to the President)	1985–87	**Thomas Dawson**— Deputy Assistant to the President and Executive Assistant to the Chief of Staff	1985–87
			Craig Fuller— Assistant to the Chief of Staff	1985–89
	James A. Baker III (Chief of Staff and Assistant to the President)	1981–85	**Michael K. Deaver**— Deputy Chief of Staff and Assistant to the President	1981–85

ADMINISTRATION	CHIEF OF STAFF	DATES	DEPUTY (Served during some part or all of term of chief of staff shown at left.)	DATES
			Richard Darman— Assistant to the President and Deputy to the Chief of Staff; Deputy Assistant	1983–85 1981–83
			Margaret Tutwiler— Special Assistant to the President and Executive Assistant to the Chief of Staff	1981–89
			James W. Cicconi— Special Assistant to the President and Special Assistant to the Chief of Staff	1981–85
			Francis S.M. Hodsoll— Deputy Assistant to the President and Deputy to the Chief of Staff	1981
CARTER	**Jack H. Watson Jr.**[a]	1979–80		
	Hamilton Jordan	July, 1979–1980	**Landon Butler**— Deputy Assistant to the President	1979–80
			Leslie Francis— Deputy Assistant to the President	1979–81
	Hamilton Jordan	1977–79	**Alonzo McDonald**[b]	
FORD	**Richard B. Cheney** (Staff Coordinator)	Nov., 1975– Jan., 1977		
	Donald H. Rumsfeld (Staff Coordinator)	Sept., 1974– Nov., 1975	**Richard B. Cheney** Deputy Assistant to the President	Oct., 1974–Nov., 1975
	Alexander M. Haig	Aug.–Sept., 1974		
NIXON	**Alexander Haig**	1973–74	**John Bennett**	1973–74
	H. R. Haldeman	1969–73	**Alexander Butterfield**	1969–73

[a]When Watson became chief of staff, Butler and McDonald continued as deputies, but Francis did not.
[b]McDonald, though listed formally as assistant to the president and staff director, administered the office and staff on a day-to-day basis moreso than Jordan.

White House Office of Staff Secretary: 1969–2001

ADMINISTRATION	STAFF SECRETARY	DATES	DEPUTY (Served during some part or all of term of staff secretary shown at left.)	DATES
CLINTON	**Lisel Loy**	Summer, 2000– Jan., 2001	**Adam Rosman**	Summer, 2000– Jan., 2001
			Lisel Loy—Deputy Assistant to the President and Deputy Staff Secretary	1999–Spring, 2000
			Vacant	1999–2000
	Sean P. Maloney	1999–Spring, 2000		
	Phillip Caplan	Spring, 1998– Spring, 1999	**Sean P. Maloney** **David Goodfriend**	1998–99
	Todd Stern	Fall, 1995–	**Philip M. Caplan**	Fall, 1995– Spring, 1998
		Fall, 1997	**Sean P. Maloney**	Fall, 1997– Spring, 1999
			Helen Howell	Spring, 1996–1997
	John D. Podesta	Spring, 1993– Spring, 1995	**R. Paul Richard**	Spring, 1994– Spring, 1995
			Todd Stern	Spring, 1993– Spring, 1995
			Brant Lee	Spring, 1993– Fall, 1993
BUSH	**Phillip D. Brady** (Assistant to the President and Staff Secretary)	Jan. 13, 1991– Oct. 15, 1992	**Dean McGrath Jr.**—Deputy Assistant to the President and Deputy Staff Secretary	Aug. 9, 1992– Nov. 4, 1992
	James W. Cicconi (Assistant to the President and Deputy Chief of Staff [Staff Secretary])	Jan. 21, 1989– Dec. 28, 1990	**John S. Gardner**—Special Assistant to the President and Deputy Staff Secretary; Special Assistant to the President and Assistant Staff Secretary	Aug. 4, 1991– Aug. 25, 1992 Jan. 24, 1989– Aug. 4, 1991
REAGAN	**Rhett Dawson** (Assistant to the President for Operations)	Apr., 1987– Fall, 1988	**Katherine D. Ladd**— Director, White House Secretariat; White House Secretariat; Executive Assistant	1988 Fall, 1987 Spring, 1987 1985–Spring, 1987
	David L. Chew (Assumed Staff Secretary responsibilities under Rhett Dawson)			
	Richard Darman (Assumed Staff Secretary responsibilities)	1981–83		
CARTER	**Richard G. Hutcheson III**	Jan., 1977– Jan., 1981	**William D. Simon**	Jan., 1977– Jan., 1981

ADMINISTRATION	STAFF SECRETARY	DATES	DEPUTY (Served during some part or all of term of staff secretary shown at left.)	DATES
FORD	**James E. Connor**	June, 1975– Jan., 1977	**David Hoopes**	Aug., 1974– Jan., 1977
	Jerry H. Jones	Aug., 1974– May, 1975		
NIXON	**Jerry H. Jones**	Apr., 1974– Aug., 1974	**David Hoopes**	Apr., 1971– Aug., 1974
	Bruce A. Kehrli	Jan., 1972– May, 1974		
	Jon M. Huntsman	Feb., 1971– Feb., 1972		
	John R. Brown, III	1969–Mar., 1971		
	Ken Cole	1969		

Sources: U.S. Government Manual, Capital Source, Nixon Presidential Materials Project, Ford Presidential Library, Carter Presidential Library, and presidential press releases.

White House Presidential Personnel Office: 1969–2001

ADMINISTRATION	PERSONNEL DIRECTOR	DATES	DEPUTY (Served during some part or all of term of personnel director shown at left.)	DATES
CLINTON	**Bob J. Nash** (Assistant to the President and Director of Presidential Personnel)	1995–2001	**Maria Luisa Haley**	1999–2001
			Marsha Scott	1998–2001
			D. Vanessa Weaver,	
			Patsy L. Thomasson	1995–97
			Antonella Pianalto	1994–95
			Craig Smith	1994–95
	Veronica J. Biggins (Assistant to the President and Director of Presidential Personnel)	1994	**John Emerson**	1993–94
			Jan Piercy	1993–94
	Bruce Lindsey (Assistant to the President and Senior Advisor and Director, Office of Presidential Personnel)	1993		
BUSH	**Constance Horner** (Assistant to the President and Director of Presidential Personnel)	Aug. 25, 1991– Jan. 19, 1993	**Jeanette L. Naylor**[a]— Deputy Assistant to the President and Deputy Director of Presidential Personnel	Jan. 21, 1989– Nov. 16, 1990
	Charles G. "Chase" Untermeyer (Assistant to the President for Presidential Personnel)	Jan. 21, 1989– Aug. 24, 1991	**Roscoe B. Starek III**— Deputy Assistant to the President and Deputy Director of Presidential Personnel	Feb. 13, 1989– Nov. 17, 1990
			Ronald C. Kaufman—Deputy Assistant to the President for Presidential Personnel	Feb. 13, 1989–1991 ("between January and June")
REAGAN	**Robert H. Tuttle** (Deputy Assistant to the President and Director of Presidential Personnel)	1985–89	No deputies listed, just eight "associate" directors.	
	John Herrington (Assistant to the President for Presidential Personnel)	1983–85		

ADMINISTRATION	PERSONNEL DIRECTOR	DATES	DEPUTY (Served during some part or all of term of personnel director shown at left.)	DATES
	Helene von Damm (Assistant to the President for Presidential Personnel; Deputy Assistant to the President and Director of Presidential Personnel)	1982–83 1981–82	**John Schrote**—Deputy Director of Presidential Personnel	1982–83
			Becky Norton Dunlop— Deputy Assistant to the President and Deputy Director of Presidential Personnel	1983–85
	E. Pendleton James (Assistant to the President for Presidential Personnel)	1981	**Lynn Rose Wood**—Deputy Director of Presidential Personnel	1981–85
			Mike Farrell—Deputy Director of Presidential Personnel	1981–82
			William Spartin—Deputy Director of Presidential Personnel	1981
			Richard Shelby—Deputy Director of Presidential Personnel	1981
			Wayne Roberts—Deputy Director of Presidential Personnel	1981
CARTER	**Arnie Miller** (Director of the Presidential Personnel Office)	1978–80	**Harley Frankel**—Deputy Director of the Presidential Personnel Office	1979–80
	James F. Gammill Jr. (Director, Presidential Personnel Office)	1977–78	**James B. King**—Special Assistant to the President for Personnel	1977–78
FORD	**Douglas P. Bennett**	June, 1975– Jan., 1977	**Peter M. McPherson**	Aug., 1975– Jan., 1977
	William N. Walker	Oct., 1974– June, 1975	**M. Alan Woods**	Dec., 1974– Aug., 1975
	David J. Wimer	Aug.–Sept., 1974	**Samuel Schulhof**	Aug.–Dec., 1974
NIXON	**Dave Wimer**	Apr. 15, 1973–1974		
	Jerry Jones	Jan. 21, 1973–1974		
	Frederick V. Malek	1970	**Dan Kingsley**	Feb. 08, 1971–1973
	Harry Flemming	1969–70	**Al Kaupinen**	1971–72

Note: In 1978 the Presidential Personnel Office was designated as the White House Office of the Assistant to the President for Political Affairs and Personnel.
ᵃ Naylor during this tenure is listed as "Special Assistant to the President and Associate Director of Presidential Personnel."

White House Counsel's Office: 1969–2001

ADMINISTRATION	COUNSEL	DATES	DEPUTY (Served during some part or all of term of counsel shown at left.)	DATES
CLINTON	**Beth Nolan**	Aug., 1999–Jan., 2001	**Bruce Lindsey**—Assistant to the President and Deputy Counsel	Jan., 1993–Jan., 2001
			William Marshall—Deputy Assistant to the President and Deputy Counsel	Dec., 1999–Jan., 2001
	Charles F. Ruff	Feb., 1997–Aug., 1999	**Cheryl Mills**—Deputy Assistant to the President and Deputy Counsel	1996–Aug., 1999
	John M. "Jack" Quinn	Nov., 1995–Feb., 1997	**Kathleen M. Wallman**—Deputy Counsel to the President	1995–96
	Abner J. Mikva	Sept., 1994–Nov., 1995	**James Castello**—Deputy Counsel to the President	Mar., 1995–1996
	Lloyd N. Cutler (Special Counsel to the President)	Mar., 1994–Sept., 1994	**Joel I. Klein**—Deputy Counsel to the President	July, 1993–Mar., 1995
	Bernard Nussbaum	Jan., 1993–Mar., 1994	**Vincent Foster**—Deputy Counsel to the President	Jan., 1993–July, 1993
BUSH	**C. Boyden Gray**	Jan. 21, 1989–Jan. 19, 1993	**John Schmitz**—Deputy Counsel to the President	Feb., 13, 1989–Jan., 20, 1993
REAGAN	**Arthur B. Culvahouse Jr.**	Mar., 1987–Jan., 1989	**Phillip Brady**—Deputy Counsel to the President	May, 1988–Jan., 1989
			Jay B. Stephens—Deputy Counsel to the President	Apr., 1986–Mar., 1988
	Peter J. Wallison	Apr., 1986–Mar., 1987		
	Fred F. Fielding	Jan., 1981–Apr., 1986	**Richard Hauser**—Deputy Counsel to the President	Mar., 1981–June, 1986
			Herbert Ellingwood—Deputy Counsel to the President	Mar., 1981–Dec., 1981
CARTER	**Lloyd N. Cutler**	Oct., 1979–Jan., 1981	**Michael Cardozo**—Deputy Counsel to the President	Oct., 1979–Jan., 1981
			Joseph Onek—Deputy Counsel to the President	Sept., 1979–Jan., 1981
	Robert J. Lipshutz	Jan., 1977–Aug., 1979	**Margaret A. McKenna**—Deputy Counsel to the President	1977–80
FORD[a]	**Philip W. Buchen**	Aug., 1974–Jan., 1977	**Edward C. Schmults**—Counsel to the President	Oct., 1975–Jan., 1977
			William E. Casselman II—Counsel to the President	1975–76
			Roderick N. Hills—Counsel to the President	Mar.–Nov., 1975
			Philip E. Areeda—Counsel to the President	Sept., 1974–Feb., 1975

ADMINISTRATION	COUNSEL	DATES	DEPUTY (Served during some part or all of term of counsel shown at left.)	DATES
NIXON[b]	**J. Fred Buzhardt**	Jan., 1974– Aug., 1974		
	Leonard Garment	May, 1973– Jan., 1974	**Fred Fielding**—Deputy Counsel to the President	May, 1973– Jan., 1974 (on Counsel staff since Oct., 1970)
	John Wesley Dean III	July, 1970– Apr., 1973		
	John Ehrlichman	Jan., 1969– Nov., 1969		

[a] Under President Ford, several listed as "deputy" (i.e., top assistant) in the Counsel's Office—Areeda, Hills, Casselman, and Schmults—were so named because they did much of the office's legal work and because the title earned them higher pay and more prestige.

[b] Although presidents from FDR through Nixon had aides with the titles of special counsel or counsel, such staffers typically had wider-ranging policy responsibilities. Under Nixon, Ehrlichman focused on domestic policy and political issues. Dean introduced the first law-focused White House Counsel's Office. (See also chapter 10, note 6.)

White House Office of Press Secretary: 1969–2001

ADMINISTRATION	PRESS SECRETARY	DATES	DEPUTY DIRECTOR (Served during some part or all of term under press secretary shown at left.)	DATES
CLINTON	**Richard "Jake" Siewert Jr.**	2000–2001	**Elliot Diringer**	2000–2001
			Nanda Chitre	2000–2001
	Joseph Lockhart	1998–2000	**Jennifer Palmieri**—Deputy Assistant to the President and Deputy Press Secretary for Operations	1999
			Richard "Jake" Siewert Jr., Barry Toiv, Beverly Barnes, Amy Weiss Tobe, James Kennedy— all Deputy Assistants to the President and Deputy Press Secretaries	1997–2000 1996–2000 1997–2000 1997–2000 1995–2000 2000–2001
	Mike McCurry	1995–98	**Joseph Lockhart**—Deputy Assistant to the President and Deputy Press Secretary	1997–98
			Mary Ellen Glynn—Deputy Assistant to the President and Deputy Press Secretary	1995–97
			Lorraine McHugh Wytkind— Deputy Assistant to the President and Deputy Press Secretary for Operations and Media Affairs	1995–97
			Virginia M. Terzano—Deputy Assistant to the President and Deputy Press Secretary	1994–96
			Evelyn Lieberman—Deputy Assistant to the President and Deputy Press Secretary for White House Operations	1994–95
	Dee Dee Myers (Press Secretary and Assistant to the President)	1993–94	**Arthur Jones**—Deputy Assistant to the President and Deputy Press Secretary	1993–94
			Lorraine Voles—Deputy Assistant to the President and Deputy Press Secretary	1993
			Donald K. Steinberg—Special Assistant to the President, Deputy Press Secretary, and Senior Director	1993–94
BUSH	**Marlin Fitzwater** (Assistant to the President and Press Secretary)	Jan. 20, 1989– Jan. 20, 1993	**Judy A. Smith**—Special Assistant to the President and Deputy Press Secretary	Apr. 14, 1991– Jan. 20, 1993

ADMINISTRATION	PRESS SECRETARY	DATES	DEPUTY DIRECTOR (Served during some part or all of term under press secretary shown at left.)	DATES
			Walter H. Kanstiner III—Special Assistant to the President and Deputy Press Secretary for Foreign Affairs (detailed from State Department)	May 27, 1992–Jan. 20, 1993
			Gary L. Foster—Special Assistant to the President and Deputy Press Secretary	May 12, 1991–May 18, 1992
			Stephen T. Hart—Special Assistant to the President and Deputy Press Secretary	Jan. 30, 1989–May 8, 1991
			Alixe Glen—Special Assistant to the President and Deputy Press Secretary	Jan. 30, 1989–Nov. 24, 1990
			Roman Popadiuk—Deputy Assistant to the President and Deputy Press Secretary	Jan. 30, 1989–May 26, 1992
REAGAN	**Marlin Fitzwater** (Assistant to the President for Press Relations;	1987–88	**B. Jay Cooper**—Special Assistant to the President and Deputy Press Secretary	1987–88
	Special Assistant to the President and Deputy Press Secretary for Domestic Affairs)	1983–85	**Mark D. Weinberg**—Special Assistant to the President and Assistant Press Secretary	1987–88
			Leslye Arsht—Special Assistant to the President and Deputy Press Secretary to the President	1987–88
			Roman Popadiuk—Special Assistant to the President and Deputy Press Secretary for Foreign Affairs	1988
			Dan Howard—Special Assistant to the President and Deputy Press Secretary for Foreign Affairs;	1987–88
			Deputy Press Secretary to the President	1986–87
	Larry Speakes (Assistant to the President and Principal Deputy Press Secretary;	1983–87	**Rusty Brashear**—Special Assistant to the President and Deputy Press Secretary for Domestic Affairs	1985–87
	Deputy Assistant to the President and Deputy Press Secretary to the President)	1981–83	**Edward P. Djerejian**—Special Assistant to the President and Deputy Press Secretary for Foreign Affairs	1985–86
			Robert Sims—Special Assistant to the President and Deputy Press Secretary for Foreign Affairs	1983–85

ADMINISTRATION	PRESS SECRETARY	DATES	DEPUTY DIRECTOR (Served during some part or all of term under press secretary shown at left.)	DATES
			Peter Roussel—Special Assistant to the President and Deputy Press Secretary;	1983–87
			Deputy Press Secretary to the President	1981–83
			Leslie A. Janka—Special Assistant to the President and Deputy Press Secretary for Foreign Affairs	1983
			Lyndon "Mort" Allin—Deputy Press Secretary to the President;	1982–83
			Assistant Press Secretary	1981
	James Scott "Jim" Brady[a] (Assistant to the President and Press Secretary)	1981–88	**Karna Small Stringer**—Deputy Assistant to the President and Deputy Press Secretary	1981–82
CARTER	**Joseph "Jody" Powell Jr.** (Press Secretary to the President)	1977–81	**Patricia Y. Bario**—Deputy Press Secretary	1979–80
			Rex L. Granum—Deputy Press Secretary	1977–80
			Walter W. Wurfel—Deputy Press Secretary	1977–79
			C. Ray Jenkins—Special Assistant to the President	1979–81
FORD	**Ronald H. Nessen**	Sept., 1974–Jan., 1977	**John G. Carlson**	Jan., 1976–Jan., 1977
			John W. Hushen	Aug., 1974–Feb., 1976
	Jerald F. TerHorst	Aug.–Sept., 1974	**Andrew T. Falkiewicz**—Deputy Press Secretary	1974–75
			William I. Greener Jr.—Deputy Press Secretary	1975–76
			Gerald L. Warren—Deputy Press Secretary	1972–76(?)
NIXON	**Ronald L. Ziegler**	1969–74	**Andrew T. Falkiewicz**—Deputy Press Secretary	1973–74
			Ken W. Clawson—Deputy Press Secretary	1973–74
			Neal Ball—Deputy Press Secretary	1971–73
			Gerald L. Warren—Deputy Press Secretary	1969–72

[a]Although Brady was incapacitated in a 1981 attempt on President Reagan's life, he held the title press secretary until 1989. Speakes's title was assistant to the president and principal deputy press secretary; Fitzwater's title was assistant to the president for press relations. Fitzwater's title became White House press secretary in the George H. W. Bush administration.

White House Office of Communications: 1969–2001

ADMINISTRATION	DIRECTOR	DATES	DEPUTY (Served during some part or all of term under director shown at left.)	DATES
CLINTON	**Loretta Ucelli**	1999–2001	**Stephanie Cutter**	1999–2001
			Thomas D. Janenda	1999–2001
			Stacie Spector	1998–99
	Ann Lewis	1997–99		
	Donald Baer (Assistant to the President and Coordinator of Strategic Planning and Communications)	Aug., 1995–1997	**Ann Lewis**	1996–97
			Victoria Radd	1996–97
			Tara Sonenshine— Special Assistant to the President and Deputy Director of Communications	1994–95
	Mark D. Gearan (Assistant to the President and Coordinator of Strategic Planning and Communications)	May, 1993– Aug., 1995	**Rahm I. Emanuel**—Assistant to the President and Deputy Director of Communications	1993–94
			David Dreyer—Deputy Assistant to the President and Deputy Director of Communications	1993–94
	George Stephanopoulos (Assistant to the President and Director of Communications)	Jan.–May, 1993	**Ricki Seidman**	1993
BUSH	**Margaret Tutwiler** (Assistant to the President for Communications)	Aug. 23, 1992– Jan. 7, 1993	**Karen Groomes**—Deputy Assistant to the President for Communications	Aug. 23, 1992– Apr. 30, 1991
	David F. Demarest Jr. (Assistant to the President for Communications)	Jan. 21, 1989– July 13, 1992	**Chriss Winston**—Deputy Assistant to the President for Communications	Feb. 13, 1989– Apr. 30, 1991
			Deborah A. Amend—Special Assistant to the President for Communications	Jan. 2, 1990– Sept. 29, 1991
REAGAN	**Mari Maseng** (Assistant to the President for Communications)	July, 1988– Jan., 1989		
	Thomas C. Griscom (Assistant to the President for Communications and Planning)	Apr., 1987– June, 1988	**John O. Koehler**—Assistant to the President and Director of Communications	1987
	John O. Koehler (Assistant to the President and Director of Communications)	Feb., 1987		

ADMINISTRATION	DIRECTOR	DATES	DEPUTY (Served during some part or all of term under director shown at left.)	DATES
	Patrick Buchanan (Assistant to the President and Director of Communications)	Feb., 1985– Feb., 1987		
	Michael A. McManus Jr. (Acting Director, Assistant to the President and Deputy to the Deputy Chief of Staff)	Jan., 1984– Jan., 1985		
	David R. Gergen (Assistant to the President for Communications)	June, 1981– Jan., 1984	**Joanna E. Bistany**—Deputy Assistant to the Assistant to the President for Communications	1981–84
	Frank A. Ursomarso (Deputy Assistant to the President for Communications and Director of the Office of Communications)	Feb.–June, 1981		
CARTER	**None**[a]	Sept., 1979– Jan., 1981		
	Gerald Rafshoon	June, 1978– Aug., 1979	**Gregory S. Schneiders**—Deputy Assistant to the President for Communications	1978–79
			Barry Jagoda—Special Assistant to the President for Media and Public Affairs	1977–78
	None[a]	Jan., 1977– June, 1978		
FORD	**David R. Gergen**	July, 1976– Jan., 1977		
	Margita E. White[b]	June, 1975– July, 1976		
	Gerald Warren[b]	Nov., 1974– June, 1975		
	Office did not exist	Aug.–Nov., 1974		
NIXON	**Ken W. Clawson**	Jan.–Aug., 1974	**Jeb Magruder**	1972–73
	Herbert G. Klein	Jan., 1969– June, 1973	**Charles Colson**	Nov. 6, 1969– Mar. 10, 1973

[a]The functions of the Office of Communications were performed by the deputy press secretaries and the Office of Media Liaison.
[b]The Communications Office was under the jurisdiction of the Press Office.

White House Office of Management and Administration: 1978–2001

ADMINISTRATION	DIRECTOR	DATES	DEPUTY (Served during some part or all of term under the director shown at left.)	DATES
CLINTON	**Mark F. Lindsay** (Assistant to the President for Management and Administration)	1999–2001	**Bradley J. Kiley**	2000–2001
	Virginia M. Apuzzo (Assistant to the President for Management and Administration)	1997–99	**Michael D. Malone**—Deputy Assistant to the President for Management and Administration; Special Assistant for Management and Administration	1996–2000
	Jodie R. Torkelson (Deputy Assistant to the President for Management and Administration)	1995–97	**Franklin Reeder**— Director, Office of Administration	1995–96
	Vacant	1994–95	**Patsy L. Thomasson**—Special Assistant to the President for Management and Administration and Director of the Office of Administration	1994–95
	David Watkins (Assistant to the President for Management and Administration)	1993–94	**Patsy L. Thomasson**— Director, Office of Administration	1993
BUSH	**Timothy J. McBride** (Assistant to the President for Management and Administration)	Jan. 14, 1992– Jan. 20. 1993	**Paul Bateman**—Deputy Assistant to the President for Management and Director of the Office of Administration	Jan. 31, 1989– Jan. 11, 1993
	Vacant	Feb. 2, 1991– Jan. 14, 1992		
	J. Bonnie Newman (Assistant to the President for Management and Administration)	Jan. 21, 1989– Feb. 2, 1991		
			Hector F. Irastorza Jr.— Special Assistant to the President and Deputy Director of the Office of Administration	Jan. 30, 1989– early 1991 (position abolished)
			Rose M. Zamaria—Deputy Assistant to the President and Director of White House Operations	Jan., 1991– Oct. 13, 1992

ADMINISTRATION	DIRECTOR	DATES	DEPUTY (Served during some part or all of term under the director shown at left.)	DATES
			Rose M. Zamaria—Special Assistant to the President and Director of White House Operations	Jan. 30, 1989– Jan., 1991
REAGAN	**Rhett B. Dawson** (Assistant to the President for Operations)	1987–88	**Vacant**—Deputy Assistant to the President for Management and Administration	1987–88
			David L. Chew—Deputy Assistant to the President (for Operations)	1987
			Claire M. O'Donnell—Special Assistant to the President for White House Operations (under Dawson)	1987
			Gordon G. Riggle—Deputy Assistant to the President and Director of the Office of Administration	1987
			Johnathan Miller—Deputy Assistant to the President for Administration	1986–87
	Christopher Hicks (Deputy Assistant to the President for Administration)	1985–86	**John P. Brady**—Deputy Director, Office of Administration	1985
			Charles Kupperman—Special Assistant to the President for Administration (under Hicks and Miller)	1985–87
	John F. W. Rogers (Assistant to the President for Management and Administration and Director of the Office of Administration)	1982–84	**Vacant**	1983
	Richard Darman (Assistant to the President and Deputy to the Chief of Staff)	1981–84	**John F. W. Rogers**—Special Assistant to the President for Administration	1981–82 (under Darman)
			Sarah Kadec—Deputy Director, Office of Administration	1981
CARTER	**Hugh A. Carter Jr.** (Special Assistant to the President for Administration)	1977–80	**Richard Harden**—Special Assistant to the President for Information Management and Director of the Office of Administration	1978–81
			Valerio L. Giannini—Deputy Special Assistant for Administration	1979–80
			Daniel Malachuk Jr.—Deputy Special Assistant for Administration–White House Operations	1979–80

CONTRIBUTORS

PERI E. ARNOLD, University of Notre Dame

MARYANNE BORRELLI, Connecticut College

JOHN P. BURKE, University of Vermont

GEORGE C. EDWARDS III, Texas A&M University and editor,
Presidential Studies Quarterly

JOHN FORTIER, American Enterprise Institute

KAREN HULT, Virginia Polytechnic Institute and State University

CLAY JOHNSON III, executive director, Bush-Cheney transition

NANCY KASSOP, State University of New York-New Paltz

JOHN H. KESSEL, The Ohio State University

MARTHA JOYNT KUMAR, Towson University and director, White
House 2001 Project

G. CALVIN MACKENZIE, Colby College and visiting fellow,
Brookings Institution

NORMAN ORNSTEIN, American Enterprise Institute

BRADLEY H. PATTERSON, JR., National Academy of Public
Administration

JAMES P. PFIFFNER, George Mason University

TERRY SULLIVAN, University of North Carolina at Chapel Hill and
White House 2001 Project

KATHRYN DUNN TENPAS, University of Pennsylvania

CHARLES E. WALCOTT, Virginia Polytechnic Institute and State
University

SHIRLEY ANNE WARSHAW, Gettysburg College

STEPHEN J. WAYNE, Georgetown University

INDEX

ISBN 1-58544-223-2

90000